THE ENCYCLOPEDIA
OF BAKING

THE ENCYCLOPEDIA
OF BAKING

REBO
PRODUCTIONS

Rebo Productions
EDITOR'S GUARANTEE
Despite the great care taken in producing this book, it is
unfortunately possible that there could be printing or
production faults in this work.
In such an event, your book will be replaced free of charge.
Please take it to the bookshop where you bought it or write to
us at the address given below, telling us the exact nature of
the fault found.
In either case, your complaint will be dealt with immediately.
Gründ Bookshop - 60, rue Mazarine - 75006 Paris

© Ceres-Verlag Rudolf-August Oetker KG, Bielefeld
© 1997 Published by Rebo Productions Ltd
Printed in Slovenia
Translation: First Edition Translations Ltd, Cambridge, UK
Typesetting: Hof&Land Typografie, Maarssen, the Netherlands

ISBN 1901094 146

BISCUITS

To eat with a cup of tea or coffee, to go with a dessert or just for sheer enjoyment.

——————— *Page 118*

Getting ready for Christmas
Hazelnuts, almonds, honey, spices... the festive season!

——————— *Page 148*

CONFECTIONERY AND PETITS FOURS

Just as good as a treat for yourself as they are to give: tempting and sophisticated, with marzipan, fruits, chocolate or flavoured with liqueurs and spices, they are heaven for those with a sweet tooth.

——————— *Page 186*

GENOESE SPONGES

Anyone learning the art of baking starts with sponge cakes: light and moist, they are good for a whole host of delicate fillings and iced decorations.

——————— *Page 226*

RICH FLAN PASTRY

Easy to make, light and crisp, this pastry is ideal for fruit pies and poppy seed cakes.

————— Page 272

FATLESS SPONGES

With their light and delicate texture, they have many uses: perfect for mocha cakes, cream gâteaux or filled with fruit, they are just as good when used for a jam Swiss roll.

————— Page 316

SWEET YEAST COOKERY

Light and fragrant, this dough is used for delicious, traditional cakes, such as honey crisps, buns and doughnuts.

————— Page 340

CREAM CHEESE PASTRY

Soft and sumptuously filled, quick and easy to make, it stays fresh for several days.

—————————— *Page 376*

CHOUX PASTRY

Light and airy. Prepared on the hob first of all, then baked in the oven, cakes made using choux pastry are temptingly light, whether filled with cream or fruit, or simply iced.

—————————— *Page 388*

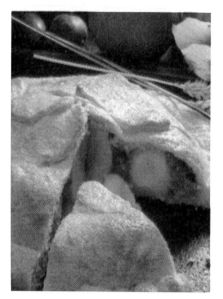

BAKING WITH FRUITS AND NUTS

Wholemeal flours are no longer taboo: fruit cakes, spicy sponge cakes and dried fruit sponge cakes.

—————————— *Page 398*

SAVOURY BREAD AND ROLLS

Sandwich loaves, mixed grain loaves, loaves with fillings, filled pancakes ... lots of tasty recipes to try when playing at being an apprentice baker.

——————————— *Page 424*

PIZZAS AND PANCAKES

Crusty, flaky pizzas and wholemeal pancakes for main dishes, starters or a buffet.

——————————— *Page 452*

USEFUL TIPS

What you need to know about baking: recipes for traditional mixtures, how to make various fillings and icings, essential equipment, simple ways to avoid or correct mistakes.

——————————— *Page 464*

RHUBARB MERINGUE
Serves 8

150 g (5 oz) plain flour
1 pinch of baking powder
565 g (1 lb 22 oz) caster sugar
1 egg
Rind of 1 unwaxed lemon
65 g (22 oz) butter

1.5 kg (32 lb) rhubarb
2 sachets vanilla sugar
5 tablespoons cornflour
6 tablespoons white wine
Lemon juice
6 egg whites

Sift the flour and baking powder on to the work surface and make a well in the centre. Add 65 g (22 oz) sugar, the egg and half the grated lemon rind. Combine with some of the flour to form a soft dough. Cut the butter into pieces and add to the dough, covering them with the remaining flour. Knead all the ingredients until the dough is smooth. Chill for 30 minutes in a refrigerator. Grease a 24 cm (92 in) round, fluted flan ring, roll out the dough and then line the flan ring with it. Prick the base with a fork and place in a preheated oven at 200° C (400° F, Gas Mark 6) for 25-30 minutes. Remove from the oven and leave to cool in the flan ring.

For the rhubarb: trim and clean the rhubarb, cut the stalks into chunks about 3 cm (1¼ in) long. Sprinkle with 250 g (8 oz) sugar and all the vanilla sugar and leave to

soak. Put the rhubarb in a large pan, add the remaining lemon rind, then cook over a low heat for 5 minutes (the rhubarb must stay firm). Remove the lemon rind, sprinkle with the cornflour, add the white wine and mix together. Leave to cool.

For the meringue: whisk 5 egg whites into peaks and gradually add the remaining sugar, whisking continuously; add the lemon juice. Fill an icing bag fitted with a star-shaped nozzle with the meringue mixture.

Spread the rhubarb over the base of the flan, cover with a thick layer of meringue mixture, then place under a hot grill for 2-3 minutes until golden.

REDCURRANT MERINGUE
Serves 8

250 g (8 oz) plain flour
250 g (8 oz) caster sugar
1 sachet vanilla sugar
A pinch of salt
1 egg
125 g (4 oz) butter

500 g (1 lb) redcurrants
2-3 tablespoons crushed rusks or dried breadcrumbs
5 egg whites

Sift the flour on to the work surface and make a well in the centre. Add 65 g (22 oz) sugar, the vanilla sugar, salt and egg. Using some of the flour, work the mixture into a soft dough. Cut the butter into pieces and add to the dough, cover with the remaining flour, combine all the ingredients until the dough is soft.

Chill for 1 hour in a refrigerator. Place two-thirds of the dough in a 28 cm (11 in) deep, round cake tin. Using the remaining third, roll out a strip 4 cm (12 in) wide and press this around the sides of the tin. Prick the base with a fork and place in a preheated oven at 200-220° C (400-425° F, Gas Mark 6-7) for 10-15 minutes.

For the filling: wash and drain the redcurrants, remove from the stalk using a fork. Whisk the egg whites into peaks, then gently fold in the remaining sugar and the redcurrants. While still hot, sprinkle the base of the flan with the crushed rusks or breadcrumbs. Fill it with the redcurrant meringue mixture before returning the flan to the oven.

Bake for 5-10 minutes until the meringue is golden. Leave the flan to cool for 1-2 hours. Carefully remove from the tin and serve with whipped cream.

Below: Rhubarb meringue

Above: *Redcurrant meringue*
Pages 10 and 11: *Yoghurt cake (recipe on page 62)*

Above: *Strawberry meringue flan*

STRAWBERRY MERINGUE FLAN

Serves 8

150 g (5 oz) plain flour	jelly
100 g (32 oz) ground	7 tablespoons raspberry
almonds	syrup
200 g (7 oz) caster sugar	3 tablespoons raspberry
1 sachet vanilla sugar	brandy
1 egg	3 egg whites
125 g (4 oz) butter	A few pistachio nuts for
750 g (12 lb) strawberries	decoration
5 tablespoons strawberry	

Sift the flour and ground almonds on to the work surface, then make a well in the centre. Add 65 g (22 oz) sugar, the vanilla sugar and egg. Using some of the flour, work the mixture into a soft dough. Cut the butter into pieces, cover with the remaining flour and combine all the ingredients into a smooth dough. Chill for 30 minutes in a refrigerator. Spread the mixture out in a deep, 26 cm (102 in) round cake tin, making the sides 2-3 cm (14 in) deep. Prick the base with a fork and bake in a preheated oven at 200° C (400° F, Gas Mark 6) for 20-25 minutes.

For the filling: wash, drain and carefully hull the strawberries, and if necessary halve them, sprinkle with 1 tablespoon sugar.
In a small pan, melt the strawberry jelly and the raspberry syrup, thinned down with a bit of water; bring to the boil. Remove from the heat and add some of the raspberry brandy, then spread the mixture on the base of the cold flan. Place the strawberries on the flan, sprinkle with the remaining raspberry brandy.

For the meringue: whisk 3 egg whites into peaks and gradually add the remaining sugar, whisking continuously. Spread over the flan. Decorate with a few pistachio nuts and place under a hot grill for 3-5 minutes.

APRICOT AND ALMOND FLAN

Serves 8

175 g (6 oz) plain flour	125 g (4 oz) ground
1 pinch of baking powder	almonds
150 g (5 oz) caster sugar	500 g (1 lb) apricots,
2 sachets vanilla sugar	blanched and halved
2 tablespoons white wine	4 tablespoons apricot jam
250 g (8 oz) butter	1 leaf gelatine
4 eggs, separated	1-2 tablespoons toasted
Rind of 2 lemon, unwaxed	flaked almonds

Sift the flour and baking powder on to the work surface and make a well in the centre. Combine 25 g (1 oz) sugar, 1 sachet of vanilla sugar and the white wine with some of the flour to form a soft dough. Add 125 g (4 oz) butter cut into pieces, cover with flour and knead the ingredients into a smooth dough. Grease a deep, 26 cm (102 in) round cake tin and line it with the pastry, making the sides 2-3 cm (w-14 in) deep. Prick the base with a fork. Bake in a preheated oven at 200-220° C (400-425° F, Gas Mark 6-7) for 15 minutes.

Apricot filling: cream the remaining butter and gradually add the remaining sugar and vanilla sugar, 4 egg yolks, the lemon rind and ground almonds. Whisk the egg whites into stiff peaks and gently fold in the almond cream mixture. Spread the mixture over the pastry case and smooth off evenly. Bake in a preheated oven at 160° C (325° F, Gas Mark 3) for 30-35 minutes. Leave to cool. Drain the apricots, reserving the juice, and place them on the almond filling.
For the glaze: heat the apricot juice with the jam, leave to cool. Dissolve the gelatine in 2 tablespoons water and

mix it with the cooled juice. Coat the apricots with this
mixture. Decorate with the toasted almonds.

Below: *Apricot and almond flan*

BANANA AND APRICOT FLAN

Serves 8

300 g (10 oz) plain flour
2 teaspoons baking
powder
100 g (3½ oz) caster sugar
1 sachet vanilla sugar
A pinch of salt
1 egg
125 g (4 oz) butter
500 g (1 lb) tinned
apricots in syrup

4 bananas
5 teaspoons lemon juice
1 teaspoon apricot liqueur
25 g (1 oz) crushed
almonds
150 g (5 oz) icing sugar
2-3 spoons banana
essence

Sift the flour and baking powder on to the work surface
and make a well in the centre. Combine the sugar, vanilla
sugar, salt, egg and some of the flour into a soft dough.

Add the butter cut into pieces, cover with the remaining
flour and knead the ingredients into a smooth dough.
Leave to rest in a refrigerator for 30 minutes.

Below: *Banana and almond flan*

For the filling: drain the apricots, peel the bananas.
Slice the apricots into a mixing bowl, add the lemon juice,
the apricot liqueur and the crushed almonds and leave to
soak. Grease a deep, 28 cm (11 in) round cake tin and line
it with two-thirds of the pastry, making the sides 2 cm
(¾ in) deep. Prick the base with a fork. Bake in a
preheated oven at 200-220° C (400-425° F, Gas Mark 6-7)
for about 10 minutes.

Spread the fruit over the base of the cooked flan case.
Roll out the remaining pastry into a circle the same size
as the tin. Prick the circle with a fork and cover the fruit
with it. Return to the oven and bake for 35 minutes.

For the glaze: mix the icing sugar with the banana
essence and coat the cake while still hot. The icing will
set as it cools.

GOOSEBERRY
AND MACAROON FLAN

Serves 8

200 g (7 oz) plain flour
250 g (8 oz) caster sugar
A pinch of salt
1 egg
125 g (4 oz) butter
750 g (1½ lb) gooseberries
500 ml (18 fl oz) white
wine
1 sachet vanilla sugar

Grated rind of 1 lemon
75 g (3 oz) cornflour
2 rusks
200 g (7 oz) marzipan
50 g (2 oz) icing sugar
2 egg yolks
1 tablespoon lemon juice
2 tablespoons apricot jam

Sift the flour on to the work surface and make a well in
the centre. Add 65 g (2½ oz) sugar, the salt and egg and
combine with some of the flour to form a soft dough.
Add the butter cut into pieces, cover with flour and
knead the ingredients quickly to form a smooth dough.
Leave to rest in a refrigerator for 1 hour.
Grease a deep, 28 cm (11 in) round cake tin. Roll out the
pastry and use it to line the tin, making the sides about
4 cm (1½ in) deep. Prick with a fork. Bake in a preheated
oven at 200°C (400°F, Gas Mark 6) for 25 minutes.

For the gooseberries: wash, drain, and top and tail the
gooseberries.
In a pan, bring the white wine (reserving 5 tablespoons)
to the boil with the remaining sugar, the vanilla sugar
and the lemon rind. Add the gooseberries, bring back to
the boil and leave to simmer until the gooseberries are
soft (they must not disintegrate). Remove the
gooseberries with a slotted spoon and strain them. Mix
the cornflour with the reserved white wine and the juice
from the gooseberries. Carefully mix in the fruit and

Above: *Gooseberry and macaroon flan*

leave to cool. Crush the rusks into crumbs and spread them over the base of the cooled flan case, then fill with the gooseberry mixture.

For the macaroon: knead the marzipan, icing sugar, egg yolks and the lemon juice. Transfer this mixture to an icing bag and decorate the flan, creating a lattice. Leave the macaroon mixture to dry for 30 minutes, then return to a preheated oven at 200-220° C (400-425° F, Gas Mark 6-7) for 5 minutes.

For the glaze: thin the apricot jam with 2 tablespoons water, bring to the boil and brush over the flan when it has cooled.

Right:
Fruit tartlets

FRUIT TARTLETS

Makes 12-14 tartlets

200 g (7 oz) plain flour
1 teaspoon baking powder
100 g (3½ oz) caster sugar
2 sachets vanilla sugar
A pinch of salt
4 drops concentrated
lemon juice
100 g (3½ oz) butter
500-750 g (1-1½ lb) fresh

fruit and tinned fruit in
syrup
2 tablespoons jam
(depending on the fruits
used)
1 leaf gelatine
250 ml (8 fl oz) double
cream

Sift the flour and baking powder on to the work surface and make a well in the centre. Add 75 g (3 oz) sugar, 1 sachet vanilla sugar, the salt, lemon juice and 2 tablespoon water and combine with some of the flour to form a soft dough. Add the butter cut into pieces, cover with the remaining flour and knead the ingredients into a smooth dough. Leave to rest in a refrigerator for 1 hour. Roll out the pastry to about 3 cm (1¼ in) thick. Cut into 10 cm (4 in) circles, prick with a fork, then place the tartlets on a greased baking sheet. Bake in a preheated oven at 180-200° C (350-400° F, Gas Mark 4-6) for 10-15 minutes.

For the filling: wash and drain the fruits. Sprinkle with the remaining sugar and leave to soak, then place them in half of the tartlets. Strain the tinned fruits in syrup (reserve the juice) and use them to cover the remaining tartlets.

For the glaze: thin down the jam with a little of the fruit juice, bring to the boil. Add the gelatine, leave to cool and then coat the tartlets with the mixture.
Whip the cream, flavour with the remaining vanilla sugar. Serve the cream separately.

RASPBERRY GÂTEAU

Serves 8

125 g (4 oz) plain flour
75 g (3 oz) caster sugar
A pinch of salt
1 egg
65 g (2½ oz) butter
750 g (1½ lb) raspberries

125 ml (4 fl oz) white wine
1 tablespoon raspberry jam
1 leaf gelatine
40 g (1½ oz) toasted flaked almonds

Sift the flour on to the work surface and make a well in the centre. Add 25 g (1 oz) sugar, the salt and egg and combine with some of the flour to form a soft dough. Add the butter cut into pieces, cover with flour and quickly knead the ingredients into a smooth dough. Leave to rest in a refrigerator for 1 hour.

Grease a deep, 23 cm (9 in) round cake tin. Roll out the pastry and line the tin, making the sides about 4 cm (1½ in) deep. Prick the base with a fork. Bake in a preheated oven at 200° C (400° F, Gas Mark 6) for 20-25 minutes. Remove the flan base from the tin and leave to cool.

For the raspberries: in a pan, bring half of the raspberries (reserving the rest) to the boil with the white wine, the remaining sugar and 125 ml (4 fl oz) water. Lower the heat and leave to reduce for 5 minutes.

Pass the cooked raspberries through a sieve. Heat the juice with the jam. Dissolve the gelatine leaf in a little water and add the raspberry syrup. Place the pan in a container full of cold water until the mixture starts to set.

Arrange the reserved raspberries close together in the flan case, reserve 3 tablespoons glaze and coat the raspberries with the rest. Place in a refrigerator. Reheat the remaining glaze, brush it over the sides of the flan and decorate with the toasted flaked almonds.

TROPICAL FRUIT FLAN

Serves 5

200 g (7 oz) plain flour
100 g (3½ oz) softened butter
A pinch of salt
100 g (3½ oz) caster sugar
4 egg yolks
250 ml (8 fl oz) milk
1 tablespoon orange

flower water
1 tablespoon cornflour
2 limes
1 pineapple
1 mango
3 kiwi fruits
2 bananas
2 gelatine leaves

Place the flour, butter, salt and 6 tablespoons of tepid water in a bowl. Combine until the mixture forms a smooth dough. Leave to rest in a refrigerator for 1 hour. Beat the egg yolks and the sugar together. Heat the milk, pour on to the mixture. Add the orange flower water. Heat slowly, stirring all the time. Leave to cool.

Place the dough in a greased baking tin, making sure it is evenly spread. Bake in a preheated oven at 200° C (400° F, Gas Mark 6) for 25 minutes. When cooked, spread the cream mixture over the base of the flan. Peel the fruits; use them to decorate the flan as you wish.
Brush the fruits with the gelatine dissolved in the juice from the fruits. Chill in the refrigerator before serving.

Right: *Raspberry gâteau*

Above: *Rhubarb and frangipane tart*

ingredients quickly into a smooth dough.
Form a ball of dough and leave to rest in a refrigerator for 1 hour.
Knead the dough for 5 minutes, roll it out and line a greased, 28 cm (11 in) round cake tin. Prick the base with a fork. Bake in a preheated oven at 200° C (400° F, Gas Mark 6) for 15 minutes.

For the frangipane: beat the marzipan, 1 whole egg and 1 egg yolk to a cream. Cover and put to one side. Spread half of this mixture over the base of the cooled pastry case and smooth off evenly. Transfer the remaining mixture to an icing bag fitted with a star-shaped nozzle and decorate the edge of the tart. Place on a low shelf in a preheated oven at 200° C (400° F, Gas Mark 6) for 12 to 15 minutes.

For the rhubarb: clean the rhubarb and cut into 4-5 cm (1½-2 in) pieces. Bring to the boil with the white wine, the red wine, the remaining sugar and the cinnamon. Let it reduce, making sure that the rhubarb does not disintegrate. Drain the rhubarb well, reserving the juice. Arrange the pieces of rhubarb on the frangipane.

For the glaze: melt the redcurrant jelly in the rhubarb juice, add the gelatine leaf. As soon as the mixture gels, coat the tart with it. Serve with whipped cream.

RHUBARB AND FRANGIPANE TART

Serves 6

Serves 6	1 kg (2 lb) rhubarb
275 g (9 oz) plain flour	125 ml (4 fl oz) white wine
150 g (5 oz) caster sugar	125 ml (4 fl oz) red wine
1 sachet vanilla sugar	A pinch of cinnamon
A pinch of salt	250 ml (8 fl oz) rhubarb
2 eggs	juice
Rind of 2 lemons	2 tablespoons redcurrant
100 g (3½ oz) butter	jelly
400 g (13 oz) marzipan	1 leaf gelatine
1 egg yolk	

Sift the flour on to the work surface and make a well in the centre. Add 50 g (2 oz) of the sugar, the vanilla sugar, the salt, egg and grated rind of 1 lemon and combine with some of the flour to form a soft dough. Add the butter cut into pieces, cover with flour and knead the

REDCURRANT GÂTEAU

Serves 6

175 g (6 oz) plain flour	2 tablespoons ground
400 g (13 oz) caster sugar	almonds
1 sachet vanilla sugar	50 g (2 oz) cornflour
2 pinches of salt	2 tablespoons redcurrant
5 eggs, separated	jelly
75 g (3 oz) butter	20 g (¾ oz) flaked
1 kg (2 lb) redcurrants	almonds

Sift 150 g (5 oz) flour on to the work surface and make a well in the centre. Combine 40 g (1½ oz) sugar, the vanilla sugar, a pinch of salt and 2 egg yolks. Then add the butter chopped into pieces, cover with flour and quickly knead the ingredients to form a smooth dough. Roll out the pastry and use it to line a greased, 28 cm (11 in) round flan tin. Prick the base with a fork. Bake in a preheated oven at 200-220°C (400-425°F, Gas Mark 6-7) for 15 minutes. Remove from the tin immediately and leave to cool.
For the almond sponge layer: whisk the egg whites into peaks, add 40 g (1½ oz) sugar and another pinch of

Above: *Redcurrant gâteau*

salt. Incorporate the remaining egg yolks. Sift the remaining flour and the ground almonds and gently fold into the egg whites.

Turn the mixture into a lined, 28 cm (11 in) round flan tin, and bake in a preheated oven at 180-200°C (350-400°F, Gas Mark 4-6) for about 15 minutes. Remove from the baking tin immediately and leave to cool.

For the filling: wash and drain the redcurrants, then strip them from the stalks using a fork. Place them in a pan and sprinkle with 175 g (6 oz) sugar. Bring to the boil.

Dissolve the cornflour in 5 tablespoons water and use to thicken the redcurrants. Leave to cool, stirring from time to time. Brush the base of the tart with the redcurrant jelly, cover with the almond sponge layer and cover that with the redcurrant filling.

Whisk the egg whites into peaks and gradually add the remaining sugar.

Spread half the egg whites over the fruits. Put the remainder in an icing bag fitted with a star-shaped nozzle and use for decoration.

Scatter the flaked almonds on the edge of the gâteau and bake in a preheated oven at 220-240°C (425-475°F, Gas Mark 7-9) for about 5 minutes until the meringue is golden. Serve with whipped cream.

KIWI GÂTEAU

Serves 4

175 g (6 oz) sponge fingers
150 g (5 oz) softened butter
125 g (4 oz) icing sugar
1 sachet vanilla sugar
3 egg yolks
500 ml (18 fl oz) double
cream
150 g (5 oz) ground almonds
6 kiwi fruits
1 teaspoon caster sugar
Some toasted flaked almonds

*P*lace the sponge fingers in a plastic bag, then crush them using a rolling pin. Spread half of them over the base of a lined deep, 26 cm (10½ in) round cake tin. In a bowl, cream the butter and first the icing sugar, then the vanilla sugar, egg yolks, ground almonds and half the double cream.

Peel 3 kiwi fruits, dice them and incorporate them in the mixture. Spread the kiwi mixture over the crushed sponge fingers and cover with the remaining sponge fingers. Cover the tin and place in a refrigerator for 5-6 hours. Remove from the cake tin and transfer to a plate.

Peel the remaining kiwi fruits and arrange them on the gâteau. Whip the remaining cream and the caster sugar, transfer to an icing bag and decorate the cake with this mixture. Cover the sides of the gâteau with the toasted flaked almonds.

Opposite: *Kiwi gâteau*

CHERRY CHEESECAKE

Serves 8

175 g (6 oz) sponge
fingers
125 g (4 oz) softened
butter
200 g (7 oz) cream cheese
50-75 g (2-3 oz) caster
sugar
1 sachet vanilla sugar
3 tablespoons lemon juice

250 ml (8 fl oz) double
cream
500-625 g (1-1¼ lb)
preserved Morello
cherries
2 tablespoons cherry jam
1 leaf gelatine
Some white chocolate
curls

Place the sponge fingers in a plastic bag and crush them with a rolling pin. Mix the resultant crumbs with the butter to form a smooth dough. Grease a deep, springform cake tin, line it with greaseproof paper and fill with the mixture.

For the filling: combine the cream cheese, sugar, vanilla sugar and lemon juice. Whip the cream for 30 seconds. Incorporate with the cream cheese mixture, then transfer the entire mixture to the cake tin. Drain the cherries and reserve 500 ml (18 fl oz) of the juice. Arrange them on the cream cheese mixture.

For the cherry glaze: melt the jam in the cherry juice over a medium heat. Remove from the heat and add the gelatine. Coat the cherries as soon as the mixture starts to gel. Leave the cheesecake in a refrigerator for 2-3 hours.

Remove the sides of the cake tin before serving and decorate the edge of the cake with the white chocolate curls.

PINEAPPLE WAFFLES

Serves 4

100 g (3½ oz) marzipan
2 egg whites
300 ml (½ pint) milk
25 g (1 oz) plain flour
65 g (2½ oz) icing sugar
A pinch of cinnamon
500 g (1 lb) pineapple,
from 1 kg (2 lb) pineapple

400 ml (14 fl oz) double
cream
2-3 tablespoons orange
liqueur
Some chopped pine
kernels for decoration
Quartered strawberry for
decoration

Knead the marzipan with the egg whites, milk and flour. Sift the icing sugar and cinnamon over the dough. Make the waffles one after another in a round waffle iron or in a frying pan like pancakes. Leave to cool on a muslin cloth spread over a wire rack.

For the filling: cut half of the pineapple into thin chunks and liquidize the rest. Whip the cream and beat vigorously until stiff. Gently fold in the pineapple purée and the orange liqueur. Spread some of the pineapple mixture on the first waffle, garnish with pineapple chunks, lay the second waffle on top and repeat the operation.

Transfer the remaining cream to an icing bag fitted with a star-shaped nozzle and decorate the top waffle. Decorate with the pine kernels, the pineapple chunks and the quartered strawberry.

Suggestion: fill the waffles just before serving.

Left: *Cherry cheesecake*

Opposite: *Pineapple waffles*

MOZART

Serves 8

225 g (7½ oz) plain flour
140 g (4½ oz) caster sugar
3 sachets vanilla sugar
A pinch of salt
6 eggs
100 g (3½ oz) butter
25 g (1 oz) cornflour
4 teaspoons cocoa powder
2 teaspoons baking
powder
50 g (2 oz) raisins

2 tablespoons rum
1 sachet gelatine
750 ml (1¼ pints) double
cream
75 g (3 oz) hazelnut
chocolate spread
40 g (1½ oz) icing sugar
2-3 tablespoons
cranberries
Some chocolate curls

Sift 150 g (5 oz) flour on to the work surface and make a well in the centre. Mix in 40 g (1½ oz) sugar, 2 sachets vanilla sugar, the salt and 2 eggs. Add the butter cut into pieces, cover with flour and quickly knead the ingredients until they form a smooth dough.

Roll out the dough and use it to line a greased, 28 cm (11 in) round flan tin. Prick the base with a fork. Bake in a preheated oven at 200-220° C (400-425° F, Gas Mark 6-7) for 15 minutes.

Remove the base of the cake from the tin immediately, but do not put on the plate until it has cooled.

For the sponge layers: in a mixing bowl, beat the remaining eggs with 2 tablespoons of hot water using an electric mixer at high speed for 1 minute until they are thick and frothy. Add the remaining sugar and vanilla sugar, whisking continuously for 2 minutes.

Incorporate the remaining flour, the cornflour, cocoa powder and baking powder using an electric mixer at low speed.

Turn the mixture into a lined, greased, deep, 28 cm (11 in) round cake tin, smoothing it out evenly.

Bake in a preheated oven at 180-200° C (350-400° F, Gas Mark 4-6) for about 30 to 35 minutes.

Remove from the tin, place on a wire rack and quickly remove the greaseproof paper. When cool, cut the sponge into two layers.

For the filling: leave the raisins to soak in the rum for a few hours.
Put the gelatine and 3 tablespoons of cold water in a small pan, leave to soak for 10 minutes, then heat until the gelatine has completely dissolved.
Whip the cream. Gradually add the gelatine to the cream, whisking continuously until very firm. Divide the cream into three.
Melt the hazelnut chocolate spread in a bowl over a pan of hot water and mix it with the first portion of cream.

Drain the raisins, reserving the rum. Fold the raisins (reserving about 20 for decoration) and 20 g (¾ oz) icing sugar into the second portion of cream, finally add the rum.
Mix the remaining icing sugar with the final portion of cream.

Spread the cranberries (reserving about 10 for decoration) over the pastry base and cover with one

Above: *Mozart*

sponge layer. Spread with the hazelnut chocolate cream, cover with the second layer of sponge. Cover the top and the sides of the cake with the raisin cream. Transfer the remaining cream to an icing bag fitted with a star-shaped nozzle and decorate the cake.

Decorate with the reserved raisins and cranberries.

KIWI MOUSSE GÂTEAU

Serves 4

125 g (4 oz) plain flour
175 g (6 oz) caster sugar
A pinch of salt
½ teaspoon grated lemon rind
1 egg
75 g (3 oz) butter
4 gelatine leaves
3 egg yolks

Juice of 2 lemons
500 g (1 lb) cottage cheese
250 ml (8 fl oz) double cream
1 small glass orange liqueur
5-6 kiwi fruits
250 ml (8 fl oz) fruit juice

Sift flour on to the work surface and make a well in the centre. Mix in 25 g (1 oz) sugar, the salt, lemon rind and egg. Add the butter cut into pieces, cover with flour and quickly knead the ingredients until they form a smooth dough.
Leave the pastry to rest for 30 minutes in a refrigerator.

Roll out the pastry and use it to line the base of a greased, 24 cm (9½ in) flan tin. Bake in a preheated oven at 200° C (400° F, Gas Mark 6) for 15-20 minutes. Then leave to cool.

For the filling: soak 2 gelatine leaves in 3 tablespoons cold water for 10 minutes. Beat the cottage cheese with the remaining sugar, the egg yolks and lemon juice. Heat the gelatine, stirring constantly, until it has dissolved. Add it to the cottage cheese and chill until the mixture starts to set.

Whip the cream and fold into the mixture, add the orange liqueur.

Transfer the base of the tart to a plate, place the sides of a deep, 24 cm (9½ in) springform cake tin around it, then cover the base with the cream cheese mixture, smooth it out evenly and leave in a refrigerator for 5-6 hours. Peel the kiwi fruits, slice them and arrange them on the top of the cake.

Below: *Kiwi mousse gâteau*

For the glaze: soak the remaining gelatine leaves in a little fruit juice.
Heat until dissolved, use to coat the cake as soon as it starts to gel.

STRAWBERRY MERINGUE CHARLOTTE

Serves 8

4 eggs, separated
350 g (11½ oz) caster sugar
1 kg (2 lb) strawberries
Grated rind of 1 lemon
3 tablespoons raspberry brandy
200 g (7 oz) plain superfine

cooking chocolate
450 ml (¾ pint) double cream
1 sachet gelatine
1 sachet vanilla sugar
36 sponge fingers

Above: *Strawberry meringue charlotte*

Whisk the egg whites into peaks, then gradually add 200 g (7 oz) sugar. Transfer this mixture to an icing bag. Cut out three circles of greaseproof paper about 28 cm (11 in) in diameter, and line two baking sheets with greaseproof paper. Divide the meringue mixture between the three circles and bake in a preheated oven at 110-130° C (225-250° F, Gas Mark ¼-½) for 1½-1¾ hours. Leave the meringues in the cold oven overnight to dry.

For the filling: wash, drain and hull the strawberries, purée half the fruits in a blender, add the lemon rind, 50 g (2 oz) sugar and 1 tablespoon raspberry brandy. Dice the remaining strawberries, sprinkle with the remaining raspberry brandy and put to one side.

Melt the chocolate in a bowl over a pan of hot water, stirring until it becomes smooth.
Remove the paper from the meringues, spread one side of each meringue layer with chocolate, leave to set and then repeat the procedure on the other side.

Beat the egg yolks with the remaining sugar until they become thick and frothy. Whip 250 ml (8 fl oz) cream. Add three-quarters of the strawberry purée and the egg yolks to the cream.

Cover a plate with a sheet of aluminium foil and place the side section of a deep, springform cake tin about 28 cm (11 in) in diameter) on the plate. Lift up the edges of the aluminium foil to seal the tin. Put the first meringue layer in the tin, with the smooth side facing downwards, spread half of the strawberry cream over the meringue and finish off with the diced strawberries.
Cover with the second meringue layer and repeat the procedure, alternating the meringue with

the cream. Leave to set in a refrigerator for 6 hours. Soak the gelatine in 2 tablespoons of cold water for 10 minutes. Whip the remaining cream and add the vanilla sugar and gelatine.

Take the cake out of the refrigerator, remove the cake tin and the foil, spread the whipped cream over the cake, covering it completely. Cut the remaining strawberries in two and arrange them on the cream, leaving a space of 2-3 cm (¾-1¼ in) around the edge. Transfer the remaining cream to an icing bag and use to decorate the edge. Cut the sponge fingers to match the depth of the cake and arrange them round it, gently pressing them in. Serve immediately.

the flour, cornflour and baking powder using the electric mixer at slow speed until a smooth dough is formed.

Transfer the mixture to a lined, 28 cm (11 in) round cake tin and bake in a preheated oven at 180-200° C (350-400° F, Gas Mark 4-6) for 20-30 minutes.

Remove from the tin immediately and place on a wire rack, remove the greaseproof paper. Cut the sponge into three layers, sprinkle with the strawberry liqueur.

For the filling: mix the gelatine with 5 tablespoons cold water, leave to soak for 10 minutes, then heat until the gelatine has dissolved. Add the lemon juice and the remaining sugar to the strawberry purée and mix, finally adding the gelatine while still warm. Chill.

When the strawberry purée starts to gel, whip the cream and fold into the mixture. Spread this cream over the three sponge layers and place them one on top of the other.

Cover the cake with the cream, reserving some to put in an icing bag and decorate the cake. Finish off by decorating the cake with the halved strawberries.

Above : *Strawberry sponge*

STRAWBERRY SPONGE

Serves 8

4 eggs	liqueur
250 g (8 oz) caster sugar	500 ml (18 fl oz)
1 sachet vanilla sugar	strawberry purée
100 g (3½ oz) plain flour	1-2 tablespoons lemon
100 g (3½ oz) cornflour	juice
2 teaspoons baking	600 ml (1 pint) double
powder	cream
2 sachets gelatine	Some halved strawberries
8 tablespoons strawberry	

*B*eat the eggs and 2 tablespoons of hot water using an electric mixer at high speed for 1 minute until the mixture is thick and frothy. Add 150 g (5 oz) sugar and the vanilla sugar, beating continuously for 2 minutes. Incorporate

EMDEN GÂTEAU

Serves 8

2 eggs	750 ml (1¼ pints) double
100 g (3½ oz) caster sugar	cream
1 sachet vanilla sugar	3 tablespoons cranberries
75 g (3 oz) plain flour	1-2 tablespoons lemon
50 g (2 oz) cornflour	juice
2 teaspoons baking	100 g (3½ oz) plain
powder	chocolate
20 g (¾ oz) cocoa powder	

*B*eat the eggs and 2 tablespoons hot water using an electric mixer at high speed for 1 minute until the mixture is thick and frothy. Add the sugar and vanilla sugar, beating continuously for 2 minutes. Incorporate the flour, cornflour and baking powder using the electric mixer at low speed until a smooth consistency is achieved.

Transfer half the mixture to a deep, 28 cm (11 in) round cake tin, lined with greaseproof paper. Bake in a preheated oven at 180-200° C (350-400° F, Gas Mark 4-6) for about 15 minutes.

Add the cocoa powder to the remaining mixture and bake as for the plain sponge. Leave to cool.

For the filling: whip the cream until firm. Reserve one-third of the cream. Add the cranberries (reserving a few for decoration) and the lemon juice. Spread the mixture on the chocolate sponge layer. Cover with the plain sponge layer.

Break the plain chocolate into pieces and melt in a bowl over a pan of hot water, stirring well until it is smooth. Add the remaining cream, folding it in gently. Spread half of this chocolate cream over the cake and fill an icing bag with the rest. Use it to decorate the cake and finish off with the reserved cranberries.

Below: *Emden gâteau*

WALNUT GÂTEAU

Serves 8-10

7 eggs	1 vanilla pod
250 g (8 oz) caster sugar	5 egg yolks
2 pinches of salt	125 ml (4 fl oz) coffee
A pinch of ground	liqueur
cinnamon	500 ml (18 fl oz) double
Grated rind of 1 lemon	cream
300 g (10 oz) ground	75 g (3 oz) chopped
walnuts	walnuts
75 g (3 oz) semolina	50 walnut halves
1 sachet gelatine	Some chocolate curls
350 ml (11 fl oz) milk	

Grease a deep, 28 cm (11 in) round cake tin and line with greaseproof paper. Mix the eggs with 4 tablespoons hot water. Beat for 1 minute using an electric mixer at high speed until the mixture is creamy. Add 150 g (5 oz) sugar, one pinch of salt, the cinnamon and the lemon rind, beating continuously for 2 minutes. With the mixer at low speed, incorporate the ground walnuts and the semolina.

Spread the mixture in the cake tin and bake in a preheated oven at 180-200° C (350-400° F, Gas Mark 4-6) for 30 to 35 minutes.

Remove from the cake tin immediately and place on a wire rack. Remove the greaseproof paper, leave to cool and cut into three layers.

For the filling: mix the gelatine with 5 tablespoons cold water, leave to soak for 10 minutes and heat until the gelatine has dissolved. Heat the milk with the remaining salt and the vanilla pod and bring to the boil. Beat the egg yolks and the remaining sugar until the mixture is thick and frothy. Remove the vanilla pod from the milk and add the beaten eggs to the hot milk, stirring continuously, finally add the melted gelatine and the coffee liqueur. Place in a refrigerator. When the cream starts to set, whip the double cream (reserving 3 tablespoons) and gently fold it into the coffee mixture.

Put a layer of walnut sponge on a plate, surround it with the side-section of a deep, springform cake tin and cover with one-third of the cream. Sprinkle with half the chopped walnuts. Cover with the second layer of sponge, pressing down gently. Repeat the procedure and finish off by spreading the remaining cream on the cake. Decorate with the walnut halves.

Leave the cake to set in a refrigerator for at least 1 hour. Remove the cake tin. Cover the sides with the remaining cream and decorate with the chocolate curls.

Right:
Nut gâteau

PEAR AND CREAM TART

Serves 8

150 g (5 oz) plain flour
100 g (3½ oz) desiccated coconut
140 g (4½ oz) caster sugar
1 sachet vanilla sugar
Grated rind of 1 lemon
1 egg
125 g (4 oz) butter
1 kg (2 lb) Williams pears
375 ml (12 fl oz) white wine
A pinch of cinnamon
1 sachet gelatine
2 egg yolks
125 ml (4 fl oz) milk
250 ml (8 fl oz) double cream
2 tablespoons redcurrant jelly

Above: *Pear and cream tart*

Sift the flour and coconut on to the work surface and make a well in the centre. Add 75 g (3 oz) sugar, the vanilla sugar, the lemon rind and 1 egg. Mix with some of the flour to form a soft dough. Cut the butter into pieces, incorporate it with the dough and the remaining flour, kneading well. Leave to rest for 30 minutes in a refrigerator.

Grease a 28 cm (11 in) round flan tin.
Roll out the pastry and use it to line the dish, making the sides about 3 cm (1¼ in) deep. Bake in a preheated oven at 200-220° C (400-425° F, Gas Mark 6-7) for 20-25 minutes. Remove from the dish immediately and leave to cool.

To prepare the pears: peel the pears, remove the pips and cut them in half. Bring the wine, 40 g (1½ oz) sugar and cinnamon to the boil. Add the pears and leave to simmer for about 6 minutes. Drain, reserving the cooking juices, and leave to cool.

For the cream: soak the gelatine in 3 tablespoons cold water for 10 minutes. Heat the milk, egg yolks and remaining sugar. Add the gelatine, stirring continuously. Put this cream in a bowl above a pan of hot water and continue to stir until the cream thickens. Gradually add 250 ml (8 fl oz) of the juice in which the pears were cooked and leave the cream to cool over the pan of hot water.

When this creamy mixture starts to set, whip the double cream. Transfer half of the creamy egg mixture to another bowl and add some of the whipped cream to it. Spread the other half over the base of the tart, arrange the halved pears on it.

Transfer the remaining whipped cream to an icing bag fitted with a star-shaped nozzle and decorate the cake. Gently heat the redcurrant jelly, stirring continuously. Leave to cool, but do not let it set again, and use it to coat the pears.

BLACKBERRY GÂTEAU

Serves 8

6 eggs
250 g (8 oz) caster sugar
Grated rind of 1 lemon
175 g (6 oz) buckwheat
flour
750 g (1½ lb) blackberries
1 sachet gelatine

2 sachets vanilla sugar
2 tablespoons lemon juice
750 ml (1¼ pints) double
cream
225 g (7½ oz) blackberry
or raspberry jelly

*I*n a large mixing bowl, beat the eggs with 2 tablespoons hot water for 1 minute using an electric mixer at high speed. Add 125 g (4 oz) sugar and the lemon rind, beating continuously for 2 minutes.
Sift half the buckwheat flour on to the creamy egg mixture. Mix in, using the mixer at slow speed. Incorporate the remaining flour. Grease a deep, 28 cm (11 in) round cake tin and line with greaseproof paper, then pour in the mixture.

Bake in a preheated oven at 180-200° C (350-400° F, Gas Mark 4-6) for 30 to 35 minutes. Remove the cake from the tin and place on a wire rack. Remove the greaseproof paper and leave to cool. Cut the cake into three equal layers.

For the filling: wash, drain and hull half the blackberries. Purée them in a blender and strain through a sieve.

Soak the gelatine in some water for 10 minutes, then heat in a small pan until it dissolves. Add 100 g (3½ oz) sugar, 1 sachet vanilla sugar, the lemon juice and gelatine to the blackberry purée. When it starts to set, whip 500 ml (18 fl oz) cream and fold into the blackberry purée.

Spread half the jelly on the first sponge layer, cover with half the blackberry cream, smooth it out evenly, then cover with the second sponge layer and repeat the procedure. Finish off with the third layer, pressing it down gently.

Wash and drain the remaining blackberries and arrange them in the centre of the cake. Melt the remaining jelly with the remaining vanilla sugar, leave to cool, but do not let it set, and use to coat the blackberries.

Whip the remaining cream with the remaining sugar. Transfer to an icing bag fitted with a star-shaped nozzle and decorate the rim of the cake.

RASPBERRY CHOCOLATE GÂTEAU

Serve 8

150 g (5 oz) plain
chocolate
5 eggs, separated
65 g (2½ oz) caster sugar
1 tablespoon plain flour
1 pinch of baking powder

375 ml (12 fl oz) double
cream
1 sachet vanilla sugar
250 g (8 oz) raspberries
Some chocolate curls

*B*reak the chocolate into pieces and melt it in a bowl over a pan of hot water, stirring until it is smooth and glossy. Pour the melted chocolate into a bowl and gradually add the egg yolks and 50 g (2 oz) sugar, mixing well. Add the flour and baking powder. Whisk the egg whites into peaks and gently fold them into the mixture.

Grease a deep, 28 cm (11 in) round cake tin and line it with greaseproof paper, then pour in the mixture. Bake in a preheated oven at 150° C (300° F, Gas Mark 2) for 45 minutes. Leave to cool in the tin.

For the filling: whip the double cream for 30 seconds, then add the remaining sugar and the vanilla sugar. Beat until firm. Transfer half the cream to an icing bag fitted with a star-shaped nozzle.

Wash and hull the raspberries and mix them with the rest of the cream. Spread this mixture over the cake, decorate it with the cream in the icing bag and sprinkle with the chocolate curls and some raspberries.

Opposite: *Blackberry gâteau*

KIWI SPONGE CAKE

Serves 4-5

5 eggs, separated
200 g (7 oz) honey
200 g (7 oz) very fine plain
flour or buckwheat flour
2 teaspoons baking
powder
1 tablespoon melted
butter

750 ml (1¼ pints) double
cream
2 teaspoons caster sugar
1 sachet vanilla sugar
2-3 kiwi fruits
Some chopped pistachio
nuts

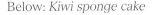

In a bowl, beat the egg yolks with the honey into a creamy consistency. In a separate bowl, whisk the egg whites into stiff peaks.

In a mixing bowl, mix the flour, baking powder and beaten eggs. Gently fold in the egg whites, followed by the melted butter.

Grease a deep, 26 cm (10½ in) round cake tin and line with greaseproof paper. Spread the mixture out in the tin and bake in a preheated oven at 180° C (350° F,

Gas Mark 4) for about 20-30 minutes. Remove from the tin immediately, take off the greaseproof paper, leave to cool and cut into three layers.

For the filling: whip the double cream for 30 seconds, then add the sugar and vanilla sugar, whisking continuously until very firm.

Peel the kiwi fruits and cut them into 3 mm (⅛in) thick slices (reserving a few for decoration).
Spread 4 tablespoons cream and some kiwi slices on the first layer of sponge, cover with the second layer and repeat the process. Place the final layer of sponge on the cream, pressing down gently.

Transfer the remaining cream to an icing bag fitted with a star-shaped nozzle and decorate the cake all over with rosettes. Garnish with some kiwi slices and chopped pistachio nuts.

Tip: leave the cake to rest for several hours in a refrigerator.

Below: *Kiwi sponge cake*

PEAR AND BLACKBERRY GÂTEAU

Serves 8

65 g (2½ oz) butter
5 eggs
200 g (7 oz) caster sugar
A pinch of salt
Grated rind of 1 lemon
75 g (3 oz) plain flour
65 g (2½ oz) cornflour
2 kg (4½ lb) medium-sized ripe pears
4 tablespoons lemon juice
500 ml (18 fl oz) white wine
1 vanilla pod
300 g (10 oz) blackberry jam
1 sachet gelatine
8 tablespoons pear brandy
500 ml (18 fl oz) double cream

*I*n a pan, melt the butter and leave to cool for a few moments. In a mixing bowl, beat the eggs with 4-5 tablespoons hot water using an electric mixer for 1 minute. Add 125 g (4 oz) sugar, the salt and lemon rind, beating continuously for 2 minutes. Add half the flour and cornflour to the beaten egg mixture, using an electric mixer at low speed. Add the remaining flour and cornflour in the same way. Skim the froth from the butter and work the butter into the mixture.

Grease a deep, 28 cm (11 in) round cake tin and line it with greaseproof paper. Spread the mixture out in the tin and bake in a preheated oven at 180-200° C (350-400° F, Gas Mark 4-6) for 20-30 minutes. Remove from the tin immediately it is taken out of the oven, take off the greaseproof paper, leave to cool and cut into two layers.

For the filling: peel the pears, sprinkle them with 2 tablespoons lemon juice, quarter them and remove the pips. In a pan, bring the white wine, 75 g (3 oz) sugar and the vanilla pod to the boil. Add the pears to this wine mixture. Cook over a low heat until the pears are soft, but do not let them disintegrate (set the 14 largest pieces to one side). Leave them to cool in the juice.

Spread half the blackberry jam on the first sponge layer and arrange half the remaining pears on the jam.

Purée the remaining pears with 125 ml (4 fl oz) of the juice in which they were cooked, 4 tablespoons pear brandy and the remaining lemon juice.

Soak the gelatine in a little cold water for 10 minutes, then heat in a small pan until it dissolves. Add it to the fruit purée, mixing well. When the purée begins to set, whip 375 ml (12 fl oz) double cream with an electric mixer until the cream is firm, fold it into the pear mixture.

Place the side section of a deep, springform cake tin around the cake and spread the pear cream over the fruits. Cover with the second sponge layer.

Mix 125 ml (4 fl oz) of the juice in which the pears were cooked with the remaining pear brandy and sprinkle on to the cake. Leave to rest for 1 hour in a refrigerator.

Whip the remaining double cream, spread it all over the cake. Arrange the reserved pear pieces around the edge and decorate the centre with the remaining blackberry jam.

Suggestion: serve with a glass of sherry.

PEACH AND HAZELNUT CHOCOLATE GÂTEAU

Serves 8

3 eggs
150 g (5 oz) caster sugar
2 sachets vanilla sugar
100 g (3½ oz) plain flour
100 g (3½ oz) cornflour
2 teaspoons baking powder
1 sachet gelatine
8 peaches
2 tablespoons lemon juice
4 tablespoons orange liqueur
500 ml (18 fl oz) double cream
400 g (13 oz) marzipan
3-4 tablespoons lemon marmalade
200 g (7 oz) icing sugar
200 g (7 oz) hazelnut chocolate spread

*I*n a large bowl, beat the eggs with 4-5 tablespoons hot water for 1 minute using an electric mixer. Add the sugar and 1 sachet vanilla sugar and continue beating for 2 minutes. Add half the flour and the cornflour to the beaten eggs and mix well with the mixer at minimum speed, add the remaining flour and beat until the mixture is smooth.

Grease a deep, 28 cm (11 in) round cake tin and line it with greaseproof paper. Spread the mixture in the tin and bake in a preheated oven at 180-200° C (350-400° F, Gas Mark 4-6) for 30-35 minutes. Remove from the tin as soon as it is taken out of the oven, take off the greaseproof paper, leave to cool. Cut the cake into two layers and place in the side section of a deep, springform cake tin.

For the filling: soak the gelatine in a little cold water for 10 minutes, then heat in a small pan until it dissolves.

Below: *Peach and hazelnut chocolate gâteau*

Plunge the peaches into some boiling water and refresh them under the cold tap. Peel the fruits, reserve 5 peaches and cover them with a sheet of aluminium foil. Purée the remaining peaches, add the lemon juice, orange liqueur, remaining vanilla sugar and the gelatine, mixing well. When the peaches begin to set, whip the double cream and fold in the peach mixture.

Halve the reserved peaches, remove the stones and arrange the fruits on the first layer of sponge, add the peach cream and smooth it out evenly. Cover with the second layer of sponge, pressing down gently.

Knead the marzipan with the lemon marmalade and the icing sugar, roll out into a 28 cm (11 in) diameter circle. Place this on the cake. With the remaining marzipan, make a band the same depth as the cake. Place this around the cake, pressing gently.

For the icing: melt the hazelnut chocolate spread in a bowl over a pan of hot water, stirring constantly, and use this to cover the cake. Place in a refrigerator.

STRAWBERRY AND CREAM TORTE

Serves 8

2 eggs, separated
125 g (4 oz) caster sugar
A pinch of salt
2 heaped tablespoons plain flour
2 heaped tablespoons ground almonds
1 sachet gelatine
1 kg (2 lb) strawberries
2 sachets vanilla sugar
1 tablespoon lemon juice
600 ml (1 pint) double cream
2 spoons strawberry jam

*I*n a mixing bowl, whisk the egg whites using an electric mixer for 1 minute. Gradually add 2 tablespoons sugar, the salt and egg yolks. Sift the flour and the ground almonds together and gently fold into the mixture. Grease a deep, 28 cm (11 in) round cake tin and line it with greaseproof paper. Spread the mixture in the tin and bake in a preheated oven at 180-200° C (350-400° F, Gas Mark 4-6) for 14 minutes. Remove from the tin as soon as it is taken out of the oven. Take off the grease-proof paper and leave to cool. Place the base of the tart on a plate and put the side section of a deep, springform cake tin around it.

For the filling: soak the gelatine in a little cold water for 10 minutes, then heat in a small pan until it dissolves.

Above: *Strawberry cream torte*

Wash, drain and hull 300 g (10 oz) strawberries and purée the fruit with 75 g (3 oz) sugar, 1 sachet vanilla sugar and the lemon juice. Add the gelatine, mixing well. When the strawberry purée begins to set, whip 375 ml (12 fl oz) double cream and fold into the strawberry mixture. Spread this mixture on to the pastry, smooth it out evenly and leave to rest in a refrigerator.

Wash and drain the remaining strawberries, halve them and dredge them with the remaining sugar. Leave to soak for a while in a sieve placed over a bowl. Save the juice and arrange the strawberries over the strawberry cream.

Heat the strawberry juice with the jam, leave to cool and use to coat the fruits.
Whip the remaining double cream for 30 seconds, add the remaining vanilla sugar. Continue to whisk until the cream is very firm.

Transfer this cream to an icing bag fitted with a fluted nozzle and decorate the sides of the tart.

BLACKCURRANT GÂTEAU

Serves 8

5 eggs
200 g (7 oz) caster sugar
1 sachet vanilla sugar
A pinch of salt
A pinch of cinnamon
Grated rind of 1 lemon
50 g (2 oz) plain flour
50 g (2 oz) cornflour
25 g (1 oz) cocoa powder
100 g (3½ oz) bitter

cooking chocolate
625 g (1¼ lb)
blackcurrants
1 sachet gelatine
125 ml (4 fl oz)
blackcurrant liqueur
600 ml (1 pint) double
cream
150 g (5 oz) milk cooking
chocolate

*I*n a bowl, beat the eggs with 3-4 tablespoons hot water using an electric mixer for 1 minute. Add half the sugar, the salt, cinnamon and lemon rind and continue beating for 2 minutes. Sift the flour, cornflour and cocoa powder on to the beaten eggs and mix in well using the electric mixer at low speed.

Break the bitter chocolate into pieces and melt it in a bowl over a pan of hot water, stirring so that it becomes smooth and glossy. Add to the mixture.

Grease a deep, 28 cm (11 in) round, lined cake tin. Spread the mixture in the tin and bake in a preheated oven at 180° C (350° F, Gas Mark 4) for 30-35 minutes.

When cooked, remove the cake from the tin, take off the greaseproof paper and leave to cool. Cut into three layers.

For the filling: wash, drain and remove the blackcurrants from their stalks using a fork. Put two-thirds of the fruit

in a pan with the remaining sugar, bring to the boil and cook for 2-3 minutes. Leave to cool.

Soak the gelatine in a little cold water for 10 minutes.

Mix the remaining blackcurrants with the cooked blackcurrant sauce and spread two-thirds of this mixture on the first layer of sponge. Heat the gelatine in a small pan until it dissolves, then add the remaining blackcurrant mixture, stirring constantly. Add the liqueur.

When the sauce begins to thicken, whip 500 ml (18 fl oz) double cream and fold it into the mixture.

Spread the blackcurrant cream over the fruit, making a dome shape. Cover with the remaining layer of sponge. Sprinkle with blackcurrant liqueur.

Whip the remaining double cream and spread all over the cake. Grate the milk chocolate and decorate the cake with the chocolate curls, pressing down gently with a broad-bladed knife.
Leave to rest in a refrigerator for about 2 hours.

Below: *Blackcurrant gâteau*

NECTARINE GÂTEAU

Serves 8

5 eggs
275 g (9 oz) caster sugar
1 sachet vanilla sugar
A pinch of salt
Grated rind of 1 lemon
100 g (3½ oz) plain flour
125 g (4 oz) cornflour
65 g (2½ oz) butter
1.2 kg (2¾ lb) nectarines
500 ml (18 fl oz) white wine

2 tablespoons lemon juice
4 egg yolks
1 sachet gelatine
6-8 tablespoons apricot liqueur
750 ml (1¼ pints) double cream
100 g (3½ oz) apricot jam

Beat 5 eggs, 165 g (5½ oz) sugar, the vanilla sugar, salt and lemon rind in a bowl placed over a pan of hot water for 7 minutes, using an electric mixer at high speed. Add the flour and 100 g (3½ oz) cornflour to the beaten eggs and continue to beat using the mixer for a further 7 minutes. Melt the butter and incorporate into the mixture.

Grease a deep, 28 cm (11 in) round cake tin and line with greaseproof paper. Spread the mixture into the tin and

Right:
Nectarine gâteau

bake in a preheated oven at 180-200° C (350-400° F, Gas Mark 4-6) for 30 to 35 minutes.
Remove from the tin as soon as the cake is taken out of the oven, take off the greaseproof paper and leave to cool. Cut into three layers.

For the filling: blanch the nectarines in boiling water (the water must not return to the boil), refresh the fruits under the cold tap, peel and halve them and remove the stones. In a pan, bring the white wine, 12 ml (4 fl oz) water, the remaining sugar and the nectarines to the boil. Cook for 3-4 minutes.

For the cream: take 500 ml (18 fl oz) of the juice in which the nectarines were cooked, add the lemon juice. Incorporate 4 egg yolks, beaten, with one-third of this juice, add the remaining cornflour and mix well. Leave to cool.

Soak the gelatine in a little cold water for 10 minutes. Cut one-third of the nectarines into small cubes and sprinkle them with 3-4 tablespoons apricot liqueur.

Whip 500 ml (18 fl oz) double cream. Melt the gelatine in a small pan. Mix the pieces of fruit with the nectarine cream, incorporate the gelatine, then the whipped cream.

Mix the remaining apricot liqueur with a little of the nectarine juice and pour over the three layers of sponge.

Line the sides of a deep, 28 cm (11 in) round cake tin with greaseproof paper and insert the first layer of sponge. Spread with half the fruit cream, then cover with the second layer, repeat the operation and finish with the third layer, placing it on top while pressing down gently. Leave to rest for 1 hour in a refrigerator.

Cut the remaining nectarines into slices. Whip the remaining double cream.

Remove the cake from the tin and spread the rest of the cream all over the cake. Decorate the top with the nectarine slices. Sieve the apricot jam, heat it and use to coat the nectarine slices.

FRIESIAN CHRISTMAS CAKE

Serves 8

400 g (13 oz) plain flour	100 g (3½ oz) caster sugar
1 pinch of baking powder	A pinch of cinnamon
? sachets vanilla sugar	450 g (15 oz) tinned
1 litre (1¾ pints) double cream	prunes, drained and puréed
275 g (9 oz) butter, cut into pieces	Icing sugar for decoration

Sift 250 g (8 oz) flour and the baking powder on to the work surface, make a well in the centre. Add 2 sachets vanilla sugar, 500 ml (18 fl oz) double cream and 175 g (6 oz) butter, then work into a flexible and smooth dough. If it is too soft, add a little more flour. Leave to rest in a refrigerator for a few moments, then divide the mixture into four.

Grease a 28 cm (11 in) sandwich tin. Roll out each portion of dough and line the base of the tin with the dough. Do not make any sides. Prick the base with a fork. Repeat this process for each portion of dough. For the crumble: sift the remaining flour, 75 g (3 oz) sugar and 1 sachet vanilla sugar into a bowl. Add the cinnamon and gradually incorporate the remaining butter cut into pieces. Using the fingertips or two forks, rub in the butter until a mixture resembling breadcrumbs is formed. Spread this mixture evenly over each pastry layer.

Bake the four pastry layers one after the other in a preheated oven at 200-220° C (400-425° F, Gas Mark 6-7) for 15 minutes. Remove from the tin immediately and cut one of the pastry bases into 12 portions. Leave to cool on a muslin cloth on a wire rack.

For the filling: whip the remaining 500 ml (18 fl oz) double cream for 30 seconds. Sprinkle the remaining sugar and vanilla sugar over the cream, whipping continuously until a firm consistency is achieved. Transfer to an icing bag fitted with a fluted nozzle.

Spread one-third of the puréed prunes over each pastry layer, cover them with whipped cream. Stack the filled layers one on top of the other, finishing with the layer which has been cut into portions. Dredge with icing sugar and leave to rest in a refrigerator. Before serving, cut the portions with a serrated knife.

Opposite: *Friesian Christmas Cake*

Above: *Chocolate dome*

CHOCOLATE DOME

Serves 8

700 g (1 lb 6 oz) plain
superfine cooking
chocolate
150 g (5 oz) butter
3 eggs
125 g (4 oz) caster sugar
2 pinches of salt
2 sachets vanilla sugar
150 g (5 oz) plain flour
2 teaspoons baking

powder
100 g (3½ oz) chopped
walnuts
5 egg yolks
3 tablespoons brandy
600 ml (1 pint) double
cream
1 tablespoon cocoa
powder
2 tablespoons icing sugar

Melt 100 g (3½ oz) chocolate and the butter in a bowl over a pan of hot water, stirring until a smooth consistency is achieved.

In a bowl, beat 3 eggs with 1 tablespoon hot water for 1 minute, using an electric mixer. Add the sugar, a pinch of salt and 1 sachet vanilla sugar. Continue beating for 2 minutes until the mixture is creamy. Sift the flour and baking powder over the beaten eggs and mix well using the electric mixer at low speed. Add the chopped walnuts and continue to mix well.

Line a deep, 26 cm (10½ in) round cake tin. Spread the mixture in the tin and bake in a preheated oven at 200° C (400° F, Gas Mark 6) for 25-30 minutes.

Remove from the tin as soon as it is taken out of the oven, take off the greaseproof paper and leave to cool.

For the chocolate mousse: melt 300 g (10 oz) chocolate in a bowl over a pan of hot water, stirring well, then leave to cool for a few moments.

Beat 5 egg yolks with 5 tablespoons hot water, the remaining vanilla sugar and the 2 tablespoons brandy using the mixer for 5 minutes. Gently fold into the warm chocolate.

Whip 375 ml (12 fl oz) double cream, then whisk the egg whites into peaks. Gently fold them into the chocolate cream to make a mousse.

Pour the mousse into a round-bottomed bowl, 500 ml (18 fl oz) capacity, 28 cm (11 in) in diameter. Smooth the top and leave to set overnight in a refrigerator.

For the filling: melt the remaining chocolate in a bowl over a pan of hot water, stirring well, then spread it over a baking sheet using a spatula. Before the chocolate hardens, make curls by scraping the chocolate with a broad-bladed knife.

Place the cooled pastry layer on a plate. Put the bowl containing the mousse into hot water for a moment to loosen, then turn the mousse out on to the pastry layer.

Whip the remaining double cream. Add the cocoa powder, 1 tablespoon icing sugar and the remaining brandy. Spread this mixture carefully over the dome of mousse. Decorate with the chocolate curls and dredge with the remaining icing sugar.

COINTREAU CREAM GÂTEAU

Serves 8

150 g (5 oz) softened
butter
175 g (6 oz) caster sugar
1 sachet vanilla sugar
4 eggs
200 g (7 oz) ground
hazelnuts
4 tablespoons cocoa
powder

2 teaspoons baking
powder
500 g (1 lb) tinned
apricots in syrup
500 ml (18 fl oz) double
cream
5 tablespoons Cointreau
2 tablespoons apricot jam

Cream the butter, gradually adding 150 g (5 oz) sugar, the vanilla sugar and eggs. Incorporate the ground hazelnuts, cocoa and baking powder.

Line a deep, 28 cm (11 in) round cake tin. Spread the mixture in the tin and bake in a preheated oven at 180-200° C (350-400° F, Gas Mark 4-6) for 30 to 35 minutes.

Remove from the tin immediately it has been taken out of the oven, take off the greaseproof paper and leave to cool. Cut into two layers.

For the filling: drain the apricots and arrange them on the first layer of sponge, leaving a 2 cm (¾ in) gap on the edge.
Whip the double cream for 30 seconds, add the remaining sugar, beating continuously until the cream is very firm. Add the Cointreau.

Reserve a quarter of the cream and transfer this to an icing bag fitted with a round-ended nozzle. Spread half the cream over the apricots, cover with the remaining layer of sponge, pressing down gently. Spread the rest of the cream over the cake and pipe 16 rings using the icing bag.

Sieve the apricot jam and decorate each ring and the centre of the cake with some jam.

Below: *Cointreau cream gâteau*

Above: *Yoghurt and white wine gâteau*

YOGHURT AND WHITE WINE GÂTEAU

Serves 8

4 eggs
285 g (9½ oz) caster sugar
1 sachet vanilla sugar
150 g (5 oz) plain flour
85 g (3¾ oz) cornflour
2 teaspoons baking powder
2 sachets gelatine
300 g (10 oz) cherry jam
450 ml (¾ pint) white wine
3 egg yolks
Juice of 1 lemon
500 ml (18 fl oz) double cream
150 g (5 oz) yoghurt
Some chopped pistachio nuts

In a bowl, beat the eggs and 2 tablespoons hot water with an electric mixer at high speed for 1 minute until the mixture is thick and frothy. Add 200 g (7 oz) sugar and the vanilla sugar, beating continuously for 2 minutes. Incorporate the flour, 65 g (2½ oz) cornflour and the baking powder using an electric mixer at low speed until a smooth consistency is achieved.

Line a baking sheet. Spread three-quarters of the mixture about 1 cm (½ in) thick on the baking sheet and fold up the greaseproof paper to form a rim. Place the baking sheet in a hot oven for 10-15 minutes.

Turn the remaining mixture into a lined, deep, 28 cm (11 in) round cake tin and bake in a preheated oven at 200-220° C (400-425° F, Gas Mark 6-7) for 15-20 minutes.

After 15 minutes, turn the Swiss roll sponge out on to a sheet of paper dredged with granulated sugar. Sprinkle some cold water over the greaseproof paper and remove it carefully. Spread the cherry jam over the sponge and roll it up lengthwise. Leave to cool and cut into 16 equal portions. Arrange them in a deep, springform cake tin lined with greaseproof paper and put on a plate.

For the filling: soak a sachet of gelatine in 3 tablespoons cold water for 10 minutes. Put the remaining cornflour, 200 ml (7 fl oz) white wine, 65 g (2½ oz) sugar, 3 egg yolks and the lemon juice in a pan and heat, beating continuously, until it begins to bubble. Add the gelatine. Leave to cool, beating from time to time, until it begins to set.

Whip the double cream, add the yoghurt, then the cream mixture, and spread this mixture over the Swiss roll layer.

Remove the greaseproof paper from the round sponge and put this layer of sponge on the cream, pressing down well. Leave to set in a refrigerator.

Place the tin upside down on a plate, remove the tin together with the greaseproof paper. Replace the side section of the springform tin.

Soak the remaining gelatine in a little cold water for 10 minutes. Then heat with the remaining white wine and sugar, stir until it has completely dissolved and leave to cool. When it begins to set, pour it over the cake. Decorate the edge with chopped pistachio nuts.

STRAWBERRY MERINGUE

Serves 8

750 g (1½ lb) strawberries
3-4 tablespoons kirsch
1-2 tablespoons icing sugar
4 egg whites
250 g (8 oz) caster sugar
1 tablespoon lemon juice
600 ml (1 pint) double cream
3 sachets vanilla sugar

Wash and drain the strawberries. Set aside 250 g (8 oz) and cut the remainder in four, sprinkle with kirsch and dredge with icing sugar. Cover and leave to soak for about 3 hours.

For the meringue: cover two baking sheets with greaseproof paper and draw three 22 cm (8½ in) diameter circles using a cake tin.

Whisk the egg whites in a bowl over a pan of hot water together with the sugar and lemon juice using an electric mixer at high speed until a firm consistency has been achieved.

Below: *Strawberry meringue*

Spread one-third of this mixture on the circles and place the baking sheets in a preheated oven at 100° C (200° F) for about 3 hours. Change the baking sheets around after 1½ hours.

At the end of the cooking time, remove the meringues from the paper and place one layer of meringue on a plate. Place the sides of a deep, springform cake tin around the meringue.

For the cream: whip 500 ml (18 fl oz) double cream and gradually add 2 sachets vanilla sugar. Gently fold in the strawberries soaked in kirsch and spread half the cream mixture over the first layer of meringue. Cover with another layer of meringue, spread with the remaining cream and finish with the third layer of meringue. Leave to set for at least 5 hours in the freezing compartment of a refrigerator.

Half an hour before serving, whip the remaining double cream together with the remaining vanilla sugar. Spread this mixture over the cake. Decorate with the remaining strawberries.

Variation: alternatively, the cake can be decorated by dredging it with sifted icing sugar or cocoa powder.

MOCHA CREAM

Serves 8

225 g (7½ oz) plain flour
2 tablespoons caster sugar
3 sachets vanilla sugar
A pinch of salt
100 g (3½ oz) butter
2 eggs
75 g (3 oz) cornflour
2 teaspoons baking powder

250 g (8 oz) tinned Morello cherries in syrup
2 teaspoons instant coffee
2-4 spoons cherry jam
750 ml (1¼ pints) double cream
2 tablespoons icing sugar
16 confectioner's coffee beans for decoration

Sift 150 g (5 oz) flour on to a work surface and make a well in the centre. Quickly rub in the sugar, 1 sachet vanilla sugar, the salt and the butter cut into pieces. Cover with flour and rub in using the fingertips until the mixture resembles breadcrumbs. Gradually add 150 ml (¼ pint) water. Quickly work the mixture into a dough which is easy to roll out. Leave to rest.

Roll out the pastry and use it to line a greased, 28 cm (11 in) flan tin. Prick the base with a fork.

Bake in a preheated oven at 180-200° C (350-400° F, Gas Mark 4-6) for 15-20 minutes. Remove from the tin as soon as the cake is taken out of the oven and leave to cool.

For the sponge: beat the eggs and 2 tablespoons hot water using an electric mixer at high speed for 1 minute until the mixture is thick and frothy. Add 1 sachet vanilla sugar and continue to beat for 2 minutes. Incorporate the remaining flour, 50 g (2 oz) cornflour and the baking powder using an electric mixer at low speed until a smooth consistency is achieved.

Turn the mixture into a lined, deep, 28 cm (11 in) round cake tin, smoothing it out evenly.

Bake in a preheated oven at 180-200° C (350-400° F, Gas Mark 4-6) for 25-30 minutes. Remove from the tin as soon as the cake is taken out of the oven and take off the greaseproof paper.

When the sponge has cooled, cut it into two equal layers.

Above: *Mocha cream*

For the filling: drain the cherries and reserve 200 ml (7 fl oz) of the juice. Mix the remaining cornflour with the juice and bring to the boil. Add the cherries and sugar to taste and leave to set in a refrigerator.

Mix the coffee with 2 spoons boiling water and leave to cool. Spread 2 spoonfuls of cherry jam on the pastry base, cover with the first layer of sponge and spread the cherries over the sponge.

Whip the double cream for 30 seconds and gradually add the icing sugar and the remaining vanilla sugar. Set aside one-third of this cream and mix the rest with the coffee. Spread the coffee cream over the cherries and cover with the second layer of sponge.

Cover the cake with half of the remaining cream. Transfer the rest to an icing bag and pipe 16 cream rosettes around the edge of the cake. Place a coffee bean on the top of each rosette.

RUM GÂTEAU

Serves 8

200 g (7 oz) butter
3 pinches of salt
200 g (7 oz) caster sugar
275 g (9 oz) plain flour
6 eggs
1 teaspoon grated lemon
rind
375 g (12 oz) cherries in
syrup
4 tablespoons cornflour
A pinch of cinnamon

2 sachets gelatine
7 egg yolks
375 ml (12 fl oz) milk
1 vanilla pod
750 ml (1¼ pints) double
cream
3-4 tablespoons rum
50-65 g (2-2½ oz) flaked
almonds
Icing sugar to finish

Place 250 ml (8 fl oz) water, 125 g (4 oz) butter, a pinch of salt and 15 g (½ oz) sugar in a pan and bring to the boil. Remove the pan from the heat and add 125 g (4 oz) flour to the hot water. Combine quickly to form a smooth ball. Cook for 1 minute over a very low heat, stirring constantly.

Transfer the mixture immediately to a bowl. Incorporate the eggs, one by one, and, using an electric mixer with a kneading attachment, beat until the paste retains its shape. Divide the mixture into three portions and leave to cool. Spread out into three circles. Bake these one after the other in a deep, 28 cm (11 in) round cake tin, greased and dusted with flour, in a preheated oven at 220° C (425° F, Gas Mark 7) for 15-20 minutes. Make sure that the edges are not too thin, as otherwise the pastry may burn.
Loosen the pastry layers immediately, put them back on the base of the cake tin and bake for a further 3-5 minutes. Leave to cool on a muslin cloth on a wire rack.

For the shortcrust pastry: sift the remaining flour on to a work surface and make a well in the centre. Add 50 g (2 oz) sugar, a pinch of salt and the remaining butter, cut into pieces. Add the lemon rind and cover with flour. Quickly rub in the butter, using the fingertips, until the mixture resembles breadcrumbs. Gradually add 150 ml (¼ pint) water. Quickly work the mixture to a consistency which is easy to roll out. Leave to rest.

Below: *Rum gâteau*

Roll out the pastry and use to line a greased, 28 cm (11 in) round flan tin. Prick the base with a fork. Bake in a preheated oven at 200° C (400° F, Gas Mark 6) for 15 minutes. Remove from the tin immediately and leave to cool.

For the filling: drain the cherries and reserve 250 ml (8 fl oz) of the juice. Mix the cornflour with 4 tablespoons juice and bring to the boil with the remaining juice, the cinnamon and 15 g (½ oz) sugar. Add the cherries and leave to cool in a refrigerator.

For the rum cream: soak the gelatine in 6 tablespoons cold water for 10 minutes. Beat the egg yolks and 100 g (3½ oz) sugar until the mixture is thick and frothy. Put the milk in a pan, add the vanilla, the remaining sugar and the last pinch of salt. Bring to the boil. Gradually add the milk to the eggs, beating constantly until a thick creamy consistency is achieved, then add the gelatine and continue to beat to ensure it dissolves.

As soon as it starts to set, whip the double cream and fold it into the vanilla cream. Add the rum.

Put the pastry base on a plate and place the side section of a deep, 28 cm (11 in) round springform cake tin around it. Spread the cherry mixture over the pastry, cover with a choux pastry layer, pressing down gently, fill with half the rum cream, cover with the second choux pastry layer, repeat the procedure with the third choux pastry layer. Leave the cake to set in the refrigerator for 4-5 hours.

Toast the almonds in a frying pan and arrange them on the sides of the cake, pressing them in gently. Decorate the top with the icing sugar.

Above: *Redcurrant and wine cream gâteau*

REDCURRANT AND WINE CREAM GÂTEAU

Serves 8

275 g (9 oz) plain flour
240 g (7¾ oz) caster sugar
2 sachets vanilla sugar
2 pinches of salt
Grated rind of 1 lemon
100 g (3½ oz) butter
6 eggs
2 teaspoons baking powder
80 g (3¼ oz) cornflour

700 g (1 lb 6 oz) redcurrant jelly
1 sachet gelatine
2 egg yolks
150 ml (¼ pint) white wine
1 tablespoon lemon juice
600 ml (1 pint) double cream
500 g (1 lb) redcurrants

Sift 150 g (5 oz) flour on to a work surface and make a well in the centre. Quickly incorporate 50 g (2 oz) sugar, 1 sachet vanilla sugar, a pinch of salt, the lemon rind and the butter cut into pieces. Cover with flour and rub in lightly using the fingertips until the mixture resembles breadcrumbs. Gradually add 150 ml (¼ pint) water. Quickly work the mixture into a dough which is easy to roll out. Leave to rest.
Roll the pastry out and use to line a greased, 28 cm (11 in) round flan tin. Prick the base with a fork.

Bake in a preheated oven at 180-200° C (350-400° F, Gas Mark 4-6) for 15-20 minutes.
Remove from the tin immediately and leave to cool.

For the sponge: beat the eggs and 6 tablespoons hot water using an electric mixer at high speed for 1 minute until the mixture is thick and frothy. Add 90 g (3¼ oz) sugar and the remaining vanilla sugar, beating continuously for 2 minutes. Incorporate the remaining flour, the baking powder and cornflour using an electric mixer at low speed until a smooth consistency is achieved.

Grease a baking sheet and line it with greaseproof paper. Spread the mixture on the paper and bake in an oven preheated to 180-200° C (350-400° F, Gas Mark 4-6) for 10 minutes.

When the sponge is cooked, turn it out on to a sheet of greaseproof paper dredged with sugar and spread 300 g (10 oz) redcurrant jelly on the sponge.

For the white wine cream: soak the gelatine in 3 tablespoons cold water for 10 minutes.
Put the white wine, the remaining sugar and the lemon juice in a pan and heat, beating constantly. Remove from the heat, add the gelatine and 2 egg yolks. Continue to beat while leaving the mixture to cool over a pan of cold water.
When the cream starts to set, whip up 500 ml (18 fl oz) double cream and fold it into the white wine mixture. Spread the cream over the sponge.
Cut the sponge into strips roughly 4 cm (1½ in) wide.

Spread 100 g (3½ oz) redcurrant jelly over the pastry base. Roll the first strip of sponge to form a Swiss roll, place it in the centre of the pastry base and arrange the remaining strips of sponge cake in a spiral around it until the cake is completed.
Place the side section of a deep, springform cake tin around the cake and leave to set in a refrigerator for 1 hour.

For the filling: wash and drain the redcurrants and remove them from their stalks using a fork. Arrange them on the cake. Heat the remaining redcurrant jelly and coat the redcurrants with this liquid jelly. Leave to cool for 10 minutes.

Whip the remaining cream.

Remove the side section of the cake tin and decorate the sides of the cake with the whipped cream.

SNOWBALL

Serves 8

125 g (4 oz) butter
125 g (4 oz) caster sugar
2 sachets vanilla sugar
4 eggs, separated
A pinch of salt
100 g (3½ oz) plain flour
2 teaspoons baking powder
100 g (3½ oz) desiccated coconut
3 tablespoons raspberry or cherry jam
500 ml (18 fl oz) double cream
Icing sugar to finish

Cream the butter and add the sugar, 1 sachet vanilla sugar, the egg yolks and salt. Add the flour and baking powder, incorporate well, finally add 65 g (2½ oz) desiccated coconut.

Whisk the egg whites into peaks and gently fold them into the mixture.

Turn the mixture into a greased, deep, 28 cm (11 in) round cake tin, smoothing it out evenly. Bake in a preheated oven at 180oC (350oF, Gas Mark 4) for 30 minutes.

Remove the cake from the tin and cut into two layers.

For the filling: spread the jam over the first layer of sponge.

Whip the cream for 30 seconds, add the remaining vanilla sugar, continuing to beat until the cream is very firm. Spread half the cream over the jam, cover with the second layer of sponge and spread the rest of the cream over the top and sides of the cake. Sprinkle the remaining coconut over the cake. Dredge with icing sugar just before serving.

Opposite: *Snowball*

CRANBERRY AND ADVOCAT GÂTEAU

Serves 8

3 eggs
110 g (3¾ oz) caster sugar
100 g (3½ oz) ground hazelnuts
100 g (3½ oz) grated plain chocolate
225 g (7½ oz) cranberries

in syrup
375 ml (12 fl oz) double cream
1 sachet vanilla sugar
4-5 tablespoons advocat

Beat the eggs with 2 tablespoons hot water using an electric mixer at high speed for 1 minute until the mixture is thick and frothy. Add 100 g (3½ oz) sugar, beating constantly for 2 minutes. Mix the ground hazelnuts with the chocolate and gradually add to the eggs.

Turn the mixture into a lined, deep, 26 cm (10½ in) round cake tin, smoothing it out evenly.

Bake in a preheated oven at 180-200° C (350-400° F, Gas Mark 4-6) for 25-20 minutes. Remove from the tin immediately, peel off the greaseproof paper and leave to cool.

Right:
Cranberry and advocat gâteau

For the filling: arrange the cranberries on the cake. Whip the cream for 30 seconds, add the remaining sugar and the vanilla sugar, then continue to beat until the cream is very firm. Spread two-thirds of the cream over the cranberries and smooth it out evenly. Transfer the remaining cream to an icing bag fitted with a round nozzle. Decorate the edge of the cake and pipe the checkerboard pattern on the top. Pour the advocat into some of the squares.

APRICOT GÂTEAU

Serves 8

250 g (8 oz) plain flour
200 g (7 oz) butter
A pinch of salt
50 g (2 oz) cornflour
275 ml (9 fl oz) white wine
100 g (3½ oz) caster sugar
Juice of 2 lemons
Grated rind of 1 lemon
2 egg yolks
1 kg (2 lb) ripe apricots
4 tablespoons apricot liqueur

8 tablespoons apricot jam
500 ml (18 fl oz) double cream
2 teaspoons powdered gelatine or 1 gelatine leaf
4 tablespoons apricot brandy
4 tablespoons apricot juice
150 g (5 oz) rectangular chocolate slices

Above: *Apricot Gâteau*

Sift the flour on to a work surface and make a well in the centre. Cut the butter into pieces, place in the well with the salt and 100 ml (3½ fl oz) water, knead, drawing the flour into the centre, until a smooth dough is formed.

Roll out the pastry into a rectangle measuring approximately 32 x 22 cm (12¾ x 8½ in). Fold one-third of the pastry to the middle and cover with the other side, pressing down gently, roll out again and repeat the procedure until there are six layers of pastry. Leave to rest in a refrigerator for 30 minutes.

Divide the pastry into three equal parts. Roll out each one and cut into circles 28 cm (11 in) in diameter. Place each pastry circle on a baking sheet, previously rinsed in cold water. Prick the pastry with a fork and leave to rest for 10 minutes. Bake in a preheated oven at 200° C (400° F, Gas Mark 6) for 15 minutes.

Remove the tart base carefully from the baking sheet and leave to cool.

For the cream: mix the cornflour with 5 tablespoons wine. Pour the remaining wine into a pan with the sugar, the lemon rind and juice, then bring to the boil. Thicken using the cornflour mixture. Remove from the heat, add the egg yolks, stirring well. Leave to cool, stirring constantly.

Blanch the apricots and refresh under the cold tap. Remove the skin, cut the fruit in two and remove the stone. Set two-thirds of the fruit to one side. Dice the remaining third and sprinkle with apricot liqueur.

For the filling: thin down the apricot jam with 4 tablespoons water, bring to the boil and cook for 5-8 minutes over a low heat. Coat two of the pastry bases with the hot jam on both sides, the third one on only one side.

Beat the double cream until floppy. Whip up 100 ml (3½ fl oz) until firm. Gently fold in the diced apricot.

Take the side section of a deep, 28 cm (11 in) round springform cake tin, put it on a plate and place the third pastry base, jam side uppermost, in the tin. Spread half the apricot cream over this layer of pastry, cover with another pastry layer, press down gently and repeat the procedure.

Mix the gelatine with 2 tablespoons cold water and leave to soak for 10 minutes. In a separate bowl, mix the brandy, apricot juice and 2 tablespoons jam. Heat the gelatine, stirring until it has completely dissolved, then add the brandy mixture. Arrange the halved fruits on the top of the cake and coat with the apricot jelly. Leave to set in the refrigerator for 15 minutes.

Whip the remaining double cream until it is very firm. Remove the side section of the cake tin and cover the sides of the cake with a thick layer of cream. Press the chocolate slices into the cream all around the cake and decorate the edge with the whipped cream, using an icing bag.

Above: *Raspberry nut gâteau*

RASPBERRY NUT GÂTEAU

Serves 8

100 g (3½ oz) coarsely
chopped hazelnuts
100 g (3½ oz) coarsely
chopped walnuts
325 g (11 oz) icing sugar
4 eggs
50 g (2 oz) caster sugar
1 sachet vanilla sugar
100 g (3½ oz)
breadcrumbs
2 pinches of salt
2 sachets powdered

gelatine or 4 gelatine
leaves
200 g (7 oz) redcurrant
jelly
4 egg yolks
500 g (1 lb) raspberries
750 ml (1¼ pints) double
cream
5-6 spoons raspberry
brandy
25 g (1 oz) plain superfine
cooking chocolate

Mix the hazelnuts and walnuts together. Melt 250 g
(8 oz) icing sugar in a pan until it caramelizes and turns
light brown, add the walnuts and hazelnuts and stir.
Spread this nut mixture on to a baking sheet, leave to set,
then crush the praline.

For the pastry: beat the eggs with 1 tablespoon hot
water using an electric mixer at high speed for 1 minute,
add the caster sugar and vanilla sugar and continue to
beat for 2 minutes. Combine the breadcrumbs with half
the praline and gradually add to the eggs.

Cut out three 28 cm (11 in) diameter circles in
greaseproof paper. Lay them on greased baking sheets
and cover with the mixture. Bake in a preheated oven at
220° C (425° F, Gas Mark 7) for 5-6 minutes. Remove from

the tin immediately, place on a muslin cloth on a wire rack, and peel off the greaseproof paper. Leave to cool.

For the filling: mix the gelatine with 2 tablespoons cold water and leave to soak for 10 minutes.

Melt the redcurrant jelly with 2 spoons water in a small pan, bring to the boil and cook over a low heat for 5-6 minutes. Add one-third of the gelatine, stirring well.

Put the egg yolks and the remaining icing sugar in a bowl over a pan of hot water and beat until the mixture thickens. Add the remaining gelatine, stirring constantly. Put a praline pastry layer on a plate and place the side section of a deep, 28 cm (11 in) round springform cake tin around it.

Arrange half the raspberries (keep the best ones for decoration) on the praline pastry layer, leaving a 1 cm (½ in) gap around the edge. Coat with half the redcurrant jelly.

Whip 500 ml (18 fl oz) double cream until it is very firm and fold in half of the remaining praline mixture, the egg cream mixture and the raspberry brandy. Spread half of this mixture over the raspberries, cover with another pastry layer, press down gently.

Arrange the remaining raspberries on the pastry layer and repeat the above procedure. Leave the cake to set in a refrigerator for 1 hour.

For the decoration: melt the chocolate in a bowl over a pan of hot water, stirring until smooth.

Make a small funnel out of greaseproof paper and cut an opening 3 mm (⅛ in) wide.

Whip the remaining double cream until firm and cover the entire cake with this cream. Pour the chocolate into the paper funnel and draw a spiral on the top of the cake. Using a cocktail stick, mark out 16 portions. Finish by decorating with raspberries.

PLUM AND COCONUT GÂTEAU

Serves 8

4 eggs	200 g (7 oz) creamed
300 g (10 oz) caster sugar	coconut
2 sachets vanilla sugar	75 g (3 oz) desiccated
100 g (3½ oz) plain flour	coconut
100 g (3½ oz) cornflour	4 tablespoons coconut
2 teaspoons baking	liqueur
powder	Grated rind of ½ lemon
2 sachets gelatine	2 tablespoons lemon juice
1.5 g (3½ lb) plums	750 ml (1¼ pints) double
3 egg yolks	cream

*B*eat the eggs with 4 tablespoons hot water using an electric mixer at high speed for 1 minute until the mixture is thick and frothy. Add 150 g (5 oz) sugar and 1 sachet vanilla sugar, beating constantly for 2 minutes. Incorporate the flour, cornflour and baking powder using an electric mixer at low speed until a smooth consistency is achieved.

Turn the mixture into a lined, deep, 28 cm (11 in) round cake tin, taking care to smooth it out evenly.
Bake in a preheated oven at 180-200° C (350-400° F, Gas Mark 4-6) for 35 minutes. Remove from the tin immediately and peel off the greaseproof paper.
When the sponge is cool, cut it into three equal layers.

Right: *Plum and coconut gâteau*

For the filling: in a pan, mix the gelatine with 6 table-spoons cold water and leave to soak for 10 minutes.

Wash the plums, remove the stones and reserve 8 fruits for decoration. Pour 125 ml (4 fl oz) water and 125 g (4 oz) sugar into a pan, bring to the boil. Add the plums. Bring back to the boil and leave to cool. Stew 300 g (10 oz) plums slightly longer to make a compôte.

Heat half the gelatine, stirring constantly, until it dissolves and add to the fruit compôte. Place in a refrigerator.

Beat 3 egg yolks with 15 g (½ oz) sugar and the remaining vanilla sugar until the mixture is thick and frothy. Mix the creamed coconut and the desiccated coconut (reserving 2 tablespoons for decoration), moisten with the liqueur, the lemon rind and juice. Combine all these ingredients with the egg mixture. Heat the remaining gelatine, stirring constantly until it melts, and stir into the mixture. Place in a refrigerator. When the mixture starts to set, whip 500 ml (18 fl oz) double cream until it is very firm.

Mix 6 spoons whipped cream with the plum compôte and incorporate the rest with the coconut cream.

Line the side of a deep, round cake tin with a sheet of aluminium foil higher than the side of the tin and create a solid upper rim. Place the first sponge layer in the tin.

Spread the plum compôte over the sponge, cover with the second layer of sponge, pressing down gently, spread the cooked plums over the second layer, cover with the coconut cream (reserve 4 tablespoons) and finish by covering the coconut cream with the third layer of sponge.

Spread the remaining coconut cream over the top of the cake and leave to set in a refrigerator for 6 hours.

Whip the remaining cream for 30 seconds, add the remaining sugar, then continue beating until the cream is very firm. Transfer this cream to an icing bag fitted with a star-shaped nozzle.

Carefully remove the side section of the cake tin and the aluminium foil and decorate the sides of the cake using the icing bag.

Arrange the remaining plums around the centre of the cake and finish by dredging the centre with desiccated coconut.

CARDINAL CAKE

Serves 8

3 eggs	Morello cherries in syrup
125 g (4 oz) caster sugar	2-3 tablespoons
75 g (3 oz) plain flour	redcurrant jelly
1 packet caramel custard	1 sachet gelatine
2 teaspoons baking	350 ml (11 fl oz) double
powder	cream
3 tablespoons rum	Some chocolate curls
250-300 g (8-10 oz) stoned	

*B*eat the eggs with 2 to 3 tablespoons hot water using an electric mixer at high speed for 1 minute until the mixture is thick and frothy. Add the sugar and continue to beat for 2 minutes. Combine the flour and the caramel custard mix, then gradually mix them into the eggs, beating constantly with the mixer at low speed.

Turn the mixture into a lined, deep, 28 cm (11 in) round cake tin and smooth it out evenly. Preheat the oven to 180-200° C (350-400° F, Gas Mark 4-6).
Bake for 3-4 minutes.

Remove from the tin immediately and leave to cool on a muslin cloth on a wire rack. Carefully peel off the greaseproof paper. When cool, cut into two equal layers.

For the filling: drain the cherries, reserve some for decoration and save the juice. Sprinkle the cherries with rum. Spread the redcurrant jelly over the first sponge layer. Cover with the second layer of sponge, drain the rum-soaked cherries (save the juice) and arrange them on top of the second layer of sponge.
Soak the gelatine in 5 tablespoons cherry juice for 10 minutes, then place over a low heat until it has dissolved. Whip the double cream until firm, reserve a few spoonfuls for decoration and mix in the cooled gelatine; cover the cake with the cherry cream. Decorate with the chocolate curls and the remaining cream and reserved cherries.

Above: *Cardinal cake*

KIWI AND WILD STRAWBERRY GÂTEAU

Serves 8

1 packet vanilla instant
whip mix
300 ml (½ pint) milk
1 sachet vanilla sugar
200 g (7 oz) butter
12 kiwi fruits

200 g (7 oz) wild
strawberries
1 ready-made genoese
sponge
100 g (3½ oz) strawberry
jam

First whisk the contents of the packet with the milk using an electric mixer at low speed. Increase the speed and continue to whisk for 2 minutes. Add the vanilla sugar and the softened butter. Continue to whisk until the mixture is thick and frothy. Place this cream in a refrigerator.

Peel the kiwi fruits, slice them. Wash and hull the strawberries.

Cut the genoese sponge into three layers. Place the first layer on a plate.

Spread 50 g (2 oz) strawberry jam over the first layer, then quarter of the butter mixture and cover with the equivalent of 4 kiwis cut into slices. Cover with the second layer of sponge, repeat the procedure and finish with the third layer, pressing down gently.

Spread the remaining cream over the entire cake and decorate with slices of kiwis and the wild strawberries.

Below: *Kiwi and wild strawberry gâteau*

GRAPE AND WHITE WINE GÂTEAU

Serves 8

100 g (3½ oz) marzipan
225 g (7½ oz) caster sugar
2-3 tablespoons brandy
A pinch of salt
1 teaspoon grated lemon rind
12 eggs, separated
100 g (3½ oz) plain flour
1 sachet gelatine

1 kg (2 lb) white grapes
1 tablespoon lemon juice
250 ml (8 fl oz) white wine
150 g (5 oz) apricot jam
500 ml (18 fl oz) double cream
125 g (4 oz) bitter chocolate leaves

Above: *Grape and white wine gâteau*

*I*n a mixing bowl, combine the marzipan with 100 g (3½ oz) sugar and the brandy. Add the salt, lemon rind and egg yolks. Beat using an electric mixer until a creamy consistency is achieved.
Whisk the egg whites into peaks and place them on the marzipan mixture. Cover with the flour and gently combine all these ingredients.

Turn the mixture into a greased, deep, 28 cm (11 in) round cake tin and smooth it out evenly. Bake in a preheated oven at 180-200° C (350-400° F, Gas Mark 4-6) for 25-30 minutes. Remove from the tin once the cake is cool and cut into two equal layers.

For the filling: soak the gelatine in 5 tablespoons cold water for 10 minutes.
Wash and drain the grapes, then remove the pips, set aside about 20 for decoration.

Put the remaining egg yolks, the remaining sugar, the lemon juice and wine in a bowl over a pan of hot water. Beat until the mixture thickens.

Heat the gelatine, stirring constantly until it has completely dissolved, then add it to the wine cream. Cool the mixture by placing the bowl in cold water.

Spread the apricot jam over the first layer of sponge and cover with grapes. Place the side section of a deep, springform cake tin around this layer. Fill the spaces between the grapes with 3-4 spoonfuls wine cream. Place the cake in a refrigerator.

Whip 250 ml (8 fl oz) double cream until firm and fold into the wine cream. Spread over the grapes and cover with the second layer of sponge. Leave the cake overnight in the refrigerator.

Remove the side section of the tin, cut reserved the grapes in two.

Whip the remaining 250 ml (8 fl oz) cream until firm and spread over the cake.

Take the halved grapes and make two bunches of grapes as decoration. Melt the leaves of chocolate in a bowl over a pan of hot water. Pour half into small leaf-shaped moulds and leave to cool. Make a small funnel out of greaseproof paper, fill with the remaining melted chocolate and draw vine shoots on the top of the cake.

Take the chocolate leaves out of the moulds and decorate the sides and top of the cake with these vine leaves

YOGHURT GÂTEAU

Serves 8

3 eggs
225 g (7½oz) caster sugar
2 sachets vanilla sugar
75 g (3 oz) plain flour
110 g (3¾ oz) cornflour
25 g (1 oz) cocoa powder
2 teaspoons baking powder
625 g (1¼ lb) Morello

cherries in syrup, stones removed
1 sachet gelatine
150 g (5 oz) plain yoghurt
4 tablespoons lemon juice
Grated rind of ½ lemon
500 ml (18 fl oz) double cream

Beat the eggs with 3 tablespoons hot water using an electric mixer at high speed for 1 minute until the mixture is thick and frothy. Add 125 g (4 oz) sugar and 1 sachet vanilla sugar, beating constantly for 2 minutes. Incorporate the flour, 75 g (3 oz) cornflour, the baking powder and 20 g (¾ oz) cocoa powder using an electric mixer at low speed until a smooth consistency is achieved.

Turn the mixture into a lined, deep, 28 cm (11 in) round cake tin, taking care to smooth it out evenly.
Bake in a preheated oven at 180-200° C (350-400° F, Gas Mark 4-6) for 25-30 minutes. Remove from the tin immediately and peel off the greaseproof paper.

When the sponge is cold, cut it into two equal layers.

For the filling: drain the cherries, reserve some for decoration, save 375 ml (12 fl oz) juice. Add the remaining cornflour to the cherry juice and mix well; bring to the boil with the cherries, finally add 25 g (1 oz) sugar and leave to cool.

Soak the gelatine in 4 tablespoons cherry juice for 10 minutes, then heat gently until it has dissolved.

Beat the yoghurt with the remaining sugar and vanilla sugar, the lemon juice and rind. Add the gelatine, stirring constantly.

Whip the double cream until firm, then fold into the yoghurt cream.

Spread the cherry mixture over the first layer of sponge, spread half the yoghurt cream over the cherries and smooth it out evenly.

Cover with the second sponge layer and cover the cake with the rest of the cream. Decorate with the remaining cherries and dredge with the remaining cocoa powder.

CHOCOLATE GÂTEAU

Serves 8

3 eggs
100 g (3½ oz) caster sugar
1 sachet vanilla sugar
75 g (3 oz) plain flour
50 g (2 oz) cornflour
2 teaspoons baking powder
100 g (3½ oz) icing sugar

750 ml (1¼ pints) double cream
4 tablespoons cocoa powder
Superfine cooking chocolate
Some chocolate curls

Beat the eggs with 3 tablespoons hot water using an electric mixer at high speed for 1 minute until the mixture is thick and frothy. Add the sugar and the vanilla sugar, beating constantly for 2 minutes. Incorporate the flour, cornflour and baking powder using an electric mixer at low speed until a smooth consistency is achieved.

Turn the mixture into a lined, deep, 28 cm (11 in) round cake tin, taking care to smooth it out evenly.
Bake in a preheated oven at 180-200° C (350-400° F, Gas Mark 4-6) for 25-30 minutes. Remove from the tin immediately and peel off the greaseproof paper.

When the sponge is cool, cut it into two equal layers.

For the cream: whip the double cream for 1 minute. Add the icing sugar and whip constantly until it is very firm. Transfer 3 tablespoons cream to an icing bag.

Mix 3 tablespoons cocoa powder into the cream. Spread two-thirds of this cream over the first layer of sponge.

Melt the chocolate in a bowl over a pan of hot water, stirring constantly, and use to coat the second layer. Place this layer of sponge on the cream. Coat the sides of the cake with the remaining chocolate cream and dredge with the remaining cocoa powder. Decorate the edge of the cake with whirls of cream using the icing bag.

Above: *Chocolate gâteau*

Above: *English mocha cake*

ENGLISH MOCHA CAKE

Serves 8

450 g (15 oz) butter
200 g (7 oz) caster sugar
1 sachet vanilla sugar
200 g (7 oz) chocolate
5 eggs
A pinch of salt
150 g (5 oz) plain flour
50 g (2 oz) cornflour
2 teaspoons baking
powder
75 g (3 oz) ground

hazelnuts
1 packet vanilla
blancmange mix
500 ml (18 fl oz) milk
5 teaspoons instant coffee
100 g (3½ oz) coffee-
flavoured chocolate
Cocoa powder
Some coffee beans to
finish

Cream 200 g (7 oz) butter and incorporate 150 g (5 oz) sugar, the vanilla sugar, the melted chocolate, the eggs and salt. Mix the flour, cornflour and baking powder, and incorporate them into the mixture. Add the hazelnuts and mix well. Turn the mixture into a lined, deep, 28 cm (11 in) round cake tin, taking care to smooth it out evenly. Bake in a preheated oven at 180-200° C (350-400° F, Gas Mark 4-6) for 45 minutes. Remove from the tin immediately, place on muslin cloth on a wire rack, and carefully peel off the greaseproof paper. Leave to cool and cut into three equal layers.

For the cream: make up the vanilla blancmange using the milk and the remaining sugar, following the instructions given on the packet. Dissolve the coffee in the mixture while it is still hot. Leave to cool, stirring occasionally. Cream the remaining softened butter and add, together with the coffee-flavoured chocolate, to the blancmange mixture. Beat the cream until smooth, transfer a quarter to an icing bag. Spread part of the cream mixture over the first layer of chocolate sponge, cover with the second layer, repeat the procedure, and finish off with the third layer. Cover the cake with the remaining cream and decorate using the icing bag. Dredge the sides with cocoa powder. Decorate with the coffee beans.

CHOCOLATE MARZIPAN GÂTEAU

Serves 8

250 g (8 oz) butter
150 g (5 oz) caster sugar
1 sachet vanilla sugar
A pinch of salt
4 eggs
125 g (4 oz) plain flour
125 g (4 oz) cornflour
2 teaspoons baking powder
125 g (4 oz) hazelnut chocolate spread
75 g (3 oz) chopped blanched almonds
150 ml (¼ pint) double cream
4 teaspoons instant coffee
275 g (9 oz) icing sugar
250 g (8 oz) coffee-flavoured chocolate
450 g (15 oz) plain superfine cooking chocolate
500 g (1 lb) marzipan
4 tablespoons orange liqueur
4 tablespoons marmalade

Cream the butter and gradually incorporate the sugar, vanilla sugar, salt and eggs.
In a separate bowl, mix the flour, cornflour and baking powder together and then add them to the creamed mixture.

Melt the hazelnut chocolate spread in a bowl over a pan of hot water, stirring until creamy. Add to the mixture, together with the chopped almonds, mixing well.

Turn the mixture into a lined, deep, 26 cm (10½ in) round cake tin, taking care to smooth it out evenly.
Bake in a preheated oven at 180-200° C (350-400° F, Gas Mark 4-6) for 45-50 minutes.

Remove from the tin immediately and carefully peel off the greaseproof paper. Leave to cool. Cut the cake into three equal layers.

For the cream: heat the cream, instant coffee and 2 tablespoons icing sugar. Bring to the boil. Break the coffee-flavoured chocolate and 250 g (8 oz) plain chocolate into little pieces, add to the hot cream, allow to melt, mixing well. Leave to cool.

In a mixing bowl, knead the marzipan with 250 g (8 oz) icing sugar and the orange liqueur. Divide the mixture into five portions.

Roll out three portions on a work surface covered with the remaining icing sugar. Using the side section of a deep, springform cake tin, cut out three 26 cm (10½ in) diameter marzipan circles.

Spread half the cream over the first layer of sponge. Drape a marzipan circle over the rolling pin and place it on top of the cream. Cover with the second sponge layer. Spread the rest of the cream, then place another marzipan layer on top and finish off by placing the remaining sponge layer on top of the cake.

Heat the orange marmalade. Spread over the final layer and cover with the third marzipan circle.

Roll out the two remaining portions of marzipan and cut a strip the same depth as the cake (put the rest to one side). Cover the sides of the cake, pressing down gently.

For the icing: melt the remaining plain chocolate in a bowl over a pan of hot water, stirring until very smooth. Coat the cake with this mixture.

Use the remaining marzipan to make decorative shapes and place on the cake before the icing has fully set.

Below: *Chocolate marzipan gâteau*

RASPBERRY YOGHURT CREAM

200 g (7 oz) plain flour
125 g (4 oz) caster sugar
2 sachets vanilla sugar
A pinch of salt
125 g (4 oz) butter
2 sachets powdered
gelatine or 4 gelatine
leaves
2 eggs, separated
Grated rind of 1 lemon
4 tablespoons lemon juice
300 g (10 oz) plain

yoghurt
400 ml (14 fl oz) double
cream
500 g (1 lb) raspberries
2 tablespoons icing sugar
4 spoons raspberry juice
4 tablespoons red fruit
jelly
125 g (4 oz) ground
almonds
Some toasted flaked
almonds to finish

Sift the flour on to a work surface and make a well in the centre. Incorporate 50 g (2 oz) sugar, 1 sachet vanilla sugar, the salt and 1-2 tablespoons water with some of the flour to form a soft dough. Add the butter, cut into pieces, cover with flour and knead the ingredients into a smooth dough. Leave to rest in a refrigerator for 1 hour.

Grease a 28 cm (11 in) round flan tin and line with the pastry. Prick the base with a fork. Bake in a preheated oven at 200-220° C (400-420° F, Gas Mark 6-7) for 20-25 minutes.

Remove from the tin immediately and leave to cool in the upturned tin. When cold, transfer this pastry layer to a plate.

Cover the side section of a deep, springform cake tin with aluminium foil and place around the pastry layer.

For the filling: soak the gelatine in 4 tablespoons cold water for 10 minutes.

Beat the egg yolks, the remaining sugar and vanilla sugar until creamy. Add the lemon rind and juice, yoghurt and double cream, mixing well.

Heat the gelatine until it has dissolved and incorporate with the cream mixture. Place in a refrigerator and stir from time to time until it starts to set.

Whisk the egg whites into peaks. Gently fold them into the cream mixture. Spread this mixture over the pastry base and smooth it out evenly.

Carefully wash and drain the raspberries, dredge with the icing sugar, leave to soak for a few minutes, saving the juice. Arrange the raspberries on the cake.

Reduce the raspberry juice and the red fruit jelly and use to coat the raspberries. Place the cake in a refrigerator.

Before serving, remove the cake tin and decorate the sides of the cake with the ground almonds and the toasted flaked almonds.

PINEAPPLE AND NUT GÂTEAU

3 eggs
265 g (8½ oz) caster sugar
1 sachet vanilla sugar
100 g (3½ oz) plain flour
100 g (3½ oz) cornflour
2 teaspoons baking
powder
1 packet vanilla
blancmange mix

500 ml (18 fl oz) milk
265 g (8½ oz) butter
125 g (4 oz) chopped
blanched almonds
500 g (1 lb) tinned
pineapple in syrup
2-3 tablespoons pineapple
or apricot jam

Beat the eggs with 3 tablespoons hot water using an electric mixer at high speed for 1 minute until the mixture is thick and frothy. Add 150 g (5 oz) sugar and the vanilla sugar, beating constantly for 2 minutes. Incorporate the flour, cornflour, and baking powder using an electric mixer at low speed until a smooth consistency is achieved.

Turn the mixture into a lined, deep, 28 cm (11 in) round cake tin, taking care to smooth it out evenly.
Bake in a preheated oven at 180-200° C (350-400° F, Gas Mark 4-6) for 20-30 minutes. Remove from the tin immediately and peel off the greaseproof paper.

When the sponge is cold, cut it into three equal layers.

For the cream: make up the vanilla blancmange using the milk and 50 g (2 oz) sugar following the instructions on the packet. Leave to cool, stirring from time to time.

For the nut brittle: in a pan, heat 15 g (½ oz) butter and the remaining sugar. When they start to brown, add the almonds, continue to cook, stirring until the mixture caramelizes. Spread the nut mixture on a greased baking sheet, leave to set, and crush with a rolling pin.

For the filling: cream the remaining butter and

Opposite: *Pineapple nut gâteau*

gradually incorporate it in the cooled vanilla cream. Transfer half of this butter cream mixture to a mixing bowl, add half the nut brittle and mix well.

Drain the pineapple and cut into chunks. Reserve 16 chunks for decoration.

Spread the jam over the first sponge layer, arrange the pineapple chunks, then cover with some of the nut brittle cream. Place the second sponge layer on top and cover with the rest of the cream. Place the remaining layer of sponge on top.

Cover the cake with the remaining butter cream mixture (transfer a little to an icing bag). Using a knife, mark out 16 portions on the top. Decorate each portion using the icing bag and arrange the 16 reserved pineapple chunks. Cover the sides of the cake with crushed nut brittle.

Suggestion: flavour the butter cream mixture with 2-3 spoons rum or brandy

ALMOND PRALINE GÂTEAU

Serves 8

500 g (1 lb) plain flour
4 teaspoons baking powder
150 g (5 oz) caster sugar
2 sachets vanilla sugar
A pinch of salt
2 teaspoons grated lemon rind
500 g (1 lb) butter
50 g (2 oz) marzipan
3 eggs
200 g (7 oz) flaked blanched almonds
400 g (13 oz) hazelnut chocolate spread
250 g (8 oz) plain superfine cooking chocolate

Sift the flour and baking powder on to a work surface and make a well in the centre. Incorporate the sugar, vanilla sugar, salt, lemon rind and 1-2 tablespoons water with some of the flour to make a soft dough.
Add 250 g (8 oz) butter cut into pieces, then the marzipan, cover with flour and knead the ingredients to form a smooth dough. Place in a refrigerator overnight.

Divide the dough into 6 balls and roll each of them out into 3 mm (⅛ in) thick circles, cutting them out using the side section of a deep, 28 cm (11 in) round, springform cake tin.

Beat 1 egg and coat each pastry layer with the beaten egg. Sprinkle the almonds over each layer.

Grease a baking sheet and cover it with greaseproof paper. Bake the pastry layers one after the other in a preheated oven at 200° C (400° F, Gas Mark 6) for 8-10 minutes each. Leave the pastry layers to cool.

For the cream: cream the remaining softened butter with the remaining eggs. Melt the hazelnut chocolate spread in a bowl over a pan of hot water, stirring until smooth and creamy. Add the butter.

Spread 3 tablespoons of the hazelnut chocolate cream over each pastry layer and place them one on top of the other. Cover with the remaining cream. Place in a refrigerator for at least 1 hour.

For the icing: melt the chocolate in a bowl over a pan of hot water, beating constantly until a smooth, creamy consistency is achieved. Use to ice the cake.

Chill in a refrigerator for 24 hours before serving.

Left: *Almond praline gâteau*

CHOCOLATE PRALINE GÂTEAU

Serves 8

400 g (13 oz) butter
200 g (7 oz) caster sugar
1 sachet vanilla sugar
4 eggs
1 bottle rum flavouring
200 g (7 oz) plain flour
20 g (¾ oz) cocoa powder
2 teaspoons baking
powder
300 ml (½ pint) milk

1 packet vanilla
blancmange mix
3 tablespoons rum
100 g (3½ oz) chocolate
40 g (1½ oz) grated
chocolate
Chocolate pralines to
finish

In a mixing bowl, cream 200 g (7 oz) butter and gradually incorporate the sugar, vanilla sugar, eggs and rum flavouring. Sift the flour, cocoa powder and baking powder into a bowl and spoon them gradually into the butter, mixing well.

Turn the mixture into a greased, 28 cm (11 in) round cake tin, taking care to smooth it out evenly.

Bake in a preheated oven at 180-200° C (350-400° F, Gas Mark 4-6) for 40 minutes. Leave the cake to cool. When completely cold, cut into two equal layers.

For the cream: make up the vanilla blancmange mix using the milk following the instructions on the packet. Incorporate the remaining butter and the rum, mixing well. Melt the chocolate in a bowl over a pan of hot water and incorporate it with the butter cream mixture.

Spread half the cream over the first layer, cover with the second, pressing down gently. Transfer one-third of the remaining cream to an icing bag, spread the remaining two-thirds over the top and sides of the cake. Cover the sides of the cake with the grated chocolate, decorate with the cream in the icing bag and the chocolate pralines.

Above: *Chocolate praline gâteau*

EASTER CAKE

Serves 8

450 g (15 oz) marzipan
25 g (1 oz) caster sugar
6 eggs, separated
2 pinches of salt
75 g (3 oz) plain flour
A pinch of baking powder
265 g (8½ oz) icing sugar
1 tablespoon cocoa
powder

150 g (5 oz) butter
100 g (3½ oz) plain
superfine cooking
chocolate
1-2 tablespoons brandy
Marzipan leaves and
flowers to finish

*G*rease a deep, 16 cm (6¼ in) round cake tin and raise the sides of the tin by 3 cm (1¼ in) with a sheet of aluminium foil.

In a bowl, knead 50 g (2 oz) marzipan and the sugar, then add 3 egg yolks, 3 tablespoons hot water and a pinch of salt. Beat until frothy, using an electric mixer.

Whisk the egg whites into peaks. Fold some of the egg white into the marzipan cream. Sift the flour and the baking powder on to this cream, mix well, and finally gently fold in the remaining egg white.

Transfer this mixture to the tin, smooth out evenly, bake in a preheated oven at 180° C (350° F, Gas Mark 4) for 30-35 minutes.

Remove from the tin immediately and peel off the foil. Leave to cool and cut the cake into three equal layers.

For the decoration: knead the remaining marzipan with 175 g (6 oz) icing sugar and the cocoa powder. Wrap this mixture in aluminium foil and put to one side.

For the cream: cream the softened butter. Melt the chocolate in a bowl over a pan of hot water and incorporate the butter, 2 egg yolks, one after the other, 75 g (3 oz) icing sugar, the second pinch of salt and the brandy.

Spread a third of this cream over the first sponge layer, cover with the second, pressing down gently, and repeat the procedure. Coat the completed cake with the rest of the cream. Place in a refrigerator for 30 minutes.

Roll out half of the marzipan which had been put to one side. Cut a strip of the same depth as the cake, put the unused marzipan to one side, dredge the remaining icing sugar over the marzipan strip, drape the marzipan strip over a rolling pin and press the marzipan lightly on to the cake.

Knead the unused marzipan, roll it out. Cut out a circle using the side section of a deep, 16 cm (6¼ in) round, springform cake tin and place it on the cake.

Roll out the remaining marzipan until about 3 mm (⅛ in) thick. Cut into strips about 1 cm (½ in) wide. Taking two strips, make a cross in the centre of the cake. Interweave the other strips until the top of the cake is completely covered.

Knead the unused strips and make into thin rolls, 3-5 mm (½-¼ in) wide and 47 cm (18½ in) long. Moisten with a bit of water and the remaining egg yolk. Stick them around the cake. Make a pattern on them using a special cutter or a knife. Decorate with marzipan flowers and leaves.

Left: *Easter cake*

Above: *Pink parfait*

PINK PARFAIT

Serves 8

3 eggs
350 g (11 oz) caster sugar
1 sachet vanilla sugar
100 g (3½ oz) plain flour
100 g (3½ oz) cornflour
2 teaspoons baking powder
500 g (1 lb) frozen red fruits

4 tablespoons kirsch
150 g (5 oz) butter
100 g (3½ oz) marzipan, coloured pink using food colouring
50 g (2 oz) icing sugar
Silver balls and other cake decorations

*B*eat the eggs with 3 tablespoons hot water using an electric mixer at high speed for 1 minute until the mixture is thick and frothy. Add 150 g (5 oz) sugar and the vanilla sugar, beating constantly for 2 minutes. Incorporate the flour, cornflour, and baking powder using an electric mixer at low speed until a smooth consistency is achieved.

Turn the mixture into a lined, deep, 28 cm (11 in) round cake tin, taking care to smooth it out evenly.
Bake in a preheated oven at 180-200° C (350-400° F, Gas Mark 4-6) for 45-50 minutes. Remove from the tin immediately and peel off the greaseproof paper.
When cool, cut the sponge into three equal layers.

For the filling: defrost the fruits. Cook with 200 g (7 oz) sugar and let them reduce. The juice should drip from the spoon. Strain and keep the juice. Sprinkle the fruits with kirsch. Leave to cool.

Spread a third of the fruit mixture over the first layer of sponge, cover with the second and repeat the procedure. Finish with the remaining layer of sponge.

Soften the butter by beating with the remaining sugar and incorporate about 5 spoonfuls of red fruits. Spread this cream on the top and sides of the cake, transfer the remaining cream to an icing bag.

For the decoration: knead the marzipan with the icing sugar and a little of the juice from the red fruits. Roll it out and cut out a 24 cm (9½ in) diameter circle. Place this circle on the cake, leaving 2 cm (¾ in) around the edge. Decorate with whirls of cream using the icing bag, then finish off with silver balls and flowers.

SCHÖNBRUNN

Serves 8

100 g (3½ oz) plain chocolate
450 g (15 oz) butter
165 g (5½ oz) icing sugar
3 eggs
3 egg yolks
75 g (3 oz) plain flour
2 teaspoons baking powder

150 g (5 oz) ground hazelnuts
3 egg whites
125 g (4 oz) whole hazelnuts
1 packet chocolate blancmange mix
500 ml (18 fl oz) milk

*B*reak the chocolate into small pieces and melt in a bowl over a pan of hot water, stirring until it is very creamy.

In a mixing bowl, cream 200 g (7 oz) butter, mix it into the chocolate and finally add 100 g (3½ oz) icing sugar, 3 eggs and 3 yolks.

Mix the flour, baking powder and ground hazelnuts and add them to the chocolate mixture. Whisk the egg whites into peaks and gently fold them into the mixture.

Turn the mixture into a greased, deep, 28 cm (11 in) round cake tin, and smooth it out evenly using a spatula. Bake in a preheated oven at 180-200° C (350-400° F, Gas Mark 4-6) for 45-50 minutes. Remove from the tin immediately. Leave to cool and cut the cake into three layers.

For the cream: place the whole hazelnuts on a baking sheet in a preheated oven at 200 ° C (400° F, Gas Mark 6) for about 8-10 minutes until the skin breaks. Transfer the hazelnuts to a sieve, leave to cool, remove the skin by rubbing them together. Reserve 18 hazelnuts and grind the rest.

Make up the chocolate blancmange using the milk and following the instruction on the packet. Place in a refrigerator and stir from time to time.

Cream the remaining butter and icing sugar. Gradually fold this mixture into the chocolate cream. Beat until the mixture is very smooth and creamy. Transfer a quarter of

Above: Schönbrunn

the cream mixture to an icing bag fitted with a star-shaped nozzle.

Add the ground hazelnuts to the cream and mix well.

Cover the three layers of sponge with the chocolate hazelnut cream and place them one on top of the other to make up the cake. Cover the entire cake with the remaining cream. Smooth it out evenly.
Pipe the top of the cake decoratively using the icing bag and finish off with the whole hazelnuts.

Above: *Pistachio marzipan gâteau*

PISTACHIO MARZIPAN GÂTEAU

Serves 8

300 g (10 oz) caster sugar	500 ml (18 fl oz) milk
50 g (2 oz) blanched	1 vanilla pod
almonds	6 egg yolks
5 eggs	100 g (3½ oz) butter
2 pinches of salt	100 g (3½ oz) pistachio
75 g (3 oz) plain flour	nuts
125 g (4 oz) cornflour	200 g (7 oz) marzipan
Grated rind of 1 lemon	4 tablespoons Arrack

Melt 1 teaspoon sugar in a small, greased pan, then add a further 100 g (3½ oz). Stir constantly until the sugar caramelizes. Add the almonds.

Spread this nut mixture on a greased baking sheet. Leave to cool and set. Crush the nut brittle with a rolling pin.

For the sponge: beat 5 eggs with 5 tablespoons hot water using an electric mixer at high speed for 1 minute until the mixture is thick and frothy. Add 125 g (4 oz) sugar and a pinch of salt, beating constantly for 2 minutes. Incorporate the flour, 75 g (3 oz) cornflour and the lemon rind using an electric mixer at low speed until a smooth consistency is achieved.

Turn the mixture into a lined, deep, 28 cm (11 in) round cake tin, taking care to smooth it out evenly.
Bake in a preheated oven at 180-200° C (350-400° F, Gas Mark 4-6) for 45-50 minutes. Remove from the tin immediately and peel off the greaseproof paper.

When cold, cut the sponge into three equal layers.

For the cream: heat the milk with the vanilla pod, the remaining sugar and the second pinch of salt. Bring to the boil.

Combine the remaining cornflour and 6 egg yolks. Remove the vanilla pod from the milk and gradually add the egg mixture to the milk, mixing well. Bring back to the boil, stirring well. Remove from the heat and add the softened butter. Leave to cool.

Reserve 18-24 pistachio nuts and grind the rest.

Knead 100 g (3½ oz) marzipan with half the ground pistachio nuts and 3 tablespoons Arrack.

Beat the cream using an electric mixer and incorporate the marzipan.

Put a quarter of this cream to one side and spread the rest over the three layers of sponge. Place them one on top of the other to make the cake and transfer to a refrigerator.

Knead the remaining marzipan with 1 tablespoon ground pistachio nuts, 1 tablespoon crushed nut brittle and the remaining Arrack. Make into a roll and divide it up into 12-16 little balls.

Spread the remaining cream all over the cake.

Mix the remaining nut brittle with the ground pistachios and sprinkle over the top and sides of the cake. Mark out the slices using a pointed knife and place a marzipan ball on each one.

Halve the whole pistachios and stick them into the marzipan balls. Leave the cake to rest in a refrigerator for 2 hours.

CONTINENTAL WEDDING CAKE

Serves about 40

750 g (1½ lb) butter
400 g (13 oz) caster sugar
1 sachet vanilla sugar
5 eggs
1 egg yolk
1 bottle rum flavouring
300 g (10 oz) plain flour
100 g (3½ oz) cornflour
2 teaspoons baking
powder
100 ml (3½ fl oz) milk
2 packets vanilla

blancmange mix
100 g (3½ oz) ground
toasted hazelnuts
75 g (3 oz) plain chocolate
350 g (11½ oz) marzipan
625 g (1¼ lb) icing sugar
1 tablespoon kirsch
1 egg white
Green and yellow food
colouring
Sugar flowers to finish

In a bowl, cream 250 g (8 oz) butter and gradually incorporate 250 g (8 oz) sugar, the vanilla sugar, 5 whole eggs, 1 yolk and the rum flavouring. Then incorporate the flour, cornflour and baking powder into the mixture, adding 2 tablespoons milk if necessary.

Turn the mixture into two greased, lined, deep, 28 cm (11 in) round cake tins and smooth it out evenly using a spatula. Bake the cakes one after the other in a preheated oven at 180-200° C (350-400° F, Gas Mark 4-6) for 45-55 minutes. Take each cake out of the oven, leave in the tin for 5 minutes, then remove and leave to cool.

Cut each cake into 8 equal layers.

Take two layers and cut out four 14 cm (5½ in) diameter circles using a saucer. Then cut out three 20 cm (8 in) diameter circles using a plate.

For the cream: mix the contents of the packet of vanilla blancmange with 5 tablespoons milk. Bring the remaining milk to the boil and add the thinned down pudding mixture and the remaining sugar, stirring constantly. Leave to cool and beat from time to time.

Cream the remaining butter and gradually add to the vanilla cream.

Put half this cream mixture to one side and add the ground hazelnuts to the remaining half.

Break the plain chocolate into small pieces, melt them in a bowl over a pan of hot water, stirring until very smooth.

Below: *Continental wedding cake*

Fold into the vanilla cream mixture which had been put to one side.

Spread the hazelnut cream over two 28 cm (11 in) layers. Place them one on top of the other and cover with the third 28 cm (11 in) layer.

Spread the chocolate cream over two 20 cm (8 in) layers and cover with the third 20 cm (8 in) layer.

Cover three 14 cm (5½ in) layers with hazelnut cream. Spread the remaining chocolate cream on top of the last tier of the cake.

Knead the marzipan with 200 g (7 oz) icing sugar.

Colour one-third of the marzipan with the green colouring, roll it out and cut out the flowers and leaves using a template. Stick the sugar flowers in the marzipan leaves.

Roll out the remaining marzipan about 1 mm (¹/₁₆ in) thick. Cut out a 28 cm (11 in) diameter circle and place on the first tier of the cake.

Knead the remaining marzipan again and make a strip as

deep as the first tier of the cake. Proceed in the same way for the other two tiers.

Mix 300 g (10 oz) icing sugar with the kirsch, the yellow food colouring and the reserved egg white to form a thick icing. Use to coat the whole cake and leave to set. Place the first tier on a large plate, place the second on the first, and so on. Decorate with the sugar and marzipan flowers.

Beat the remaining icing sugar with the remaining egg white, transfer to an icing bag and add the finishing touches to the decoration.

PRINCE REGENT

Serves 8-10

500 g (1 lb) butter
350 g (11½ oz) caster sugar
1 sachet vanilla sugar
4 eggs
A pinch of salt
200 g (7 oz) plain flour
50 g (2 oz) cornflour
2 teaspoons baking
powder
1 packet chocolate blancmange mix
500 ml (18 fl oz) cold milk
20 g (¾ oz) cocoa powder
100 g (3½ oz) chocolate
Chocolate fans to finish

*I*n a mixing bowl, cream 250 g (8 oz) butter and gradually incorporate 250 g (8 oz) sugar, the vanilla sugar, eggs and salt. Gradually spoon in the flour, cornflour and baking powder, mixing well. If necessary, add 2 tablespoons milk.

Make eight circles with this mixture. For each one, turn the mixture into a greased, deep, 28 cm (11 in) round cake tin, and spread it out evenly using a spatula.

Bake each circle in a preheated oven at 180-200° C (350-400° F, Gas Mark 4-6) for 8-10 minutes. Take out of the oven and leave in the tin for 5 minutes, then leave to cool.

For the cream: make up the chocolate blancmange using the milk and following the instructions on the packet. Add the cocoa powder and the remaining sugar.

Cream the remaining butter and gradually incorporate into the chocolate cream, making sure that the cream and the butter are not too cold.

Coat each layer of pastry with the chocolate cream (reserve 2-3 tablespoons of cream for decoration).

Below: *Prince regent*

Place the pastry layers one on top of the other to make up the cake, finishing with a layer without cream.

For the icing: break the chocolate into small pieces and melt in a bowl over a pan of hot water, beating until smooth. Coat the cake. Decorate with the remaining cream in an icing bag and the chocolate fans.

FOUR-LEAFED CLOVER

Serves 8-9

3 eggs
150 g (5 oz) caster sugar
1 sachet vanilla sugar
100 g (3½ oz) plain flour
100 g (3½ oz) cornflour
2 teaspoons baking
powder
2 tablespoons sherry
5 tablespoons apricot jam
225 g (7½ oz) icing sugar

2-3 tablespoons lemon
juice
Green and red food
colouring
200 g (7 oz) marzipan,
coloured green
Hundreds and thousands
to finish
Silver balls to finish

Above: *Four-leafed clover*

Beat the eggs with 3 tablespoons hot water using an electric mixer at high speed for 1 minute until the mixture is thick and frothy. Add the caster sugar and the vanilla sugar, beating constantly for 2 minutes. Incorporate the flour, cornflour and baking powder using an electric mixer at low speed until a smooth consistency is achieved.

Turn the mixture into a lined, deep, 28 cm 911 in) round cake tin, taking care to smooth it out evenly. Bake in a preheated oven at 180-200° C (350-400° F, Gas Mark 4-6) for 20-30 minutes. Remove from the tin immediately and peel off the greaseproof paper.

When cold, cut the sponge into two equal layers.

Make a template in the shape of a four-leafed clover, place it on the cake and cut to shape.

For the filling: sprinkle the first layer of sponge with the sherry, spread with 2 heaped tablespoons apricot jam, then cover with the second sponge clover leaf. Press down gently and coat with the remaining jam.

For the decoration: mix 125 g (4 oz) icing sugar with the lemon juice, add some green colouring and coat the sides of the cake. Decorate with hundreds and thousands.

Knead the marzipan with the remaining icing sugar. Roll it out, place the clover leaf template on the marzipan and cut to shape. Cover the cake with the marzipan clover leaf. Decorate the edge with silver balls. Colour the remaining marzipan red and use to decorate the cake.

SWEETHEART

Serves 8

500 g (1 lb) plain flour	6 eggs
500 g (1 lb) butter	175 g (6 oz) caster sugar
2 teaspoons baking powder	2 spoons cornflour
2 sachets vanilla sugar	160 ml (5½ fl oz) lemon juice
A pinch of salt	225 g (7½ oz) icing sugar
Grated rind of 3 lemons	16 pistachio nuts to finish

Sift the flour into a bowl and using the fingertips quickly and lightly rub in 300 g (10 oz) butter, 1 sachet vanilla sugar, a pinch of salt, the rind of 1 lemon and 3 eggs, until the mixture resembles breadcrumbs. Gradually add 150 ml (¼ pint) water. Quickly bring the mixture together until it forms a smooth dough which is easy to roll out.

Leave to rest for at least 2 hours wrapped in a cloth.

Roll out a little pastry and cut out 32 fluted circles of pastry, about 2 cm (¾ in) in diameter.

Grease a baking sheet and place in a preheated oven 180-200° C (350-400° F, Gas Mark 4-6) for 8-10 minutes.

Divide the remaining pastry into five portions. Make into balls and roll out. Grease a flan tin and line it with one pastry layer, prick the base with a fork. Bake in a preheated oven at 180-200° C (350-400° F, Gas Mark 4-6) for 12-15 minutes. Repeat the procedure for each layer of pastry. Remove from the tin immediately and leave to cool.

For the cream: place the rind of 1 lemon, the sugar, the remaining vanilla sugar and the cornflour in a pan and moisten with 150 ml (¼ pint) lemon juice. Stir, add 3 beaten eggs and mix well.

Heat this mixture, stirring constantly, bring to the boil and immediately remove from the heat.

Gradually incorporate the remaining butter and leave the cream to cool, stirring from time to time.

Sandwich the little pastry circles together in pairs using a bit of this cream.

Spread the rest of the cream over each pastry layer, then place them one on top of the other to make up the cake. Cover the sides of the cake with the cream mixture and place the mixture in a refrigerator.
Mix the icing sugar with the remaining lemon juice to form a thick paste. Spread some icing on the top of the little pastry circles, decorate each with a pistachio nut. Coat the cake with the remaining lemon icing, arrange the little pastry circles on the top before the icing sets and place in a refrigerator.

Opposite: *Sweetheart*

Above: *Chocolate truffle cake*

CHOCOLATE TRUFFLE CAKE

Serves 8-10

5 eggs
175 g (6 oz) caster sugar
2 sachets vanilla sugar
100 g (3½ oz) plain flour
100 g (3½ oz) cornflour
125 g (4 oz) cocoa powder
2 teaspoons baking
powder

125 g (4 oz) butter
150 g (5 oz) icing sugar
1 bottle rum flavouring
100 g (3½ oz) chocolate
Creamed coconut
75 g (3 oz) chocolate
hundreds and thousands
to finish

*B*eat 4 eggs with 4 tablespoons hot water using an electric mixer at high speed for 1 minute until the mixture is thick and frothy. Add the sugar and 1 sachet vanilla sugar, beating constantly for 2 minutes. Incorporate the flour, cornflour, 25 g (1 oz) cocoa powder and the baking powder using an electric mixer at slow speed until a smooth consistency is achieved.

Turn the mixture into a lined, deep, 28 cm (11 in) round cake tin, taking care to smooth it out evenly.
Bake in a preheated oven at 180-200° C (350-400° F, Gas Mark 4-6) for 20-30 minutes. Remove from the tin immediately and peel off the greaseproof paper.

When cold, cut the sponge into three equal layers.

For the cream: in a mixing bowl, cream the butter with the icing sugar and the remaining cocoa powder. Beat the remaining egg with the rum flavouring and add to the cream mixture.

Take 16 teaspoons of the cream mixture and roll into little cherry-sized truffles. Place them in a refrigerator.

Dissolve the remaining vanilla sugar in 2 tablespoons water and add to the chocolate cream, stirring well. Spread the cream over two layers of sponge, place them one on top of the other and cover with the third layer to complete the cake.

For the icing: break the chocolate into small pieces and melt with the creamed coconut in a bowl over a pan of hot water, beating until a smooth consistency is achieved. Coat the cake, making a 2 cm (¾ in) wide rim around the edge of the cake.

Press the chocolate hundreds and thousands on to the sides of the cake.

Take the truffles out of the refrigerator, roll them in the chocolate hundreds and thousands and use to decorate the cake.

BLACK AND WHITE

Serves 8-10

4 eggs
250 g (8 oz) caster sugar
1 sachet vanilla sugar
65 g (2½ oz) plain flour
75 g (3 oz) cornflour
2 teaspoons baking
powder
40 g (1½ oz) cocoa
powder

100 g (3½ oz) icing sugar
250 g (8 oz) butter
50 g (2 oz) chopped
almonds
500 ml (18 fl oz) milk
6 tablespoons rum
6 tablespoons
blackcurrant jelly

Beat the eggs with 4 tablespoons hot water using an electric mixer at high speed for 1 minute until the mixture is thick and frothy. Add 125 g (4 oz) sugar and the vanilla sugar, beating constantly for 2 minutes. Incorporate the flour, 50 g (2 oz) cornflour, the baking powder and 25 g (1 oz) cocoa powder using an electric mixer at low speed until a smooth consistency is achieved.

Grease a baking sheet or line it with greaseproof paper, spread the mixture 1 cm (½ in) thick, fold up the edges of the paper so that the mixture stays level. Bake in a preheated oven at 180-200° C (350-400° F, Gas Mark 4-6) for 10-15 minutes.

Turn the sponge out immediately on to a sheet of paper dredged with icing sugar, carefully peel off the grease-proof paper and leave to cool.

For the nut brittle: heat a knob of butter and 25 g (1 oz) sugar, stirring until the sugar turns brown. Add the chopped almonds, spread the mixture on to a baking sheet and crush the nut brittle when cold.

For the cream: mix the remaining cornflour and the remaining sugar with 5 tablespoons milk. Bring the rest of the milk to the boil, remove from the heat and add the cornflour, stirring constantly, bring back to the boil, leave to cool, stirring from time to time.

Cream the remaining butter and gradually add it to the cream mixture, making sure that neither is too cold.

Take 3 teaspoons of the cream mixture, mix with the remaining cocoa powder and transfer to an icing bag.

Melt the blackcurrant jelly in the rum and spread over the sponge, then cover with two-thirds of the cream mixture.

Below: *Black and white*

Cut out 6 long strips of sponge 5 cm (2 in) wide. Roll up the first strip to form a central spiral, place it on its end on a plate. Cut the other strips in half and continue to make the spiral until the cake is complete.

Spread the remaining third of the cream mixture on the top and sides of the cake.

Make circles on the top using a fork, press the nut brittle around the sides and decorate with the cream in the icing bag.

CHERRY BRANDY PARFAIT

Serves about 8

4 eggs	mix
350 g (11½ oz) caster sugar	1 teaspoon blackberry liqueur
2 sachets vanilla sugar	500 ml (18 fl oz) milk
75 g (3 oz) plain flour	250 g (8 oz) butter
50 g (2 oz) cornflour	6 tablespoons cherry brandy
1 teaspoon baking powder	
3 egg whites	50 g (2 oz) flaked almonds
100 g (3½ oz) ground almonds	25 g (1 oz) icing sugar to finish
1 packet caramel custard	

*B*eat 4 eggs with 2-3 tablespoons hot water using an electric mixer at high speed for 1 minute, until the mixture is thick and frothy. Gradually add 100 g (3½ oz) sugar and 1 sachet vanilla sugar. Beat for a further 2 minutes. Mix the flour with the cornflour and baking powder. Sift half this mixture on to the creamy egg mixture. Mix using an electric mixer at low speed, then add the remaining flour mixture. Turn the mixture into a greased or lined, 28 cm (11 in) round springform cake tin. Smooth it out well and bake in a preheated oven at 180-200° C (350-400° F, Gas Mark 4-6) for 25-30 minutes. Remove the sponge from the tin immediately, turning it out on to a plate, and leave to cool.

For the meringue: whisk the egg whites into peaks, fold in 150 g (5 oz) sugar and the remaining vanilla sugar. Gently fold in the ground almonds. Transfer the meringue mixture to two greased or lined, 28 cm (11 in) round springform cake tins. Smooth the mixture out well and bake in a preheated oven at 100-125° C (200-250° F, Gas Mark 2-½) for 30-40 minutes. Turn the oven off and leave the meringue to rest for about 20 minutes. When the two layers of meringue are cooked, moisten the greaseproof paper and peel it off. Transfer the meringue layers to an air-tight tin so that they do not become soft.

For the filling: mix the packet of caramel custard mix with the remaining sugar, 6 tablespoons cold milk and the blackberry liqueur. Pour this mixture into a pan containing the remaining milk. Bring to the boil and leave to cool, stirring from time to time.

Soften the butter and gradually add the custard mixture to the softened butter, making sure that the butter and the custard mixture are not too cold so as to prevent lumps forming.

For the syrup: boil up 6 tablespoons water with the remaining sugar. Leave to cool, then add the 6 table-spoons brandy.

Spread one of the meringue layers with a quarter of the cream mixture, place the layer of sponge on top, moisten it with the syrup, cover with about half of the remaining cream mixture. Place the second layer of meringue on top, pressing down firmly, and coat the sides and the top of the cake with the remaining cream mixture.

Lightly toast the flaked almonds on a baking sheet, turning them from time to time, and press on to the sides of the cake.

Plunge a knife into the hot water and make a lattice pattern on the cake. Dredge with icing sugar.

Suggestion: this cake is easier to cut if made the day before.

Above: *Cherry brandy parfait*

LEMON GÂTEAU

Serves 8-10

4 eggs
375 g (12 oz) caster sugar
1 sachet vanilla sugar
100 g (3½ oz) plain flour
100 g (3½ oz) cornflour
2 teaspoons baking
powder
375 g (12 oz) butter

4 egg yolks
125 ml (4 fl oz) lemon
juice
1 packet vanilla
blancmange mix
500 ml (18 fl oz) milk
Lemon slices and mint
leaves to finish

Beat the eggs with 4 tablespoons hot water using an electric mixer at high speed for 1 minute until the mixture is thick and frothy. Add 150 g (5 oz) sugar and the vanilla sugar, beating constantly for 2 minutes. Incorporate the flour, cornflour and baking powder using an electric mixer at low speed until a smooth consistency is achieved.

Turn the mixture into a lined, deep, 28 cm (11 in) round cake tin, taking care to smooth it out evenly. Bake in a preheated oven at 180-200° C (350-400° F, Gas Mark 4-6) for 25-30 minutes. Remove from the tin immediately, peel off the greaseproof paper and leave to cool.

When cold, cut the sponge into 4 equal layers.

For the lemon cream: melt 125 g (4 oz) butter in a bowl over a pan of hot water and gradually incorporate 175 g (6 oz) sugar and the egg yolks, beating until the mixture thickens. Add the lemon juice, beating constantly. Reheat the mixture and remove from the heat just before it boils. Leave to cool, stirring regularly.

For the butter cream: make up the vanilla blancmange using the milk and the remaining sugar following the instruction on the packet. Soften and cream the remaining butter and gradually incorporate it into the cream mixture.

Spread half the lemon cream on the first sponge layer, cover with the second, pressing down gently. Spread a third of the butter cream over the second sponge layer and cover with the third, which is then covered with the lemon cream. Finish with the remaining layer and press down gently.

Below: *Lemon gâteau*

Spread half of the remaining butter cream all over the cake, transfer the rest to an icing bag fitted with a star-shaped nozzle. Decorate the cake and finish with the lemon slices and mint leaves.

WHITE CHOCOLATE GÂTEAU

Serves 8-10

1 ready-made genoese sponge	cream
400 g (13 oz) white chocolate	125 g (4 oz) apricot jam
200 g (7 oz) marzipan	2 packets chocolate leaves
200 ml (7 fl oz) milk	100 g (3½ oz) plain superfine cooking chocolate
8 gelatine leaves	Some ratafia biscuits to finish
500 ml (18 fl oz) double	

Cut the genoese sponge into two layers.

For the filling: melt 300 g (10 oz) white chocolate in a bowl over a pan of hot water and incorporate the marzipan and the milk. Soak the gelatine in a little cold water, heat in a small pan until it has completely dissolved.

Whip the double cream until firm, add the cooled gelatine, continue beating, then mix into the marzipan mixture. Place in a refrigerator until the cream sets.

Sieve 100 g (3½ oz) apricot jam and spread some jam over each layer of genoese sponge.

Place one layer of sponge, jam side up, inside the side section of a deep, springform cake tin. Insert the chocolate leaves firmly between the sponge cake and the side of the tin, then spread out the marzipan cream. Cover with the second layer of sponge, jam side down. Press down gently. Leave to set in a refrigerator overnight.

Remove the cake tin and transfer the cake to a plate.

For the icing: in separate bowls, melt the remaining 100 g (3½ oz) white chocolate and the plain chocolate.

Spread the remaining apricot jam all over the cake. Using the plain chocolate, make a lattice design, filling the spaces with the white chocolate, and create a marbling effect using a spoon handle. Finish with the ratafia biscuits.

ZUGER

(A Swiss speciality)

Serves 8-10

4 eggs	almonds
400 g (13 oz) caster sugar	1 packet raspberry
2 sachets vanilla sugar	blancmange mix
75 g (3 oz) plain flour	500 ml (18 fl oz) milk
50 g (2 oz) cornflour	250 g (8 oz) butter
2 teaspoons baking powder	6 spoons kirsch
3 egg whites	50 g (2 oz) flaked almonds
100 g (3½ oz) ground	25 g (1 oz) icing sugar

Beat 4 eggs with 4 tablespoons hot water using an electric mixer at high speed for 1 minute until the mixture is thick and frothy. Add 100 g (3½ oz) sugar and 1 sachet vanilla sugar, beating constantly for 2 minutes. Incorporate the flour, cornflour and baking powder with the mixer at low speed until a smooth consistency is achieved.

Turn the mixture into a lined, deep, 28 cm (11 in) round cake tin, taking care to smooth it out evenly.
Bake in a preheated oven at 180-200° C (350-400° F, Gas Mark 4-6). Remove from the tin immediately and peel off the greaseproof paper.

For the meringue: whisk 3 egg whites into peaks, fold in 150 g (5 oz) sugar, the remaining vanilla sugar and the ground almonds.

Turn half the egg whites into a well-greased, lined, deep, 28 cm (11 in) round cake tin, smooth out evenly, bake in a preheated oven at 100-125° C (200-250° F, Gas Mark 2½) for 30-40 minutes.

Turn the oven off and leave to dry out in the oven for about 20 minutes. Repeat the procedure with the remaining egg whites.

Keep the meringues in an air-tight container so that they do not go soft.

For the cream: mix the contents of the raspberry blancmange packet with 5 tablespoons of milk. Heat the remaining milk with 100 g (3½ oz) sugar, bring to the boil, add the blancmange mixture, bring back to the boil, stirring constantly, and leave to cool, beating from time to time.
Cream the butter and gradually incorporate it in the blancmange mixture, making sure that neither is too cold.

Put 6 spoons water and the remaining sugar in a small pan, bring to the boil, leave to cool, and add the kirsch. Spread a quarter of the raspberry cream over the meringue layer, cover with the sponge, sprinkle with the kirsch syrup, then spread on half of the remaining cream, cover with the second meringue layer, pressing down gently. Spread the remaining cream over the top and sides of the cake.

Toast the flaked almonds on a baking sheet and use to decorate the sides of the cake. Make a lattice pattern on the top of the cake and dredge with icing sugar.

Suggestion: this cake will be easier to cut if made the day before.

PISCHINGER

(an Austrian speciality)

Serves 8

250 g (8 oz) butter	300 g (10 oz) plain
65 g (2½ oz) caster sugar	chocolate
125 g (4 oz) chopped	2 packets large, round
blanched almonds	waffles (5 waffles in each
50 g (2 oz) icing sugar	packet)
3 eggs	

*H*eat a knob of butter and the sugar, stirring until the sugar turns brown. Add the chopped almonds, caramelize and spread on a baking sheet. When cold, crush the nut brittle with a rolling pin.

For the cream: cream the remaining softened butter and the icing sugar using an electric mixer until smooth and creamy. Incorporate the eggs, one at a time, beating constantly.
Break 200 g (7 oz) chocolate into pieces, melt in a bowl over a pan of hot water, then leave to cool slightly.

Mix the melted chocolate with the butter cream. Reserve 2 spoons chocolate cream and mix the crushed nut brittle with the rest of the cream.

Spread this nut brittle cream over the waffles, stack them one on top of the other to make up the cake. Cover the sides with the reserved chocolate cream.
Melt the remaining chocolate in a bowl over a pan of hot water, beating until the mixture is smooth. Use to coat the cake. Place in a refrigerator for several hours.

Cut the cake using a very sharp knife dipped in boiling water.

ALMOND AND CHOCOLATE GÂTEAU

Serves 8-10

5 eggs	blancmange mix
2 spoons rum	500 ml (18 fl oz) milk
175 g (6 oz) caster sugar	250 g (8 oz) softened
1 sachet vanilla sugar	butter
100 g (3½ oz) plain flour	1 spoon apricot jam
2 teaspoons baking	100 g (3½ oz) plain
powder	superfine cooking
25 g (1 oz) cocoa powder	chocolate
100 g (3½ oz) ground	1 spoon creamed coconut
almonds	1 spoon oil
1 packet vanilla	32 blanched almonds

*B*eat the eggs with 5 tablespoons boiling water using an electric mixer at high speed for 1 minute until the mixture is thick and frothy. Add 125 g (4 oz) sugar and the vanilla sugar, beating constantly for 2 minutes. With the mixer at low speed, incorporate the flour, baking powder, cocoa and ground almonds until a smooth consistency is achieved.

Turn the mixture into a lined, deep, 28 cm (11 in) round cake tin, taking care to smooth it out evenly.
Bake in a preheated oven at 180-200° C (350-400° F, Gas Mark 4-6) for 25-35 minutes. Remove from the tin immediately and peel off the greaseproof paper. When cold, cut the sponge into three equal layers.

For the cream: make up the vanilla blancmange following the instructions on the packet, using the remaining sugar and the milk, leave to cool, stirring from time to time.

Cream the softened butter and gradually incorporate into the cream.

Transfer 3 spoons cream to an icing bag fitted with a round nozzle.

Spread the rest of the cream over the first two layers of sponge and assemble the cake. Cover the sides with the cream. Sieve the apricot jam and spread it over the top of the cake.

For the icing: break the chocolate into small pieces and melt them with the creamed coconut in a bowl over a pan of hot water, beating until the mixture is smooth and glossy. Use to coat the cake.

Opposite: *Chocolate and almond gâteau*

Make a spiral on the cooled icing using the butter cream in the icing bag.

Toast the blanched almonds in an oiled frying pan and use to decorate the cake.

Suggestion: sprinkle the sponge layer with some rum or cognac before spreading on the cream.

PRALINE SWISS ROLL

Serves 8-10

225 g (7½ oz) plain flour	A pinch of baking powder
350 g (11½ oz) butter, softened	1 packet vanilla blancmange mix
225 g (7½ oz) caster sugar	500 ml (18 fl oz) milk
200 g (7 oz) marzipan	200 g (7 oz) hazelnut praline
6 eggs, separated	
Grated rind of 1 lemon	2 spoons redcurrant jelly
75 g (3 oz) cornflour	25 g (1 oz) icing sugar

Sift 150 g (5 oz) flour into a bowl and, using the fingertips, quickly rub in 100 g (3½ oz) softened butter and 50 g (2 oz) sugar until the mixture resembles breadcrumbs. Gradually add 150 ml (¼ pint) water. Quickly bring the mixture together to form a dough which is easy to roll out.

Leave to rest for at least 2 hours wrapped in a cloth.

Roll out the pastry and use to line a 28 cm (11 in) round flan tin, prick the base using a fork and bake in a preheated oven at 200-220° C (400-425° F, Gas Mark 6-7) for about 15 minutes.
Leave to cool in the tin.

For the sponge: place 150 g (5 oz) marzipan, the egg yolks and the remaining sugar in a bowl, sprinkle with 2 spoons hot water and mix using an electric mixer. Add the lemon rind.

Whisk the egg whites into peaks, add them to the egg yolks.
In a mixing bowl, mix the remaining flour, the cornflour and baking powder and gently incorporate the ingredients.
Turn the mixture on to a greased, lined baking sheet, pull up the edges of the paper to stop the mixture running.
Place the baking sheet in a preheated oven at 200-220° C (400-425° F, Gas Mark 6-7) for 10-15 minutes.

Turn the sponge out on to a sheet of paper dredged with sugar, peel off the greaseproof paper and leave to cool (photo no. 1).

For the cream: make up the vanilla blancmange mix using the milk and following the instructions on the packet.

Cut the praline into small pieces and mix into the hot cream. Beat using an electric mixer until the mixture is smooth, leave to cool, stirring from time to time.

Cream the remaining butter and gradually add to the cream mixture.

Spread half of this cream mixture over the sponge. Cut it into 4 cm (1½ in) wide strips (photo no. 2). Spread the redcurrant jelly over the pastry layer (photo no. 3). Roll up the strips of sponge into a spiral, starting from the centre of the cake (photo no. 4). Spread half of the remaining cream all over the cake. Make vertical grooves in the sides of the cake using a fork.

Knead the remaining marzipan with the icing sugar. Roll it out. Cut out simple leaves. Make fine stalks with the rest of the marzipan and use to decorate the cake. Serve well chilled.

Opposite: *Praline Swiss roll*

HAZELNUT AND VANILLA CREAM GÂTEAU

Serves 8-10

7 eggs
1 egg white
175 g (6 oz) caster sugar
1 sachet vanilla sugar
A pinch of cinnamon
A pinch of salt
325 g (11 oz) ground hazelnuts
2 teaspoons baking powder
50 g (2 oz) sponge fingers
1 packet vanilla blancmange mix
125 ml (4 fl oz) milk
150 ml (¼ pint) double cream
1 egg yolk
25 g (1 oz) butter, softened
5-6 spoons apricot jam
5 to 5 spoons rum or brandy
75 g (3 oz) ground hazelnuts or almonds

Beat the eggs and the egg white using an electric mixer at high speed for 1 minute until the mixture is thick and frothy. Add 165 g (5½ oz) sugar, the vanilla sugar, cinnamon and salt and continue beating for 2 minutes. With the mixer at low speed, incorporate the ground hazelnuts and the baking powder.

Place the sponge fingers in a plastic bag, then crush them with a rolling pin. Add these crumbs to the other ingredients and fold in gently.

Turn the mixture into a lined, deep, 28 cm (11 in) round cake tin, taking care to smooth it out evenly.
Bake in a preheated oven at 180° C (350° F, Gas Mark 4) for 45-50 minutes.

Leave to cool and cut the cake into three layers.

For the cream: mix the contents of the vanilla blancmange mix with the remaining sugar and the milk, add the double cream and the egg yolk, then bring to the boil, stirring constantly. Incorporate the softened butter, leave to cool, stirring from time to time. Spread the cream over the first two layers of sponge. Assemble the cake and cover with the third layer.

Sieve the apricot jam. Thin it down with the alcohol and bring to the boil. Sprinkle this syrup over the cake.

Dredge the cake with the powdered hazelnuts or almonds.
Leave to rest in a refrigerator before serving.

PANAMA

Serves 8-10

250 g (8 oz) plain chocolate
9 eggs
150 g (5 oz) caster sugar
1 sachet vanilla sugar
25 g (1 oz) plain flour
2 teaspoons baking powder
150 g (5 oz) ground hazelnuts
150 g (5 oz) butter
50 g (2 oz) icing sugar
25 g (1 oz) toasted flaked almonds

Break 150 g (5 oz) chocolate into small pieces and melt it in a bowl over a pan of hot water, stirring until smooth and glossy.

Beat 7 eggs using an electric mixer at high speed for 1 minute, add the sugar and the vanilla sugar and continue beating for a further 2 minutes. Mix the flour and baking powder together in a mixing bowl, add to the eggs, finally add the chocolate and the ground hazelnuts and beat with the mixer at low speed.

Turn the mixture into a lined, deep, 28 cm (11 in) round cake tin, smoothing it out evenly with a spatula.
Bake in a preheated oven at 150-180° C (300-350° F, Gas Mark 2-4) for 50 minutes. Leave to cool.

For the cream: in a mixing bowl, cream the butter, add the icing sugar and incorporate the 2 remaining eggs one by one.

Break the remaining 100 g (3½ oz) chocolate into small pieces and melt it in a bowl over a pan of hot water, stirring until smooth and glossy. Gradually combine the melted chocolate and the butter cream.

Cut the cake into two layers.

Spread half the chocolate cream over the first layer of sponge, cover with the second. Spread the rest of the cream all over the cake. Create a wavy effect on the top of the cake using a fork. Decorate the sides of the cake with the toasted flaked almonds.

Above: *Surprise*

SURPRISE

Serves 8

500 ml (18 fl oz) milk
1 level spoonful cornflour
3 egg yolks
275 g (9 oz) plain
chocolate

150 g (5 oz) butter,
softened
2 teaspoons vanilla sugar
200 sponge fingers
1 knob creamed coconut

*P*our 250 ml (8 fl oz) milk into a pan, add the cornflour and 3 egg yolks. Heat, stirring constantly, until it starts to bubble.

Break 250 g (8 oz) chocolate into small pieces and melt in a bowl over a pan of hot water, stirring until smooth and glossy. Cream the butter using an electric mixer at high speed for 30 seconds, gradually incorporate the melted chocolate, then the butter cream, beating constantly.

Line the side section of a deep, 24 cm (9½ in) round springform cake tin with greaseproof paper and place it on a plate.

Mix the remaining milk with the vanilla sugar. Briefly dip half the sponge biscuits in the milk and cover the base of the tin with some of the sponge fingers. Cover with half the chocolate cream. Dunk the remaining biscuits in the milk and use to make a second layer of sponge. Cover it with the chocolate cream and smooth it out evenly. Leave to set.

Melt the remaining chocolate and the creamed coconut in a bowl over a pan of hot water and sprinkle this mixture over the chocolate cake to create an irregular pattern. Serve well chilled.

OTHELLO

Serves 8-10

5 eggs
125 g (4 oz) caster sugar
Grated rind of 1 lemon
A pinch of salt
75 g (3 oz) plain flour
75 g (3 oz) cornflour
50 g (2 oz) butter, melted
and cooled

625 g (1¼ lb) marzipan
150 g (5 oz) icing sugar
450 g (15 oz) apricot jam
5 spoons rum
2 egg yolks
75 g (3 oz) toasted pine
kernels
Whipped cream to serve

Beat 5 eggs with 5 tablespoons hot water using an electric mixer at high speed for 1 minute until the mixture is thick and frothy. Add the sugar, lemon rind and salt, beating constantly for 2 minutes. With the mixer at low speed, incorporate the flour and cornflour until a smooth consistency is achieved.

Turn the mixture into a lined, deep, 28 cm (11 in) round cake tin, taking care to smooth it out evenly.
Bake in a preheated oven at 180° C (350° F, Gas Mark 4) for 40 minutes. Remove from the tin immediately and leave to cool overnight.

Cut the sponge into two or three equal layers.

For the filling: in a mixing bowl, knead 400 g (13 oz) marzipan, 100 g (3½ oz) icing sugar, 250 g (8 oz) apricot jam and 4 spoons rum into a smooth dough. Reserve a quarter of this mixture. Spread the rest over the sponge layers and assemble the cake. Spread the reserved mixture over the cake.

For the decoration: mix the remaining marzipan and the remaining icing sugar with the egg yolks and the last spoon of rum into a soft cream. Transfer the mixture to an icing bag fitted with a round nozzle. Make two lines of marzipan in the centre of the cake to form a cross. Leave a gap of 1 cm (½ in) around the edge. Repeat the process, leaving 5 mm (¼ in) between the lines until the entire cake is covered with the lattice-work. Using a knife, mark out 16 slices.

Leave to rest for 30 minutes for the marzipan to dry out.

Place the cake under the grill until golden.

Heat the remaining apricot jam with 3 spoons water. Spread this syrup over the cooled cake. Decorate with toasted pine kernels. Serve with whipped cream.

Left: *Othello*

Above: *Hazelnut and carrot gâteau*

HAZELNUT AND CARROT GÂTEAU
(A Swiss speciality)

Serves 8-10

500 g (1 lb) carrots
500 g (1 lb) ground hazelnuts
4 teaspoons baking powder
8 eggs, separated
3 tablespoons orange juice
Grated rind of 1 orange

300 g (10 oz) caster sugar
2 spoons orange marmalade
150 g (5 oz) plain chocolate
1 knob creamed coconut
Some marzipan carrots to finish
Whipped cream to serve

Clean and wash the carrots, grate them finely.
In a bowl, mix the ground hazelnuts and the baking powder. In a mixing bowl, beat the egg yolks, the orange juice and the grated rind until smooth, thick, and creamy. Add the sugar. Whisk the egg whites into peaks and gradually fold into the creamy egg mixture. Add the hazelnuts and finally the carrots.

Turn the mixture into a lined, deep, 28 cm (11 in) round cake tin, taking care to smooth it out evenly.
Bake in a preheated oven at 180-200° C (350-400° F, Gas Mark 4-6) for 55-60 minutes.

Turn the cake out of the tin on to a plate immediately, peel off the greaseproof paper and leave to cool.

For the coating: thin down the orange marmalade with 2 teaspoons water and bring to the boil. Coat the cake with this syrup.

For the icing: melt the chocolate and the creamed coconut in a bowl over a pan of hot water, stirring until the mixture is smooth and glossy, and use to coat the cake.
Decorate with marzipan carrots. Serve with slightly sweetened whipped cream.

COTTAGE CHEESECAKE

Serves 8

175 g (6 oz) butter,
softened
150 g (5 oz) caster sugar
7 eggs, separated
Grated rind of 1 lemon

2-3 tablespoons lemon
juice
750 g (1½ lb) cottage
cheese
75 g (3 oz) semolina

*I*n a mixing bowl, cream the butter and incorporate the sugar, egg yolks, lemon rind and juice, beat until smooth. Add the cheese and the semolina.

Whisk the egg whites into peaks and gently fold into the mixture.

Turn the mixture into a greased, deep, 28 cm (11 in) round cake tin and smooth it out evenly. Bake in a preheated oven at 180oC (350oF, Gas Mark 4) for 70 minutes.

When cooked, leave the cake to rest in the oven for 30 minutes, leaving the oven door half open, then cool in the tin.

SACHERTORTE

Serves 8-10

6 eggs
175 g (6 oz) caster sugar
1 sachet vanilla sugar
100 g (3½ oz) plain flour
4 tablespoons cocoa
powder
2 teaspoons baking

powder
100 g (3½ oz) butter,
melted and cooled
200 g (7 oz) apricot jam
125 g (4 oz) plain
chocolate
1 knob creamed coconut

*B*eat the eggs with 6 tablespoons hot water using an electric mixer at high speed for 1 minute until the mixture is thick and frothy. Add the sugar and vanilla sugar, beating constantly for 2 minutes. With the mixer at low speed, incorporate the flour, cocoa powder and baking powder until a smooth consistency is achieved.

Turn the mixture into a lined, deep, 28 cm (11 in) round cake tin, taking care to smooth it out evenly.
Bake in a preheated oven at 180-200° C (350-400° F, Gas Mark 4-6) for 35-40 minutes. When cool, cut the sponge into two equal layers. Leave until completely cooled.

For the icing: mix the apricot jam well.

Spread two-thirds of the jam over the first layer, assemble the cake and spread the remaining jam over the top and sides.

Melt the chocolate and the creamed coconut in a bowl over a pan of hot water, stirring until the mixture is smooth and glossy, then coat the cake.

When the icing begins to set, mark out 16-20 slices using a knife.

OLD-FASHIONED CHOCOLATE CAKE

Serves 8-10

250 g (8 oz) plain
chocolate
175 g (6 oz) butter,
softened
225 g (7½ oz) caster sugar
3 eggs

4 egg yolks
5 egg whites
125 g (4 oz) fine
breadcrumbs
6 tablespoons apricot jam
Cocoa powder to finish

*M*elt 175 g (6 oz) chocolate in a bowl over a pan of hot water, stirring until smooth. Transfer the mixture to a bowl and then add the softened butter, 175 g (6 oz) sugar, 3 whole eggs and 4 egg yolks, mixing well. Finally, gradually add the breadcrumbs. Whisk 4 egg whites into peaks and gently fold them into the mixture.

Turn the mixture into a greased, deep, 28 cm (11 in) round cake tin and smooth it out evenly using a spatula. Bake in a preheated oven at 180° C (350° F, Gas Mark 4) for 35 to 40 minutes.

Leave the cake to cool completely and cut into two equal layers. Spread 3 tablespoons apricot jam over the first layer of sponge, cover with the second layer. Sieve the remaining jam and spread all over the cake.

For the icing: melt the remaining chocolate in a bowl over a pan of hot water, stirring until the mixture is smooth and glossy. Add the remaining sugar and 1 egg white. Beat until the chocolate icing become glossy, coat the cake and leave to set.
Dredge with cocoa powder.

Opposite: *Old-fashioned chocolate cake.*

Above: *Viennese chocolate cake*

VIENNESE CHOCOLATE CAKE

Serves 8 to 10

350 g (11½ oz) plain
chocolate
250 g (8 oz) butter,
softened
150 g (5 oz) caster sugar
5 egg yolks
3 eggs
250 g (8 oz) ground
almonds

100 g (3½ oz) fine
breadcrumbs
2 teaspoons baking
powder
5 egg whites
3 spoons redcurrant jelly
Creamed coconut
Chocolate curls to finish

Melt 250 g (8 oz) chocolate in a bowl over a pan of hot water, stirring until the mixture is smooth and glossy. Leave to cool slightly. In a mixing bowl, cream the butter, add the melted chocolate, 50 g (2 oz) sugar, 5 egg yolks and 3 whole eggs, mixing well. In a separate bowl, sift the ground almonds, breadcrumbs and baking powder and incorporate into the chocolate mixture.

Whisk the egg whites into peaks, add the remaining sugar, beating constantly, and gently fold the egg whites into the mixture. Turn the mixture into a well-greased, deep, 28 cm (11 in) round cake tin. Smooth it out evenly using a spatula. Bake in a preheated oven at

CARROT CAKE
(Ruebli, Swiss speciality)

Serves 8

300 g (10 oz) carrots
4 eggs, separated
200 g (7 oz) caster sugar
1 sachet vanilla sugar
Grated rind of ½ lemon or ½ orange
2 spoons lemon juice
300 g (10 oz) ground almonds

65 g (2½ oz) plain flour
2 teaspoons baking powder
A pinch of salt
150 g (5 oz) icing sugar
8 marzipan carrots to finish
Whipped cream to serve

*C*lean, wash and finely grate the carrots.
Mix the egg yolks, sugar, vanilla sugar, lemon or orange rind, and 2 spoons lemon juice until the mixture is thick, smooth and creamy. Add the carrots and mix.

Sift the ground almonds, flour, baking powder and salt, and incorporate them into the mixture.

Whisk the egg whites into peaks, reserve 3 tablespoons egg whites, and fold the rest into the mixture.

Turn the mixture into a lined, deep, 24 cm (9½ in) round cake tin, taking care to smooth it out well.
Bake in a preheated oven at 180-200° C (350-400° F, Gas Mark 4-6) for 40 minutes. Remove from the tin immediately and transfer to a muslin cloth over a wire rack.

For the icing: mix the icing sugar with the remaining lemon juice and use to coat the cake while still warm. Leave to cool. Decorate with marzipan carrots and serve with whipped cream.

150-180° C (300-350° F, Gas Mark 2-4) for 70 minutes. Leave to cool.

For the filling: thin down the redcurrant jelly with 3 spoons water and bring to the boil. Cook for several minutes. Pour this redcurrant syrup over the cake.

For the icing: melt the remaining plain chocolate with the creamed coconut in a bowl over a pan of hot water, stirring until the mixture is smooth and glossy, and use to coat the cake. Decorate with curls of chocolate before the icing sets.

Below: Carrot cake

Below: *Baden walnut gâteau*

BADEN WALNUT GÂTEAU

Serves 8

200 g (7 oz) marzipan
7 eggs, separated
Grated rind of 1 lemon
1 sachet vanilla sugar
A pinch of salt
175 g (6 oz) caster sugar
200 g (7 oz) ground
walnuts
125 g (4 oz) plain flour
2 teaspoons baking
powder

100 g (3½ oz) butter,
melted
200 g (7 oz) walnut
chocolate
1 knob creamed coconut
20 g (¾ oz) plain superfine
cooking chocolate
Some walnut halves to
finish

Cut the marzipan into small pieces and cream with the egg yolks, lemon rind, vanilla sugar and salt, then beat using an electric mixer until the mixture is thick and frothy.

Whisk the egg whites into peaks and incorporate the sugar, beating constantly. Combine the ground walnuts, flour and baking powder in a mixing bowl and incorporate into the mixture. Finally add the melted butter.

Turn the mixture into a greased, deep, 26 cm (10½ in) round cake tin, taking care to smooth it out evenly. Bake in a preheated oven at 180-200° C (350-400° F, Gas Mark 4-6) for 40 minutes. Remove from the tin immediately and transfer to a muslin cloth over a wire rack.

For the icing: melt the walnut chocolate in a bowl over a pan of hot water, stirring constantly. Use to coat the cake.
In a separate bowl, melt the chocolate and the creamed coconut over a pan of hot water.

Make a small funnel out of greaseproof paper, fill it with the melted chocolate and, starting from the centre of the cake, draw a spiral on the praline while it is still warm. Again starting from the centre, mark out the slices using a cocktail stick and decorate with walnut halves.

Above: *Linzertorte*

LINZERTORTE

Serves about 8

200 g (7 oz) plain flour
1 teaspoon baking powder
125 g (4 oz) caster sugar
1 sachet vanilla sugar
1 teaspoon oil
A pinch of ground cloves
1 teaspoon cinnamon
1 egg, separated

125 g (4 oz) butter
125 g (4 oz) ground
almonds or hazelnuts
400 g (13 oz) raspberry
jam
1 teaspoon milk
Icing sugar to finish

Sift three-quarters of the flour and the baking powder. Make a well and add the sugar, vanilla sugar, oil, cloves and cinnamon, egg white and half the yolk. Knead.

Cut the butter into pieces and dredge with the ground almonds or hazelnuts. Cover with the remaining flour. Then, drawing the ingredients into the centre, quickly knead them into soft dough. If the mixture is too sticky, place it in a refrigerator for a while.

Spread out half the mixture into a 28 cm (11 in) diameter circle. Cut into even strips. Line a springform tin of the same size with the rest of the dough and spread it with jam, leaving 1 cm (½ in) free of jam. Place the strips of dough over the jam, pressing down at the edges. Beat the remaining half egg yolk with 1 teaspoon milk and brush on to the strips of dough. Bake in a preheated oven at 180-200° C (350-400° F, Gas Mark 4-6) for 25-30 minutes. When cold, decorate by dredging with icing sugar.

MOCHA

Makes 12-16 slices

8 eggs	2 teaspoons instant coffee
450 g (15 oz) caster sugar	300 g (10 oz) bitter
2 sachets vanilla sugar	superfine cooking
150 g (5 oz) plain flour	chocolate
375 g (12 oz) butter,	1-2 tablespoons coffee
softened	liqueur
100 g (3½ oz) icing sugar,	1 egg yolk
sifted	40 g (1½ oz) flaked
Salt	almonds

*B*eat 4 eggs with 2 teaspoons hot water using an electric mixer at high speed for 1 minute until the mixture is thick and frothy.

Gradually sift 100 g (3½ oz) sugar and 1 sachet vanilla sugar on to the egg mixture. Beat for a further 2 minutes.

Sift 40 g (½ oz) flour on to this creamy mixture. With the mixer at low speed, incorporate the flour, then add a further 40 g (1½ oz) flour in the same way.

Using 4-5 tablespoons of the mixture make a thin layer in a greased or lined, deep, 28 cm (11 in) round springform cake tin. Bake in a preheated oven at 200° C (400° F, Gas Mark 6) for about 10 minutes. Remove the layer of sponge from the tin immediately, turning it out on to a sheet of greaseproof paper covered in sugar. Repeat the procedure for the rest of the mixture, making three more layers of sponge.

For the second mixture: mix 4 eggs, 100 g (3½ oz) sugar and the remaining vanilla sugar and flour. Proceed as above, making four layers of sponge. Leave the eight layers of sponge to cool.

For the filling: combine the softened butter, salt and remaining sugar. If using, dissolve the instant coffee in 1 teaspoon hot water. Add to the creamed mixture. Melt the chocolate in a bowl over a pan of hot water. When cool, add the coffee liqueur and the egg yolk and mix well.

Spread a thin layer of butter cream over each layer (reserve some for decoration).
Place the layers one on top of the other and cover the cake all over with butter cream.

For the icing: heat the remaining sugar with a little water in a stainless steel pan until the mixture turns brown. Place the remaining layer of sponge on a plate and pour the caramel on to it, spreading it out quickly.

When the caramel begins to set, cut the sponge layer into 12-16 portions. Cut the cake into 12-16 slices too. Arrange the caramel sponge portions on top of the cake, slightly tilted at an angle. Spread the remaining butter cream over the sides of the cake and sprinkle on the flaked almonds.

Left: *Mocha*

Above: *Cheesecake*

CHEESECAKE

Serves about 8

150 g (5 oz) plain flour
2 sachets vanilla sugar
350 g (11½ oz) butter
250 g (8 oz) caster sugar
7 eggs, separated
Salt

Rind of 1 lemon
3 tablespoons lemon juice
1 kg (2 lb) drained cream cheese
2 tablespoons cornflour

Sift the flour and make a well in the centre. Add 1 sachet vanilla sugar. Cut 100 g (3½ oz) butter into pieces and mix with 40 g (1½ oz) sugar. Knead all the ingredients, drawing the flour into the centre, to form a smooth ball of dough. Roll out the pastry and place in a deep, 28 cm (11 in) round springform cake tin.

For the filling: incorporate the remaining softened butter, the remaining sugar and vanilla sugar, the egg yolks, a pinch of salt, the lemon rind and juice, stirring well. Add the cottage cheese and cornflour to this mixture.

Whisk the egg whites into peaks and gently fold into the mixture.

Pour on to the tart base, smooth out evenly and place in a preheated oven at 160-180° C (325-350° F, Gas Mark 3-4) for 70-80 minutes. Leave the cooked cheesecake to cool in the oven for 30-45 minutes with the door half open. Then remove from the oven and leave to cool in the tin.

KAISERIN FRIEDRICH CAKE

Serves 8

300 g (10 oz) butter,
softened
300 g (10 oz) caster sugar
1 sachet vanilla sugar
5 eggs
1 egg white
1 egg yolk
3 drops bitter almond
essence

½ bottle rum flavouring
Salt
300 g (10 oz) plain flour
75 g (3 oz) cornflour
2 teaspoons baking
powder
175 g (6 oz) candied peel
175 g (6 oz) icing sugar
3 tablespoons lemon juice

Cream the softened butter, sugar and vanilla sugar until the mixture is light and pale. Then add 5 eggs, 1 egg white and half the egg yolk, the bitter almond essence, rum and a pinch of salt. Then combine and sift the flour, cornflour and baking powder. Gradually spoon into the egg mixture. Finally add 125 g (4 oz) candied peel. Turn the mixture into a flower-shaped tin (or a deep, springform cake tin). Place in a preheated oven at 180-200° C (350-400° F, Gas Mark 4-6) for 65-75 minutes. For the icing: sift the icing sugar and mix with the remaining egg yolk and the lemon juice to make a thick syrup. Use to coat the cooled cake. Using the remaining candied peel, cut out flowers and stems and arrange them on the cake to finish.

SPANISH VANILLA CAKE

Serves 6

150 g (5 oz) marzipan
6 eggs, separated
100 g (3½ oz) caster sugar
Grated rind of 1 lemon
3 sachets vanilla sugar
A pinch of salt
200 g (7 oz) superfine
cooking chocolate
50 g (2 oz) flaked almonds

9 spoons Marsala
2 teaspoons baking
powder
75 g (3 oz) plain flour
75 g (3 oz) cornflour
2 spoons apricot jam
150 g (5 oz) icing sugar
1 spoon lemon juice
200 g (7 oz) walnuts

Cut the marzipan into pieces and combine with the egg yolks until smooth and creamy. Then add the sugar, lemon rind, and 2 sachets vanilla sugar. Mix well. Coarsely chop the cooking chocolate with the flaked almonds, sprinkle with the Marsala. Add the baking powder, flour and cornflour to the marzipan cream, stirring until the mixture is smooth. Whisk 5 egg whites into peaks, then gently fold them into the mixture, alternating with the chocolate.
Turn the mixture into a lined, deep, 24 cm (9½ in) round

cake tin, smoothing it out evenly with a spatula. Bake in a preheated oven at 180° C (350° F, Gas Mark 4) for about 45 minutes.

Take the cake out of the oven and remove from the tin after about 8 minutes.
Spread the sieved apricot jam all over the cake.

For the icing: mix the icing sugar, the remaining vanilla sugar and egg white and the lemon juice until a smooth consistency is achieved, then coat the cake with this icing.

Coarsely chop the walnuts and spread over the top and the sides of the cake, pressing down gently.

Opposite: *Kaiserin Friedrich cake*
Below: *Spanish vanilla cake*

APPLE AND NUT CAKE

Serves 8-10

6 eggs
200 g (7 oz) caster sugar
1 sachet vanilla powder
A pinch of cinnamon
75 g (3 oz) semolina
1 spoon cocoa powder
125 g (4 oz) ground
hazelnuts

250 g (8 oz) apples, peeled
and grated
3 spoons apple jelly
100 g (3½ oz) plain
chocolate
1 knob creamed coconut
Some flaked hazelnuts

Beat the eggs and sugar in a bowl using an electric mixer at high speed for 1 minute until the mixture is thick and frothy. Add the vanilla sugar and the cinnamon, continue beating for 2 minutes. In a mixing bowl, mix the semolina, cocoa powder and the ground hazelnuts, add them to the egg cream, beating with the mixer at low speed. Incorporate the apples.

Turn the mixture into a lined, deep, 28 cm (11 in) round cake tin, smoothing it out evenly with a spatula. Bake in a preheated oven at 180-200° C (350-400° F, Gas Mark 4-6) for about 30-35 minutes. Remove from the tin immediately, spread the apple jelly over the cake and leave to cool.

For the icing: melt the chocolate and the creamed coconut in a bowl over a pan of hot water, stirring until the mixture is smooth and glossy. Coat the cake and decorate the sides with the flaked hazelnuts.

GÂTEAU D'ANNA

Serves 8-10

250 g (8 oz) butter
250 g (8 oz) caster sugar
1 sachet vanilla sugar
4 eggs
½ bottle rum flavouring
250 g (8 oz) plain flour
2 teaspoons baking
powder

125 g plain chocolate,
grated
100 g (3½ oz) ground
almonds
50 g (2 oz) candied peel,
finely chopped
Icing sugar to finish

Cream the butter in a bowl and then add the sugar, vanilla sugar, eggs and rum flavouring. Gradually add the flour and baking powder to the other ingredients. Incorporate the plain chocolate, ground almonds and finely chopped candied peel and beat the mixture until it holds its shape.

Turn the mixture into a greased, deep, 28 cm (11 in) round cake tin, smoothing it out evenly. Bake in a preheated oven at 180-200° C (350-400° F, Gas Mark 4-6) for about 1 hour.

Remove from the tin and leave to cool. Dredge with icing sugar.

Left: *Gâteau d'Anna*

Above: *Grilled gâteau*

GRILLED GÂTEAU

Serves 6

250 g (8 oz) butter
250 g (8 oz) caster sugar
1 sachet vanilla sugar
2 eggs
4 egg yolks
4 egg whites
4-5 spoons rum or brandy
150 g (5 oz) plain flour

100 g (3½ oz) cornflour
2 teaspoons baking
powder
125 g (4 oz) icing sugar
5-6 spoons lemon juice
25 g (1 oz) plain chocolate
15 g (½ oz) creamed
coconut

Cream the butter in a bowl and then incorporate the sugar, followed by the vanilla sugar, the whole eggs and egg yolks, then the rum or brandy. Gradually mix the flour, the cornflour and the baking powder into the other ingredients. Whisk the egg whites into peaks and gently fold into the mixture.

Grease a deep, 28 cm (11 in) round cake tin, line it with greaseproof paper and spread 1-2 heaped spoonfuls of the mixture in the tin. Place about 20 cm (8 in) below the grill and grill until the mixture browns slightly (2 minutes).

Spread 1-2 spoonfuls of the mixture over the first layer and place under the grill for a further 2 minutes. Repeat the same process until all the mixture has been used. Carefully remove the cake from the tin by first loosening the edges with a knife and then turning it out on to a baking sheet. Peel off the greaseproof paper and return to a hot oven for 5 minutes.

For the glacé icing: mix the icing sugar and lemon juice into a smooth paste and use to coat the cake.

For the chocolate icing: melt the chocolate and the creamed coconut in a bowl over a pan of hot water, stirring until the mixture is smooth and glossy. Make a small funnel out of greaseproof paper and fill with the melted chocolate. Draw a spiral on the glacé icing before it sets. Take a cocktail stick and mark out 16 slices in the soft icing, working alternately to and from the centre.

Suggestion: if wrapped up well in a sheet of aluminium foil, this cake will keep for several weeks in a refrigerator, and is thus very useful for unexpected guests.

Above: *Belgrade coffee cake*

BELGRADE COFFEE CAKE

Serves 8-10

200 g (7 oz) marzipan
6 eggs, separated
100 g (3½ oz) caster sugar
A pinch of salt
Grated rind of 1 lemon
100 g (3½ oz) plain flour
2 teaspoons baking powder
6 tablespoons orange

liqueur
4 tablespoons apricot jam
225 g (7½ oz) icing sugar
1-2 teaspoons instant coffee
1-2 teaspoons rum
1 teaspoon cocoa powder
Whipped cream

Using an electric mixer, mix 100 g (3½ oz) marzipan with 3 tablespoons water, add 6 egg yolks and continue beating until the mixture is smooth and creamy. Then add 50 g (2 oz) sugar, followed by the salt and lemon rind. Whisk 5 egg whites into peaks, add the remaining sugar, mix well and fold the egg whites into the other ingredients. Incorporate the flour and baking powder in the mixture using an electric mixer at slow speed.

Turn the mixture into a greased and lined, deep, 28 cm (11 in) round cake tin, smoothing it out well. Bake in a preheated oven at 180-200° C (350-400° F, Gas Mark 4-6) for 30 minutes.
Remove from the tin immediately, peel off the greaseproof paper and cut the cake into two layers.

For the filling: moisten the first layer of sponge with 3 tablespoons orange liqueur. Mix 2 rounded tablespoons apricot jam with 2 spoons orange liqueur and spread over the sponge. Cover with the second layer of sponge. Sprinkle with orange liqueur. Sieve 2 tablespoons jam, add 1 spoon water and one spoon orange liqueur. Bring to the boil and use to coat the cake.

Knead the remaining marzipan with 50 g (2 oz) icing sugar, roll the mixture out and cut out a 28 cm (11 in) diameter circle. Place on the cake.

For the icing: dissolve the instant coffee in the rum, mix the remaining icing sugar and egg white into a smooth paste. Reserve one rounded tablespoon of icing and spread the rest over the cake.

Add the cocoa powder to the reserved icing, thinning it down with a little water if necessary. Make a small funnel out of greaseproof paper and trace a chocolate lattice pattern on the cake. Serve with slightly sweetened whipped cream.

ORANGE GÂTEAU

Serves 8

2 large oranges
250 g (8 oz) caster sugar
4 spoons orange liqueur
250 g (8 oz) butter, softened
4 eggs
A pinch of salt
250 g (8 oz) plain flour

A pinch of baking powder
100 g (3½ oz) orange marmalade
150 g (5 oz) candied orange slices
100-150 g (3½-5 oz) plain superfine chocolate

Wash the oranges, shred the peel and cut into thin strips, put to one side. Squeeze the oranges and save 150 ml (¼ pint) juice, add 50 g (2 oz) sugar and bring to the boil, add the orange liqueur, cover and leave to soak.

Cream the softened butter with the remaining sugar, add the eggs, then the salt. Incorporate the flour and baking powder to make a smooth paste. Turn the mixture into a greased, deep, 22 cm (8½ in) round cake tin, smoothing it out well. Bake in a preheated oven at 180-200° C (350-400° F, Gas Mark 4-6) for 45 minutes.

Leave the cake in the tin, prick with a fork and pour on the orange liqueur syrup. Leave to cool, turn out on to a wire rack.

Spread the jam all over the cake. Cut the candied orange slices in half, arrange on the top of the cake, and reserve some for decoration.

For the icing: melt the chocolate in a bowl over a pan of hot water, stirring until the mixture is smooth and glossy. Coat the cake and decorate the sides with the reserved orange slices.

Right: *Orange gâteau*

HAZELNUT AND REDCURRANT GÂTEAU

Serves 6-8

200 g (7 oz) marzipan
6 eggs, separated
300 g (10 oz) caster sugar
1 sachet vanilla sugar
A pinch of salt
Grated rind of ½ lemon
A pinch of cinnamon
100 g (3½ oz) ground
hazelnuts
200 g (7 oz) ground
toasted hazelnuts
100 g (3½ oz)
breadcrumbs

125 g (4 oz) plain flour
3 teaspoons baking
powder
75 g (3 oz) butter
5 tablespoons redcurrant
jelly
200 ml (7 fl oz) rum
100 g (3½ oz) icing sugar
125 g (4 oz) coffee-
flavoured glacé icing
1 tablespoon cocoa
powder
Some marzipan leaves

Using an electric mixer, combine 50 g (2 oz) marzipan with 3 spoons water, add 6 egg yolks and continue beating until the mixture is smooth and creamy. Then add 100 g (3½ oz) sugar, followed by the vanilla sugar, salt, lemon rind and cinnamon, beating constantly.

Whisk the egg whites into peaks (reserve 2 tablespoons for decoration), add 100 g (3½ oz) sugar, mix well and incorporate this mixture into the other ingredients. Finally add the ground hazelnuts, roasted hazelnuts, breadcrumbs, 25 g (1 oz) flour and 2 teaspoons baking powder and fold in gently.

Turn the mixture into a lined, deep, 26 cm (10½ in) round cake tin, smoothing it down well. Bake in a preheated oven at 180-200° C (340-400° F, Gas Mark 4-6) for 45 minutes. Remove from the tin immediately, peel off the greaseproof paper and leave to cool.

For the pastry: place the remaining flour in a bowl with the remaining teaspoon of baking powder and 2 tablespoons sugar. Quickly rub the cold butter into the ingredients, using the fingertips, until the mixture resembles breadcrumbs.
Gradually add 150 ml (¼ pint) water. Quickly bring the mixture together into a dough which is easy to roll out.

Leave to rest for at least 2 hours in a cloth.

Grease a smooth-sided, 28 cm (11 in) round flan tin. Roll out the pastry, place in the tin and prick the base well with a fork. Bake in a preheated oven at 200-220° C (400-425° F, Gas Mark 6-7) for 15 minutes. Remove from the tin immediately and leave to cool.

For the filling: spread 2 tablespoons redcurrant jelly over the pastry layer. Heat the remaining 75 g (3 oz) sugar in 150 ml (¼ pint) water, bring to the boil, cook until the sugar has dissolved, then add the rum.

Place the hazelnut sponge on the pastry layer. Prick the hazelnut sponge with a fork and pour over the syrup. Spread the remaining redcurrant jelly over the sides of the cake.

Knead the remaining marzipan with 75 g (3 oz) icing sugar, roll it out into a thin layer, place the marzipan over the cake, pressing down gently. Remove any excess marzipan and knead it up into a ball again. Cut out a strip for the sides of the cake.

For the icing: coat the hazelnut sponge with the coffee-flavoured glacé icing.
Make a small amount of glacé icing with the remaining icing sugar and egg white.
Make a small funnel out of greaseproof paper and decorate the cake, dredge with cocoa powder and finish by decorating the cake with the marzipan leaves.

QUICK HAZELNUT GÂTEAU

Serves 6-8

6 eggs
100 g (3½ oz) caster sugar
1 sachet vanilla sugar
150 g (5 oz) ground
hazelnuts

50 g (2 oz) breadcrumbs
150 g (5 oz) plain
chocolate
1 knob creamed coconut
Whipped cream to serve

Beat the eggs and the sugar using an electric mixer at high speed for 1 minute until the mixture is thick and frothy. Add the vanilla sugar and continue to beat for 2 minutes. Combine the ground hazelnuts and the breadcrumbs, add to the other ingredients, beating with the mixer at low speed.

Turn the mixture into a lined, deep, 26 cm (10½ in) round cake tin, smoothing it out evenly using a spatula.
Bake in a preheated oven at 180-200° C (350-400° F, Gas Mark 4-6) for 35-40 minutes. Remove from the tin immediately, peel off the greaseproof paper and leave to cool on a muslin cloth on a wire rack. Wrap the cake in a sheet of aluminium foil and leave in a refrigerator for 1-2 days.

Above: *Hazelnut and redcurrant gâteau*

For the icing: melt the chocolate and the creamed coconut in a bowl over a pan of hot water, stirring until the mixture is smooth and glossy. Use to coat the cake and leave to set. Serve with whipped cream.

FRENCH CHOCOLATE CAKE

Serves 8-10

250 g (8 oz) butter, softened
250 g (8 oz) caster sugar
1 sachet vanilla sugar
A pinch of salt
6 eggs
250 g (8 oz) plain flour
2 teaspoons baking powder
350 g (11½ oz) plain chocolate
100 g (3½ oz) ground almonds
250 ml (8 fl oz) brandy or rum
2 spoons apricot jam
1 knob creamed coconut
Pistachio nuts and crushed nut brittle to finish

Using an electric mixer, cream the butter in a bowl for 30 seconds, then incorporate first the sugar, followed by the vanilla sugar, salt and finally the eggs. Continue beating until all the ingredients are incorporated. Gradually mix the flour and the baking powder into the other ingredients.

Grate 250 g (8 oz) chocolate and mix with the ground almonds, then incorporate into the mixture.

Turn the mixture into a greased, deep, 28 cm (11 in) round cake tin. Bake in a preheated oven at 180-200° C (350-400° F, Gas Mark 4-6) for 1 hour. Remove from the tin and sprinkle with the rum or brandy.

Sieve the apricot jam, thin it down with 1 tablespoon water, bring to the boil and use to coat the cake.

For the icing: melt the remaining chocolate and the creamed coconut, stirring until the mixture is smooth and glossy. Spread the icing over the cake. Decorate with the pistachio nuts and the crushed nut brittle and leave to set.

CHOCOLATE HAZELNUT CAKE

Serves 6-8

200 g (7 oz) butter, softened
200 g (7 oz) caster sugar
1 teaspoon orange flower water
A pinch of salt
4 eggs
150 g (5 oz) plain flour
100 g (3½ oz) cornflour
3 teaspoons cocoa powder
2 teaspoons baking powder
2 spoons milk
150 g (5 oz) ground hazelnuts
250 ml (8 fl oz) brandy or rum
2 spoons apricot jam
3 tablespoons rum
200 g (7 oz) icing sugar
Chopped hazelnuts and almonds to finish

Using an electric mixer, cream the butter in a bowl for 30 seconds and then incorporate first the sugar, followed by the orange flower water, the salt and finally the eggs. Continue beating until all the ingredients are incorporated.

Sift the flour, cornflour, cocoa powder and baking powder together, gradually add to the other ingredients, then add the milk and finally gently fold in the ground hazelnuts and 100 ml (3½ fl oz) rum or brandy.

Turn the mixture into a greased, deep, 26 cm (10½ in) round cake tin. Bake in a preheated oven at 180-200° C (350-400° F, Gas Mark 4-6) for 60 to 70 minutes. Remove from the tin and leave to cool on a muslin cloth on a wire rack.

For the icing: combine the icing sugar with the remaining 150 ml (¼ pint) rum or brandy and 5-6 tablespoons water into a smooth paste. Use to coat the cake and decorate it with chopped hazelnuts and almonds.

Opposite: *French chocolate cake*

Above: *Viennese sponge cake*

VIENNESE SPONGE CAKE

Serves 8-10

6 eggs
375 g (12 oz) caster sugar
2 sachets vanilla sugar
175 g (6 oz) plain flour
175 g (6 oz) cornflour
2 teaspoons baking
powder

375 g (12 oz) butter,
melted
2 tablespoons apricot jam
3 tablespoons apricot
liqueur
1 teaspoon rum
25 g (1 oz) icing sugar

*B*reak the eggs into a bowl and reserve 2 teaspoons egg white. Beat the eggs, caster sugar and vanilla sugar using an electric mixer at high speed for 2-3 minutes, add 1-2 spoons water and continue beating.

Incorporate the flour, cornflour and baking powder into the egg mixture, finishing with the melted butter.

Turn the mixture into a greased flower-shaped cake tin or alternatively a deep, 28 cm (11 in) round cake tin.
Bake in a preheated oven at 150-180° C (300-350° F, Gas Mark 2-4) for 60-85 minutes.
Remove from the tin and leave to cool slightly.

Sieve the apricot jam, mix with the apricot liqueur, 1 teaspoon water and the rum.
Bring to the boil and spread the syrup over the cake.

Mix the icing sugar with the reserved egg white and a little water to form a smooth icing.
Transfer it to an icing bag made out of greaseproof paper and use to decorate the cake.

MALAKOFF

Serves 8-10

150 g (5 oz) butter
165 g (5½ oz) caster sugar
2 sachets vanilla sugar
3 egg yolks
150 g (5 oz) ground almonds
375 ml (12 fl oz) double cream
250 ml (8 fl oz) milk
5-6 spoons rum
250 g (8 oz) sponge fingers
Glacé cherries to finish

Cream the butter using an electric mixer at high speed for 30 seconds, add 150 g (5 oz) caster sugar, 1 sachet vanilla sugar and beat until the mixture holds its shape. Gradually add the egg yolks, beating constantly.

Mix the ground almonds with the remaining vanilla sugar, add 125 ml (4 fl oz) cream, the milk and rum. Dunk the sponge fingers in this mixture.

Line the side section of a 28 cm (11 in) round springform cake tin with aluminium foil, put on a plate and arrange half the moist sponge fingers on the base. Spread on half the cream mixture, cover with the remaining sponge fingers, then with the rest of the cream mixture. Smooth it out evenly and chill in a refrigerator for 5-6 hours.

Remove the side section of the cake tin.
Whip the remaining cream for 30 seconds, add the remaining sugar, continue beating until the cream is very firm. Place half the cream in an icing bag. Spread the other half of the cream over the cake. Decorate using the icing bag and finish with the glacé cherries.

Line the side section of the tin with aluminium foil.

Arrange half the moist sponge fingers.

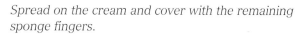

Spread on the cream and cover with the remaining sponge fingers.

BITTER ORANGE CHRISTMAS CAKE

Serves 6-8

4 eggs	flavouring
200 g (7 oz) caster sugar	300 g (10 oz) almond
1 teaspoon orange flower	paste
water	200 g (7 oz) icing sugar
150 g (5 oz) plain flour	150 g (5 oz) plain cooking
75 g (3 oz) cornflour	chocolate
2 teaspoons baking	2 teaspoons grated
powder	chocolate
1 jar marmalade	300 g (10 oz) ground
3 teaspoons rum	almonds

Beat the eggs with 2 tablespoons hot water using an electric mixer at high speed for 1 minute, until the mixture is thick and frothy. Add the sugar, stirring well. Beat for a further 2 minutes.

Combine the orange flower water, flour, cornflour and baking powder, sift half this mixture over the egg cream mixture. Beat with the mixer at slow speed, then add the remaining flour mixture in the same way.
Turn the mixture into a greased or lined deep, 26 cm (10½ in) round springform cake tin. Bake in a preheated oven at 180-200° C (350-400° F, Gas Mark 4-6) for about 45 minutes.
Leave the sponge to cool and cut into two layers.

For the filling: mix the marmalade with the rum flavouring. Spread some over the first layer of sponge and the rest over both sides of the second layer.
Combine the almond paste with the icing sugar and roll two-thirds of it out into a thin layer between two pieces of cling film. When it is very smooth, remove the top layer of cling film, carefully lift the second layer and lay the almond paste on to the cake.

For the icing: melt the chocolate in a bowl over a pan of hot water, pour on to the almond paste and leave to set.

Draw a 22 cm (8½ in) wide star on a sheet of paper. Roll out the remaining almond paste, place the star on top. Cut out the star and place on the cake.
Sprinkle with the grated chocolate. Decorate the sides of the cake with ground almonds.

MACAROON CAKE

Serves 8

5 eggs	paste
125 g (4 oz) caster sugar	150 g (5 oz) icing sugar
Salt	450 g (15 oz) apricot jam
Rind of 1 lemon	5 tablespoons rum
75 g (3 oz) plain flour	2 egg yolks
75 g (3 oz) cornflour	75 g (3 oz) toasted pine
50 g (2 oz) butter, melted	kernels (optional)
625 g (1¼ lb) almond	

Using an electric mixer, beat the eggs, sugar, a pinch of salt and the lemon rind in a bowl over a pan of hot water until the mixture is thick and frothy. Remove the bowl from the water and continue beating until the mixture is cold. Add the flour, cornflour and the cooled, melted butter.

Turn the mixture into a greased, deep, 28 cm (11 in) round springform cake tin. Dust with a little flour, spread the mixture out evenly and bake in a preheated oven at 180° C (350° F, Gas Mark 4) for about 40 minutes. Remove the sponge cake from the tin immediately and turn out on to a plate. Leave to rest overnight, then cut into 2-3 layers.

For the filling: combine 400 g (13 oz) almond paste, 100 g (3½ oz) icing sugar, 250 g (8 oz) apricot jam and 4 tablespoons rum until the ingredients are incorporated. Set aside a quarter of this mixture and use the rest to cover the layers of sponge cake. Use the reserved mixture to cover the top and sides of the cake.

For the decoration: combine the remaining almond paste, 2 egg yolks, the remaining sifted icing sugar and 1 tablespoon rum. Transfer this mixture to an icing bag and decorate the cake. Leave to rest for about 30 minutes to let the almond paste dry out. Place the cake under a preheated grill and brown lightly.

Bring the remaining apricot jam, thinned down with 3 tablespoons water, to the boil, stirring constantly. Use the jam to ice the cake once it has cooled a little. If you wish, you may decorate the sides of the cake with the toasted pine kernels.

Opposite: *Macaroon cake*

ut the sponge into two or three
yers.

Cover the layers of sponge with the
almond paste cream.

Decorate the cake using an icing
bag.

Crush the sponge fingers using a rolling pin.

Spread the crushed sponge finger and butter mixture evenly over the base of the tin.

Incorporate the whipped cream into the cream cheese mixture.

Spread the filling over the sponge finger base using spatula.

QUICK CHEESECAKE

Serves 6-8

175 g (6 oz) sponge
fingers
75 g (3 oz) butter
1 sachet or 3 leaves
gelatine
200 g (7 oz) cream cheese

125 g (4 oz) sugar
1 sachet vanilla sugar
Juice of 1 lemon
500 ml (18 fl oz) double
cream

Place 125 g (4 oz) sponge fingers in a plastic bag and
crush them using a rolling pin. Transfer the crumbs to a
bowl.

Melt the butter and pour over the crumbs, mix well.
Spread the mixture, pressing it down into an even layer
in a deep, 28 cm (11 in) round springform cake tin.

For the filling: put the gelatine in 2 tablespoons cold
water. Leave to soak for 10 minutes, then heat until
dissolved. Leave to cool.

Mix the cream cheese with the sugar, vanilla sugar and
lemon juice. Combine with the gelatine. Whip the cream
into soft peaks and add to the cheese mixture. Transfer
the filling to the biscuit crumb base. Smooth it out
evenly.

For the decoration: crush the remaining sponge
fingers and sprinkle over the cheesecake. Keep in a
refrigerator until just about to serve.

Opposite: *Quick cheesecake*

HAZELNUT GÂTEAU

Serves 6-8

4 eggs
250 g (8 oz) caster sugar
1 teaspoon orange flower
water
65 g (2½ oz) plain flour
75 g (3 oz) cornflour
2 teaspoons cocoa powder
1½ teaspoons baking
powder

5 tablespoons rum
500 ml (18 fl oz) double
cream
100 g (3½ oz) ground
hazelnuts
½ teaspoon cinnamon
200 g (7 oz) icing sugar
Red food colouring
Sugar flowers to finish

Beat the eggs with 4 tablespoons hot water using an
electric mixer at high speed for 1 minute until the mixture
is thick and frothy.
Gradually add 200 g (7 oz) sugar and beat for 2 minutes.
With the mixer at low speed, add the orange flower
water. Combine the flour, cornflour, cocoa essence and
baking powder. Sift half of this mixture over the eggs.
Beat at low speed, then add the rest of the mixture in the
same way.

Turn the mixture into a greased or lined, deep,
28 cm (11 in) round springform cake tin. Smooth the
mixture out evenly and place in a preheated oven at
180-200° C (350-400° F, Gas Mark 4-6) for about
30 minutes. Leave to cool, then cut the sponge into three
layers. Moisten the layers with 3 tablespoons rum.

For the filling: whip the cream and the remaining sugar
until firm. Gently fold in the ground hazelnuts and
cinnamon. Spread the cream over two layers of sponge
and place them one on top of the other. Place the third
layer on top.

For the icing: sift the icing sugar and mix with
2 tablespoons rum. Colour a quarter of this mixture with
red food colouring, then transfer it to an icing bag.
Cover the top of the cake with the white icing and make
lines with the red icing. Smooth the icing using the blade
of a knife.

Decorate the cake with the sugar flowers.

BISCUITS AND COOKIES

Above : *Austrian shortbread biscuits*

AUSTRIAN SHORTBREAD BISCUITS

Makes about 5

350 g (1½ oz) plain flour
100 g (3½ oz) icing sugar
1 sachet vanilla sugar
2 egg yolks
A pinch of cinnamon
Grated rind of ½ lemon

300 g (10 oz) butter
200 g (7 oz) ground almonds
Raspberry jam
Icing sugar to finish

Sift the flour onto a work surface and make a well in the centre. Add the icing sugar (reserve 1 teaspoonful for decoration), vanilla sugar, egg yolks, cinnamon and lemon rind; then, using part of the flour, work the ingredients into a soft dough. Finally add the cold butter, cut into pieces, and the ground almonds, cover with the remaining flour and knead the ingredients into a smooth dough. Leave to rest in a refrigerator for several hours.

Roll out the dough until 3 mm (¼ in) thick. Cut out the biscuits using a 6 cm (2½ in) round cutter, make a hole 1.5 cm (1 in) wide in the middle of half of the biscuits. Place all the biscuits on a baking sheet covered with greaseproof paper and bake in a preheated oven at 180-200° C (350-400° F, Gas Mark 4-6) for 10 minutes.

When cool, spread some raspberry jam over the whole biscuits, then cover each of them with a biscuit with a hole in. Dredge with icing sugar.

VANILLA CRESCENTS

Makes about 6

250 g (8 oz) plain flour	200 g (7 oz) butter
A pinch of baking powder	125 g (4 oz) ground
125 g (4 oz) caster sugar	almonds
2 sachets vanilla sugar	50 g (2 oz) icing sugar
3 egg yolks	

Sift the flour and baking powder onto a work surface and make a well in the centre. Add the sugar, 1 sachet vanilla sugar and the egg yolks; then, using some of the flour, work the ingredients into a soft dough. Add the cold butter, cut into pieces, and the ground almonds, cover with the remaining flour, and knead the ingredients into a smooth dough.

Make the dough into a roll about as thick as your thumb and cut into pieces 2 cm (¾ in) long. Roll these out until they are 5 cm (2 in) long. Make points at each end, then turn the points towards you, making small crescent shapes, and transfer them to a greased baking sheet. Bake in a preheated oven at 180-200° C (350-400° F, Gas Mark 4-6) for 10 minutes. Mix the icing sugar and the remaining vanilla sugar and toss the biscuits in the sugar while still hot.

PEAR BRANDY SHORTBREAD BISCUITS

Makes about 10

175 g (6 oz) plain flour	2 spoons apricot jam
A pinch of baking powder	200 g (7 oz) superfine milk
40 g (1½ oz) caster sugar	cooking chocolate
1 sachet vanilla sugar	50 g (2 oz) icing sugar
A pinch of salt	6-7 teaspoons pear
2 tablespoons milk	brandy
165 g (5½ oz) butter	

Sift the flour and baking powder onto a work surface. Add the sugar, vanilla sugar, salt and milk; then, using some of the flour, work the ingredients into a soft dough. Finally add 100 g (3½ oz) cold butter, cut into pieces, cover with the remaining flour, and knead into a smooth dough. Leave to rest in a refrigerator for several hours.

Roll the dough out until 5 mm (¼ in) thick. Cut out the biscuits using a 3 cm (1¼ in) fluted round cutter. Transfer them to a baking sheet lined with greased greaseproof paper and bake in a preheated oven at 200°C (400˚F, Gas Mark 6) for 10-12 minutes.

For the filling: sieve the apricot jam and spread over the cold biscuits. Melt the chocolate in a bowl over a pan of hot water, stirring constantly. Leave to cool slightly. Cream the remaining softened butter together with 20 g (¾ oz) icing sugar and 2-3 teaspoons pear brandy. Add to the chocolate and beat using an electric mixer. Transfer the mixture to an icing bag and pipe a circle on each biscuit.
Mix the remaining icing sugar with the remaining pear brandy and put a drop in the centre of each chocolate cream circle. Leave to set in a refrigerator.

Right: *Vanilla crescents*
Page 118: *Pignolati (recipe on page 162)*
Page 119: *Pear brandy shortbread biscuits*

LITTLE KISSES

Makes about 6

100 g (3½ oz) caster sugar
1 spoon cocoa powder

50 g (2 oz) plain
chocolate, grated

In a mixing bowl, whisk the egg whites into very stiff peaks, then gently fold in the sugar. Mix the cocoa powder with the grated chocolate and add to the egg whites.

Line a baking sheet with greased greaseproof paper and, using a wooden spoon, place some little piles of the mixture about the size of a walnut on the baking sheet. Bake in a preheated oven at 130-150°C (250-300°F, Gas Mark ½-2) for 25-30 minutes.
Leave the biscuits to cool before peeling off the greaseproof paper.

FLORENTINE BISCUITS

Makes about 6

2 egg whites
150 g (5 oz) plain flour
2 pinches of baking powder
150 g (5 oz) caster sugar
2 sachets vanilla sugar
1 egg
125 g (4 oz) butter
2 spoons honey

140 ml (4½ fl oz) double cream
100 g (3½ oz) flaked almonds
100 g (3½ oz) chopped hazelnuts
25 g (1 oz) glacé cherries, chopped
75 g (3 oz) plain chocolate

Sift the flour and baking powder onto a work surface and make a well in the centre. Add 50 g (2 oz) sugar, 1 sachet vanilla sugar, the egg and 2 tablespoons water; then, using some of the flour, work the ingredients into a soft dough. Finally add 75 g (3 oz) cold butter, cut into pieces, cover with flour and knead the ingredients into a smooth dough. Leave to rest in a refrigerator for several hours.

Roll the dough out until 3 mm (¼ in) thick. Using a 5 cm (2 in) round pastry cutter, cut out the biscuits, transfer them to a baking sheet lined with greased greaseproof paper, and bake in a preheated oven at 200-220°C (400-425°F, Gas Mark 6-7) until they brown slightly (about 8 minutes).

For the filling: heat the remaining butter and sugar with the remaining vanilla sugar and the honey. As soon as the mixture turns brown, add the double cream and

Above: *Little kisses*

stir until the caramel makes threads. Finally add the flaked almonds, hazelnuts and glacé cherries; leave over the heat, stirring until all the ingredients are coated.

Spread the mixture over the cooked biscuits using a wooden spoon. Return them to a preheated oven at 180-200°C (350-400°F, Gas Mark 4-6) and bake for 10 minutes. Leave to cool.

Melt the chocolate in a bowl over a pan of hot water and coat the smooth side of the biscuits when they are absolutely cold.

VANILLA RINGS

Makes about 20

250 g (8 oz) plain flour	1 egg
2 teaspoons baking powder	125 g (4 oz) butter
75 g (3 oz) caster sugar	Jam
1 sachet vanilla sugar	Superfine cooking chocolate
1 bottle rum flavouring	

Sift the flour and baking powder onto a work surface and make a well in the centre. Add the sugar, vanilla sugar, rum flavouring and egg. Then, using some of the flour, work the ingredients into a soft dough. Finally add the cold butter, cut into pieces, cover with the remaining flour, and knead into a smooth dough. Leave to rest in a refrigerator for several hours.

Roll the dough out until 3 mm (¼ in) thick, then cut out the biscuits, using a 5 cm (2 in) round pastry cutter. Using a smaller cutter, cut out the centre of each biscuit to make them into rings. Transfer them to a greased baking sheet and bake in a preheated oven at 180-200° C (350-400° F, Gas Mark 4-6) for 8-10 minutes.

Spread a thin layer of jam over half of the rings and then cover them with the remaining ones.
Melt the chocolate in a bowl over a pan of hot water. Dip the rings into the chocolate, coating half of each biscuit.

Above: *White wine cookies*

WHITE WINE COOKIES

Makes about 20

325 g (11 oz) plain flour
175 g (6 oz) caster sugar
1 sachet vanilla sugar
3 tablespoons white wine
200 g (7 oz) butter

2 egg whites
A pinch of cinnamon
Some chopped almonds to finish

Sift the flour onto a work surface and make a well in the centre. Add 125 g (4 oz) sugar, the vanilla sugar and white wine; then, using some of the flour, work the ingredients into a soft dough. Finally add the cold butter, cut into pieces, cover with the remaining flour, and knead the ingredients into a smooth dough. Leave to rest in a refrigerator for several hours.

Roll the dough out until 3 mm (¼ in) thick, then cut out the biscuits using a 4 cm (1½ in) round pastry cutter. Place on a greased baking sheet.

For the filling: whisk the egg whites into very stiff peaks and spread them on the biscuits. Combine the cinnamon, the remaining sugar and the chopped almonds, sprinkle this mixture over the egg whites. Bake in a preheated oven at 180-200° C (350-400° F, Gas Mark 4-6) for 10-15 minutes.

LITTLE TERRACES

Makes about 6

300 g (10 oz) plain flour
2 teaspoons baking powder
100 g (3½ oz) caster sugar
1 sachet vanilla sugar
1 egg
150 g (5 oz) butter
Icing sugar to finish
Jam or jelly to finish

Sift the flour and baking powder onto a work surface and make a well in the centre. Add the sugar, vanilla sugar and egg; then, using some of the flour, work the ingredients into a soft dough. Finally add the cold butter, cut into pieces, cover with the remaining flour, and knead the ingredients into a smooth dough. Leave to rest for several hours in a refrigerator.

Roll the dough out until 3 mm (¼ in) thick. Cut out the biscuits using pastry cutters of the same shape but of three different sizes, (the same number of each size). Prick with a fork and transfer to a greased baking sheet. Bake in a preheated oven at 180-200° C (350-400° F, Gas Mark 4-6) for 8-10 minutes.

Spread a thin layer of jam on one side of the small biscuits and on both sides of the medium-sized biscuits, place them on the large biscuits, dredge with icing sugar and put a drop of jam in the centre.

COCONUT OR HAZELNUT TRIANGLES

Makes about 10

150 g (5 oz) plain flour
1 teaspoon baking powder
165 g (5½ oz) caster sugar
2 sachets vanilla sugar
1 egg
165 g (5½ oz) butter
2 spoons apricot jam
100 g (3½ oz) ground hazelnuts and
100 g (3½ oz) chopped hazelnuts or
200 g (7 oz) desiccated coconut
50 g (2 oz) plain chocolate

Sift the flour and baking powder onto a work surface. Add 65 g (2½ oz) sugar, 1 sachet vanilla sugar and the egg; then, using some of the flour, work the ingredients into a soft dough. Finally add 65 g (2½ oz) cold butter, cut into pieces, cover with the remaining flour, and knead all the ingredients into a smooth dough. Leave to rest for several hours in a refrigerator.
Roll the dough out into a rectangle, 32 x 24 cm (12¾ x 9½ in), and spread with the apricot jam.

For the filling: in a pan, heat the remaining butter, sugar and vanilla sugar with 2 spoons water. Add the ground hazelnuts and the chopped hazelnuts (or the desiccated coconut), bring briefly to the boil, leave to cool, and spread evenly over the dough.

Transfer the dough to a baking sheet lined with a sheet of aluminium foil. Fold the foil over the edges to make a cake tin and bake in a preheated oven at 180-200° C (350-400°F, Gas Mark 4-6) for 20-30 minutes. Leave to cool slightly. Cut first into squares, 8 x 8 cm (3 x 3 in), and then into triangles.
For the icing: melt the chocolate in a bowl over a pan of hot water, and dip the two acute angles of the triangles into the melted chocolate.

Below: *Little terraces*

ANISEED BISCUITS

Makes about 20

3 eggs
200 g (7 oz) caster sugar
1 sachet vanilla sugar
125 g (4 oz) plain flour
125 g (4 oz) cornflour
15 g (½ oz) ground
aniseed

In a mixing bowl, beat the eggs until thick and frothy, gradually add the sugar and the vanilla sugar, beating constantly so that they hold their shape. Gradually spoon the flour and baking powder and finally the aniseed, into the mixture and combine the ingredients.

Grease one or more baking sheets and dust them with some flour. Using a spoon, make balls of dough about the size of a walnut and place them on the baking sheet, leaving enough space between them. Leave to dry overnight in a warm place. Bake in a preheated oven at 130-150° C (250-300° F, Gas Mark ½-2) for about 35 minutes.

SPRITS
(Dutch shortbread biscuits)

Makes about 20

375 g (12 oz) butter,
softened
250 g (8 oz) caster sugar
2 sachets vanilla sugar
A pinch of salt
500 g (1 lb) plain flour
125 g (4 oz) ground
almonds
4 teaspoons cocoa powder

Cream the butter using an electric mixer for 30 seconds, then gradually add the sugar and vanilla sugar. Continue beating until the mixture is light and fluffy.
Gradually incorporate the flour, finally add the almonds. Knead on a work surface. Make rolls of dough. Transfer some of this mixture to a piping bag and pipe the biscuits straight on to the baking sheet.

Knead the cocoa powder into the remaining mixture, add some of the cocoa mixture to the plain mixture and pipe more biscuits. Bake in a preheated oven at 180-200° C (350-400° F, Gas Mark 4-6) for 10 minutes.

ALMOND THINS

Makes about 10

250 g (8 oz) butter,
softened
100 g (3½ oz) marzipan
100 g (3½ oz) demerara
sugar
250 g (8 oz) plain flour

In a mixing bowl, cream the butter using an electric mixer with a kneading attachment, incorporate the marzipan and gradually add the sugar and the flour, kneading well.

Make the dough into a roll and leave to rest in a refrigerator for 2-3 hours. Roll the dough out until about 15 mm (⅛ in) thick, cut into strips about 15 mm x 6 cm (⅛ x 2½ in) and return to the refrigerator for 30 minutes.

Transfer the rectangles to a greased baking sheet. Make grooves on each biscuit, using a fork, and sprinkle with demerara sugar.

Bake in a preheated oven at 150-180° C (300-350° F, Gas Mark 2-4) for 25-30 minutes.

Below: *Sprits*

Opposite: *Almond thins*

Above: *Spiced fruit cookies*

SPICED FRUIT COOKIES

Makes about 8

75 g (3 oz) butter, softened
150 g (5 oz) caster sugar
1 sachet vanilla sugar
2 eggs
A pinch of salt
A large pinch of cardamom
A large pinch of cinnamon
250 g (8 oz) plain flour
2 teaspoons baking powder
65 g (2½ oz) candied mixed peel, chopped
75 g (3 oz) chopped almonds
150 g (5 oz) icing sugar
5-6 spoons lemon juice

Cream the butter in a mixing bowl, and gradually add the sugar, vanilla sugar, eggs, salt, cardamom and cinnamon. Gradually incorporate the flour and baking powder, kneading well. Add the chopped mixed peel and almonds.

Shape the mixture into balls the size of walnuts using a spoon, and place them on a baking sheet lined with aluminium foil. Bake in a preheated oven at 180-200° C (350-400° F, Gas Mark 4-6) for 10-15 minutes.

For the icing: combine the icing sugar with the lemon juice to make a thick cream and use to coat the cookies when cold.

MARZIPAN BISCUITS

Makes about 16

150 g (5 oz) plain flour
1 teaspoon baking powder
65 g (2½ oz) caster sugar
1 sachet vanilla sugar
1 egg yolk
½ egg white

65 g (2½ oz) butter
4 tablespoons apricot jam
150 g (5 oz) icing sugar
250 g (8 oz) marzipan
200 g (7 oz) plain
chocolate

Sift the flour and baking powder onto a work surface and make a well in the centre. Add the sugar, vanilla sugar and egg yolk; then, using some of the flour, work the ingredients into a soft dough. Finally add the cold butter, cut into pieces, cover with the remaining flour, and knead the ingredients into a smooth dough. Leave to rest in a refrigerator for several hours.

Roll the dough out into a square, 25 x 25 cm (10 x 10 in), prick with a fork, transfer to a greased baking sheet, and bake in a preheated oven at 200-220° C (400-425° F, Gas Mark 6-7) for 10-15 minutes.

Sieve the apricot jam and spread on the cooled biscuit mixture.

For the filling: knead the icing sugar with the marzipan. Roll the mixture out into a square, 25 x 25 cm (10 x 10 in). Place this square on the jam-covered biscuit layer, pressing down well. Using a knife, mark out a pattern on the marzipan layer and coat with the egg white.

Bake at the top of a preheated oven at 240° C (475° F, Gas Mark 9) for 10-15 minutes until golden. Leave to cool and cut into square-shaped biscuits.

Melt the chocolate in a bowl over a pan of hot water, stirring until smooth and glossy, then dip the marzipan biscuits into the chocolate, coating half of each biscuit. Photo (page 129 of original)

Above:
Egg rings

EGG RINGS

Makes about 10

250 g (8 oz) butter
125 g (4 oz) caster sugar
2 sachets vanilla sugar
1 egg
3 egg yolks

250 g (8 oz) plain flour
150 g (5 oz) cornflour
Glacé cherries (red and
green) to finish

Cream the butter in a mixing bowl, then gradually add the sugar, vanilla sugar, egg and egg yolks. Gradually incorporate the flour and cornflour, kneading well. Transfer the mixture to a piping bag fitted with a fluted nozzle and pipe the rings, about 4 cm (1½ in) in diameter, on to a greased baking sheet.

Cut the cherries into strips and use to decorate the biscuits. Bake in a preheated oven at 180-200° C (350-400° F, Gas Mark 4-6) for 12 minutes.

Suggestion: put the egg rings in a pretty box and gift-wrap it. Alternatively, put the rings in little baskets wrapped up in a table napkin and tied with a ribbon.

baking powder with the cocoa on to a work surface and make a well in the centre. Add the remaining sugar, vanilla sugar and rum flavouring, and 3 spoons water. Using some of the flour, work the ingredients into a soft dough. Add the remaining cold butter, cut into pieces, cover with the remaining flour, and knead the ingredients into a smooth dough. Leave to rest in a refrigerator for several hours.

Roll both doughs into sausage shapes about 3 cm (1¼ in) thick. Roll them in the granulated sugar and return them to the refrigerator.

Cut into slices 5 mm (¼ in) thick and dredge with the granulated sugar. Transfer the biscuits to a greased baking sheet and bake in a preheated oven at 180-200° C (350-400° F, Gas Mark 4-6) for 10 minutes.

Suggestion: serve with a cup of fruit tea.

CHEQUERBOARDS AND SPIRALS

Makes about 15

250 g (8 oz) plain flour	1 egg
2 teaspoons baking powder	2 egg whites
	125 g (4 oz) butter
165 g (5½ oz) caster sugar	20 g (¾ oz) cocoa powder
1 sachet vanilla sugar	1 spoon milk
1 bottle rum flavouring	

Sift the flour and baking powder on to a work surface and make a well in the centre. Add 150 g (5 oz) sugar, vanilla sugar, rum flavouring and egg; then, using some of the flour, work the ingredients into a soft dough.

Finally add the cold butter, cut into pieces, cover with the remaining flour, and knead the ingredients into a smooth dough. Leave to rest for several hours in a refrigerator.

In a mixing bowl, combine the cocoa powder, the remaining sugar and the milk. Add this mixture to half of the dough, kneading well.

For the spirals: roll out half of each type of dough separately into two squares of the same size. Coat one of the squares with half the egg white, cover with the other square, and roll out the two squares one on top of the other, pressing down well.

For the chequerboards: cut six strips, 1 cm (½ in) wide, of plain dough and six of chocolate dough. Coat them with the remaining egg white and arrange them one on top of the other, alternately. Roll out either the plain or the chocolate mixture into a square and roll

FRIESIAN ISLAND BISCUITS

Makes about 30

500 g (1 lb) plain flour	2 bottles rum flavouring
2 teaspoons baking powder	200 g (7 oz) butter
	2 spoons cocoa powder
200 g (7 oz) caster sugar	Granulated sugar to finish
2 sachets vanilla powder	

Sift 250 g (8 oz) flour and 1 teaspoon baking powder onto a work surface. Add 100 g (3½ oz) sugar, 1 sachet vanilla sugar, 1 bottle rum flavouring and 2 spoons water. Using some of the flour, work the ingredients into a soft dough. Finally add 100 g (3½ oz) cold butter, cut into pieces, cover with the remaining flour, and knead into a smooth dough. Leave to rest for several hours in a refrigerator.
For the brown biscuits: sift the remaining flour and

round the chequerboard log. Return the log to the refrigerator.

Cut the dough into even slices and arrange them on a greased baking sheet. Bake in a preheated oven at 180-200° C (350-400° F, Gas Mark 4-6) for 10-15 minutes.

Opposite page: Friesian Island biscuits
Below: Chequerboards and spirals

Above: *Cherry and chocolate whirls*

remaining biscuits, spread the melted chocolate over the smooth side, and place a plain biscuit on top of the chocolate before it sets.

Take half of the remaining biscuits and spread apricot jam over the smooth side, proceed as for the chocolate whirls. Finally, dunk one edge of each biscuit into the melted chocolate.

CHOCOLATE AND PINEAPPLE CRISPS

Makes about 20

325 g (11 oz) plain flour	200 g (7 oz) butter
2 teaspoons baking powder	Pineapple jam
100 g (3½ oz) caster sugar	75 g (3 oz) plain chocolate
1 sachet vanilla sugar	1 knob creamed coconut
1 egg	

*S*ift the flour and baking powder on to a work surface and make a well in the centre. Add the sugar, vanilla sugar and egg; then, using some of the flour, work the ingredients into a soft dough. Finally, add the cold butter, cut into pieces, cover with the remaining flour, and knead the ingredients into a smooth dough. Leave to rest for several hours in a refrigerator.

Roll the dough out and, using a 4 cm (1½ in) fluted round pastry cutter, cut out the biscuits. Cut out a smaller circle - about 1 cm (½ in) - from the centre of half the biscuits to make rings.

Transfer the plain biscuits and the rings to a greased baking sheet and bake in a preheated oven at 180-200° C (350-400° F, Gas Mark 4-6) for 8-10 minutes. Leave to cool.

For the filling: sieve the pineapple jam and spread over the smooth side of the rings. Stick the rings to the plain biscuits.

Melt the chocolate and creamed coconut in a bowl over a pan of hot water, stirring until smooth and glossy, and place a drop of melted chocolate in the centre of each biscuit.

CHERRY AND CHOCOLATE WHIRLS

Makes about 20

250 g (8 oz) butter	75 g (3 oz) ground almonds
175 g (6 oz) caster sugar	
1 sachet vanilla sugar	Glacé cherries to finish
1 egg	100 g (3½ oz) superfine cooking chocolate
175 g (6 oz) plain flour	
175 g (6 oz) cornflour	Apricot jam

*C*ream the butter in a mixing bowl and gradually add the sugar, vanilla sugar and egg. Gradually incorporate the flour and cornflour into the other ingredients, kneading well. Finally add the ground almonds. Transfer the mixture to a piping bag fitted with a fluted nozzle and pipe the biscuits on to a greased baking sheet. Bake in a preheated oven at 180-200° C (350-400° F, Gas Mark 4-6) for 10-15 minutes.

Place half a glacé cherry in the centre of some of the biscuits.

Melt the chocolate in a bowl over a pan of hot water, stirring until smooth and glossy. Take a quarter of the

Opposite: *Fried egg biscuits*

FRIED EGG BISCUITS

Makes about 12

150 g (5 oz) plain flour
1 sachet vanilla sugar
A pinch of salt
150 g (5 oz) cornflour
150 g (5 oz) butter

250 g (8 oz) apricots in
syrup
75 g (3 oz) icing sugar
1 spoon lemon juice

Sift the flour, vanilla sugar, salt and cornflour on to a work surface. Incorporate the cold butter, cut into pieces.

Knead all the ingredients into a smooth dough. Leave to rest for 1 hour in a refrigerator.

Roll half the dough out into a 40 x 20 cm (16 x 8 in) rectangle. Cut lengthwise into 1 cm (½ in) wide strips. Roll up two strips of dough into a snail shape, sealing the ends. Press down lightly in the middle and fill with a drained apricot half. Transfer to a greased baking sheet and bake in a preheated oven at 200-220° C (400-425° F, Gas Mark 6-7) for 25 minutes. Leave to cool.

Beat the icing sugar and lemon juice together and spread the icing over the 'fried eggs' while they are still hot.

SHORTBREAD CRESCENTS

Makes about 15

250 g (8 oz) plain flour
2 teaspoons baking powder
75 g (3 oz) caster sugar
1 sachet vanilla sugar
A pinch of salt

1 bottle rum flavouring
100 g (3½ oz) butter
Granulated sugar
25 g (1 oz) chocolate
1 knob creamed coconut

Sift the flour and baking powder on to a work surface and make a well in the centre. Add the sugar, vanilla sugar, salt, rum flavouring and 2 tablespoons water; then, using some of the flour, work the ingredients into a soft dough. Finally add the cold butter, cut into pieces, cover with the remaining flour, and knead the ingredients into a smooth dough. Leave to rest for several hours in a refrigerator.

Roll the dough into a sausage shape about as thick as your thumb and cut into 2 cm (¾ in) long pieces. Roll them until they are 6 cm (½ in) long, toss them in the granulated sugar, make into crescent shapes, transfer to a greased baking sheet and bake in a preheated oven at 180-200° C (350-400° F, Gas Mark 4-6) for 10 minutes and leave to cool.

Melt the chocolate and creamed coconut in a bowl over a pan of hot water, stirring until smooth and glossy. Dip the edges of the little crescents into this icing.

ORANGE VIENNESE FINGERS

Makes about 25

300 g (10 oz) butter
150 g (5 oz) icing sugar
1 sachet vanilla sugar
A pinch of salt
4 egg yolks
Grated rind of 1 orange
3 tablespoons orange

juice
300 g (10 oz) plain flour
100 g (3½ oz) hazelnut chocolate spread
100 g (3½ oz) chocolate cake covering

Cream the butter in a mixing bowl and gradually add the sugar, vanilla sugar, salt, egg yolks, orange rind and juice. Incorporate the flour, kneading well. Transfer this mixture to a piping bag fitted with a star-shaped nozzle. Pipe 6 cm (2½ in) long fingers on to a greased, lined baking sheet.
Bake in a preheated oven at 180-200° C (350-400° F, Gas Mark 4-6) for 7 minutes.

For the filling: melt the hazelnut chocolate spread in a bowl over a pan of hot water, stirring until it is smooth and glossy. Spread the hazelnut chocolate spread over the smooth side of half the fingers. Cover with the other fingers.

Melt the chocolate cake covering in a bowl over a pan of hot water. Dip one end of each finger in the melted chocolate.

ALMOND HALF-MOONS

Makes about 20

250 g (8 oz) plain flour
110 g (3¾ oz) caster sugar
1 sachet vanilla sugar
A pinch of salt
2 eggs, separated
200 g (7 oz) butter
50 g (2 oz) ground almonds

65 g (2½ oz) candied orange peel
Condensed milk (optional)
50 g (2 oz) chopped almonds
125 g (4 oz) superfine cooking chocolate
1 knob creamed coconut

Sift the flour on to a work surface and make a well in the centre. Add 100 g (3½ oz) sugar, the vanilla sugar, salt and egg yolks; then, using some of the flour, work the ingredients into a soft dough.
Incorporate the cold butter, cut into pieces, cover with the remaining flour and knead the ingredients into a smooth dough. Finally add the ground almonds and finely chopped candied orange peel.
Leave to rest in a refrigerator for 1 hour.

Roll the dough out until 3 mm (¼ in) thick. Cut out half-moon shapes and transfer them to a lined, greased baking sheet.

Whisk the egg whites into stiff peaks, fold in the remaining sugar, and spread over the half-moons. If there is not enough egg white, coat the remaining half-moons with condensed milk and sprinkle with chopped almonds. Bake in a preheated oven at 180-200° C (350-400° F, Gas Mark 4-6) for 10 minutes and leave to cool.

For the filling: melt the chocolate and the creamed coconut in a bowl over a pan of hot water, stirring until smooth and glossy. Dip one point of each half-moon in this icing. Leave the biscuits to set on the greaseproof paper.
Store them in an airtight container.

Left: *Orange Viennese fingers*

Above: *Milanese stars*

MILANESE STARS

Makes about 20

400 g (13 oz) butter, softened
250 g (8 oz) icing sugar
2 sachets vanilla sugar
A pinch of salt
3 small eggs
Grated rind of 1 lemon
500 g (1 lb) plain flour
4 teaspoons baking powder
65 g (2½ oz) caster sugar

Cream 350 g (11½ oz) butter in a bowl, and gradually add the icing sugar, 1 sachet vanilla sugar, the salt, eggs and lemon rind. Gradually incorporate the flour and baking powder, kneading well. Leave the mixture to rest overnight in a refrigerator.

Roll out the dough until 5 mm (¼ in) thick, press a grater down on to the dough to make a pattern, and cut out small pointed stars with rounded points.
Transfer the stars to a lined, greased baking sheet. Bake in a preheated oven at 180-200° C (350-400° F, Gas Mark 4-6) for 12 minutes.
Melt the remaining butter and use to coat the biscuits. Dredge with caster sugar and the remaining vanilla sugar.

PRINCESS PRETZELS

Makes about 20

375 g (12 oz) plain flour
40 g (1½ oz) cocoa powder
175 g (6 oz) caster sugar
1 sachet vanilla sugar
A pinch of salt
1 egg
250 g (8 oz) butter
100 g (3½ oz) plain superfine cooking chocolate
65 g (2½ oz) chopped toasted almonds

Sift the flour and cocoa powder on to a work surface and make a well in the centre. Add the sugar, vanilla sugar, salt and egg; then, using some of the flour, work the ingredients into a soft dough. Incorporate the cold butter, cut into pieces, cover with the remaining flour and knead the ingredients into a smooth dough.

Roll the dough into a long, thin sausage, about the diameter of a pencil. Cut into strips about 17 cm (6½ in) long, twist them to form pretzels. Transfer the pretzels to a greased, lined baking sheet. Bake in a preheated oven at 180-200° C (350-400° F, Gas Mark 4-6) for 12-15 minutes. Leave to cool.

Melt the chocolate in a bowl over a pan of hot water, stirring until smooth and glossy. Spread the melted chocolate over the biscuits, sprinkle with chopped almonds.

BUTTER RINGS

Makes about 12

150 g (5 oz) butter, softened
75 g (3 oz) icing sugar
1 sachet vanilla sugar
1 egg
½ teaspoon ground coriander
175 g (6 oz) plain flour
25 g (1 oz) cornflour

Melt the butter and leave to cool, then add the icing sugar, vanilla sugar, egg and coriander.
Gradually incorporate the flour and cornflour, kneading well. Transfer the mixture to a piping bag fitted with a fluted nozzle and pipe rings on to a greased baking sheet. Bake in a preheated oven at 180-200° C (350-400° F, Gas Mark 4-6) for 8-10 minutes.

Below: *Princess pretzels*

Above: *Pineapple meringue wafers*

RYE BISCUITS

Makes about 20

300 g (10 oz) rye flour
2 teaspoons baking
powder
100 g (3½ oz) caster sugar
1 sachet vanilla sugar

4 tablespoons milk
A pinch of salt
2 pinches of cinnamon
150 g (5 oz) butter
Condensed milk

Sift the flour and baking powder on to a work surface and make a well in the centre. Add the sugar, vanilla sugar, milk, salt and a pinch of cinnamon and, using some of the flour, work the ingredients into a soft dough. Add the cold butter, cut into pieces, cover with the remaining flour and knead the ingredients into a smooth dough. Leave to rest in a refrigerator for 1-2 hours.

Roll out until 3 mm (¼ in) thick and cut into rectangles, 3 x 6 cm (1¼ x ½ in). Combine a little condensed milk with the remaining cinnamon. Spread this mixture over the biscuits.
Transfer to a lined baking sheet. Bake in a preheated oven at 180-200° C (350-400° F, Gas Mark 4-6) for 10 minutes.

PINEAPPLE MERINGUE WAFERS

Makes about 55

4 egg whites
125 g (4 oz) caster sugar
125 g (4 oz) ground
almonds

100 g (3½ oz) pineapple in
syrup
55 wafers, 5 cm (2 in) in
diameter, or rice paper

Whisk the egg whites into peaks in a mixing bowl. Gently fold in the sugar, then the ground almonds. Drain the pineapple slices, chop them and add them to the mixture. Place a spoonful of this mixture over each wafer or rice paper circle. Transfer the wafers to a greased and lined baking sheet and bake in a preheated oven at 150° C (300° F, Gas Mark 2) for 30 minutes.

SPRINGERLE
(A speciality of southern Germany)

Makes about 15

2 eggs
200 g (7 oz) icing sugar
1 sachet vanilla sugar
225 g (7½ oz) plain flour

A pinch of baking powder
Some aniseed seeds to
finish

Beat the eggs until thick and frothy using an electric mixer. Gradually add the sugar and vanilla sugar, beating constantly, until the mixture holds its shape. Gradually incorporate the flour and baking powder and knead the dough until it is very smooth. If the dough is still too sticky, add a little more flour.

Roll out until 1 cm (½ in) thick and cut into 4 x 6 cm (1½ x 2½ in) rectangles. Dust a concave mould imprinted with a decorative pattern with flour. Press each rectangle of dough into this mould so that the pattern is transferred. Arrange the biscuits on a greased baking sheet sprinkled with aniseed. Bake in a preheated oven at 130-150° C (250-300° F, Gas Mark ½-2) for 30 minutes.

Tip: as the raised patterns on the surface of these biscuits must remain visible, it is advisable to place another baking sheet on top of the first one to prevent the biscuits from becoming too brown.

ORANGE BISCUITS

Makes about 15

1 egg	Some slices of candied
1 bottle lemon flavouring	orange to finish
300 g (10 oz) plain flour	175 g (6 oz) butter
175 g (6 oz) icing sugar	100 g (3½ oz) caster sugar
4-5 spoons orange liqueur	1 sachet vanilla sugar

Cream the butter in a bowl and gradually add the sugar, vanilla sugar, egg and lemon flavouring. Gradually spoon in and incorporate the flour. Leave to rest in a refrigerator for 30 minutes.

Roll out the dough until it is 5 mm (¼ in) thick and cut out round biscuits, 4 cm (1½ in) in diameter. Transfer them to a greased baking sheet and bake in a preheated oven at 180-200°C (350-400°F, Gas Mark 4-6) for 10-15 minutes.

Below: *Orange biscuits*

Combine the icing sugar with the orange liqueur to make a smooth icing. Spread this icing over the cooled biscuits, decorate with chopped candied orange peel. Serve with a glass of orange liqueur.

VANILLA SHORTBREAD BISCUITS

Makes about 30

250 g (8 oz) plain flour	softened
1 bottle vanilla essence	Condensed milk
150 g (5 oz) double cream	75 g (3 oz) granulated
175 g (6 oz) butter,	sugar

Sift the flour into a bowl and add all the ingredients. Incorporate them using an electric mixer at slow speed first, then increase the speed. Knead this dough on a work surface. If it is still too sticky, place in a refrigerator for 15 minutes.

Roll the dough out until it is 5 mm (¼ in) thick and cut out circles, 6 cm (2½ in) in diameter. Make into rings by cutting out 4 cm (1½ in) circles from the centre to form the biscuits. Brush the dough with condensed milk and dredge with granulated sugar.

Transfer the rings to a greased baking sheet, bake in a preheated oven at 180-200° C (350-400° F, Gas Mark 4-6) for 10-15 minutes.

DATE MACAROONS

Makes about 20

125 g (4 oz) butter	100 g (3½ oz) caster sugar
250 g (8 oz) rolled oats	1 sachet vanilla sugar
250 g (8 oz) dates	2 teaspoons baking
2 eggs	powder

Melt the butter in a pan and gradually incorporate the rolled oats. Leave to cool.

Stone the dates and cut into small pieces.

Beat the eggs until thick and frothy. Add the sugar, vanilla sugar and baking powder, beating constantly. Incorporate the rolled oats and the dates.
Using a spoon, make balls of dough about the size of a walnut. Transfer to a greased baking sheet, and bake in a preheated oven at 180° C (350° F, Gas Mark 4) for 15-20 minutes.

CHOCOLATE FINGERS

Makes about 15

1 egg	75 g (3 oz) plain chocolate
1 egg yolk	200 g (7 oz) ground
125 g (4 oz) caster sugar	almonds
1 sachet vanilla sugar	A pinch of baking powder
A pinch of salt	1 egg white
1 teaspoon instant coffee	65 g (2½ oz) icing sugar

Put the egg, egg yolk, sugar, vanilla sugar, salt and coffee in a bowl and beat using an electric mixer until the mixture holds its shape. Melt the chocolate in a bowl over a pan of hot water and incorporate into the mixture. Combine the ground almonds and baking powder in a mixing bowl, add to the mixture, and knead well. Place in a refrigerator.

Whisk the egg white into peaks, fold in the icing sugar.

Roll out the dough into a rectangle, 12 x 40 cm (4½ x 16 in), spread the icing all over the dough and cut into fingers measuring 6 x 1 cm (2½ x ½ in). Transfer to a greased baking sheet. Bake in a preheated oven at 180-200° C (350-400°F, Gas Mark 4-6) for 10-15 minutes.

ORANGE AND CHOCOLATE CHIP COOKIES

Makes about 30

200 g (7 oz) plain flour	Grated rind of 1 orange
65 g (2½ oz) cornflour	1 egg
2 teaspoons baking	125 g (4 oz) butter,
powder	softened
100 g (3½ oz) caster sugar	100 g (3½ oz) plain
1 sachet vanilla sugar	chocolate

Combine the flour, cornflour and baking powder; add the sugar, vanilla sugar, orange rind, egg and butter. Combine all the ingredients using an electric mixer fitted with a kneading attachment first at slow and then at high speed (photograph no. 1).
Cut the chocolate into small pieces, add to the dough and knead well. Make three rolls of dough, 3 cm (1¼ in) thick. Flatten them so that they are about 5 cm (2 in) wide and 1 cm (½ in) deep (photograph no. 2).
Place in a refrigerator until the dough is firm, then cut it into 5 mm (¼ in) thick slices. Arrange the cookies on a greased baking sheet (photograph no. 3) and bake in a preheated oven at 180-200° C (350-400° F, Gas Mark 4-6) for 10 minutes.

Right:
Orange and chocolate chip cookies

1

2

3

HAZELNUT MERINGUES

Makes about 20

3 egg whites
200 g (7 oz) caster sugar
A pinch of cinnamon
200 g (7 oz) ground

roasted hazelnuts
100 g (3½ oz) whole
hazelnuts

Whisk the egg whites into firm peaks using an electric mixer. Gradually incorporate the sugar, whisking constantly. Set 5-6 spoons egg white to one side.

Gently fold the cinnamon and ground hazelnuts into the egg whites. Transfer the mixture to a piping bag fitted with a fluted nozzle. Pipe walnut-sized mounds of the hazelnut meringue on to a greased, lined baking sheet.

Transfer the reserved egg white to a piping bag fitted with a round nozzle and pipe on to the hazelnut meringues. Place a whole hazelnut in the centre of each, pressing down gently. Bake in a preheated oven at 130-150° C (250-300° F, Gas Mark ½-2) for 25 minutes.

Tip: the hazelnut meringues should still be soft when removed from the oven.

ICED HEARTS

Makes 30-40

300 g (10 oz) butter
200 g (7 oz) caster sugar
A pinch of salt
2 drops almond essence
1 sachet vanilla sugar
1 egg
1 egg yolk

400 g (13 oz) plain flour
200 g (7 oz) ground
almonds
125 g (4 oz) icing sugar
1 egg white
1 teaspoon lemon juice

Cream the butter in a bowl using an electric mixer fitted with a kneading attachment, then add the sugar, followed by the salt, almond essence, vanilla sugar, egg and egg yolk. Beat for 1 minute. Mix the flour and the ground almonds together and gradually incorporate them, beating constantly, with the mixer at low speed. Leave the dough to rest in a refrigerator overnight.

Roll out the dough until 5 mm (¼ in) thick and cut out little hearts using a heart-shaped pastry cutter. Transfer the biscuits to a lined, greased baking sheet.

Combine the icing sugar with the egg white and the lemon juice to form a thick syrup. Spread the icing over the hearts and bake in a preheated oven at 200° C (400° F, Gas Mark 6) for 8-10 minutes.

SCOTS BUTTER
SHORTBREAD BISCUITS

Makes 40-50

375 g (12 oz) plain flour
200 g (7 oz) brown sugar
1 sachet vanilla sugar

250 g (8 oz) butter,
softened

Put the flour, brown sugar, vanilla sugar and butter in a bowl. Using an electric mixer, work the mixture first at low speed, then at high speed. Finally, knead the dough well.

Make rolls of dough 2.5 cm (1 in) in diameter and place in a refrigerator until the dough is firm. Cut 5 mm (¼ in) thick slices and arrange them on a greased baking sheet. Bake in a preheated oven at 180-200° C (250-400° F, Gas Mark 4-6) for 10 minutes.

CHERRY CRUMBLES

Makes about 30

500 g (1 lb) plain flour
2 teaspoons baking
powder
225 g (7½ oz) caster sugar
2 sachets vanilla sugar
A pinch of salt
275 g (9 oz) butter,

softened
75 g (3 oz) ground
almonds
A pinch of cinnamon
Some glacé cherries to
finish

Sift 250 g (8 oz) flour and the baking powder into a bowl, add 100 g (3½ oz) sugar, 1 sachet vanilla sugar, the salt, 150 g (5 oz) butter and the ground almonds. Incorporate the ingredients using an electric mixer fitted with a kneading attachment, first at low speed, then at high speed. Then knead the dough well. If it is too sticky, place in a refrigerator for a short while.
Roll the dough out until 3 mm (¼ in) thick and cut out the biscuits using a pastry cutter 6 cm (2½ in) in diameter. Place them on a greased baking sheet.
For the filling: combine the remaining flour, sugar, vanilla sugar, butter and the cinnamon. Rub in with the fingertips until the mixture resembles breadcrumbs. Spread over the biscuits. Decorate with glacé cherries and bake in a preheated oven at 180-200° C (350-400° F, Gas Mark 4-6) for 15 minutes.

Above: *Sugar marzipan biscuits*

SUGAR MARZIPAN BISCUITS

Makes 20-25

200 g (7 oz) marzipan
125 g (4 oz) butter, softened
200 g (7 oz) caster sugar
1 sachet vanilla sugar
3 drops lemon flavouring
1 egg

250 g (8 oz) plain flour
125 g (4 oz) cornflour
2 teaspoons baking powder
100 ml (3½ fl oz) milk
1 teaspoon cinnamon

*C*ream the marzipan and butter in a bowl using an electric mixer fitted with a kneading attachment, first at low speed, then at high speed. Then add 75 g (3 oz) sugar, the vanilla sugar and lemon flavouring. Continue beating until the ingredients are incorporated.

Mix in the egg. Spoon in the flour, cornflour and baking powder, reducing the speed of the mixer. If the dough is too sticky, place in a refrigerator until firm.

Roll out the dough and cut out into different shapes. Place the biscuits on a greased baking sheet and brush with milk.

Mix the remaining sugar with the cinnamon and dredge over the biscuits.
Bake in a preheated oven at 180-200° C (350-400° F, Gas Mark 4-6) for 8-10 minutes.

PRAGUE CURRANT COOKIES

Makes about 40

375 g (12 oz) plain flour
2 teaspoons baking powder
50 g (2 oz) caster sugar
1 sachet vanilla sugar
3 eggs, separated

250 g (8 oz) butter, softened
200 g (7 oz) icing sugar
75 g (3 oz) chopped almonds
175 g (6 oz) currants

Sift the flour and baking powder into a bowl; add the sugar, vanilla sugar, egg yolks and butter. Combine the ingredients using an electric mixer, first at low speed, then at high speed. If it is too sticky, place in a refrigerator for a short while. Roll out and cut into biscuits 4 cm (1½ in) in diameter. Place on a greased baking sheet.

For the filling: whisk the egg whites into peaks, gradually fold in the icing sugar. Transfer this mixture to an icing bag fitted with a round nozzle and pipe a whirl of meringue on to each biscuit. Sprinkle with chopped almonds and currants. Bake in a preheated oven at 180-200° C (350-400° F, Gas Mark 4-6) for 10-15 minutes.

PEANUT BUTTER COOKIES

Makes about 20

125 g (4 oz) butter
125 g (4 oz) brown sugar
125 g (4 oz) caster sugar
A pinch of salt
1 sachet vanilla sugar
2 eggs

350 g (11½ oz) peanut butter
250 g (8 oz) plain flour
2 teaspoons baking powder

Cream the butter in a bowl using an electric mixer fitted with a kneading attachment. Add first the brown sugar, then the caster sugar, salt, vanilla sugar and eggs. Mix until the ingredients are incorporated. Add the peanut butter and continue beating at medium speed.

Gradually spoon in the flour and baking powder, mixing all the ingredients well.
Using a spoon, make walnut-sized balls, place them on a greased baking sheet and flatten slightly.
Bake in a preheated oven at 180-200° C (350-400° F, Gas Mark 4-6) for 10 minutes.

ALMOND CHOCOLATE DROPS

Makes about 20

3 egg whites
250 g (8 oz) icing sugar
300 g (10 oz) ground almonds

200 g (7 oz) plain chocolate, grated
50 g (2 oz) cocoa powder
1 knob creamed coconut

Whisk the egg whites into peaks using an electric mixer, and gradually incorporate the sugar, beating constantly.

Gently fold the ground almonds, 50 g (2 oz) grated chocolate and the cocoa powder into the whisked egg whites. Transfer this mixture to a piping bag with a no. 10 nozzle. Pipe meringues on to a lined, greased baking sheet.
Bake in a preheated oven at 200-220° C (400-425° F, Gas Mark 6-7) for 10 minutes.

Melt the remaining chocolate and the creamed coconut in a bowl over a pan of hot water, stirring until smooth and glossy. Dip the cookies into the melted chocolate. Leave to set on greaseproof paper.

CHOCOLATE CREAM BISCUITS

Makes 20-30

250 g (8 oz) plain flour	coconut
2 teaspoons baking powder	185 g (6½ oz) icing sugar
75 g (3 oz) caster sugar	75 g (3 oz) chocolate, grated
2 sachets vanilla sugar	50 g (2 oz) ground almonds
A pinch of salt	1 bottle rum flavouring
2 eggs	1 heaped tablespoon cocoa powder
125 g (4 oz) butter, softened	
50 g (2 oz) creamed	

Sift the flour and baking powder into a bowl, add the sugar, 1 sachet vanilla sugar, salt, 1 egg and the butter. Combine the ingredients using an electric mixer, first at low speed, then at high speed. Knead the dough on a work surface. If it is too sticky, place in a refrigerator for a short while.

Roll out the dough as thinly as possible and cut out the biscuits using an oval pastry cutter. Transfer the biscuits to a greased baking sheet, bake in a preheated oven at 180-200° C (350-400° F, Gas Mark 4-6) for 7-10 minutes until golden.

For the filling: melt the creamed coconut in a small pan together with 40 g (1½ oz) icing sugar, the remaining vanilla sugar, the grated chocolate, almonds and rum flavouring. Remove from the heat.

Beat the remaining egg and add it to the chocolate cream filling. Spread the cream over the smooth side of half of the biscuits and stick the other half on top.

In a pan, combine the remaining icing sugar, the cocoa powder and 2-3 tablespoons hot water to form a thick syrup. Dip the biscuits in the icing so that they are half-covered with icing.

SOVEREIGNS

Makes 30-40

250 g (8 oz) plain flour	softened
2 teaspoons baking powder	125 g (4 oz) creamed coconut
75 g (3 oz) caster sugar	75 g (3 oz) icing sugar
2 sachets vanilla sugar	4 tablespoons cocoa powder
A pinch of salt	1 spoon rum flavouring
2 eggs	75 g (3 oz) superfine cooking chocolate
1 tablespoon milk	
125 g (4 oz) butter,	

Sift the flour and baking powder into a bowl and add the sugar, 1 sachet vanilla sugar, salt, 1 egg, the milk and butter. Combine the ingredients using an electric mixer first at low speed, then at high speed. Knead the dough on a work surface. If it is too sticky, place in a refrigerator for 10 minutes.

Roll out the dough as thinly as possible and cut out circles, 4 cm (1½ in) in diameter, prick them with a fork and transfer to a greased baking sheet. Bake in a preheated oven at 180-200° C (350-400° F, Gas Mark 4-6) for 10 minutes.

For the filling: put a knob of creamed coconut to one side and melt the rest in a pan. Leave to cool. Sift the icing sugar, the remaining vanilla sugar and cocoa powder into a bowl and add the rum flavouring. Mix with the creamed coconut. When the mixture starts to set, spread it over the smooth side of half of the biscuits and stick the remaining half on top.

Melt the chocolate and the remaining creamed coconut in a bowl over a pan of hot water, stirring until smooth and glossy.
When the biscuits have set sufficiently, dip them into the mixture so that they are half-covered with icing.

LEMON HEARTS

Makes about 20

3 egg yolks	200-250 g (7-8 oz) ground almonds
125 g (4 oz) caster sugar	
1 sachet vanilla sugar	100 g (3½ oz) icing sugar
Grated rind of ½ lemon	1-2 spoons lemon juice
A pinch of baking powder	

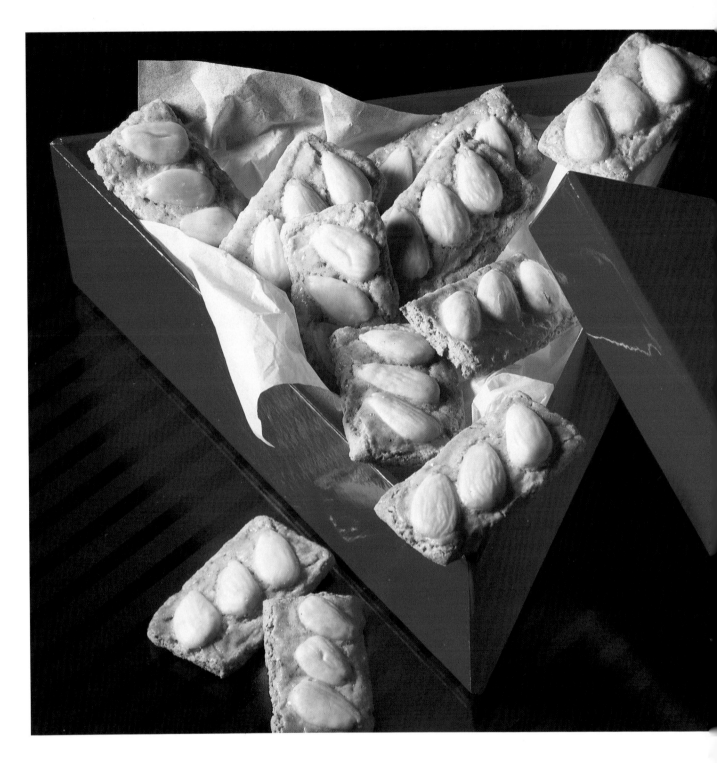

Above: *Almond and cinnamon crisps*

Put the egg yolks, sugar and vanilla sugar in a bowl and beat using an electric mixer at high speed for 1 minute. Add the lemon rind, baking powder and ground almonds (the amount of ground almonds depends on the size of the egg yolks), and combine the ingredients into a smooth dough. It should not be at all sticky.

Dredge a work surface with 1 tablespoon icing sugar and roll out the dough until 5 mm (¼ in) thick. Using a heart-shaped pastry cutter, cut out little hearts. Transfer them to a lined, greased baking sheet and bake in a preheated oven at 180-200°C (350-400°F, Gas Mark 4-6) for 10 minutes.

Combine the remaining icing sugar with the lemon juice to make a smooth, thick cream.
Spread over the hearts as soon as they are out of the oven.

ALMOND AND CINNAMON CRISPS

Makes 20-30

3 eggs
250 g (8 oz) granulated sugar
3 teaspoons ground cinnamon
A pinch of ground cloves
65 g (2½ oz) candied lemon peel, finely

chopped
75-100 g (3-3½ oz) ground almonds
250 g (8 oz) plain flour
2 teaspoons baking powder
75-100 g (3-3½ oz) halved blanched almonds

Break 2 eggs into a bowl, add the sugar and beat using an electric mixer for 30 seconds. Add the cinnamon, cloves, chopped lemon peel and ground almonds, then mix well. Gradually spoon in the flour and baking powder, beating with the mixer at medium speed.

Roll the dough out until 3 mm (¼ in) thick and cut out rectangles, 3 x 5 cm (1¼ x 2 in). Place them on a greased baking sheet lined with greaseproof paper.

Beat the remaining egg, brush over the biscuits and decorate with blanched almonds.
Bake in a preheated oven at 180-200° C (350-400° F, Gas Mark 4-6) for 12-15 minutes.

Tip: the almond and cinnamon crisps can be stored in an airtight container for about ten days.

RAISIN FINGERS

Makes about 15

200 g (7 oz) raisins
4-6 spoons rum
275 g (9 oz) plain flour
2 sachets vanilla sugar
A pinch of salt
2 tablespoons milk
250 g (8 oz) butter,

softened
3 tablespoons icing sugar
100 g (3½ oz) plain chocolate (optional)
2 knobs creamed coconut (optional)

Soak the raisins in the rum in a bowl. Sift the flour into a bowl, add the vanilla sugar, salt, milk and butter. Knead the ingredients using an electric mixer first at low speed, then at high speed.
Knead the dough on a work surface. If it is too sticky, place it in a refrigerator for a short while. Drain the raisins.

Roll out the dough until 3 mm (¼ in) thick. Cut out rectangles, 5 x 4 cm (2 x 1½ in), and place a few raisins on each rectangle. Fold the rectangles over to make turnovers. Transfer the biscuits to a greased baking sheet. Bake in a preheated oven at 180-200° C (350-400° F, Gas Mark 4-6) for 15 minutes.
Dredge with icing sugar.

Alternative: make an icing by melting the chocolate and the creamed coconut in a bowl over a pan of hot water.

ALMOND BISCUITS

Makes about 40

125 g (4 oz) caster sugar
1 sachet vanilla sugar
A pinch of salt
Grated rind of ½ lemon
1 egg
250 g (8 oz) softened butter
100 g (3½ oz) flaked

almonds
100 g (3½ oz) superfine cooking chocolate
1 knob creamed coconut
375 g (12 oz) plain flour
2 teaspoons baking powder

Sift the flour and baking powder into a bowl; add the sugar, vanilla sugar, salt, lemon rind, egg and butter. Combine the ingredients using an electric mixer, first at low speed, then at high speed. Finally incorporate the flaked almonds.

Knead the dough on a work surface. Make rolls of dough about 2.5 cm (1 in) in diameter and place in a refrigerator until the dough is firm. Cut into 5 mm (⅓ in) thick slices.

Transfer the biscuits to a greased baking sheet. Bake in a preheated oven at 180-200° C (350-400° F, Gas Mark 4-6) for 10-15 minutes.

Make the icing by melting the chocolate with the creamed coconut in a bowl over a pan of hot water, stirring until the mixture is smooth and glossy. Spread it over the biscuits.

ALMOND PRALINE CREAMS

Makes about 30

4 egg yolks
200 g (7 oz) caster sugar
A pinch of salt
200 g (7 oz) plain flour
75 g (3 oz) flaked almonds

200 g (7 oz) hazelnut chocolate spread
30-40 g (¼-½ oz) superfine cooking chocolate

***P**ut the egg yolks in a bowl and beat using an electric mixer at high speed for 1 minute. Add the sugar and salt and continue beating for 2 minutes. Gradually incorporate the flour, beating constantly at low speed. Transfer the mixture to a piping bag fitted with a wide nozzle, then pipe thick biscuits on to a greased baking sheet dusted with flour. Decorate with the flaked almonds. Bake in a preheated oven at 200° C (400° F, Gas Mark 6) for 10 minutes. Remove the biscuits from the baking sheet immediately.

Melt the hazelnut chocolate spread in a bowl over a pan of hot water, stirring until it is smooth and creamy. Spread the cream over the smooth side of half of the biscuits and immediately stick the remaining biscuits on top of the hazelnut chocolate spread.

Melt the cooking chocolate in a bowl over a pan of hot water and drizzle over the biscuits.

Suggestion: arrange the creams in a pretty container, with a sheet of aluminium foil between each layer. Alternatively, arrange them on a tray lined with a paper doily.

Below: *Almond praline creams*

Above: *Almond stars*

ALMOND STARS

Makes about 20

300 g (10 oz) plain flour
20 g (¾ oz) cocoa powder
2 teaspoons baking
powder
75 g (3 oz) caster sugar
1 sachet vanilla sugar
3 drops almond essence

3 spoons milk
175 g (6 oz) butter
Condensed milk for the
icing
200 g (7 oz) flaked
almonds

Sift the flour, cocoa powder and baking powder on to a work surface and make a well in the centre. Add the sugar, vanilla sugar, almond essence and milk. Incorporate all the ingredients, using some of the flour, to form a soft dough. Cut the cold butter into pieces and place on the dough, knead with the remaining flour until the dough is smooth. Leave to rest in a refrigerator.

Roll out the dough until 3 mm (¼ in) thick and cut out stars using a star-shaped pastry cutter. Place them on a greased baking sheet. Brush with the condensed milk and decorate with the flaked almonds. Bake in a preheated oven at 180-200° C (350-400° F, Gas Mark 4-6) for 10-15 minutes.

OAT MACAROONS

Makes about 10

2 egg whites
2 spoons caster sugar
4 spoons rosehip jelly

50 g (2 oz) ground
almonds
125 g (4 oz) rolled oats

Whisk the egg whites into peaks and gradually incorporate the sugar and 2 spoons rosehip jelly, beating constantly.

Gently fold in the ground almonds and rolled oats. Using a spoon, place walnut-sized balls of meringue on a lined, greased baking sheet. Bake in a preheated oven at 150° C (300° F, Gas Mark 2) for 25 minutes.

Decorate with the remaining jelly as soon as the macaroons are taken out of the oven.

RUM RINGS

Makes about 10

100 g (3½ oz) butter
100 g (3½ oz) caster sugar
1 sachet vanilla sugar
1 bottle rum flavouring
1 egg
100 g (3½ oz) plain flour

2 teaspoons baking
powder
200 g (7 oz) rolled oats
100 g (3½ oz) icing sugar
2-3 spoons rum

Cream the butter using an electric mixer fitted with a kneading attachment and add the sugar, vanilla sugar, rum flavouring and egg, beating until the ingredients are incorporated. Gradually spoon in the flour and baking powder, mixing well. Incorporate the rolled oats and knead the dough. If it is too sticky, place in a refrigerator for a short while.

Roll out the dough until 3 mm (¼ in) thick and cut out circles, 6 cm (2½ in) in diameter. Then cut out circles 4 cm (1½ in) in diameter from the centre of each biscuit. Remove the small circles to create the rings. Transfer the rings to a greased baking sheet and bake in a preheated oven at 180-200° C (350-400° F, Gas Mark 4-6) for 10-15 minutes.

For the icing: combine the icing sugar and the rum to form a thick cream. Coat the rings while they are still hot.

LITTLE ROUND BISCUITS

(Rondjes, a Dutch speciality)

Makes about 20

50 g (2 oz) caster sugar
175 g (6 oz) butter
75 g (3 oz) cane sugar

1 teaspoon golden syrup
125 g (4 oz) plain flour

Heat the sugar in a pan until it caramelizes, pour the caramel over a sheet of aluminium foil, leave to cool and crush it finely.

Cream the butter in a bowl using an electric mixer. Add first the cane sugar, then the syrup and 1 tablespoon water. Gradually spoon in the flour, mixing well, and finally incorporate the crushed caramel. Make balls of the mixture about the size of a walnut and arrange on a baking sheet, leaving plenty of space between them. Bake in a preheated oven at 180-200° C (350-400° F, Gas Mark 4-6) for 10 minutes.

Remove the biscuits from the baking sheet as soon as they are out of the oven and store them in an airtight container.

CINNAMON STARS

Makes 15-20

3 egg whites
250 g (8 oz) icing sugar
1 sachet vanilla sugar
3 drops almond essence
1 teaspoon ground
cinnamon

275-325 g (9-11 oz)
ground almonds or
hazelnuts
(the quantity depends on
the size of the eggs)

Whisk the egg whites into peaks and gradually fold in the icing sugar. Set 2 heaped tablespoons of this mixture to one side for the icing. Add the vanilla sugar, almond essence and cinnamon. Add half the ground almonds (or hazelnuts) and mix well. Finally incorporate enough of the remaining almonds (or hazelnuts) so that the dough is hardly sticky at all.

Roll out the dough until 5 mm (¼ in) thick and cut out stars using a star-shaped pastry cutter. Transfer the stars to a lined, greased baking sheet, brush with the reserved egg white.

Bake in a preheated oven at 130-150° C (250-300° F, Gas Mark ½-2) for 20-30 minutes.

Tip: the stars should still be soft when taken out of the oven. Store them in a cardboard container.

Above: *Cinnamon stars*

Left: *Rum rings and Little round biscuits*

GERMAN JAMMY DODGERS

(Spitzbuben, a speciality of southern Germany)

Makes about 40

375 g (12 oz) plain flour
2 teaspoons baking
powder
200 g (7 oz) caster sugar
1 sachet vanilla sugar
250 g (8 oz) butter

125 g (4 oz) ground
almonds
125 g (4 oz) redcurrant
jelly
2 tablespoons icing sugar

Sift the flour and baking powder on to a work surface and make a well in the centre. Add the sugar, vanilla sugar, cold butter, cut into pieces, and ground almonds. Quickly knead the ingredients into a smooth dough. Leave to rest in a refrigerator for a while.

Roll out until 3 mm (¼ in) thick, cut out circles, 4 cm (½ in) in diameter, and transfer to a greased baking sheet. Bake in a preheated oven at 180-200° C (350-400° F, Gas Mark 4-6) for 10 minutes.

Leave the biscuits to cool and divide into two piles. Spread the redcurrant jelly over the smooth side of half of the biscuits and cover with the other half, pressing down well. Dredge with icing sugar.

Below: *German jammy dodgers*

CINNAMON FINGERS

Makes about 20

250 g (8 oz) plain flour
75 g (3 oz) caster sugar
1 sachet vanilla sugar
½ bottle rum flavouring
1 teaspoon ground
cinnamon

1 egg, separated
125 g (4 oz) butter
Condensed milk for the
icing (optional)
Some flaked almonds to
finish

Sift the flour on to a work surface and make a well in the centre. Add the sugar, vanilla sugar, rum flavouring, cinnamon and egg yolk. Using some of the flour, work the ingredients into a soft dough. Add the cold butter, cut into pieces, cover with the remaining flour and quickly knead all the ingredients into a smooth dough. Leave to rest in a refrigerator for a while.

Roll out until 3 mm (¼ in) thick and cut out rectangles, 2 x 6 cm (¾ x 2½ in), and place on a greased baking sheet.

Whisk the egg white into peaks and spread over the biscuits. If there is not enough, spread the condensed milk over the remaining fingers. Decorate with flaked almonds. Bake in a preheated oven at 180-200° C (350-400°F, Gas Mark 4-6) for 10 minutes.

ALMOND BOATS

Makes about 10

175 g (6 oz) butter
100 g (3½ oz) icing sugar
1 sachet vanilla sugar
1 egg, separated
½ bottle rum flavouring
A pinch of cinnamon
200 g (7 oz) plain flour

25 g (1 oz) cocoa powder
A pinch of baking powder
125 g (4 oz) ground
hazelnuts
Some blanched almonds
to finish

Cream the butter and add first the sugar, then the vanilla sugar, egg yolk, rum flavouring and cinnamon and mix until all the ingredients are incorporated. Sift the flour, cocoa powder and baking powder together, gradually spoon them into the mixture, mixing well, incorporate the ground hazelnuts and knead.

Make into long, thin rolls about as thick as a pencil, cut into pieces 4 cm (1½ in) long and, using the fingers, shape into boats. Beat the egg white and brush over each boat. Place half a blanched almond on each boat and transfer them to a greased baking sheet. Bake in a

Above: *Almond boats*

preheated oven at 180-200° C (350-400° F, Gas Mark 4-6)
for 10 minutes.

SPICY TRIANGLES

(Spitz, a German speciality)

Makes about 40

175 g (6 oz) golden syrup
50 g (2 oz) caster sugar
A pinch of salt
2 tablespoons oil
1 egg
1 heaped teaspoon cocoa
powder
6 drops lemon flavouring
A pinch of allspice
1 teaspoon cinnamon

250 g (8 oz) plain flour
2 teaspoons baking
powder
75 g (3 oz) chopped
almonds
175 g (6 oz) redcurrant
jelly
200 g (7 oz) superfine
cooking chocolate

Heat the syrup, sugar, salt and oil over a low heat until melted. Pour into a bowl and leave to cool. Add the egg, cocoa powder, lemon flavouring, allspice and cinnamon, stirring well. Combine the flour and baking powder. Incorporate 175 g (6 oz) of the flour and baking powder into the mixture. Mix well and finally add the remaining flour and the chopped almonds. Knead well. Place the dough in a refrigerator.

Roll the dough into sausage shapes about 2 cm (¾ in) in diameter and the length of the baking sheet. Transfer the strips of dough to a greased baking sheet, leaving a space between them.

Bake in a preheated oven at 180-200° C (350-400° F, Gas Mark 4-6) for 12 minutes until golden. As soon as the strips of dough are cold, cut them into even triangles. Brush with redcurrant jelly.

Melt the chocolate in a bowl over a pan of hot water, stirring until it is smooth and glossy. Use to coat the biscuits.

CHOCOLATE ALMOND BISCUITS

Makes about 40

500 g (1 lb) plain flour
2 teaspoons baking
powder
150 g (5 oz) icing sugar
1 sachet vanilla sugar
A pinch of salt
1 large egg

350 g (1½ oz) butter
40 g (1½ oz) cocoa
powder
1 spoon rum
100 g (3½ oz) crushed
almonds

Sift the flour and baking powder on to a work surface and make a well in the centre. Add 140 g (4½ oz) icing sugar, the vanilla sugar, salt, the egg (reserve 2 teaspoons of the egg white), and the butter cut into pieces. Combine the ingredients, drawing the flour to the centre, then knead well to form a smooth dough. Set one-third of the dough to one side.

Incorporate the cocoa powder, the remaining icing sugar, the rum and almonds into the remaining two-thirds of the dough. Shape the dough into 4 rectangular rolls, 32 cm (12¾ in) long, 3.5 cm (1¼ in) wide and 15 mm (⅛ in) deep.

Roll out the plain dough into a rectangle measuring about 44 x 32 cm (17½ x 12 ¾ in). Cut into 4 strips measuring 11 x 32 cm (4¼ x 12¾ in) and coat them with the reserved egg white.

Wrap a strip of plain dough around each roll of almond dough. Cover with a sheet of aluminium foil and place in a refrigerator overnight.

Cut into 5 mm (¼ in) thick slices and transfer to a lined baking sheet. Bake in a preheated oven at 200° C (400° F, Gas Mark 6) for 12-15 minutes until golden.

Opposite: *Chocolate almond biscuits*

Above: *Hazelnut fingers*

Opposite: *Basel hearts and Little almond crescents*

HAZELNUT FINGERS

Makes about 20

200 g (7 oz) plain flour
140 g (4½ oz) caster sugar
1 sachet vanilla sugar
A pinch of salt
2 eggs, separated

100 g (3½ oz) butter
400 g (13 oz) ground
hazelnuts
4 spoons rum
200 g (7 oz) icing sugar

Sift the flour on to a work surface and make a well in the centre. Add 40 g (1½ oz) sugar, the vanilla sugar, salt and egg yolks, and combine with some of the flour to form a soft dough. Add the cold butter cut into pieces, cover with the remaining flour and knead well until smooth.

Roll out the dough into a rectangle measuring 40 x 30 cm (16 x 12 in).

For the filling: dissolve the remaining sugar in 140 ml (4½ fl oz) water and bring to the boil. Remove from the heat. Incorporate the ground hazelnuts and the rum, mix well. Leave to cool and spread the mixture over the dough.

Combine the icing sugar with the egg whites, stirring to make a thick cream. Coat the hazelnut cream with this icing.

Cut into fingers measuring 6 cm x 15 mm (2½ x ¼ in) and transfer to a lined, greased baking sheet.
Bake in a preheated oven at 180°C (350°F, Gas Mark 4) for 12-15 minutes until golden.

If the icing runs down the side of a slice, remove it using the tip of a knife.

BASEL HEARTS

Makes about 10

2 egg whites
250 g (8 oz) caster sugar
1 sachet vanilla sugar
1 teaspoon cinnamon
½ teaspoon ground cloves
½ bottle rum flavouring
65 g (2½ oz) cocoa

powder
15 g (½ oz) butter, melted
250 g (8 oz) ground
almonds
2 teaspoons baking
powder
1 tablespoon plain flour

Beat the egg whites until they become thick and frothy. Add first the sugar, then the vanilla sugar, cinnamon, ground cloves, rum flavouring, cocoa and melted butter. Gently combine these ingredients. Sift the ground almonds and baking powder into the egg mixture, mix well to form a firm dough.

Dust a work surface with flour and roll out the dough until 5 mm (¼ in) thick. Using a heart-shaped pastry cutter, cut out little hearts and transfer them to a greased baking sheet. Bake in a preheated oven at 180-200° C (350-400° F, Gas Mark 4-6) for 10 minutes.

LITTLE ALMOND CRESCENTS

Makes about 10

200 g (7 oz) marzipan
2 egg whites
100 g (3½ oz) caster sugar
1 sachet vanilla sugar

50 g (2 oz) plain flour
50 g (2 oz) flaked almonds
100 g (3½ oz) superfine
cooking chocolate

Beat the egg whites and the marzipan using an electric mixer fitted with a kneading attachment until the mixture is smooth and creamy. Add the sugar, followed by the vanilla sugar and flour and mix well. Transfer the mixture to a piping bag fitted with a flattened round nozzle.

Pipe crescent shapes on to a greased, floured baking sheet. Decorate with the flaked almonds and bake in a preheated oven at 180-200° C (350-400° F, Gas Mark 4-6) for 10-15 minutes.

Melt the chocolate in a bowl over a pan of hot water, stirring until smooth and glossy, and dip the ends of the crescents into it.

COCONUT CREAMS

Makes about 20

250 g (8 oz) plain flour
2 teaspoons baking
powder
175 g (6 oz) caster sugar
1 sachet vanilla sugar
3 eggs, separated

125 g (4 oz) butter
175 g (6 oz) desiccated
coconut
3 drops almond essence
1 teaspoon condensed
milk

Sift the flour and baking powder on to a work surface and make a well in the centre. Add 75 g (3 oz) sugar, the vanilla sugar and 2 egg yolks, and combine with some of the flour. Add the cold butter, cut into pieces, cover with the remaining flour and knead into a smooth dough. Leave to rest in a refrigerator for a while.

Roll out the dough and divide into two halves. For one half, cut out circles 4.5 cm (1¾ in) in diameter, for the other half circles 3 cm (1¼ in) in diameter. Place the large circles on a greased baking sheet.

For the filling: whisk the egg whites into stiff peaks. Incorporate the remaining sugar, the coconut and almond essence. Place a spoonful of this mixture on each

Opposite: *Coconut creams*

larger biscuit and top with a small biscuit. Beat the egg yolk and condensed milk together and brush the biscuits with this mixture. Bake in a preheated oven at 200ºC (400ºF, Gas Mark 6) for 12-15 minutes.

CASHEW CRUNCHIES

Makes about 40-50

150 g (5 oz) plain flour
150 g (5 oz) cane sugar
4 egg yolks
1 teaspoon ground ginger
1 teaspoon cardamom

1 sachet vanilla sugar
150 g (5 oz) butter
250 g (8 oz) ground
cashew nuts

Sift the flour on to a work surface and make a well in the centre. Add the cane sugar, egg yolks, ginger and cardamom, and combine with some of the flour. Place the cold butter, cut into pieces, on the mixture, cover with the ground cashew nuts and the remaining flour. Knead well.

Shape the dough into rolls about 2.5 cm (1 in) in diameter, leave in a refrigerator until firm, and then cut into 5 mm (¼ in) thick slices. Transfer them to a lined, greased baking sheet and bake in a preheated oven at 180-200° C (350-400° F, Gas Mark 4-6) for 12-15 minutes.

Below: *Cashew crunchies*

CHOCOLATE GINGER SLICES

Makes about 60

125 g (4 oz) butter	powder
200 g (7 oz) caster sugar	250 g (8 oz) chocolate,
1 sachet vanilla sugar	grated
2 teaspoons ground	200 g (7 oz) raisins
ginger	150 g (5 oz) superfine
4 eggs	cooking chocolate
250 g (8 oz) plain flour	Some glacé cherries to
2 teaspoons baking	finish

Cream the butter in a bowl using an electric mixer fitted with a kneading attachment. First add the sugar, then the vanilla sugar, ginger and eggs, and beat until the ingredients are incorporated. Gradually spoon in the flour and baking powder, together with the grated chocolate, and mix well. Chop the raisins into little pieces and add them to the mixture.

Spread this mixture over a greased baking sheet. Bake in a preheated oven at 180-200° C (350-400° F, Gas Mark 4-6) for 20-25 minutes. When cool, cut into 4 x 4 cm (1½ x 1½ in) squares.

Melt the chocolate in a bowl over a pan of hot water and stir until smooth and glossy. Use to coat the slices and decorate with glacé cherries.

Below: *Chocolate ginger slices*

NUTCRACKERS

Makes about 70

600 g (1 lb 3 oz) whole	4 egg yolks
hazelnuts	250 g (8 oz) icing sugar
50 g (2 oz) cornflour	70 wafers or rice paper
1 teaspoon grated lemon	circles, 4 cm (1½ in) in
rind	diameter
1 teaspoon ground	150 g (5 oz) plain
cinnamon	superfine cooking
A pinch of salt	chocolate
3 eggs	

Grind 200 g (7 oz) hazelnuts and chop the remaining hazelnuts. Combine the nuts with the cornflour, grated lemon rind, cinnamon and salt in a bowl. Put the whole eggs, egg yolks and icing sugar in a bowl over a pan of hot water and beat using a mixer at high speed for 6-8 minutes until the mixture holds its shape. Remove the bowl from the pan and incorporate the mixture into the other ingredients.

Arrange the wafers or rice paper circles over two baking sheets and place a spoonful of the mixture on each. Bake in a preheated oven at 150° C (300° F, Gas Mark 2) for 15 to 18 minutes. Leave to cool.

For the icing: melt the chocolate in a bowl over a pan of hot water, stirring well to form a smooth icing. Leave to cool slightly. Reheat as soon as it sets. Make an icing bag out of a piece of greaseproof paper and drizzle over the hazelnut sponge biscuits.

CHESTNUT COOKIES

Makes about 70

250 g (8 oz) butter	75 g (3 oz) chopped
450 g (15 oz) chestnut	pistachio nuts
purée	1 teaspoon ground
175 g (6 oz) icing sugar	coriander
A pinch of salt	½ teaspoon ground cloves
1 sachet vanilla sugar	1 teaspoon cinnamon
2 eggs	200 g (7 oz) superfine
3 egg yolks	cooking chocolate
100 g (3½ oz) plain flour	100 g (3½ oz) blanched
2 teaspoons baking	almonds
powder	200 g (7 oz) milk superfine
200 g (7 oz) chopped	cooking chocolate
walnuts	

Above: *Chestnut cookies and Hazelnut dreams*

Cream the butter and chestnut purée in a bowl, then add the icing sugar, followed by the salt, vanilla sugar, whole eggs and egg yolks. Incorporate the flour (reserve one tablespoonful for the baking sheet) and baking powder into the chestnut mixture, together with the chopped walnuts, pistachio nuts, coriander, cloves and cinnamon.

Cut the chocolate into small pieces and incorporate in the mixture. Spread the mixture evenly over a floured, greased baking sheet. Bake in a preheated oven at 200°C (400°F, Gas Mark 6) for 18-20 minutes.

Halve the almonds and roast in a hot oven for 8-10 minutes until golden.

For the icing: melt the milk chocolate in a bowl over a pan of hot water. Leave to cool. As soon as it sets, reheat it and use to coat the entire layer of sponge biscuit. Cut into little rectangles and decorate each one with a roasted almond. Leave the cakes to set before removing from the baking sheet. Store in an airtight container.

HAZELNUT DREAMS

Makes about 50

165 g (5½ oz) plain flour
150 g (5 oz) caster sugar
1 teaspoon lemon juice
2 egg yolks
150 g (5 oz) butter

150 g (5 oz) crushed
hazelnuts
40 whole hazelnuts to
finish

Sift 150 g (5 oz) flour on to a work surface and make a well in the centre. Add the sugar, lemon juice and egg yolks, and, using some of the flour, work the ingredients into a soft dough. Cut the cold butter into pieces, place on the dough, together with the hazelnuts, cover with the remaining flour and knead into a smooth dough. Shape the dough into a roll and place in a refrigerator for 1 hour.

Dust the work surface with the remaining 15 g (½ oz) flour and roll out the dough until 3 mm (⅛ in) thick. Cut out using a fluted pastry cutter 4 cm (1½ in) in diameter and transfer to a lined, greased baking sheet. Cut the hazelnuts in half and put one half on each biscuit. Bake in an oven heated to 200° C (400° F, Gas Mark 6) for 8 minutes.

PIGNOLATI

(Pine kernel macaroons)

Makes 40-50

5 egg whites
150 g (5 oz) caster sugar
50 g (2 oz) icing sugar
3 drops vanilla essence
1 teaspoon ground

cinnamon
150 g (5 oz) chopped
almonds
50 g (2 oz) cornflour
150 g (5 oz) pine kernels

Put the egg whites in a bowl over a pan of hot water and whisk them into soft peaks using an electric mixer at high speed. Gradually incorporate the caster sugar, beating constantly for 1 minute. Place the bowl in cold water and continue to beat until the eggs are cold. Add the icing sugar, vanilla, cinnamon, chopped almonds and cornflour. Mix well.

Transfer the mixture to a piping bag fitted with a plain nozzle and pipe walnut-sized balls on to a greased, lined baking sheet. Decorate the macaroons with pine kernels (about 8 per macaroon) and bake in a preheated oven at 160° C (325° F, Gas Mark 3) for 25-30 minutes.

SYRUP CRISPS

(Knusperle, a German speciality)

Makes about 40

375 g (12 oz) golden syrup
50 g (2 oz) caster sugar
100 g (3½ oz) butter
1 heaped teaspoon
ground cinnamon
1 teaspoon cloves

A pinch of nutmeg
A pinch of cardamom
500 g (1 lb) plain flour
2 teaspoons baking
powder

Heat the syrup, sugar and butter in a pan over a low heat. As soon as the ingredients have melted, put them in a bowl and leave to cool. Then add the cinnamon, cloves, nutmeg and cardamom.

Combine the flour and baking powder. Put one-third to one side. Gradually spoon the remaining two-thirds into the syrup mixture, stirring until the ingredients are incorporated. Add the reserved third and knead into a smooth dough.

Roll out the dough until very thin. Cut out the biscuits in different shapes and transfer them to a greased baking sheet.

Bake in a preheated oven at 180-200° C (350-400° F, Gas Mark 4-6) for 5-7 minutes.

MARZIPAN MACAROONS

Makes about 10

200 g (7 oz) marzipan
50 g (2 oz) icing sugar
1 spoon lemon juice
Grated rind of ½ lemon
A pinch of salt
2 egg yolks
1 glacé orange

Some glacé cherries
Some whole walnuts
1 spoon apricot jam
1 spoon rum or apricot
liqueur
A few drops of lemon
juice

Beat the marzipan using an electric mixer fitted with a kneading attachment to soften it. Then add the icing sugar, lemon rind and juice, salt and egg yolks, beating constantly.

Transfer the mixture to a piping bag fitted with a wide, round nozzle. Pipe 3 drops of the mixture side by side in the shape of a triangle (they must touch) on to a greased, lined baking sheet.

Above: *Marzipan macaroons*

Cut the glacé orange and the cherries into small pieces. Decorate each macaroon with the glacé orange and cherries and the walnuts. Bake in a preheated oven at 180-200° C (350-400° F, Gas Mark 4-6) for 10 minutes.

For the icing: sieve the apricot jam, mix it with the rum or apricot liqueur and lemon juice, bring to the boil. Brush the macaroons with this mixture as soon as they are out of the oven.

Cut out the Christmas trees with a shaped pastry cutter.

Spread the filling over the trees.

Spread the trees with jam while they are still hot

CHRISTMAS TREES

Makes 3

300 g (10 oz) plain flour
2 teaspoons baking powder
200 g (7 oz) caster sugar
3 eggs, separated
175 g (6 oz) butter
2-3 spoons shredless orange marmalade

½ teaspoon ground cinnamon
150 g (5 oz) desiccated coconut
Glacé icing or sifted icing sugar
Silver balls to finish

Sift the flour and the baking powder into a bowl, add 50 g (2 oz) sugar, the egg yolks and butter. Knead the ingredients using an electric mixer fitted with a kneading attachment, first at low speed, then at high speed. Turn the dough on to a work surface and knead well. If it is too sticky, place it in a refrigerator for a short while.

Roll out the dough until 5 mm (¼ in) thick and, using a shaped pastry cutter or a paper template you have made yourself, cut out the Christmas trees. Transfer them to a greased baking sheet and bake in a preheated oven at 200° C (400° F, Gas Mark 6) for 10 minutes.

For the filling: sieve the marmalade and spread it over the Christmas trees while they are still hot.
Whisk the egg whites into peaks, then add the remaining sugar, the cinnamon and coconut. Continue beating until all the ingredients are incorporated, then spread this mixture over the biscuits.
Return to a preheated oven at 130-150° C (250-300° F, Gas Mark ½-2) and bake for 20-25 minutes.
Leave to cool.
Decorate the biscuits with the glacé icing and the silver balls, or dredge with icing sugar.

Alternative: the trees can be decorated using chocolate icing. Melt 100 g (3½ oz) superfine cooking chocolate in a bowl over a pan of hot water, transfer to an icing bag and decorate the trees with the greeting: 'Happy Christmas'. Coloured icing may also be used.

Opposite: *Christmas trees*

CINNAMON COTTAGE

100 g (3½ oz) honey
50 g (2 oz) caster sugar
A pinch of salt
25 g (1 oz) butter
1 egg
1 egg white
½ teaspoon ground
cinnamon
2 drops almond essence
250 g (8 oz) plain flour
2 teaspoons baking
powder
175 g (6 oz) icing sugar
Some whole hazelnuts
1 chocolate flake bar
Hundreds and thousands
Some sugar flowers
Some pistachio nuts
Some glacé cherries
Some blanched almonds
White glacé icing

*B*efore starting, make a template for the cottage, based on a 6 x 6 cm (2½ x 2½ in) surface area, using a sheet of card 20 x 32 cm (8 x 12¾ in). Cut out the four walls. For the roof, cut out a strip of card and fold it in two.

For the dough: heat the honey, sugar, salt and butter over a low heat, leave to cool and pour the mixture into a bowl. Add the whole egg, the cinnamon and the almond extract. Combine using an electric mixer. Sift the flour and baking powder into a separate bowl and incorporate two-thirds of it into the honey mixture, beating constantly at medium speed. Add the remaining flour and knead into a smooth dough. Roll out into a 30 x 30 cm (12 x 12 in) square, place on a greased baking sheet and bake in a preheated oven at 180-200° C (350-400° F, Gas Mark 4-6) for 10-20 minutes. As soon as it is out of the oven, cut out the four walls and the two roof panels using the template.

To finish: mix the icing sugar and egg white into a thick cream. Use to stick the biscuit shapes to the templates for the walls. Spread the edges of the walls with this icing and join together to form a box. Spread the icing over the roof panels and stick them to the strip of card. Place the roof on the cottage, pressing down gently.

Cover the roof with icing and decorate the rooftop with the whole hazelnuts. Cut off a piece of the chocolate flake bar to make a chimney. Decorate the sides of the roof with hundreds and thousands, green and yellow icing, chocolate curls, sugar flowers and red glacé cherries secured with white icing.

Right:
*Cinnamon
cottage*

MR AND MRS SPICE

250 g (8 oz) honey
100 g (3½ oz) caster sugar
1 sachet vanilla sugar
1 egg
½ teaspoon ground cinnamon
A pinch of ground cloves
A pinch of nutmeg
3 drops lemon flavouring
½ bottle rum flavouring
500 g (1 lb) plain flour
2 teaspoons baking powder
Condensed milk

Some whole almonds
25 g (1 oz) hundreds and thousands
25 g (1 oz) chocolate vermicelli
Some sugar flowers
Some glacé cherries
Some raisins
Some chopped almonds
100 g (3½ oz) pistachio nuts
Some chopped candied peel

Put the honey, sugar, vanilla sugar, egg, cinnamon, cloves, nutmeg, lemon flavouring and rum flavouring in a bowl and mix well. Sift the flour and baking powder into a separate bowl and incorporate two-thirds into the honey mixture. Add the remaining flour and knead into a smooth dough.

Roll out the dough until 1 cm (½ in) thick and cut out the shapes using a pastry cutter or a card template. Transfer the shapes to a greased baking sheet and bake in a preheated oven at 180-200° C (350-400° F, Gas Mark 4-6) for 25 minutes. Leave them to cool, brush with condensed milk and decorate as shown in the photograph.

BREAD SHAPES

Makes 8-10 little men and 8 geese

500 g (1 lb) strong plain flour
1 sachet powdered easy-blend yeast
2 spoons caster sugar
1 teaspoon salt
2 eggs, 1 separated
100 g (3½ oz) butter,

melted140 ml (4½ fl oz) warm milk
50 currants
2 teaspoons condensed milk
Sugar crystals
8-10 little pipes to finish (optional)

Sift the flour into a bowl, add the yeast and mix well. Add the sugar, salt, 1 whole egg and 1 egg white, the melted butter and the warm milk. Knead the ingredients using an electric mixer fitted with a kneading attachment, first at low speed, then at high speed, for 5 minutes. Leave in a warm place until blisters form and the dough has doubled in bulk. Knead again on a work surface.

Below: *Bread shapes*

To make the little men: roll out the dough until 1 cm (½ in) thick. Make templates cut out from a sheet of card in the shape of people - 18 cm (7 in) tall and 8 cm (3 in) wide. Place on the dough and cut out the little men using a very sharp knife. Place the little men on a greased baking sheet and decorate them with the currants.

Mix the egg yolk with the condensed milk and spread some of this mixture over the shapes. Leave to prove for 20 minutes. Bake in a preheated oven at 200° C (400° F, Gas Mark 6) for 15-20 minutes. Decorate with the pipes immediately if using.

To make the geese: Make templates - 20 cm (8 in) high x 14 cm (5/½ in) long x 10 cm (4 in) wide. Cut out the geese from the remaining dough. Brush them with the remaining condensed milk and egg mixture. Leave to prove for 20 minutes. Sprinkle with the sugar crystals before baking for 15 minutes.

CHRISTMAS STOCKINGS

Makes 2

125 g (4 oz) honey
50 g (2 oz) caster sugar
1 sachet vanilla sugar
65 g (2½ oz) butter
1 egg, separated
A pinch of ground cinnamon
A pinch of ground cloves
250 g (8 oz) plain flour

2 teaspoons baking powder
1 teaspoon cocoa powder
100 g (3½ oz) icing sugar
5-6 glacé cherries
5-6 blanched almonds
20 coloured chocolate drops
Some pieces of angelica

Melt the honey, sugar, vanilla sugar and butter in a pan over a low heat. Remove from the heat. Add the egg yolk, cinnamon and cloves, mix well using an electric mixer, then leave to cool. Pour the mixture into a mixing bowl.

Sift the flour, baking powder and cocoa, incorporate two-thirds into the honey mixture using an electric mixer at medium speed. Add the remaining flour mixture and knead into a smooth dough.

Roll out the dough until 5 mm (¼ in) thick and, using a template made of card, cut out the stockings with a sharp knife. Transfer them to a greased baking sheet and bake in a preheated oven at 180-200° C (350-400° F, Gas Mark 4-6) for 15 minutes.

Mix the egg white with the icing sugar into a thick cream. Decorate the stockings with this icing and finally add the glacé cherries, coloured chocolate drops, pieces of angelica and blanched almonds.

Below: *Christmas stockings*

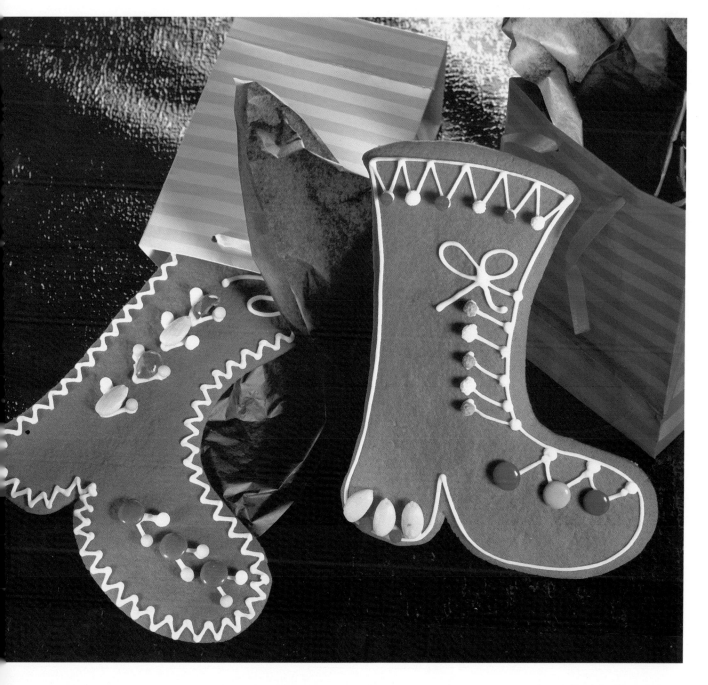

FATHER CHRISTMAS BISCUITS

Makes 4

500 g (1 lb) strong plain flour	250 ml (8 fl oz) warm milk
1 sachet powdered easy-blend yeast	2 tablespoons condensed milk
75 g (3 oz) caster sugar	10 currants
1 sachet vanilla sugar	20 blanched almonds
1 teaspoon salt	10 glacé cherries
75 g (3 oz) butter, melted	Chopped candied peel

Sift the flour into a bowl, add the yeast and mix well. Add 65 g (2½ oz) sugar, the vanilla sugar, salt, butter and milk. Knead all these ingredients together using an electric mixer fitted with a dough hook, first at low speed, then at high speed, for 5 minutes. Leave in a warm place until blisters form and the dough has doubled in bulk. Knead again on a work surface.

Divide the dough into four equal portions, roll them out into oval shapes and, using a card template, cut out the Father Christmas shapes with a sharp knife.

Transfer the figures to two greased baking sheets. Brush them with the condensed milk and decorate with the currants, almonds, cherries and candied peel. Leave to prove for 20 minutes. Bake in a preheated oven at 200-220° C (400-425° F, Gas Mark 6-7) for 15-20 minutes. Make a syrup using the remaining sugar and a little water and use to coat the figures as soon as they are out of the oven.

CHRISTMAS HEART

Makes 1

200 g (7 oz) butter, softened	1 tablespoon milk
175 g (6 oz) caster sugar	50 g (2 oz) grated chocolate
3 eggs	Orange or apricot jam
100 g (3½ oz) plain flour	200 g (7 oz) marzipan
100 g (3½ oz) cornflour	300 g (10 oz) icing sugar
1 spoon cocoa powder	Food colouring
2 teaspoons baking powder	Sugar flowers

Cream the butter in a mixing bowl using an electric mixer for 30 seconds. Add the sugar and continue beating until the mixture holds its shape. Add the eggs one at a time, beating until incorporated.

Sift the flour, cornflour, cocoa powder and baking powder into a separate bowl and gradually spoon them into the butter mixture, mixing well. Finally add the milk and the grated chocolate. Turn the mixture into a greased, deep, 24 cm (9½ in) round cake tin.

Bake in a preheated oven at 130-150ºC (250-300ºF, Gas Mark ½-2) for 50 minutes. Turn out on to a muslin cloth over a wire rack, leave to cool, then cut into a heart shape using a card template. Coat with the jam.

Knead the marzipan with 150 g (5 oz) icing sugar. Roll it out between two sheets of cling film into a very thin layer and place on top of the heart.

Mix the remaining icing sugar with some water into a thick cream. Add the food colouring and, using an icing bag, pipe a message of your choice on the heart. Decorate the heart with sugar flowers.

DUCK WITH BRIGHT-COLOURED FEATHERS

Makes 1

175 g (6 oz) butter, softened	2 teaspoons baking powder
200 g (7 oz) caster sugar	50 g (2 oz) chopped almonds
1 teaspoon orange flavouring	⅓ bottle rum flavouring
3 eggs	250 g (8 oz) icing sugar
150 g (5 oz) plain flour	Yellow food colouring
50 g (2 oz) cornflour	Hundreds and thousands
2 spoons cocoa powder	(in four separate colours)

Cream the butter in a mixing bowl using an electric mixer for 30 seconds. Add the sugar, beat constantly until the mixture holds its shape. Incorporate the orange flavouring, then add the eggs one at a time and beat until incorporated.

Sift the flour, cornflour, baking powder and cocoa, gradually spoon them into the mixture, beating at medium speed. Finally add the almonds and rum flavouring. Transfer to a greased, deep, 24 cm (9½ in) round cake tin or duck-shaped tin. Bake in a preheated oven at 130-150° C (250-300° F, Gas Mark ½-2) for 50-60 minutes.

Leave to cool in the tin, then turn out on to a muslin cloth over a wire rack. If applicable, cut out the duck shape using a card template.

For the icing: mix the icing sugar with 5-6 spoons water and the yellow food colouring until thick and creamy.

Cover the duck with icing and decorate with the hundreds and thousands.

Suggestion: wrap the duck up well in cling film and it will be an amusing present for a child's birthday.

BREAD KEYS

Makes 4

500 g (1 lb) strong plain flour	140 ml (4½ fl oz) warm milk
1 sachet powdered easy-blend yeast	50 g (2 oz) butter, melted
50 g (2 oz) caster sugar	1 small egg
A pinch of salt	Some sesame seeds

Sift the flour into a bowl, add the yeast and mix well. Then add the sugar, salt, milk and butter. Using an electric mixer fitted with a dough hook, knead all the ingredients first at low speed, then at high speed, for 5 minutes. If the dough is too sticky, add a little flour.

Leave in a warm place until blisters form and the dough has doubled in bulk. Knead again on a work surface.

Divide the dough into four equal portions and shape into four rolls about 46 cm (18 in) long. Roll them out and shape into keys (roughly like a question mark). Place a ball of tin foil in the end with the hole so that it does not disappear when cooked. To make the bits of the key, make three slanting cuts on the edge of the shaft, make three strips of dough and insert them into the cuts.

Brush with beaten egg, sprinkle with sesame seeds and leave to prove for 20 minutes. Bake in a preheated oven at 200° C (400° F, Gas Mark 6) for 15-20 minutes.

TORTOISES

Makes 4-5

125 g (4 oz) ground wheat	1 egg
375 g (12 oz) strong plain flour	1 egg yolk
1 sachet powdered easy-blend yeast	140 ml (4½ fl oz) warm milk
1 spoon caster sugar	100 g (3½ oz) butter, melted
1 teaspoon salt	

Start by grinding the wheat in an electric grinder. Sift the flour into a bowl, add the yeast and ground wheat and mix well. Then add the sugar, salt, whole egg and milk (reserve 3-4 teaspoons) and the butter.

Using an electric mixer fitted with a dough hook, knead the ingredients, first at low speed, then at high speed, for 5 minutes. Leave in a warm place until blisters form and the dough has doubled in bulk. Knead again on a work surface.

Divide the dough into as many pieces as you want tortoises, reserving some for the limbs. Use balls of dough for the body and stretch the dough out at one end for the head. Shape the remaining dough into a roll about as thick as a pencil and cut off four little pieces for each tortoise to make its limbs. Stick them underneath each ball. Transfer the tortoises to a greased baking sheet. Make the shell by etching diamond shapes using a knife.

Leave to prove for 20 minutes. Mix the egg yolk with 1-2 spoons milk, brush over the tortoises. Bake in a preheated oven at 200° C (400° F, Gas Mark 6) for 25-30 minutes.

Above: *Easter bunny and chicken*

Plait the strips of dough

When baked, the outline of the bunny will still be visible.

Make an outline of the chicken and the bunny using the template.

EASTER BUNNY AND CHICKEN

Makes 1 chicken and 1 bunny

500 g (1 lb) strong plain flour
1 sachet powdered easy-blend yeast
125 g (4 oz) caster sugar
1 sachet vanilla sugar
A pinch of salt
75 g (3 oz) butter, melted
250 ml (8 fl oz) warm milk

1 egg, separated
200 g (7 oz) icing sugar
2 teaspoons cocoa powder
Yellow food colouring
Brightly coloured sweets and hundreds and thousands to finish

Mix the flour and yeast in a bowl. Then add the sugar, vanilla sugar, salt and butter. Using an electric mixer fitted with a dough hook, knead the ingredients, first at low speed, then at high speed, for 5 minutes. Leave in a warm place until blisters form and the dough has doubled in bulk.
Knead again on a work surface.
Divide the dough into two. Roll out on two greased baking sheets into two rectangles, 32 x 35 cm (12⅓ x 13⅓ in). Cut out strips of dough 5 mm (¼ in) wide

and plait them. Attach them to the edges of the rectangles. On paper, draw and cut out a hen and a rabbit. Place the templates on the dough. Using a round-ended knife, trace around the edges.
Beat the milk with the egg yolk and brush the plaited frame with this mixture. Make a hole at the top of each rectangle.

Leave to prove for 20 minutes. Bake separately in a preheated oven at 200-220°C (400-425°F, Gas Mark 6-7) for 15 minutes each.

For the decoration: mix the icing sugar with the egg white until thick and creamy. Divide this icing into three. Mix the first portion with the cocoa powder and brush on to the rabbit as shown; add the yellow food colouring to the second portion. Decorate the hen with the yellow and the white icings, using the photograph as an example.
Decorate with the brightly coloured sweets and hundreds and thousands.

DUCHESS LEMONS

Makes about 20

250 g (8 oz) butter,
softened
150 g (5 oz) icing sugar
Grated rind of 2 lemons
6 spoons lemon juice
2 eggs

375 g (12 oz) plain flour
2 spoons lemon jelly
50 g (2 oz) plain superfine
cooking chocolate
50 g (2 oz) glacé icing

Cream the butter using an electric mixer for 30 seconds, then add the sugar, lemon rind and juice and beat until incorporated. Add the eggs, beating constantly. Gradually spoon in the flour, mixing well.

Transfer the mixture to an icing bag fitted with a round nozzle and pipe walnut-sized mounds of the mixture on to a greased and lined baking sheet.
Using the fingers, lightly flatten the cakes and bake in a preheated oven at 180-200° C (350-400° F, Gas Mark 4-6) for 12 minutes. Leave to cool.

Spread the smooth side of half of the biscuits with the lemon jelly, stick the other halves on top, pressing down gently. Melt the chocolate in a bowl over a pan of hot water, add the glacé icing. Coat one side of the biscuits with the chocolate icing.

LUCKY MUSHROOMS

Makes about 40

400 g (13 oz) plain flour
1 teaspoon baking powder
75 g (3 oz) caster sugar
1 sachet vanilla sugar
A pinch of salt
2 eggs
150 g (5 oz) butter, melted
3 teaspoons condensed

milk
200 g (7 oz) red glacé
cherries
100 g (3½ oz) green glacé
cherries
100 g (3½ oz) halved
blanched almonds
50 g (2 oz) icing sugar

Sift the flour and baking powder into a bowl. Add the sugar, vanilla sugar, salt, eggs and butter. Using an electric mixer fitted with a dough hook, knead the ingredients into a smooth dough, first at slow speed, then at high speed. Leave to rest in a refrigerator for several hours.

Roll out the dough until 3 mm (⅛ in) thick and cut out round biscuits 5 cm (2 in) in diameter. Transfer them to a greased baking sheet and brush them with condensed milk. Decorate with cherries and almonds to make them look like mushrooms. Bake in a preheated oven at 180-200° C (350-400° F, Gas Mark 4-6) for 10-12 minutes.

Combine the icing sugar with a little water until thick and creamy. Transfer the icing to an icing bag made of greaseproof paper and pipe the outlines of the mushrooms.

SPICY NUT BISCUITS

Makes about 4

150 g (5 oz) honey
125 g (4 oz) caster sugar
50 g (2 oz) butter
1 egg
½ teaspoon ground
cinnamon
A pinch of ground cloves
A pinch of nutmeg
A pinch of cardamom
Grated rind of ½ lemon
1 spoon rum
400 g (13 oz) wheat flour
150 g (5 oz) rye flour

2 teaspoons baking
powder
3 tablespoons condensed
milk
50 g (2 oz) halved
blanched almonds
50 g (2 oz) whole
hazelnuts
100 g (3½ oz) sunflower
seeds
50 g (2 oz) glacé cherries
50 g (2 oz) angelica

Put the honey, 4-5 spoons water, the sugar and the butter in a small pan and melt over a low heat. Transfer the mixture to a bowl and leave to cool. Add the egg, spices, lemon rind, 1 spoon water and the rum, and beat using an electric mixer at high speed. Sift the wheat flour, rye flour and baking powder into a separate bowl, and gradually spoon in two-thirds of this mixture, beating until incorporated. Add the remaining flour and knead on a work surface until smooth. Wrap the dough in tin foil and leave in a refrigerator for 5-6 days.

Roll out the dough until 5 mm (¼ in) thick and cut out the biscuits using a card template - 10 cm x 6 cm (4 x 2½ in). Brush with 2 tablespoons condensed milk, decorate with almonds, hazelnuts and sunflower seeds. Coat with the remaining condensed milk. Decorate with the cherries and angelica.
Transfer the biscuits to a greased baking sheet and bake in a preheated oven at 200° C (400° F, Gas Mark 6) for 12 minutes.

Above: *Spicy nut biscuits*

CHRISTMAS CROWNS

Makes about 3

3 egg whites
150 g (5 oz) caster sugar
1 teaspoon lemon juice
1 tablespoon granulated

sugar
Glacé icing
Food colouring

Whisk the egg whites into peaks and gradually incorporate the sugar and lemon juice, beating constantly until the egg whites are very firm. Transfer the meringue mixture to a large icing bag.

Pipe into rings on a greased, lined baking sheet which has been dredged with granulated sugar.
Leave to rest for several hours. Bake in a preheated oven at 110-130° C (225-250° F, Gas Mark ¼-½) for 120-140 minutes. Leave the crowns to dry on a muslin cloth over a wire rack and decorate with coloured glacé icing.

SPICY PRETZEL BISCUITS

Makes about 20

200 g (7 oz) honey
125 g (4 oz) caster sugar
75 g (3 oz) butter
100 g (3½ oz) glacé fruits
1 egg
1 egg white
1 spoon orange essence
A pinch of salt
A pinch of ground cinnamon
A pinch of ground cloves

A pinch of allspice
A pinch of ginger
A pinch of cardamom
400 g (13 oz) plain flour
2 teaspoons baking powder
250 g (8 oz) icing sugar
100 g (3½ oz) plain superfine cooking chocolate

Put the honey, sugar and butter in a small pan and melt over a low heat. Leave to cool and mix well. Transfer this mixture to a bowl and add the finely chopped glacé fruits, the whole egg, orange flavouring, salt, cinnamon, cloves, allspice, ginger and cardamom. Mix well. Gradually incorporate two-thirds of the flour-baking powder mixture, then add the remaining flour and knead into a smooth dough.

Make rolls of dough 1 cm (½ in) in diameter and 15 cm (6 in) long (photograph no. 1, page 179) and make into pretzels (photograph no. 2). Transfer to a lined baking sheet and bake in a preheated oven at

160-180° C (325-350° F, Gas Mark 3-4) for 15-20 minutes.
For the icing: combine the icing sugar with the egg white to form a thick cream. Divide the icing into two. Melt the chocolate in a bowl over a pan of hot water and gently fold it into one of the portions of icing. Coat the pretzels with these two types of icing (photograph no. 3).

CINNAMON AND ALMOND STARS

Makes 30

2 egg whites
165 g (5½ oz) icing sugar
1 teaspoon cinnamon
175 g (6 oz) ground almonds

Lemon glacé icing
100 g (3½ oz) chopped pistachio nuts
Hazelnut brittle

Whisk the egg whites into peaks using an electric mixer and gradually incorporate 150 g (5 oz) sugar and the cinnamon. Add the ground almonds and continue beating at low speed until all the ingredients are incorporated. Leave to rest in a refrigerator.

Dredge a work surface with the remaining icing sugar and roll out the dough until 5 mm (½ in) thick. Cut out the stars and transfer them to a greased and lined baking sheet. Bake in a preheated oven at 160-180° C (325-350° F, Gas Mark 3-4) for 20 minutes.

Coat the stars with the glacé icing, sprinkle with the chopped pistachio nuts and crushed nut brittle.

Tip: the stars can be stored in a container lined with greaseproof paper.

Above: *Cinnamon meringue biscuits*

CINNAMON MERINGUE BISCUITS

Makes about 20

125 g (4 oz) plain flour
50 g (2 oz) caster sugar
1 sachet vanilla sugar
2 eggs, separated
65 g (2½ oz) butter,
softened
100 g (3½ oz) icing sugar

1 teaspoon cinnamon
100 g (3½ oz) ground
almonds
Some glacé cherries to
finish
Shredded rind of ½
orange

Sift the flour into a bowl and add the sugar, vanilla sugar, egg yolks and butter. Beat the mixture using an electric mixer fitted with a dough hook, first at low speed, then at high speed. Knead the dough on a work surface. Leave the dough to firm up in a refrigerator for a few hours.

Roll out until 3 mm (⅛ in) thick, cut out round biscuits about 3-4 cm (1¼-1½ in) in diameter and arrange them on a greased baking sheet.

For the meringue: whisk the egg whites into stiff peaks and gradually incorporate the icing sugar and cinnamon. Gently fold in the almonds. Place a walnut-sized mound of meringue on each biscuit and decorate with half a glacé cherry or the shredded orange rind. Bake in a preheated oven at 180-200° C (350-400° F, Gas Mark 4-6) for 10 minutes.

LITTLE CHOCOLATE FINGERS

Makes about 20

250 g (8 oz) butter, softened	powder
150 g (5 oz) caster sugar	250 g (8 oz) icing sugar
A pinch of salt	1 egg white
1 spoon orange flavouring	150 g (5 oz) plain
1 egg	superfine cooking
1 egg yolk	chocolate
300-350 g (10-12 oz) plain flour	Some chopped pistachio nuts to finish
2 teaspoons baking	Some hundreds and thousands to finish

Cream the butter using an electric mixer for 30 seconds. Incorporate the flour, salt and orange flavouring, finally add the whole egg and egg yolk, beating constantly. Gradually incorporate two-thirds of the flour-baking powder mixture, mixing well. Finally add the remaining flour and knead into a smooth dough.

Transfer the dough to a special baker's piping bag and pipe fingers of dough 6 cm (2½ in) long on to a greased and lined baking sheet. Bake in a preheated oven at 200-220° C (400-425° F, Gas Mark 6-7) for 12-15 minutes. Leave to cool.

For the icing: combine the icing sugar with the egg white, beating into a thick cream. Melt the chocolate in a bowl over a pan of hot water, and gently fold into the icing sugar mixture. Dip the fingers into the chocolate so that they are half-covered. Sprinkle with pistachio nuts or hundreds and thousands.

OAT BISCUITS

Makes about 20

250 g (8 oz) butter, softened	1 teaspoon ginger
175 g (6 oz) caster sugar	1 teaspoon cardamom
1 spoon orange flavouring	200 g (7 oz) rolled oats
1 egg	100 g (3½ oz) ground hazelnuts
1 teaspoon ground cinnamon	100 g (3½ oz) plain flour

Cream the butter using an electric mixer for 30 seconds, add the sugar, orange flavouring, egg, cinnamon, ginger and cardamom, beating constantly until all the ingredients are incorporated.
Add the rolled oats, hazelnuts and flour, beating constantly with the mixer at low speed. Leave the dough to rest in a refrigerator for a few hours.

Roll the dough out until 1 cm (½ in) thick and cut out the biscuits in a variety of shapes (Christmas trees, circles, stars, little bells, etc.). Transfer to a lined baking sheet. Bake in a preheated oven at 200° C (400° F, Gas Mark 6) for 10-12 minutes. Leave to cool on a muslin cloth over a wire rack.

HAZELNUT CRESCENTS

Makes about 30

300 g (10 oz) plain flour	100 g (3½ oz) ground roasted hazelnuts
100 g (3½ oz) icing sugar	200 g (7 oz) butter, softened
1 sachet vanilla sugar	Icing sugar to finish
A pinch of salt	
1 small egg	

Sift the flour into a bowl and add the icing sugar, vanilla sugar, salt, egg, ground hazelnuts and butter. Mix using an electric mixer fitted with a kneading attachment, first at low speed, then at high speed.
Then knead by hand on a work surface to form a smooth dough. Cut out fingers about 6 cm (2½ in) long and make the ends into points. Shape into little crescents and transfer them to a lined baking sheet. Bake in a preheated oven at 180-200° C (350-400° F, Gas Mark 4-6) for 12 minutes. Toss the crescents in the icing sugar while still hot.

Above: *Spicy pretzel biscuits (recipe on p. 176)*

1

2

3

MARZIPAN HALF-MOONS

Makes about 30-40

200 g (7 oz) marzipan
75 g (3 oz) icing sugar
150 g (5 oz) ground lightly
roasted almonds
3 teaspoons cornflour
1 egg

40 g (1½ oz) chopped
candied lemon peel
1 spoon orange liqueur
1 spoon lemon flavouring
Icing sugar

Put all the ingredients in a bowl, reserving 1 tablespoon icing sugar. Knead the ingredients together using an electric mixer fitted with a dough hook, first at low speed, then at high speed, until the ingredients are incorporated.

Dredge a work surface with icing sugar and roll out the dough until 1 cm (½ in) thick. Cut out half-moon shapes and arrange them on a greased baking sheet. Bake in a preheated oven at 180-200° C (350-400° F, Gas Mark 4-6) for 10-12 minutes.

Dredge the half-moons with icing sugar when they are still hot to the touch.

SPICED BISCUITS

Makes about 50

500 g (1 lb) plain flour
2 teaspoons baking
powder
250 g (8 oz) caster sugar
1 sachet vanilla sugar
2 drops almond essence
2 pinches of ground
cinnamon

2 pinches of cardamom
2 pinches of cloves
A pinch of salt
2 eggs
200 g (7 oz) butter,
softened
100 g (3½ oz) ground
hazelnuts or almonds

Sift the flour and baking powder into a bowl and add the sugar, vanilla sugar, almond essence, cinnamon, cloves, salt, eggs, butter and ground hazelnuts or almonds. Knead using an electric mixer fitted with a dough hook, first at low speed, then at high speed. Finally knead into a smooth dough by hand on a work surface. Leave to rest in a refrigerator for several hours.

Roll out the dough very thinly and cut out into animal shapes. Arrange on a greased baking sheet. Bake in a preheated oven at 180-200° C (350-400° F, Gas Mark 4-6) for 10 minutes.

Alternative: if you have wooden figurine moulds, dust the moulds with flour and then press the rectangles of dough in the moulds. When the figures are imprinted in the dough, carefully remove them from the moulds and place on a baking sheet. Then bake.

Opposite: *Hazelnut crescents*

WALNUT COOKIES

300 g (10 oz) plain flour
200 g (7 oz) caster sugar
1 sachet vanilla sugar
1 bottle rum flavouring
3 drops almond essence
A pinch of ground
cardamom
Salt
200 g (7 oz) butter,

softened
150 g (5 oz) ground
hazelnuts
Redcurrant jelly
50 g (2 oz) cooking
chocolate
200 g (7 oz) walnut halves
200 g (7 oz) lemon glacé
icing

Sift the flour into a bowl, add the sugar, vanilla sugar, cardamom, salt, butter and ground hazelnuts. Combine the ingredients using an electric mixer, first at low speed, then at high speed. Then knead the dough into a soft ball by hand on a work surface. If it is too sticky, place it in a refrigerator for a while.

Roll out the dough thinly and cut out circles 4 cm (1½ in) in diameter. Arrange these on a baking sheet and bake in a preheated oven at 180-200° C (350-400° F, Gas Mark 4-6) for 5-10 minutes.

Spread the smooth side of half the biscuits with redcurrant jelly and place the remaining biscuits on top. Press down firmly.

For the filling: melt the chocolate in a bowl over a pan of hot water and dip the walnut halves in it. Leave to set on a sheet of greaseproof paper.

For the icing: coat the biscuits with the lemon glacé icing and decorate with the walnuts.

Below: *Walnut cookies*

CINNAMON BISCUITS

Makes about 10

300 g (10 oz) plain flour
1 teaspoon baking powder
75 g (3 oz) icing sugar
Salt
2 teaspoons cinnamon
225 g (7½ oz) butter

100 g (3½ oz) ground
roasted hazelnuts
40 g (1½ oz) caster sugar
3 tablespoons raspberry
jam

Sift the flour and baking powder into a bowl. Add the icing sugar, salt, 1 rounded teaspoon cinnamon, 200 g (7 oz) softened butter and the ground roasted hazelnuts. Combine all the ingredients using an electric mixer at low speed, then at high speed. Transfer the dough to a work surface and knead it into a smooth ball by hand. If it is too sticky, place in a refrigerator for a while.

Roll the dough out until 3 mm (⅛ in) thick, cut out circles about 4 cm (1½ in) in diameter. Arrange them on a baking sheet and bake in a preheated oven at 180-200°C (350-400°F, Gas Mark 4-6) for about 10 minutes.

For the decoration: melt the remaining butter. Brush over the tops of half of the biscuits. Mix the sugar with a pinch of cinnamon. Dredge the butter-coated biscuits immediately so that the sugar sticks well.

For the filling: spread the smooth surface of the remaining biscuits with the raspberry jam. Place them on top of the sugar-dredged biscuits.

CHOCOLATE HAZELNUT BISCUITS

Makes 15-20

125 g (4 oz) treacle
50 g (2 oz) caster sugar
A pinch of salt
65 g (2½ oz) butter
2 tablespoons milk
(optional)
50 g (2 oz) candy sugar
5 drops lemon flavouring
½ teaspoon ground
aniseed

½ teaspoon ground cloves
½ teaspoon cinnamon
250 g (8 oz) plain flour
3 teaspoons baking
powder
200 g (7 oz) hazelnuts
200-225 g (7-7½ oz)
superfine cooking
chocolate

Melt the treacle, sugar, salt, 50 g (2 oz) butter and 2 tablespoons milk or water over a low heat. Leave the mixture to cool in a bowl. When the mixture is lukewarm add the finely ground candy sugar, lemon flavouring, ground aniseed, cloves and cinnamon, and combine using an electric mixer at high speed.

Sift the flour and baking powder into a separate bowl. Gradually spoon in two-thirds of the flour to the treacle mixture and incorporate using an electric mixer at medium speed.
Place the dough on a work surface, add the remaining flour, and knead into a smooth ball. If it is too sticky, place in a refrigerator for a while.

Roll the dough out until 5 mm (¼ in) thick and cut out rectangles measuring 2.5 x 7 cm (1 x 2¾ in). Arrange them on a baking sheet. Place the hazelnut halves on the rectangles, pressing them into the dough. Bake in a preheated oven at 180-200° C (350-400° F, Gas Mark 4-6) for about 10 minutes.

For the icing: melt the chocolate in a bowl over a pan of hot water with a knob of butter until the mixture is creamy and use to coat the cold biscuits. Decorate with hazelnut halves.

MARZIPAN TWISTS

Makes 20-30

200 g (7 oz) marzipan
125 g (4 oz) butter,
softened
100 g (3½ oz) caster sugar
1 sachet vanilla sugar
A pinch of salt
Grated rind of 1 lemon
2 eggs
200 g (7 oz) plain flour
2 teaspoons baking
powder
200 g (7 oz) icing sugar
1 egg white
100 g (3½ oz) plain
superfine cooking
chocolate

Cream the marzipan, add the butter and beat using an electric mixer for 30 seconds. Add the sugar, vanilla sugar, salt and lemon rind, beating constantly until all the ingredients are incorporated. Add the eggs one at a time, beating each in thoroughly. Gradually spoon in the sifted flour and baking powder, beating constantly.

Transfer the mixture to a piping bag fitted with a round nozzle and pipe 5 cm (2 in) long twisted fingers on to a lined baking sheet. Bake in a preheated oven at 180-200°C (350-400°F, Gas Mark 4-6) for 8-10 minutes.

For the icing: combine the icing sugar with the egg white to form a thick cream.
Melt the chocolate in a bowl over a pan of hot water and gently fold into the icing sugar mixture. Dip the twists into the chocolate so that they are half-covered.

SPICY CHRISTMAS BISCUITS
(Nuremberg Lebkuchen)

Makes about 40

75 g (3 oz) chopped
candied peel
125 g (4 oz) ground
almonds
2 eggs
200 g (7 oz) soft brown
sugar
1 sachet vanilla sugar
A pinch of ground cloves
A pinch of cinnamon
½ bottle rum flavouring
2 drops lemon flavouring
A pinch of baking powder
50 g (2 oz) plain flour
75-125 g (3-4 oz) ground
hazelnuts
40 wafers or rice paper
circles 6 cm (2½ in) in
diameter
150 g (5 oz) icing sugar
1 egg white
75 g (3 oz) superfine
cooking chocolate

Chop the candied peel very finely, combine with the ground almonds and eggs using an electric mixer. Add the sugar, vanilla sugar, spices and flavourings, baking powder, flour and ground hazelnuts. Mix using an electric mixer at low speed.

Place a spoonful of the mixture on each wafer or rice paper circle, smoothing it down evenly. Arrange on a baking sheet and bake in a preheated oven at 130-150°C (250-300°F, Gas Mark 2-2) for 25-30 minutes.

For the icing: combine the icing sugar with the egg white to form a thick cream. Divide the creamy mixture into two portions. Melt the chocolate in a bowl over a pan of hot water and gently fold it into one of the portions of creamy icing. Coat the biscuits with the white or chocolate icing.

Opposite: *Marzipan half-moons (recipe on p. 181)*

ORANGE FLOWER MARZIPANS

Makes about 30

200 g (7 oz) marzipan
125 g (4 oz) icing sugar
1 teaspoon orange peel, dried and chopped
50 g (2 oz) candied orange peel, chopped
3 tablespoons orange liqueur

100 g (3½ oz) plain superfine cooking chocolate
1 knob creamed coconut
Orange juice
30 pieces chopped candied orange peel to finish

Knead the marzipan in a bowl with 100 g (3½ oz) icing sugar and the dried orange peel. Put a quarter of the mixture to one side wrapped in aluminium foil.

Mix the candied orange peel and 1 tablespoon orange liqueur with the remaining three-quarters.

Dredge a work surface with 2 teaspoons icing sugar and roll out the orange liqueur marzipan mixture until 1 cm (½ in) thick. Cut into circles about 3 cm (1¼ in) in diameter.

Roll out the remaining portion of marzipan very thinly and cut out flower shapes, about 5 mm (¼ in) wide. Press in the middle to form a crown, then leave to dry out for a while.

For the icing: melt the cooking chocolate and the creamed coconut in a bowl over a pan of hot water. Coat the marzipan circles by dropping them into the chocolate, removing them with a fork and letting the excess chocolate drip off. Place on a sheet of greaseproof paper.
Mix the remaining icing sugar with the remaining orange liqueur, add a little orange juice, beating until thick and creamy. Coat the flowers with this mixture.

Place one piece of chopped candied orange peel in the centre of each flower and use to decorate the chocolate marzipans, pressing down gently.

Tip: the chocolates must always be stored in a refrigerator, wrapped in cellophane or in airtight containers so that they do not absorb the flavours of the other foods in the refrigerator.

PISTACHIO PRALINES

Makes about 30

150 g (5 oz) ground roasted hazelnuts
100 g (3½ oz) chopped pistachio nuts
150 g (5 oz) icing sugar
2 tablespoons brandy

1 egg white
65 g (2½ oz) candied orange slices
100 g (3½ oz) superfine cooking chocolate
30 pistachio nuts

Mix the roasted hazelnuts, chopped pistachios, icing sugar, brandy and egg white in a mixing bowl until all the ingredients are incorporated.
Roll into balls the size of a walnut.
Finely chop the candied orange slices. Make a well in each ball, fill it with chopped candied orange and roll into a ball again. Place on a baking sheet lined with aluminium foil or greaseproof paper and press each side with the fingers to make them into little cubes. Smooth them off with a knife.

Melt the chocolate in a bowl over a pan of hot water. Coat the pralines in the melted chocolate, using a fork, and place them on a sheet of greaseproof paper. Dip the tip of each pistachio nut into the chocolate and use to decorate the sweets.

CINNAMON CREAMS

Makes about 20

100 ml (3½ fl oz) double cream
200 g (7 oz) milk superfine cooking chocolate

25 g (1 oz) butter, softened
2 teaspoons cinnamon
7 g (¼ oz) icing sugar

Bring the cream to the boil and remove from the heat. Cut the chocolate into small pieces and add to the cream, together with the butter and 1 teaspoon cinnamon. Melt these ingredients, stirring constantly, until thick and creamy. Transfer the mixture to an icing bag fitted with a round nozzle and pipe sausage-shapes about 3 cm (1¼ in) long on to a sheet of aluminium foil. Leave to set.

Mix the icing sugar with the remaining cinnamon and roll the sausage-shapes in this mixture. Store in a refrigerator.

Pages 186 and 187: *Orange flower marzipans*
Opposite: *Cinnamon creams*

Above: *Truffle surprises*

TRUFFLE SURPRISES

Makes about 30

100 g (3½ oz) caster sugar
2 eggs, separated
50 g (2 oz) plain flour
50 g (2 oz) cornflour
1 teaspoon baking powder
3 tablespoons brandy
100 ml (3½ fl oz) double cream
2 tablespoons milk
2 teaspoons instant coffee

100 g (3½ oz) coffee-flavoured chocolate
100 g (3½ oz) plain chocolate
1 sachet vanilla sugar
A pinch of salt
30 cocktail cherries
Some plain chocolate vermicelli to finish

Pour 300 ml (½ pint) water and 25 g (1 oz) sugar into a small pan and bring to the boil. Boil until the sugar has completely dissolved. Skim the mixture and leave the syrup to cool.

For the cake mixture: beat the egg yolks with 2 spoons hot water in a bowl until the mixture is thick and frothy, add 50 g (2 oz) sugar and continue beating until pale yellow.

Whisk the egg whites into peaks, fold in the remaining sugar and add to the egg yolk mixture. Combine the flour, cornflour and baking powder and incorporate into the egg yolk mixture. Turn into a deep, 24 cm (9½ in) round cake tin. Bake in a preheated oven at 200° C (400° F, Gas Mark 6) for 25-30 minutes.

Thin down the sugar syrup with the brandy, prick the sponge cake with a fork and sprinkle with the syrup. Cover and leave to cool.

For the truffle mixture: bring the cream and the milk to the boil, add the instant coffee and chocolate, broken up into small pieces. Melt in a bowl over a pan of hot water until all the ingredients are incorporated, add the vanilla sugar and salt.

Crumble the sponge cake into a bowl. Cover with the truffle mixture while still hot. Knead the ingredients together using an electric mixer fitted with a dough hook. Chill.

Cut the mixture into 30 pieces and make into balls around the cocktail cherries. Roll the truffles in the plain chocolate vermicelli.

WALNUT FANCIES

Makes about 50

7 g (¼ oz) butter, softened
25 g (1 oz) caster sugar
50 g (2 oz) chopped walnuts
200 g (7 oz) marzipan
50 g (2 oz) icing sugar
2 tablespoons rum

100 g (3½ oz) milk superfine cooking chocolate
1 knob creamed coconut
12-13 whole walnuts to finish

Put the butter and sugar in a small pan and heat, stirring constantly, until they caramelize. Add the chopped walnuts. Spread over an oiled baking sheet and leave to cool. Crush into powder using a rolling pin.

Knead the marzipan, icing sugar, rum and crushed walnut brittle. Roll this mixture out until 1 cm (½ in) thick and cut out into 2 cm (¾ in) squares.
Melt the chocolate and the creamed coconut in a bowl over a pan of hot water and drop the marzipan squares into this mixture. Remove them with a fork, letting any excess chocolate drip back into the bowl. Place on a sheet of greaseproof paper.

Cut the whole walnuts into four and arrange them on the icing before it sets, pressing down gently.

MARZIPAN PETITS FOURS

Makes about 50

200 g (7 oz) marzipan
110 g (3¾ oz) icing sugar
1 tablespoon kirsch
Hundreds and thousands

to finish
Glacé cherries to finish
Sugar flowers to finish

Put the marzipan, 100 g (3½ oz) icing sugar and the kirsch in a mixing bowl. Knead into a smooth paste. Dust moulds of various shapes with the remaining icing sugar and press the pieces of marzipan into the moulds. Remove them from the moulds carefully, using a cocktail stick. Decorate with the hundreds and thousands, the cherries and the sugar flowers.

Below: *Marzipan petits fours*

191

FRUIT AND NUT CHOCOLATES

Makes 80-90

250 g (8 oz) whole hazelnuts
175 g (6 oz) plain chocolate
250 g (8 oz) raisins
15 g (½ oz) chopped candied orange peel
500 g (1 lb) milk superfine cooking chocolate

Place the hazelnuts on a baking sheet and roast them in a preheated oven at 200° C (400° F, Gas Mark 6) for about 10 minutes. Remove from the oven as soon as the brown skin splits. Place in a sieve, leave to cool and then rub them together to remove the skin. Chop the hazelnuts coarsely.

Break the plain chocolate into small pieces and melt in a bowl over a pan of hot water. Add the hazelnuts, raisins and orange peel, mixing well. Remove from the heat and arrange small spoonfuls of this mixture on a sheet of greaseproof paper.
Chill for 1 hour.

Melt the cooking chocolate in a bowl over a pan of hot water and add the spoonfuls of mixture one by one. Remove using a fork and letting any excess chocolate drip back into the bowl. Place on a sheet of greaseproof paper. Leave to set.

Tip: if the chocolate sets too quickly, put the bowl back over a pan of hot water.
Store the chocolates in an airtight container, placing a sheet of greaseproof paper between each layer of sweets.

HAZELNUT TRUFFLES

Makes about 40

75 g (3 oz) butter
75 g (3 oz) icing sugar
1 sachet vanilla sugar
200 g (7 oz) plain
chocolate
75 g (3 oz) ground roasted hazelnuts

Cream the butter in a mixing bowl, add the icing sugar and vanilla sugar.

Break the chocolate into small pieces and melt in a bowl over a pan of hot water, stirring constantly until smooth. Incorporate the creamed butter and two-thirds of the ground hazelnuts. Leave to set in a refrigerator.

Make into small truffle balls and roll them in the remaining ground hazelnuts.

Tip: store them in a refrigerator in cellophane bags or in an airtight container.

FRUIT DELIGHTS

Makes about 100

250 g (8 oz) stoned dates
250 g (8 oz) stoned prunes
250 g (8 oz) dried apricots
Grated rind of 1 lemon
2 tablespoons honey
65 g (2½ oz) ground walnuts (or almonds, or hazelnuts)

Finely chop the dates, prunes and dried apricots. Add the lemon rind and combine all the ingredients with the honey. Run your hands under cold water and roll the mixture into balls. Roll them in the ground walnuts or nuts of your choice.

Tip: keep in a refrigerator in an airtight container, with a sheet of greaseproof paper between each layer of sweets.

Left: *Hazelnut truffles*

Above: *Fruit delights*

MOZARTKUGELN
(An Austrian speciality)

Makes about 60

200 g (7 oz) hazelnut
chocolate spread
200 g (7 oz) marzipan
2 tablespoons kirsch
7 g (¼ oz) chopped

pistachio nuts
125 g (4 oz) icing sugar
100 g (3½ oz) plain
superfine cooking
chocolate

Chill the hazelnut chocolate spread and then roll into balls about 15 mm (⅓ in) in diameter. Put to one side in a refrigerator.

Combine the marzipan with the kirsch, chopped pistachio nuts and icing sugar (reserve 2 teaspoons), and make into rolls 2 cm (¾ in) thick. Cut into as many pieces as there are balls of hazelnut chocolate spread. Roll them out on a work surface dredged with the reserved icing sugar. Place a ball of hazelnut chocolate spread in the centre of each piece of marzipan and wrap the marzipan around it, pressing gently. Roll into balls again.

Melt the chocolate in a bowl over a pan of hot water and dunk the balls in one by one. Remove with a fork, letting any excess chocolate drip back into the bowl. Place on a sheet of greaseproof paper. Leave to set, turning regularly.

Tip: keep in a refrigerator in cellophane bags or in an airtight container.

KÔNIGSBERG MARZIPANS

Makes about 50

250 g (8 oz) marzipan
125 g (4 oz) icing sugar
Red fruit jam

Hazelnut chocolate spread
1 egg white

Knead the marzipan and icing sugar. Make into a roll and cut it in two pieces, one being two-thirds of the mixture, the other one-third. Roll out the larger portion until 1 cm (½ in) thick and the other portion until 5 mm (¼ in) thick. Place one layer of marzipan on top of the other and cut out different shapes (hearts, stars, circles, etc.).

Using a pointed knife, cut out part of the thinner layer, leaving a 5 mm (¼ in) rim. Fill with the red fruit jam or the hazelnut chocolate spread. Make indentations around the edges.

Coat the fluted rims with the egg white. Place the marzipans on a baking sheet and place under a hot grill for about 1 minute until golden.

Below: *Kônigsberg marzipans*

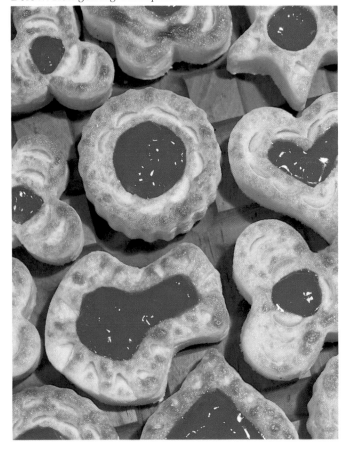

CHERRY PRALINES

Makes 50-60

10 red glacé cherries
200 g (7 oz) ground almonds
100 g (3½ oz) caster sugar

5 tablespoons kirsch
100 g (3½ oz) hazelnut praline
Icing sugar to finish

Chop the cherries and combine with the ground almonds, sugar (reserve 2 teaspoons), 3 tablespoons kirsch and 2 spoons water to form a smooth paste.

Melt the praline in a bowl over a pan of hot water, beating until creamy, add the remaining kirsch and leave to cool, stirring from time to time.
As soon as the praline thickens, roll it out on a work surface dredged with icing sugar. Carefully spread the almond mixture over the praline and cut out the sweets using a small pastry cutter. Leave to set in a refrigerator for 12-24 hours.

FLORENTINES

Makes 50-60

50 g (2 oz) butter
200 g (7 oz) caster sugar
2 sachets vanilla sugar
250 ml (8 fl oz) double cream
300 g (10 oz) flaked almonds

150 g (5 oz) chopped candied orange peel
50-60 wafers or rice paper circles, 4 cm (1½ in) in diameter
150 g (5 oz) superfine cooking chocolate

Heat the butter, sugar and vanilla sugar. As soon as it starts to brown, add the cream and continue cooking until the sugar has dissolved. Incorporate the almonds and candied orange peel and continue cooking until a smooth paste is formed. Place a teaspoon of caramel on each wafer or rice paper circle, transfer them to a baking sheet and bake in a preheated oven at 180-200°C (350-400° F, Gas Mark 4-6) for 10 minutes. Melt the cooking chocolate in a bowl over a pan of hot water and use to coat each wafer. Leave to set.

Alternative: you can use ginger instead of almonds and candied orange peel, and white chocolate instead of plain chocolate.

Tip: keep in a refrigerator in an airtight box with a sheet of greaseproof paper between each layer.

Opposite: *Florentines*

COFFEE TRUFFLE CREAMS

Makes about 55

125 g (4 oz) milk superfine
cooking chocolate
150 g (5 oz) plain
chocolate
250 ml (8 fl oz) double
cream
2 teaspoons instant coffee

50 g (2 oz) butter,
softened
75 g (3 oz) hazelnut
praline
55 gold foil cases
55 chocolate coffee beans
to finish

Break the plain and the milk chocolate into small pieces,
put in a pan, add the cream and bring to the boil.
Remove from the heat, add the instant coffee and
softened butter, stirring well. Cut the praline into small
pieces, add to the chocolate and beat until smooth and
glossy. Leave to cool.

As soon as the mixture begins to set, beat with an electric
mixer until light and creamy. Transfer this mixture to an
icing bag fitted with a star-shaped nozzle and pipe into
each foil case. Decorate with a chocolate coffee bean.

Leave to cool and store in a refrigerator in an airtight
container.

RUM TRUFFLES

Makes 15

500 g (1 lb) stale sponge
cake
4 spoons rum
125 g (4 oz) creamed
coconut
65 g (22 oz) icing sugar

20 g (w oz) cocoa powder
1 sachet vanilla sugar
1 bottle rum flavouring
1 egg
75 g (3 oz) chocolate
vermicelli

Crumble the sponge cake and place in a bowl. Mix the
rum with 250 ml (8 fl oz) water and sprinkle over the
sponge cake. Melt the creamed coconut in a pan and
leave to cool.

Sift the icing sugar, cocoa powder and vanilla sugar into
a bowl. Add the rum flavouring and the egg, then
gradually incorporate the creamed coconut and rum
sponge mixture.
Mix well and shape into 15 balls. Roll them in the
chocolate vermicelli and place in a refrigerator to set.

RUM AND RAISIN CHOCOLATES

Makes about 60

100 g (32 oz) butter
100 g (32 oz) icing sugar
1 sachet vanilla sugar
300 g (10 oz) grated
chocolate

3 teaspoons rum
125 g (4 oz) raisins,
soaked in rum
100-150 g (32-5 oz)
chocolate vermicelli

Cream the butter and incorporate the icing sugar, vanilla
sugar and chocolate. Add the rum and then the
rum-soaked raisins. Leave to rest in a refrigerator for
1-2 hours. Shape into small balls and roll them in the
chocolate vermicelli. Keep in a refrigerator in cellophane
bags or in an airtight container.

NUT BRITTLE CRUNCHIES

Makes 60-70

20 g (w oz) butter
65 g (22 oz) caster sugar
125 g (4 oz) chopped
almonds

100 g (32 oz) plain
chocolate
5 teaspoons double cream

Heat the butter and sugar. As soon as the sugar starts to
brown, add the almonds and continue cooking until the
sugar caramelizes. Spread over an oiled baking sheet
and leave to cool. Crush the nut brittle with a rolling pin.

Break the chocolate into small pieces and melt in a bowl
over a pan of hot water. Leave to cool slightly, add the
nut brittle. Place teaspoonfuls of this mixture on a sheet
of aluminium foil. Leave to set.

Opposite: *Coffee truffle creams*
Right: *Nut brittle crunchies*

Above: *Apple and calvados dreams*

APPLE AND CALVADOS DREAMS

Makes about 20

4 slices dried apple
3 tablespoons calvados
200 ml (7 fl oz) double
cream
250 g (8 oz) chocolate

100 g (32 oz) creamed
coconut
Some pistachio nuts to
finish

Finely chop the dried apple, sprinkle with calvados, cover and leave to soak for 3-4 hours.

Bring the cream to the boil and remove from the heat. Break the chocolate into small pieces, add to the cream, together with the creamed coconut, and melt, stirring constantly. Leave to cool, then beat vigorously. Incorporate the chopped apple and calvados. Transfer this mixture to an icing bag fitted with a wide, round nozzle, and pipe little mounds of chocolate into foil cases. Decorate with pistachio nuts.

PISTACHIO CHOCOLATES AND NUT BRITTLE ROUNDS

Makes about 20 chocolates and 20 rounds

100 ml (32 fl oz) double
cream
1 vanilla pod
250 g (8 oz) superfine
cooking chocolate
3 spoons icing sugar
40 g (12 oz) chopped
candied peel
40 g (12 oz) chopped

almonds
75 g (3 oz) chopped
pistachio nuts
100 g (32 oz) hazelnut
brittle
50 g (2 oz) ground
almonds
Sugar violets and rose
petals

Put the cream in a pan. Split the vanilla pod in two lengthways, scrape out the inside and add to the cream. Bring to the boil. Remove from the heat. Break the cooking chocolate into small pieces and melt in the cream, stirring constantly. Finally add the icing sugar. Divide the icing into two portions.

For the pistachio chocolates: add the candied peel together with the almonds to the first portion of chocolate, stirring well.
Leave to cool for 10 minutes. Make into a roll of chocolate, cut into slices and shape into small balls, using your hands. Roll the balls in the chopped pistachio nuts. Place in a refrigerator, then transfer to small foil cases. Keep in a refrigerator.

PEPPERMINT CREAMS

Makes 40-50

500 g (1 lb) icing sugar
1 egg white
3 teaspoons lemon juice
4 teaspoon peppermint

essence
200 g (7 oz) plain
chocolate

Put the icing sugar (reserve 1 tablespoonful) in a bowl, add the egg white, lemon juice and peppermint essence. Knead into a soft paste. Dredge a work surface with the remaining sugar and roll out the paste until 5 mm (¼ in) thick.

Cut out circles 3 cm (1¼ in) in diameter. Form the remaining paste into a ball, roll out and repeat the procedure until it has all been used up.

Melt the plain chocolate in a bowl over a pan of hot water and dunk in the creams one at a time. Remove using a fork, letting any excess chocolate drip back into the bowl. Place on a sheet of greaseproof paper or aluminium foil. Draw a fork over the icing while still hot.

For the nut brittle rounds: knead the remaining half of the chocolate mixture with the hazelnut brittle and the ground almonds. Using a spatula, spread this mixture over a baking sheet lined with aluminium foil. Place in a refrigerator.

Cut out 3 cm (1¼ in) diameter circles, press down gently in the centre using the point of a knife and decorate with sugar violets and rose petals.
These rounds can be kept in a refrigerator for 2-3 weeks.

APRICOT MARZIPANS

Makes about 20

125 g (4 oz) dried apricots
3 spoons apricot liqueur
200 g (7 oz) marzipan
100 g (32 oz) icing sugar
100 g (32 oz) plain

superfine cooking chocolate
100 g (32 oz) walnut halves

*F*inely chop the apricots, sprinkle them with the liqueur, cover and leave to soak for 2 hours. Add the marzipan and combine using an electric mixer. Incorporate the sugar. Make into 2 cm (¾ in) rolls and cut into 15 mm (⅓ in) slices.

Melt the cooking chocolate in a bowl over a pan of hot water and dunk in the marzipan circles. Remove using a fork, letting any excess chocolate drip back into the bowl. Place on a sheet of greaseproof paper and turn several times.
Decorate with the walnut halves.

Below: *Apricot marzipans*

PINEAPPLE BONBONS

Makes about 100

200 g (7 oz) marzipan
200 g (7 oz) icing sugar
200 g (7 oz) glacé
pineapple
500 g (1 lb) plain
chocolate

2 teaspoons instant coffee
125 g (4 oz) butter,
softened
1 tablespoon brandy
Sugar rose petals to finish

Knead the marzipan with 100 g (3½ oz) icing sugar and roll it out into a rectangle, 20 x 25 cm (8 x 10 in).
Cut the glacé pineapple into thin shreds and place them close together on the marzipan.

Break 200 g (7 oz) chocolate into small pieces and melt in a bowl over a pan of hot water, stirring constantly. Leave to cool. Add the instant coffee, butter, the remaining sugar and the brandy.
Beat until the mixture forms peaks when lifted with a fork. Spread the chocolate over the marzipan and the pineapple. Place in a refrigerator for several hours.
Cut into 2 cm (¾ in) squares.

Melt the remaining chocolate in a pan over a bowl of hot water. Dunk the sweets into the chocolate one at a time. Remove using a fork, letting any excess chocolate drip back into the bowl. Place on a sheet of greaseproof paper. Decorate with the sugar rose petals and leave to set.

Suggestion: place each bonbon in a little paper case, arrange in a pretty china or glass dish and gift-wrap.

PISTACHIO MARZIPAN HEARTS

Makes 40-50

200 g (7 oz) marzipan
100 g (3½ oz) icing sugar
50 g (2 oz) ground
pistachio nuts
1 tablespoon kirsch

150-200 g (5-7 oz) plain
chocolate
Some whole pistachio
nuts to finish

Knead the marzipan in a mixing bowl with the icing sugar (reserve 2 teaspoons), ground pistachio nuts and kirsch. Roll it out until 1 cm (½ oz) thick, then cut out little hearts using a small pastry cutter. Remove them carefully from the cutter and dredge with the reserved icing sugar. Leave to rest in a refrigerator on a sheet of aluminium foil for 1-2 hours.

Melt the chocolate in a bowl over a pan of hot water and dunk in the hearts one at a time. Remove using a fork, letting any excess chocolate drip back into the bowl. Place on a sheet of greaseproof paper. Decorate with the whole pistachio nuts and leave to set.

Suggestion: arrange the little hearts in a heart-shaped box lined with a paper doily.
Place a sheet of cellophane between each layer of chocolates and gift-wrap.

Opposite: *Pistachio marzipan hearts*

CONFECTIONERY AND PETITS FOURS • 201

PERNOD PRALINE BOATS

Makes about 40

200 g (7 oz) marzipan
100 g (3½ oz) ground almonds
100 g (3½ oz) ground walnuts
100 g (3½ oz) icing sugar
4 tablespoons cocoa powder

3 tablespoons Pernod
100 g (3½ oz) plain chocolate
1 knob creamed coconut
Some whole pistachio nuts
100 g (3½ oz) whole pecan nuts or walnuts

Knead the marzipan with the ground almonds, ground walnuts, icing sugar, cocoa powder and Pernod. Divide into four equal portions and make into four rolls, 15 cm (6 in) long. Cut them into 10 slices and shape into oval boat shapes using the fingers. Place on a sheet of aluminium foil, flatten gently and leave to rest in a refrigerator.

Melt the chocolate in a bowl over a pan of hot water together with the creamed coconut and dunk in the boats one at a time. Remove using a fork, letting any excess chocolate drip back into the bowl. Place on a sheet of greaseproof paper. Decorate with the pistachio or pecan nuts or the walnuts.

Below: *Butter truffles*

BUTTER TRUFFLES

Makes 50-60

150 g (5 oz) butter
100 g (3½ oz) icing sugar
1 sachet vanilla sugar
2 egg yolks
200 g (7 oz) plain

chocolate
4 tablespoons cocoa powder or chocolate vermicelli

Cream the butter. Add the icing sugar and then incorporate the vanilla sugar and egg yolks.

Break the chocolate into small pieces and melt in a bowl over a pan of hot water, stirring constantly. Combine with the butter cream mixture and place in a refrigerator.

Make into truffles the size of a walnut and return to the refrigerator. Roll the truffles in the cocoa powder or chocolate vermicelli.

Keep in a refrigerator in a cellophane bag or in an airtight container.

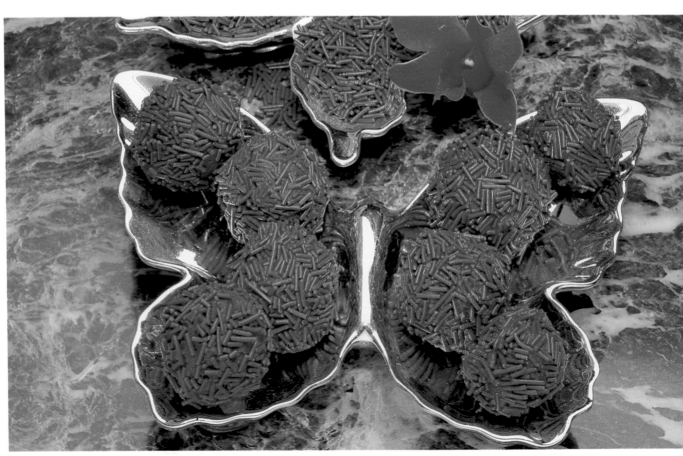

CHOCOLATE-COATED STRAWBERRIES

Makes about 30

500 g (1 lb) strawberries, stalks on
100 g (3½ oz) plain

chocolate
1 knob creamed coconut

Above: *Chocolate-coated strawberries*

Carefully wash the strawberries and wipe them. Break the chocolate into small pieces and melt in a bowl over a pan of hot water together with the creamed coconut, stirring constantly.

Dip the tips of the strawberries in the chocolate icing and place on a sheet of greaseproof paper. Serve in a basket or in a glass dish.

Above: *Rum chocolates*

RUM CHOCOLATES

Makes about 20

200 g (7 oz) plain
superfine cooking
chocolate
100 g (3½ oz) butter
40 g (1½ oz) icing sugar
1 teaspoon ground

cinnamon
3 tablespoons white rum
50 g (2 oz) milk superfine
cooking chocolate
20 sugar violets to finish

Break the plain chocolate into small pieces and melt in a bowl over a pan of hot water, stirring constantly until smooth and creamy. Leave to cool, beating from time to time.

Cream the butter and incorporate the icing sugar, cinnamon and rum. Mix into the chocolate.

Place in a refrigerator for a few minutes and beat again. If the mixture is too hard, return the bowl to a pan of hot water, beating constantly.

Transfer the mixture to an icing bag fitted with a medium-sized nozzle and pipe 4 cm (1½ in) long rolls on to a sheet of greaseproof paper or aluminium foil.

Melt the milk chocolate in a bowl over a pan of hot water, transfer to an icing bag fitted with a very fine nozzle, and pipe a thread-like design as shown.
Decorate with the sugar violets.
If stored in an airtight container, the rum chocolates will keep for 6-8 days.

CARAMEL MARZIPANS

Makes about 20

200 g (7 oz) ground
almonds
500 g (1 lb) icing sugar
50 g (2 oz) honey
50 g (2 oz) butter
1 vanilla pod

300 g (10 oz) marzipan
250 ml (8 fl oz) double
cream
100 g (3½ oz) plain
chocolate

Spread the ground almonds over a greased baking sheet
and roast in a preheated oven at 200° C (400° F, Gas Mark
6) for 6-8 minutes.
Put the sugar, honey and butter in a pan and heat,
stirring constantly, until the sugar caramelizes. Quickly
bring to the boil and remove from the heat. Split the
vanilla pod lengthways, remove the pulp. Cut the
marzipan into large chunks, beat the marzipan, vanilla
pulp and almonds together, then add them to the
caramel. Finally add the cream. Beat until all the
ingredients are incorporated.
Spread the mixture thickly over an oiled baking sheet,
leave to cool, and, using a very sharp knife, cut first into
2 cm (¾ in) strips and then into diamond shapes. Leave to
cool completely and then remove from the baking sheet.
Melt the chocolate in a bowl over a pan of hot water and
dip the points of the diamonds into the chocolate. Allow
any excess chocolate to drip back into the bowl and place
them on a sheet of greaseproof paper or aluminium foil.

DOUBLE CHOCOLATE TRUFFLES

Makes about 80

150 g (5 oz) plain
superfine cooking
chocolate
100 g (3½ oz) milk
chocolate
200 ml (7 fl oz) double
cream

100 g (3½ oz) creamed
coconut
200 g (7 oz) hazelnut
praline
80 small foil cases
Some pistachio nuts to
finish

Break the plain and the milk chocolate into small pieces,
put in a pan, add the cream and creamed coconut and
melt over a low heat, stirring constantly, until the mixture
is smooth and creamy. Bring to the boil, remove from the
heat and pour into a bowl. Incorporate the praline cut
into small pieces and mix thoroughly. Chill.

As soon as the truffle mixture is cool, beat it again using
an electric mixer so that it becomes creamy. Transfer the
mixture to an icing bag fitted with a star-shaped nozzle
and pipe a small amount of the truffle mixture into each
case.
Decorate with pistachio nuts.

Keep in a refrigerator wrapped in aluminium foil or in a
cellophane bag.

Below: *Caramel marzipans*

KÔNIGSBERG MARZIPAN EGGS

Makes 12 small or 6 large eggs

500 g (1 lb) almonds	3 teaspoons kirsch
700 g (1 lb 7 oz) icing sugar	Sugar flowers and silver balls
3 egg whites	Marzipan figures, flowers and leaves
5-6 spoons rose water	

Plunge the almonds into boiling water, drain and refresh under the cold tap, remove the skins and leave to dry overnight on a sheet of kitchen paper.

Grind the almonds. Place 500 g (1 lb) icing sugar, the ground almonds, 1 egg white and the rose water in a bowl. Beat using an electric mixer, first at low speed, then at high speed. As soon as the ingredients are incorporated, wrap the mixture in aluminium foil and leave to rest for 1-2 days at room temperature.

Divide the marzipan in two. Dredge a work surface with 2 teaspoons icing sugar and roll out one portion of marzipan until 1 cm (½ in) thick and the other portion until 5 mm (¼ in) thick. Place the thinner layer on top of the thicker layer of marzipan. Cut out large egg shapes about 15 cm (6 in) long and 10 cm (4 in) wide using a template and small eggs using an oval-shaped pastry cutter. Cut out a 5 mm (¼ in) layer from the centre of all the eggs, leaving a rim about 1 cm (½ in) wide on the large eggs, and 5 mm (¼ in) wide on the small eggs. Make indentations on the rim using a fork and a knife.

Place the eggs on a baking sheet lined with aluminium foil. Coat the rim of each egg with the 1 egg white and place under a hot grill for 2-3 minutes until golden.

Make the icing by beating the remaining icing sugar with the remaining egg white and the kirsch. Coat the centre of each egg with this icing. Decorate with the sugar flowers and silver balls and the marzipan figures, flowers and leaves.

When the icing is dry, wrap the eggs up in cellophane.

CHOCOLATE PETITS FOURS

Makes about 20

2 eggs	chocolate spread
125 g (4 oz) caster sugar	150 g (5 oz) plain chocolate
1 sachet vanilla sugar	20 g (w oz) creamed coconut
75 g (3 oz) plain flour	75 g (3 oz) marzipan
50 g (2 oz) cornflour	2 spoons icing sugar
2 teaspoons baking powder	1 spoon lemon juice
1 spoon cocoa powder	Some glacÇ cherries
25 g (1 oz) butter	
75 g (3 oz) hazelnut	

Put the eggs and 2 spoons hot water in a bowl and beat using an electric mixer at high speed until thick and frothy. Add 100 g (3½ oz) sugar and the vanilla sugar. Continue beating until thick and creamy.

Sift the flour, cornflour, baking powder and cocoa powder together and mix them into the egg mixture. Spread the mixture over a greased baking sheet lined with greaseproof paper and fold up the edges of the paper. Bake in a preheated oven at 180-200° C (350-400° F, Gas Mark 4-6) for 10-15 minutes.

Turn the sponge cake out immediately on to a sheet of greaseproof paper dredged with 2 teaspoons sugar and carefully peel the greaseproof paper off the sponge. Cut into small stars.

For the filling: cream the butter with the hazelnut chocolate spread. Spread this creamy mixture over half the stars, cover with the remaining stars.

Melt the chocolate in a bowl over a pan of hot water together with the creamed coconut and coat the sides of the stars.

Roll out the marzipan on a work surface dredged with the remaining sugar and cut out as many stars as there are petits fours. Mix the icing sugar and lemon juice into a thick icing, coat the marzipan stars and place them on the petits fours. Decorate with halved glacé cherries.

Store in an airtight container.

Opposite: *Kônigsberg marzipan eggs*

FRUIT PETITS FOURS

Makes about 20

2 eggs
100 g (3½ oz) caster sugar
1 sachet vanilla sugar
75 g (3 oz) plain flour
50 g (2 oz) cornflour
2 teaspoons baking
powder

1 teaspoon raspberry
brandy
2 tablespoons redcurrant
jelly
300 g (10 oz) icing sugar
Food colouring
Sugar flowers to finish

beating constantly for 2 minutes. With the mixer at low speed, add the flour, cornflour and baking powder, beating until all the ingredients are incorporated. Turn into a greased and lined deep, 28 cm (11 in) round cake tin, taking care to smooth the mixture out evenly. Bake in a preheated oven at 180-200° C (350-400° F, Gas Mark 4-6) for 25-30 minutes.
Remove from the tin immediately and peel off the greaseproof paper. Cut the sponge into diamond shapes.

For the icing: mix the raspberry brandy with the redcurrant jelly and spread over half the diamond sponges. Cover with the remaining half.

Make an icing using the icing sugar, a little water and some food colouring.
Use to coat the diamond sponges. Decorate with sugar flowers.

Beat the eggs and 2 tablespoons hot water using an electric mixer at high speed for 1 minute until the mixture is thick and frothy. Add the sugar and vanilla sugar,

Below: *Chocolate petits fours*

Above: *Fruit petits fours*

TRADITIONAL PETITS FOURS

Makes about 70

4 eggs
100 g (3½ oz) caster sugar
2 sachets vanilla sugar
100 g (3½ oz) plain flour
2 teaspoons baking
powder
75 g (3 oz) butter, melted
200 g (7 oz) marzipan
300 g (10 oz) icing sugar
150 g (5 oz) plain
chocolate
3 teaspoons redcurrant

jelly
75-100 g (3-3½ oz)
hazelnut praline
50 g (2 oz) creamed
coconut
1-2 teaspoons lemon juice
Silver balls
Glacé fruits
1 spoon cocoa powder
2 spoons Curaáao
Chocolate vermicelli

Put 3 eggs and 2 tablespoons hot water in a bowl and beat using an electric mixer at high speed until the mixture is thick and frothy. Add the sugar and 1 sachet vanilla sugar, then continue beating until the mixture is smooth and creamy.
In a separate bowl, combine the flour and baking

powder. First incorporate half the flour mixture into the egg mixture, then add the remaining half. Finally add the cooled, melted butter. Spread the mixture 1 cm (½ in) thick over a greased baking sheet lined with greaseproof paper. Fold up the edges of the paper to stop the mixture from running. Bake in a preheated oven at 200-220° C (400-425° F, Gas Mark 6-7) for 10-15 minutes.

Turn the sponge out immediately on to a sheet of greaseproof paper dredged with sugar and carefully peel the greaseproof paper off the cake. Cut out 32 hearts using a small pastry cutter, 36 4 cm (1½ in) diameter circles, 22 3 cm (1¼ in) squares and 22 3 x 3 cm (1½ x 1½ in) diamond shapes.

For the hearts: knead the marzipan with 50 g (2 oz) icing sugar and roll out until 5 mm (¼ in) thick. Cut out 16 hearts the same size as the sponge ones.

Break the chocolate into small pieces and melt it in a bowl over a pan of hot water, stirring constantly. Spread a little chocolate over half of the hearts, cover with a

marzipan heart, coat with a little chocolate and cover with the second sponge heart. (Reserve the remaining marzipan and chocolate.)
Mix 100 g (3½ oz) icing sugar with the redcurrant jelly and 3 spoons water to make a lovely pink icing. Use to coat the hearts.

For the round petits fours: melt the praline in a bowl over a pan of hot water, stirring constantly. Spread a little praline over half the sponge circles and cover with the remaining sponge circles. (Reserve the remaining praline.)
Mix the rest of the chocolate with 20 g (¾ oz) creamed coconut, melt in a bowl over a pan of hot water and coat the circles with this icing. Use the rest of the icing to decorate the heart-shaped petits fours.

For the square petits fours: roll out the remaining marzipan thinly and cut out 11 3 x 3 cm (1¼ x 1¼ in) squares (reserve the remaining marzipan). Spread a little praline over half the squares, place a marzipan square on top of the praline, add a layer of praline and finish with a sponge square.
Mix 125 g (4 oz) icing sugar with the lemon juice to make a thick icing and use to coat the squares. Use the remaining icing to decorate the hearts and the round petits fours.

Below: *Traditional petits fours*

For the diamonds: roll out the reserved marzipan thinly and cut out 11 3 x 3 cm (1¼ x 1¼ in) diamonds. Spread the reserved praline over half the diamonds, place a marzipan diamond over the praline, add a layer of praline and finish with a sponge diamond.

For the truffle petits fours: crumble the remaining sponge into a bowl.
Melt the remaining creamed coconut. Leave to cool in a bowl. Add the remaining icing sugar, the cocoa powder, the remaining vanilla sugar, the Curaáao and the remaining egg, stirring constantly.
Add to the crumbled sponge and shape into about ten balls. Roll them in the chocolate vermicelli.

Alternative: mix 125 g (4 oz) icing sugar with 1-2 spoons lemon juice and some yellow food colouring to form a thick icing. Use this to coat the square-shaped petits fours. Drizzle the remaining lemon or chocolate icing over the heart-shaped and round petits fours.

CARAMELIZED WALNUTS

Makes about 20 walnuts

20 whole walnuts in their shells	chocolate, grated
	1 egg white
25 g (1 oz) crushed walnuts	25 g (1 oz) icing sugar
	175 g (6 oz) sugar lumps
25 g (1 oz) plain	1 tablespoon oil

Shell the walnuts without breaking them. Place these together with the crushed walnuts on a baking sheet. Toast them quickly, turning regularly, for 7-8 minutes. Leave to cool.

Combine the crushed walnuts, grated chocolate and icing sugar, then gradually spoon in the egg white, mixing to form a smooth paste.

Spread half the walnuts with a layer of the chocolate mixture. Top with a second walnut half, pressing gently, to form a whole walnut again.

In a pan, melt the sugar lumps in 4 tablespoons water. Cook the syrup over a low heat until it turns light brown.

Remove from the heat. Dunk the reconstituted nuts into the caramel, one at a time. Turn them over using two forks to ensure they are fully coated. Transfer the caramelized walnuts to a greased baking sheet. Leave to set.

BLACKCURRANT BOATS

300 g (10 oz) plain flour
100 g (3½ oz) caster sugar
175 g (6 oz) butter
2 egg yolks
A pinch of salt

300 g (10 oz)
blackcurrants
100 g (3½ oz) redcurrant
jelly

Makes 15-20

*I*n a large bowl, mix the flour, sugar, melted butter, egg yolks and salt until all the ingredients are incorporated. Roll this dough out until 2 cm (¾ in) thick.

Turn the mixture into small, oval-shaped cake tins. Place greaseproof paper over the base and fill with dried beans. Bake blind in a preheated oven at 180° C (350° F, Gas Mark 4). The pastry must not brown.

Remove the beans and the paper, take the pastry cases out of the tins and fill with blackcurrants. Coat with redcurrant jelly.

Below: *Traditional petits fours*

HIDDEN FRUITS

Makes about 40

200 g (7 oz) ground
almonds
300 g (10 oz) caster sugar
2 teaspoon almond
essence
1 egg white
1 sachet vanilla sugar
A few drops of coffee

flavouring
Pink and green food
colourings
2 teaspoon vinegar
15 prunes
15 dates
15 dried apricots
15 glacé cherries, halved

Put the ground almonds, 100 g (3½ oz) caster sugar and
the almond essence in a bowl. Mix well.
Add the egg white and vanilla sugar. Combine until
all the ingredients are incorporated.

Divide this mixture into three equal portions. Flavour
one portion with the coffee flavouring and colour the
other two portions pink and green.
Knead each portion and roll them into sausage shapes.
Cut the rolls into slices.

Slice the dates and prunes along one side only. Remove
the stones. Replace the stones with the almond paste.
Fill the apricots. Stick the glacé cherry halves together
using a ball of almond paste.

For the icing: in a pan, mix the remaining sugar with
4 tablespoons water. Heat slowly until a very pale
caramel is formed. Add the vinegar. Put a few drops of
the mixture into cold water. If they break off, the icing is
ready.

Dunk each fruit in the caramel. Leave to cool on an oiled
baking tray. When they have cooled completely, arrange
them in paper cases and eat and enjoy within a few
hours.

CHOCOLATE CRUNCH

Makes 20

125 g (4 oz) blanched
hazelnuts
1 tablespoon oil

25 large sugar lumps
75 g (3 oz) butter
100 g (3½ oz) chocolate

Put the hazelnuts in a plastic bag. Crush them coarsely
using a rolling pin. Oil a rectangular dish.

Put the sugar lumps in a pan, add 4 tablespoons water
and the butter. Heat gently and simmer. Add 75 g
(3 oz) hazelnuts. Stir using a wooden spatula.
Pour the mixture over the oiled dish to form a
1 cm (½ in) thick layer. Leave to cool.

Melt the chocolate in a bowl over a pan of hot water.
Spread the remaining hazelnuts over the caramel and
cover with the melted chocolate. Chill for at least
2 hours, then cut the chocolate crunch into pieces.

Tip: chocolate crunch goes perfectly with hot chocolate
or pears with chocolate sauce.

Opposite: *Iced petits four*

ICED PETITS FOURS

Makes 40-50

6 eggs	200 g (7 oz) marzipan
175 g (6 oz) caster sugar	600 g (1 lb 3 oz) icing
1 teaspoon honey	sugar
100 g (3½ oz) plain flour	Food colouring
5 spoons apricot jam	Sugar violets
5 spoons raspberry jam	Chocolate vermicelli

Put the eggs and 4 tablespoons hot water in a bowl, then beat using an electric mixer at high speed until the mixture is thick and frothy.
Add the sugar and honey, then continue beating until the mixture is smooth and creamy.
Sift the flour over the egg mixture, incorporate with the mixer at low speed.
Spread half the mixture over a greased and lined baking sheet to form a 1 cm (½ in) thick layer. Fold up the edges of the paper to stop the mixture from running. Bake in a preheated oven at 200° C (400° F, Gas Mark 6) for 10 minutes. Turn the sponge out immediately on to a cloth, sprinkle the greaseproof paper with cold water and carefully peel it off. Bake the remaining sponge mixture in the same way while the first sponge cools.
Spread the apricot jam (photograph no. 1) over the first layer of sponge, cover with the second layer, and coat that layer with raspberry jam.
Knead the marzipan with 100 g (3½ oz) icing sugar and roll it out to the same size and shape as the sponge. Place the marzipan on the raspberry jam layer and cut out various shapes to make the petits fours (photographs nos. 2 and 3).

Mix the remaining icing sugar with 5-6 tablespoons water and the food colouring of your choice, knead well to form a smooth icing and use to coat the petits fours. Decorate as shown in the photographs (photograph no. 4).

2

3

4

Beat the mixture using an electric mixer.

Pipe the whirls on to a baking sheet lined with greaseproof paper.

Using an icing bag, decora the whirls with cream fillin

CHOCOLATE VIENNESE WHIRLS

Makes about 20

400 g (13 oz) butter
125 g (4 oz) caster sugar
2 teaspoon ground cinnamon
4 teaspoons milk
300 g (10 oz) plain flour

20 g (w oz) cocoa powder
25 g (1 oz) icing sugar
1 large egg
150 g (5 oz) plain chocolate, melted

Cream 275 g (9 oz) butter using an electric mixer. Then add the caster sugar, cinnamon and milk and beat until smooth. Gradually spoon in the flour and cocoa powder, beating with an electric mixer at medium speed (photograph no. 1). Transfer the mixture to a piping bag.

Pipe the whirls about 5 cm (2 in) in diameter on to a greased baking sheet lined with greaseproof paper (photograph no. 2). Bake in a preheated oven at 180-200° C (350-400° F, Gas Mark 4-6) for 15 minutes. Leave to cool.

For the filling: cream the remaining butter and then incorporate the icing sugar (reserving 1 teaspoon), the egg and the melted chocolate. Transfer this mixture to an icing bag fitted with a star-shaped nozzle and pipe on to the smooth side of half of the whirls (photograph no. 3). Cover with the remaining whirls and press down gently.

Dredge with the reserved icing sugar before serving.

HOMEMADE PETITS FOURS

Makes about 15

100 g (3½ oz) ground almonds
3 eggs
3 eggs, separated
250 g (8 oz) caster sugar
250 g (8 oz) plain flour

150 g (5 oz) butter, melted
A pinch of salt
Jam, hazelnut chocolate spread or marzipan
Liqueur or brandy
Ready-made icing

Combine the ground almonds with 1 egg. Add the sugar and 2 more eggs, then beat until smooth. Incorporate the flour, finally add the melted butter and egg yolks. Whisk the egg whites with the salt into peaks and gently fold into the mixture. Spread this mixture in a 1 cm (½ in) thick layer over a greased and lined baking sheet.

Bake in a preheated oven at 200° C (400° F, Gas Mark 6) for 12-14 minutes. Turn out on to a muslin cloth over a wire rack, peel off the greaseproof paper and leave to cool.

Cut into small squares or any other shapes you wish. Spread the jam, hazelnut chocolate spread or marzipan over half the shapes and cover with the remaining halves to make up the petits fours. Sprinkle with liqueur or brandy. Coat with ready-made icing.

Opposite: Chocolate Viennese whirls

FILLED PETITS FOURS

Makes 40-50

4 eggs
125 g (4 oz) caster sugar
A pinch of salt
125 g (4 oz) plain flour
65 g (2 oz) butter, melted
100 g (3½ oz) hazelnut
praline
Chocolate buttons
100 g (3½ oz) marzipan

2 tablespoons rum
Sugar flowers
100 g (3½ oz) raspberry
jam
Chocolate, lemon and
white glacé icings
Glacé cherries
2 spoons chopped
pistachio nuts

Put the eggs and 2 tablespoons hot water in a bowl, then beat using an electric mixer at high speed until thick and creamy. Add the sugar and salt. Continue beating until smooth and creamy. Incorporate half the flour first, then mix the remaining flour into the egg mixture. Finally add the cooled, melted butter.

Spread the mixture on to a greased and lined baking sheet to form a rectangle measuring 30 x 24 cm (12 x 9½ in). Fold up the edges of the paper to stop the mixture from running. Bake in a preheated oven at 200-220° C (350-400° F, Gas Mark 4-6) for 20-25 minutes.

Turn the sponge out immediately on to a sheet of greaseproof paper dredged with sugar and carefully peel off the greaseproof paper. Cut into 4 cm (1½ in) squares. Divide into three portions.

For the praline-filled petits fours: melt the praline in a bowl over a pan of hot water, stirring constantly. Spread a little praline over two squares of sponge, place them one on top of the other and top with a third layer of sponge. Repeat the procedure until all the sponges in the first portion have been filled.
Melt the chocolate icing in a bowl over a pan of hot water and use to coat the petits fours. Decorate with chocolate buttons.

For the marzipan-filled petits fours: knead the marzipan with the rum, roll it out until 5 mm (¼ in) thick and cut into 4 cm (1½ in) squares. Cover one sponge square with a marzipan square, top this with another sponge square, followed by a marzipan square, then finish with a sponge square. Melt the lemon icing in a bowl over a pan of hot water and use to coat the sponge cakes. Decorate with sugar flowers.

For the jam-filled petits fours: spread jam over the remaining portion of sponge squares and proceed as for the other petits fours. Make the glacé icing with some food colouring and use to coat the sponge squares. Decorate with glacé cherries and chopped pistachio nuts.

BLACKCURRANT PETITS FOURS

Makes about 20

15 g (2 oz) butter
65 g (2 oz) fresh
breadcrumbs
200 g (7 oz) blackcurrant
jam
A pinch of ground
cinnamon

A pinch of cloves
1 packet of wafers filled
with vanilla cream
300 g (10 oz) icing sugar
5 tablespoons cassis
liqueur
Glacé cherries to finish

Put the butter in a small pan and brown the breadcrumbs. Sieve the blackcurrant jam and mix with the breadcrumbs. Add the cinnamon and the cloves. Spread this mixture over the wafers (4 wafers for each petit four).

Combine the icing sugar with the liqueur to make a smooth icing. Use to coat the wafers and decorate with glacé cherries.

CHOCOLATE WAFER PETITS FOURS

Makes about 6

6 egg yolks
125 g (4 oz) caster sugar
140 g (4½ oz) chopped
hazelnuts

1 packet chocolate-filled
wafers
300 g (10 oz) icing sugar
2-3 spoons cocoa powder

Beat the egg yolks and sugar using an electric mixer until thick and frothy. Add the hazelnuts. Spread this hazelnut cream over the wafers (5 wafers to each petit four).

Combine the icing sugar, cocoa powder and 4-5 spoons water to make the chocolate icing. Use to coat the wafers. Decorate with hazelnuts.

Opposite: *Blackcurrant, chocolate wafer and orange petits fours*

ALMOND PRALINES

Makes about 40

50 g (2 oz) raisins
3 tablespoons rum
200 g (7 oz) bitter
chocolate
50 g (2 oz) glacé cherries
25 g (1 oz) desiccated

coconut
500 g (1 lb) ground
almonds
2 tablespoons icing sugar
1 egg
1 egg yolk

Soak the raisins in the rum overnight.
Break the chocolate into a bowl and place over a pan of
hot water to melt. When melted, spread over a baking
sheet lined with greaseproof paper, smoothing the
chocolate out evenly with a spatula. Place in a
refrigerator to set.

Drain the raisins. Chop the glacé cherries. Put both
ingredients in a bowl and add the coconut, ground
almonds and icing sugar. Beat the whole egg and the
egg yolk. Add to the mixture.

Remove the chocolate from the refrigerator. Spread the
mixture over the chocolate, pressing it down well. Bake
in a preheated oven at 150° C (300° F, Gas Mark 2) for
15 minutes. Leave to cool for 2 hours.

When set, remove from the baking sheet. Peel off the
greaseproof paper and cut into squares, diamonds or
other shapes.

Suggestion: the chocolates can be decorated with glacé
cherries and icing sugar. They go perfectly with a cup of
coffee.

SUGAR PUFFS

Serves 5-6

100 g (3½ oz) plain flour
A pinch of salt
3 eggs, separated

300 g (10 oz) granulated
sugar
7 g (4 oz) butter

Sift the flour and salt into a bowl. In a separate bowl,
beat the egg yolks (reserve the whites) until thick and
creamy.

In a separate bowl, whisk the egg whites into stiff peaks
with 150 g (5 oz) sugar. Mix the flour with the remaining
sugar. Gradually add the egg yolks, a little at a time.
Gently fold the egg whites into this mixture.

Transfer the mixture to a piping bag fitted with a wide
nozzle. Pipe 3 cm (1¼ in) strips or whirls on to a buttered
baking sheet.

Bake in a preheated oven at 180° C (350° F, Gas Mark 4)
for 15 minutes. Leave to cool in the oven so that the puffs
do not sink. Remove from the baking sheet with a
spatula.

Suggestion: serve with a cup of coffee or after-dinner
liqueurs instead of petits fours.

ORANGE CREAM CORNETS

Serves 10-12

1 litre (1w pints) double
cream
3 oranges
165 g (5½ oz) icing sugar
24 small ice-cream cones

100 ml (3½ fl oz)
Cointreau
150 g (5 oz) candied
orange peel
3 kiwi fruits

Pour the cream into a bowl and place in a refrigerator
with the beaters of an electric mixer for 1 hour. Wash
and dry the oranges and grate the rind finely. Then
squeeze the oranges, strain the juice and reserve
200 ml (7 fl oz) juice. Whip the chilled cream until firm.
Sprinkle over and incorporate the icing sugar, then the
orange juice and rind. Return the mixture to the
refrigerator for 4 hours.

Soak the chopped candied orange peel in the Cointreau.
Fill an icing bag fitted with a fluted nozzle with the
orange cream and fill the ice-cream cones.
Peel the kiwi fruits and chop into little triangles.
Decorate the orange cream cornets with the chopped
candied orange peel and the chopped kiwi fruits. Serve
immediately.

ORANGE PETITS FOURS

Makes about 30

500 g (1 lb) cottage cheese
5 spoons shredless orange marmalade
225 ml (7½ fl oz) freshly squeezed orange juice
100 ml (3½ fl oz) orange liqueur

2 pinches of saffron
1 packet orange-flavoured biscuits or wafers
400 g (13 oz) icing sugar
Some chopped candied orange peel to finish

Combine the cottage cheese, marmalade, 150 ml (¼ pint) orange juice and 3 tablespoons liqueur together with a pinch of saffron, using an electric mixer. Spread this cream mixture over the biscuits (6 biscuits for each petit four). Coat the top and the sides with the cream.

Combine the icing sugar, the remaining juice and orange liqueur and another pinch of saffron to make the icing. Use to coat the petits fours and decorate with the chopped candied orange peel.

COCONUT CANDIES

Makes about 30

200 g (7 oz) desiccated coconut
125 g (4 oz) soft brown sugar

2 teaspoons honey
2 teaspoons oil
1 egg white

Combine the coconut, sugar and honey in a bowl. Heat over a pan of hot water, stirring constantly until the coconut becomes transparent. Beat the egg white until frothy. Add to the bowl and cook the mixture for 10 minutes.

Remove from the heat as soon as the mixture becomes sticky and pour on to a baking sheet in an even layer. Leave to cool.

Roll the mixture into little balls and place them on a baking sheet lined with oiled greaseproof paper. Bake in a preheated oven at 150° C (300° F, Gas Mark 2) for 10 minutes.

Remove the coconut candies as soon as they start to turn golden and place on a wire rack to cool

Above: *Hazelnut marzipans, Marzipan brandy truffles, Pineapple almond crisps*

HAZELNUT MARZIPANS

Makes 15-20 marzipans

200 g (7 oz) marzipan
1 spoon icing sugar
1 spoon hazelnut liqueur
40 g (12 oz) ground,
roasted hazelnuts

75 g (3 oz) milk superfine
cooking chocolate
75 g (3 oz) plain superfine
cooking chocolate
Whole hazelnuts to finish

Knead the marzipan with the icing sugar, liqueur and ground hazelnuts. Roll out until 1 cm (½ in) thick and cut into small rectangles.

Melt the milk and plain chocolate in separate bowls over pans of hot water, stirring until smooth and creamy. Coat half the marzipans in the milk chocolate and the other half in the plain chocolate. Coat the hazelnuts in the plain chocolate and arrange them on the milk chocolate marzipans.
Drizzle the remaining milk chocolate over the plain chocolate marzipans.

MARZIPAN BRANDY TRUFFLES

Makes 15-20

200 g (7 oz) marzipan
1 spoon icing sugar
40 g (1½ oz) plain
chocolate, melted

2 spoons brandy
75 g (3 oz) milk chocolate
75 g (3 oz) plain chocolate

Knead the marzipan with the icing sugar, melted chocolate and brandy. Roll out until 1 cm (½ in) thick and cut into various shapes.

Melt the milk chocolate and the plain chocolate in separate bowls over pans of hot water, stirring well until smooth and creamy. Coat half the truffles in the milk chocolate and half in the plain chocolate.

PINEAPPLE ALMOND CRISPS

Makes 15-20

200 g (7 oz) milk chocolate
200 g (7 oz) nut brittle
25 g (1 oz) plain

chocolate, melted
65 g (2½ oz) glacé
pineapple

Melt the milk chocolate in a bowl over a pan of hot water, stirring well until smooth and creamy. Add the nut brittle and mix well. Arrange the chocolate mixture in small mounds on a sheet of greaseproof paper. Coat the chocolates in the plain chocolate and decorate with small chunks of glacé pineapple.

ALMOND CHIP TRUFFLES

Makes 15-20 truffles

125 g (4 oz) butter
1 spoon icing sugar
1 tablespoon glucose
250 g (8 oz) plain
chocolate
5 tablespoons almond

liqueur
Roasted flaked almonds
Milk superfine cooking
chocolate
White chocolate curls

Cream the butter, icing sugar and glucose in a bowl. Melt the chocolate in a bowl over a pan of hot water, stirring constantly. Leave to cool slightly (the chocolate must be cold but must not have set). Add the almond liqueur and incorporate the butter. Transfer the truffle mixture to an icing bag fitted with a round nozzle and pipe little mounds on a sheet of greaseproof paper. Stick the flaked almonds into the truffles and place in a refrigerator.

Melt the milk superfine cooking chocolate in a bowl over a pan of hot water. Use to coat the truffles and decorate them with white chocolate curls

You can use an electric mixer to make the almond chip truffles.

When the flaked almonds have been applied, the truffles are coated in milk chocolate.

HAZELNUT PRALINES

Makes about 30

125 ml (4 fl oz) double cream
250 g (8 oz) plain chocolate

150 g (5 oz) hazelnut praline
25 g (1 oz) peanut butter
15 g (2 oz) icing sugar

Bring the cream to the boil, add the chocolate, chopped into small pieces, remove from the heat and stir constantly until melted. Incorporate the praline and peanut butter. Place the bowl in a pan of cold water and beat the ingredients using an electric mixer until they have cooled completely (photograph no. 1)

Place the hazelnut chocolate mixture in an icing bag fitted with a fluted nozzle and pipe into small paper cases (photograph no. 2). Dredge with icing sugar.

Above: *making the caramel for the Almond caramels*

1

2

ALMOND CARAMELS

Makes 20-30

165 g (5½ oz) caster sugar
15 g (2 oz) butter
3 tablespoons double cream
75 g (3 oz) marzipan

75 g (3 oz) chopped almonds
Milk superfine cooking chocolate
Cocoa powder

Put the sugar in a small pan and melt it over a low heat, stirring constantly until it browns. Remove from the heat and add the butter and cream, reheat, stirring constantly. Incorporate the marzipan and chopped almonds. Roll out until 1 cm (½ in) thick and place on a greased baking sheet. Cut into rectangles measuring 1 x 3 cm (½ x 1¼ in).

Melt the cooking chocolate in a bowl over a pan of hot water, stirring constantly. Use to coat the caramels, then dredge them with cocoa powder.

Page 222: *Hazelnut pralines, Almond chip truffles (recipe on page 221), Almond caramels*
Left: *Hazelnut pralines*

GINGER CARAMELS

Makes about 50

250 g (8 oz) caster sugar
200 g (7 oz) honey
100 g (3½ oz) butter,
softened
125 g (4 oz) flaked
almonds

75-100 g (3-3½ oz)
crystallized ginger,
chopped
100 g (3½ oz) plain
superfine cooking
chocolate

Melt the sugar in a pan, add the honey and the butter, stirring constantly until it forms a smooth, thick syrup. Add the flaked almonds and the ginger, bring to the boil, stirring constantly. Using a spatula, spread the mixture 1-2 cm (½-¾ in) thick on to a greased baking sheet. Leave to cool and then cut into small diamonds, triangles or squares.
Place in a refrigerator.

Melt the cooking chocolate in a bowl over a pan of hot water, stirring constantly, and use to coat the sweets.

Arrange them on a sheet of greaseproof paper and leave to set.
Store them in an airtight container.

PRALINE CRISPS

25 g (1 oz) butter
65 g (2½ oz) caster sugar
125 g (4 oz) ground
almonds

100 g (3½ oz) chocolate
5 tablespoons double
cream

Heat the butter and sugar in a pan until the mixture turns light brown. Then add the ground almonds. Keep on the heat, stirring constantly, until the praline browns. Spread this mixture over a baking sheet using a rolling pin. Leave to cool and then cut into small pieces.

Melt the chocolate with the double cream in a bowl over a pan of hot water. Leave to cool, then use to coat the pralines. Arrange them on a sheet of aluminium foil and leave to set in a refrigerator.

Wrap the praline crisps in cellophane paper or keep them in a glass or china pot. Store in a refrigerator.

FRUIT BALLS

Makes about 100

250 g (8 oz) dates
250 g (8 oz) dried prunes
250 g (8 oz) dried apricots
Grated rind of 1 lemon

2 tablespoons honey
75 g (3 oz) ground
walnuts, hazelnuts or
almonds

Remove the stones from the dates, prunes and dried apricots. Chop them coarsely. Add the lemon rind and honey. Mix well. Wet the hands and shape the mixture into little balls. Roll them in the ground walnuts, hazelnuts or almonds.

MINIATURE MOZARTKUGELN

200 g (7 oz) hazelnut
chocolate spread
200 g (7 oz) almond paste
2 tablespoons kirsch
15 g (2 oz) chopped

pistachio nuts
125 g (4 oz) icing sugar
100 g (3½ oz) plain
superfine cooking
chocolate

Chill the hazelnut chocolate spread, roll it into balls and return to the refrigerator.
Combine the almond paste, kirsch and pistachio nuts. Add the icing sugar and knead. Make a 2 cm (¾ in) thick roll of marzipan. Cut it into as many slices as there are balls of hazelnut chocolate spread. Roll them out on a baking sheet dusted with icing sugar.

Wrap the chocolate hazelnut balls in the marzipan, sealing the edges well.

Melt the chocolate in a bowl over a pan of hot water. Use to coat the marzipan balls and leave them to dry on a plate or on a sheet of greaseproof paper. Turn them regularly so that they do not lose their shape. When set, wrap them in cellophane or place them in a glass or china pot. Store in a refrigerator.

Opposite: *Miniature Mozartkugeln*

GENOESE SPONGES

227

LINZ CHERRY SPONGE

Serves 6

250 g (8 oz) butter
200 g (7 oz) caster sugar
1 sachet vanilla sugar
A pinch of salt
5 eggs
1 teaspoon ground
cinnamon
A pinch of nutmeg

250 g (8 oz) plain flour
1 teaspoon baking powder
150 g (5 oz) ground
almonds
750 g (12 lb) Morello
cherries in syrup, stones
removed
Icing sugar to finish

Cream the butter in a bowl, then add the sugar, vanilla sugar, salt, eggs, cinnamon and nutmeg. Sift the flour and baking powder into the mixture, add the ground almonds. Turn two-thirds of this mixture into a greased, deep, 28 cm (11 in) round cake tin. Smooth it out evenly.

Drain the cherries, arrange them over the mixture, pressing them down gently. Place spoonfuls of the remaining mixture over the cherries. Bake in a preheated oven at 180-200° C (350-400° F, Gas Mark 4-6) for about 1 hour. Remove from the oven and leave to cool. Take the cake out of the tin and dredge with icing sugar.

MARBLE CAKE

Serves 8

375 g (1½ oz) butter
275 g (9 oz) caster sugar
1 sachet vanilla sugar
A pinch of salt
5 eggs
2 tablespoons rum or
brandy
375 g (1½ oz) plain flour

32 teaspoons baking
powder
50 g (2 oz) bitter chocolate
15 g (½ oz) cocoa powder
50 g (2 oz) ground
almonds
4-5 tablespoons milk
Icing sugar to finish

Cream the butter in a bowl, then add 250 g (8 oz) sugar, the vanilla sugar, salt, eggs and rum or brandy. Sift the flour and baking powder into a separate bowl and gradually add to the butter mixture. Turn two-thirds of this mixture into a fluted ring mould.

Grate the chocolate. Mix it with the cocoa powder, the remaining sugar, the ground almonds and milk. Add this chocolate mixture to the remaining sponge mixture and spread over the mixture in the mould. Create a marbling effect by making spiral movements in the mixture with a fork. Bake in a preheated oven at 160-180° C (325-350° F,

Gas Mark 3-4) for about 1 hour. Leave to cool, remove from the mould and dredge with icing sugar.

DUTCH APRICOT COOKIES

Serves about 4-6

325 g (11 oz) butter
100 g (3½ oz) icing sugar
1 sachet vanilla sugar
2 eggs
A pinch of salt

Grated rind of 1 lemon
400 g (13 oz) plain flour
1 teaspoon baking powder
6 tablespoons apricot jam
100 g (3½ oz) chocolate

Cream 300 g (10 oz) butter in a bowl, then add the icing sugar, vanilla sugar, eggs, salt and grated lemon rind. Transfer this mixture to an icing bag fitted with a broad, fluted nozzle. Pipe flattened 'S' shapes on to a greased baking sheet. Bake in a preheated oven at 180-200° C (350-400° F, Gas Mark 4-6) for about 15 minutes. Leave the cookies to cool, then sandwich them together with apricot jam.

For the chocolate coating: melt the chocolate and the remaining butter in a bowl over a pan of hot water, stirring until smooth and creamy. Dunk the broadest edge of the cookies into the melted chocolate mixture.

Opposite: *Dutch apricot cookies*
Pages 226 and 227: *Linz cherry sponge*

ALMOND AND DAMSON DELIGHT

Serves 6

1-1.2 kg (2-3 lb) damsons
165 g (5½ oz) butter,
softened
100 g (3½ oz) almond
paste
140 g (4½ oz) caster sugar
A pinch of salt
3 eggs
2 teaspoons grated lemon
rind
225 g (7½ oz) plain flour

2 teaspoons baking
powder
2 tablespoons double
cream
50 g (2 oz) blanched
almonds
2 tablespoons honey
A pinch of ground
cinnamon
150 g (5 oz) whole
blanched almonds

Wash, drain and stone the damsons. Cream 100 g (3½ oz) butter in a bowl with the almond paste, then gradually add 75 g (3 oz) sugar, the salt, eggs and grated lemon rind. Combine the flour and baking powder, then gradually add them to the butter-almond mixture. Add the double cream.

Put the blanched almonds in a non-greased frying pan and toast, stirring constantly. Leave to cool, then break into small pieces by hand. Sprinkle over a greased, deep, 28 cm (11 in) round cake tin. Add the mixture and spread it out evenly. Add the halved damsons so that they overlap slightly.

For the almond butter mixture: put the remaining butter and sugar, the honey and cinnamon in a pan. Melt them, mixing well. Halve the whole blanched almonds and add them to the mixture. Heat for a moment longer. Pour this hot mixture over the damsons.

Below: *Almond and damson delight*

Bake in a preheated oven at 200° C (400° F, Gas Mark 6) for 40-45 minutes. Leave to cool.
Run a knife round the cake tin to loosen the cake and turn out of the tin on to a plate.

Suggestion: serve with slightly sweetened whipped cream, dredged with cocoa powder if desired.

ADVOCAT CREAM DELIGHT

Serves 6

150 g (5 oz) butter
100 g (3½ oz) caster sugar
2 eggs
100 g (3½ oz) plain flour
1 teaspoon baking powder
500 g (1 lb) gooseberries
(or stoned Morello
cherries) in syrup
1 sachet powdered
gelatine or 4 gelatine

leaves
1 packet caramel custard
mix
500 ml (18 fl oz) milk
250 ml (8 fl oz) advocat
250 ml (8 fl oz) double
cream
Crushed praline and
marzipan leaves to finish

Cream the butter in a bowl, then gradually add 50 g (2 oz) sugar and the eggs. Sift the flour and baking powder and incorporate into the mixture. Turn the mixture into a greased, deep, 28 cm (11 in) round cake tin. Smooth it out evenly.

Drain the fruits, spread them over the mixture. Bake in a preheated oven at 180-200° C (350-400° F, Gas Mark 4-6) for 25-30 minutes. Leave to cool, then turn out on to a plate. Place the side section of a springform cake tin around the tart.

For the cream topping: mix the gelatine with 3 tablespoons cold water. Leave to soak for 10 minutes. Make the caramel custard by adding the milk and the remaining sugar to the powder, following the instructions on the packet. Heat the gelatine until it becomes translucent. Incorporate it into the hot custard mixture. Mix carefully. Leave to cool, then add the liqueur as soon as the mixture starts to thicken.

Whip the double cream until it is very firm, then gently fold into the mixture. Spread this mixture over the sponge. Smooth it out evenly. Leave to set in a refrigerator.

When ready to serve, decorate the dessert with crushed praline and marzipan leaves.

Above: *Advocat cream delight*

Tip: you can buy ready-made marzipan leaves or make them yourself: mix 100 g (3½ oz) plain almond paste with 50 g (2 oz) icing sugar, then add some food colouring. Roll out this mixture and cut out leaves.

COTTAGE CAKE

Serves 6

200 g (7 oz) butter
100 g (3½ oz) caster sugar
1 sachet vanilla sugar
3 eggs
1 egg yolk
A pinch of salt
Grated rind of 2 orange
or 2 lemon
150 g (5 oz) plain flour
25 g (1 oz) cornflour
1 teaspoon baking powder
2 tablespoons orange
liqueur (Grand Marnier or

Cointreau) or 2
tablespoons lemon juice
50 g (2 oz) ground
almonds
Tubes of ready-made
coloured icing to finish
Sugar strands or
hundreds and thousands
to finish
Icing sugar
2 egg whites
Food colouring (optional)

Cream the butter in a bowl, then add first the sugar, followed by the vanilla sugar, the whole eggs, egg yolk, salt and grated lemon or orange rind. Sift the flour, cornflour and baking powder into a separate bowl and gently fold into the mixture. Add the liqueur or lemon juice, then the ground almonds. Mix well, then turn the mixture into a cake tin in the shape of a house. Smooth it out evenly.

Bake in a preheated oven at 150-180° C (300-350° F, Gas Mark 2-4) for about 65 minutes. Remove from the oven and wait at least 10 minutes before removing from the tin. Leave to cool. Decorate as you wish using glacé icing (white or coloured) and patterns and greetings piped on using tubes of ready-made coloured icing, for example.

For the icing: mix sufficient icing sugar with the egg whites to form a paste which is soft enough to be piped. Add food colouring if desired.

Suggestion: cover a low-sided, square-shaped box with green tissue paper. Fill the base with hundreds and thousands or sugar strands. Place the 'house' on top. Decorate with miniature holly branches and/or ears of corn or cover the base of the box with tissue paper and wrap it in cellophane and tie with a bow.

CHOCOLATE HEART

Serves 8

250 g (8 oz) butter
100 g (3½ oz) caster sugar
1 sachet vanilla sugar
2 eggs
A pinch of salt
125 g (4 oz) plain flour
25 g (1 oz) cornflour
1 teaspoon baking powder
200 g (7 oz) chocolate

50 g (2 oz) almond paste
25 g (1 oz) icing sugar
1 tablespoon jam
1 packet vanilla
blancmange mix
400 ml (14 fl oz) milk
Chocolate flakes, sugar
flowers or silver balls to
decorate

Cream 75 g (3 oz) butter in a bowl, then incorporate first the sugar, then 1 sachet vanilla sugar, the eggs and salt.

Sift the flour, cornflour and baking powder into a separate bowl and gradually add to the creamed butter. Turn the mixture into a greased, heart-shaped cake tin. Bake in a preheated oven at 180-200° C (350-400° F, Gas Mark 4-6) for about 30 minutes. Leave to cool, then cut into three equal layers.

For the chocolate coating: break 100 g (3½ oz) chocolate into pieces and put in a bowl over a pan of hot water, together with 25 g (1
) butter. Melt, stirring constantly. Spread this mixture over the top layer of sponge. Place on one side.

For the filling: mix the almond paste with the icing sugar in a mixing bowl. Roll it out and cut out a heart the same size as the sponge. Spread the jam over the middle layer of sponge, then cover with the almond paste heart. Press down gently.

Left: *Cottage cake*

Above: *Chocolate heart*

For the confectioner's custard: sprinkle the vanilla blancmange mixture into the milk, following the instructions on the packet. Leave to cool. Cream the remaining butter. Gradually incorporate the vanilla blancmange mixture. Transfer 2 tablespoons of this mixture to an icing bag.

Cover the bottom layer of sponge with one-third of the vanilla cream. Place the middle layer of sponge, which has already been covered with jam and almond paste, on

top. Cover with the remaining confectioner's custard, then place the chocolate-covered sponge layer on top. Coat the sides of the cake with the remaining custard mixture.

Grate the remaining chocolate and sprinkle over the sides of the cake. Decorate the top of the cake with the custard mixture in the icing bag.
Sprinkle with chocolate flakes and sugar flowers and silver balls.

FRUIT LOAF

Serves 6

100 g (3½ oz) dried apricots
100 g (3½ oz) candied mixed peel
100 g (3½ oz) sultanas
100 g (3½ oz) currants
50 g (2 oz) flaked almonds
125 ml (4 fl oz) rum
200 g (7 oz) butter
125 g (4 oz) soft brown sugar
1 sachet vanilla sugar
A pinch of salt
4 eggs
1 teaspoon ground coriander
A pinch of ground nutmeg
A pinch of ground cinnamon
200 g (7 oz) plain flour
2 teaspoons baking powder
50 g (2 oz) ground hazelnuts
3 tablespoons apricot jam

Finely chop the apricots and mixed peel. Place in a bowl with the sultanas, currants and flaked almonds. Sprinkle with the rum (reserve 3 tablespoons) and leave to soak overnight.

For the sponge: cream the butter in a bowl, then add first the brown sugar, followed by the vanilla sugar, salt, eggs, coriander, nutmeg and cinnamon.

Sift the flour and baking powder into a separate bowl, then gradually incorporate into the mixture. Add the soaked fruits and the ground hazelnuts and mix well.

Turn the mixture into a greased loaf tin. Smooth it out evenly. Bake in a preheated oven at 150-180° C (300-350° F, Gas Mark 2-4) for about 1½ hours.

For the coating: sieve the apricot jam and thin it down with the reserved rum. Bring to the boil, then brush over the cake as soon as it is out of the oven.

PEACH BAKE

Serves 6-8

200 g (7 oz) butter
250 g (8 oz) caster sugar
2 sachets vanilla sugar
A pinch of salt
3 eggs
Grated rind of 1 lemon
1 tablespoon rum
2 teaspoon ground cinnamon or coriander
350 g (11½ oz) plain flour
75 g (3 oz) cornflour
32 teaspoons baking powder
1 kg (2 lb) tinned peach halves in syrup
100 g (3½ oz) raisins
50 g (2 oz) flaked almonds
2-3 tablespoons apricot jam

Cream the butter in a bowl, then add 150 g (5 oz) sugar, 1 sachet vanilla sugar, the salt, 1 egg, half the lemon rind, the rum and cinnamon or coriander.

Sift 300 g (10 oz) flour, 50 g (2 oz) cornflour and 3 teaspoons baking powder into a separate bowl, then gradually incorporate into the mixture. Spread the mixture over a greased baking sheet. Bake in a preheated oven at 200° C (400° F, Gas Mark 6) for about 15 minutes.

Drain the peach halves, then arrange them in rows on the sponge layer. Sprinkle raisins and flaked almonds on the spaces between the peaches.

Beat the remaining eggs with 2-3 tablespoons hot water using an electric mixer for about 1 minute until thick and creamy. Continue beating and gradually incorporate the remaining sugar, vanilla sugar and lemon rind. Continue beating for a further 2 minutes.

Combine the remaining flour, cornflour and baking powder.
Sift half of this mixture over the egg mixture and incorporate gently using the mixer at slow speed. Then sift the remaining flour mixture and incorporate in the same way.

Pour this mixture between the peaches. Return the baking sheet to the oven and bake at the same temperature for about 15 minutes, until cooked to your liking.

Heat the sieved apricot jam and brush over the peaches as soon as they are out of the oven.

Opposite: *Peach bake*

CHOCOLATE CHERRY TORTE

Serves 6-7

100 g (3½ oz) butter
125 g (4 oz) caster sugar
12 sachets vanilla sugar
4 eggs
A pinch of salt
100 g (3½ oz) ground hazelnuts
100 g (3½ oz) grated chocolate
125 g (4 oz) plain flour
1 teaspoon baking powder
About 450 g (15 oz) tinned stoned cherries in syrup
1 packet jelly glaze mix
250 ml (8 fl oz) double cream

Cream the butter in a bowl, then gradually add 100 g (3½ oz) sugar, 1 sachet vanilla sugar, the eggs, salt, ground hazelnuts and grated chocolate.

Sift the flour and baking powder into a separate bowl, then gradually add to the butter mixture. Turn this mixture into a deep, 28 cm (11 in) round cake tin. Smooth it out evenly.

Drain the cherries, reserving the syrup. Arrange them over the sponge mixture, pressing them down gently.

Bake in a preheated oven at 180-200° C (350-400° F, Gas Mark 4-6) for about 30 minutes. Remove from the tin and leave to cool.

For the glaze: combine the packet of glaze mix with 1 tablespoon sugar and the syrup from the cherries and make according to the instructions on the packet. Pour over the cake and leave to cool.

Whip the cream for about 30 seconds using an electric mixer. Add the remaining sugar and vanilla sugar, then continue beating until the cream is very firm. Spread in an even layer over the cake or transfer to an icing bag and pipe a lattice pattern.

Below: *Chocolate cherry torte*
Opposite, top: *Hazelnut Swiss roll*

HAZELNUT SWISS ROLL

Serves 6

0 g (3½ oz) butter, oftened	1 teaspoon baking powder
5 g (3 oz) caster sugar	300 g (10 oz) pineapple jam
sachet vanilla sugar	100 g (3½ oz) chopped hazelnuts
eggs, separated	100 g (3½ oz) superfine cooking chocolate
4 tablespoons rum	
5 g (3 oz) plain flour	

ream 75 g (3 oz) butter in a bowl, then add 65 g ½ oz) sugar, the vanilla sugar, egg yolks and tablespoons rum. Whisk the egg whites into peaks, then gently fold into the mixture. Sift the flour and baking powder into a separate bowl, then gradually incorporate into the mixture using an electric mixer. Turn this mixture on to a greased and lined baking sheet measuring about 32 x 32 cm (12¾ x 12¾ in). Bake in a preheated oven at 180-200° C (350-400° F, Gas Mark 4-6) for 12-15 minutes. Turn out of the tin immediately on to greaseproof paper dredged with the remaining sugar.

For the filling: mix the pineapple jam with the remaining tablespoons rum. Spread over the hot sponge. Sprinkle with chopped hazelnuts and roll up immediately using the greaseproof paper.

Above: *Chocolate hedgehogs*

For the icing: place the chocolate and the remaining
butter in a bowl over a pan of hot water. Melt, stirring
until smooth and creamy. Use to coat the Swiss roll.
Cut the sponge into diagonal slices as soon as the icing
begins to set.

CHOCOLATE HEDGEHOGS AND BIRTHDAY CAKE HEART

Serves 4

175 g (6 oz) butter
75 g (3 oz) caster sugar
1 sachet vanilla sugar
3 eggs
A pinch of salt
75 g (3 oz) ground hazelnuts
325 g (11 oz) bitter chocolate
75 g (3 oz) plain flour
50 g (2 oz) cornflour

2 teaspoons baking powder
15 g (½ oz) cocoa powder
Some currants to finish
50 g (2 oz) almonds cut into slivers
Sugar flowers to finish
1-2 tablespoons icing sugar
1 egg white

Cream 125 g (4 oz) butter in a bowl, then add first the sugar and vanilla sugar, followed by the eggs, salt and ground hazelnuts. Grate 100 g (3½ oz) chocolate and add to the mixture.

Sift the flour, cornflour and baking powder into a separate bowl, then gradually incorporate into the mixture.
Shape the dough into one large ball and 5-6 small ones and place on a greased baking sheet, or turn the mixture into a heart-shaped cake tin and smooth it out evenly.
Bake in a preheated oven at 150-180° C (300-350° F, Gas Mark 2-4) for the following times: about 1 hour for the large hedgehog, 30 minutes for the small ones or 50 minutes for the heart.

For the hedgehogs: melt 125 g (4 oz) chocolate and 25 g (1 oz) butter in a bowl over a pan of hot water, stirring until smooth and creamy. Spread over the hedgehog-shaped balls of dough. Add currants for the eyes and nose. Prick the hedgehogs with a cocktail stick and insert the slivered almonds into the holes.

For the heart: melt the remaining chocolate and butter in a bowl over a pan of hot water, stirring well. Use to coat the heart. Decorate with sugar flowers.
Beat the icing sugar and egg white until smooth. Transfer to an icing bag and decorate the cake with patterns or greetings.

Suggestion: if you wish to make a gift of the cake heart, present it on a gold or silver cake base or on the upturned cake tin, and attach the handwritten recipe to the cake tin with sticky tape. Wrap the cake up carefully in gift-wrap or cellophane tied with a red ribbon.

Right: *Chocolate ginger cake*

CHOCOLATE GINGER CAKE

Serves 8

100 g (3½ oz) almond paste
125 g (4 oz) caster sugar
3 eggs, separated
A pinch of salt
2 teaspoons ground cinnamon
2 teaspoon ground cloves
1 teaspoon grated lemon rind

200 g (7 oz) walnuts
200 g (7 oz) crystallized ginger
3 tablespoons rum
100 g (3½ oz) rye flour
1 teaspoon baking powder
250 g (8 oz) milk superfine cooking chocolate
100 g (3½ oz) redcurrant jelly

Cream the almond paste, sugar and egg yolks in a bowl. Add the salt, cinnamon, cloves and grated lemon rind. Chop the walnut halves coarsely, then dice the crystallized ginger.
Mix these two ingredients together well and sprinkle with the rum.

Sift the flour and baking powder into a separate bowl. Incorporate into the almond paste mixture, add the chopped walnuts and the diced ginger (reserve about 20 pieces of each for decoration).

Melt 100 g (3½ oz) chocolate in a bowl over a pan of hot water. Whisk the egg whites into stiff peaks. Fold these two ingredients into the mixture. Turn it into a greased ring mould. Smooth it out evenly.
Bake in a preheated oven at 180° C (350° F, Gas Mark 4) for 40-45 minutes.

Turn the mould upside down on to a wire rack. Leave for at least 5 minutes before removing the mould.

For the coating: spread the redcurrant jelly over the cake while still hot. Leave to cool.

For the icing: melt the remaining chocolate in a bowl over a pan of hot water, stirring until smooth and creamy. Use to cover the cake.

Before the icing sets, decorate the cake, arranging the reserved walnut halves and ginger pieces alternately

RHUBARB MERINGUE TART

Serves 7-8

250 g (8 oz) butter	250 g (8 oz) plain flour
250 g (8 oz) caster sugar	1 teaspoon baking powder
1 sachet vanilla sugar	1.5 kg (32 lb) rhubarb
1 egg	3 egg whites

Cream the butter, then add 100 g (3½ oz) sugar, the vanilla sugar and egg. Sift the flour and baking powder into a separate bowl, then incorporate them into the mixture. Spread this mixture over a greased baking sheet. If necessary, place lengths of lightly crushed aluminium foil around the edges of the mixture.

Below: *Rhubarb meringue tart*

For the filling: wash the rhubarb. Do not peel it. Cut it into chunks about 3-4 cm (1½-1½ in) long. Arrange them over the mixture. Bake in a preheated oven at 180-200° C (350-400° F, Gas Mark 4-6) for about 25 minutes.

For the meringue: whisk egg whites into very firm peaks, so stiff that a lasting mark is left when cut with a knife.
Using an electric mixer, gradually add the remaining sugar. Transfer the mixture to an icing bag.
Remove the tart from the oven after 25 minutes. Pipe a lattice pattern of meringue. Return to the top shelf of the oven, preheated to 200-220° C (400-425° F, Gas Mark 6-7), for about 8 minutes, until the meringue is golden.

ICED MADEIRA

Serves 6-8

270 g (9 oz) butter
200 g (7 oz) caster sugar
1 sachet vanilla sugar
4 eggs
A pinch of salt
A few drops of lemon or

rum essence
125 g (4 oz) plain flour
125 g (4 oz) cornflour
2 teaspoon baking powder
100 g (3½ oz) chocolate

Melt 250 g (8 oz) butter in a pan, leave to cool. When the butter starts to congeal, incorporate the sugar and vanilla sugar. Add the eggs one at a time, beating for about 2 minutes each time. Add the salt and lemon or rum essence.

Sift the flour, cornflour and baking powder into a separate bowl, then gradually add to the mixture. Turn the mixture into a greased and lined loaf tin measuring 30 x 11 cm (12 x 4½ in). Bake in a preheated oven at 160-185° c (325-350° F, Gas Mark 3-4) for 65-75 minutes. Leave to cool.

For the chocolate icing: melt the remaining chocolate and the remaining butter in a bowl over a pan of hot water, stirring until smooth and creamy. Use to coat the cake.

Above: *Iced Madeira*

MADEIRA SURPRISE

Serves 6

250 g (8 oz) butter
225 g (7½ oz) granulated sugar
1 sachet vanilla sugar
A pinch of salt
4 eggs
125 g (4 oz) plain flour
125 g (4 oz) cornflour
1 teaspoon baking powder
2 tablespoons rum
50 g (2 oz) ground almonds
1-2 tablespoons orange liqueur

25 g (1 oz) grated chocolate
2 tablespoon cocoa powder
1 tablespoon milk
50 g (2 oz) ground hazelnuts
A pinch of cinnamon
25 g (1 oz) chopped candied orange peel
Grated rind of 2 orange
1 tablespoon brandy
Icing sugar to finish

Melt the butter in a pan, leave to cool. When it starts to congeal, add 200 g (7 oz) sugar, the vanilla sugar, salt and eggs. Sift the flour, cornflour and baking powder into a separate bowl, then incorporate them into the mixture. Add 1 tablespoon rum.

Divide the mixture into four portions. Incorporate the ground almonds and orange liqueur in the first portion. Add the grated chocolate, cocoa powder, the remaining sugar and the milk to the second. Add the ground hazelnuts, cinnamon and the remaining rum to the third. Add the candied peel, orange rind and brandy to the final quarter of the mixture.

Pour the mixtures one on top of the other into a greased and lined loaf tin. Bake in a preheated oven at 180° C (350° F, Gas Mark 4) for 70 minutes.

Leave to cool and dredge with icing sugar.

MANDARIN GÂTEAU

Serves about 8

200 g (7 oz) bitter chocolate
200 g (7 oz) butter, softened
200 g (7 oz) caster sugar
3 eggs
5 egg yolks
250 g (8 oz) plain flour
2 teaspoons baking powder
1 tablespoon cocoa powder

5 egg whites
2 tablespoons orange marmalade
475 g (15½ oz) mandarin segments
600 ml (1 pint) double cream
1 teaspoon vanilla sugar
7-9 tablespoons orange liqueur (Cointreau or Grand Marnier)

Break the chocolate into pieces and put in a bowl over a pan of hot water. Melt, stirring until smooth and creamy. Leave to cool slightly. Cream the butter, incorporate the melted chocolate, then 100 g (3½ oz) sugar, the eggs and egg yolks.

Sift the flour, baking powder and cocoa powder into a separate bowl and gradually incorporate into the mixture. Whisk the egg whites into stiff peaks, then gradually add 75 g (3 oz) sugar, beating constantly. Gently fold into the mixture.

Spread over a greased and lined baking sheet. Fold the edges of the paper up if necessary to stop the mixture from running.

Bake in a preheated oven at 180-200° C

(350-400° F, Gas Mark 4-6) for about 15 minutes. Remove from the oven and turn out immediately on to greaseproof paper dredged with 2 teaspoons sugar. Leave to cool. Cut into two layers. Spread the marmalade over the bottom layer.

For the filling: peel the mandarins and cut into slices. Arrange them over the jam. Keep some for decoration. Whip the double cream, then add the remaining sugar, the vanilla sugar and 5-6 tablespoons orange liqueur.

Cover the mandarins with half of the whipped cream. Spread it out evenly. Cover with the top layer of sponge and sprinkle with the remaining orange liqueur. Cover with the remaining whipped cream.

Make parallel grooves in the cream using a knife. Add the remaining mandarin slices.

Chill for several hours before serving.

RHUBARB TART

Serves 6

125 g (4 oz) butter
150 g (5 oz) caster sugar
1 sachet vanilla sugar
1 egg
A pinch of salt
Grated rind of 2 lemon
125 g (4 oz) plain flour
1 teaspoon baking powder
100 g (3½ oz) ground

almonds
500-700 g (1 lb-1 lb 6 oz)
rhubarb, peeled
2 teaspoon ground
cinnamon
200 ml (7 fl oz) double
cream
3 egg yolks
3 egg whites

Cream the butter in a bowl, then gradually add 75 g (3 oz) sugar, the vanilla sugar, 1 egg, the salt and grated lemon rind.
Mix the flour and baking powder. Gradually add the ground almonds. Add to the creamed mixture. Turn this mixture into a well-greased 28 cm (11 in) round pie dish or cake tin. Spread it out evenly.

Wash the rhubarb and cut it into small pieces. Arrange them over the mixture. Bake in a preheated oven at 180-200° C (350-400° F, Gas Mark 4-6) for 60-65 minutes.

For the topping: in a bowl, beat the egg yolks and the remaining sugar until creamy. Add the cinnamon and double cream. Whisk the egg whites into stiff peaks and gently fold into the egg-yolk mixture. When the cake has been in the oven for 45 minutes, remove it and top with this mixture. Return it to the oven for the remaining 15-20 minutes.

TEATIME TREATS

Makes 20-25

200 g (7 oz) honey
100 g (3½ oz) butter
125 g (4 oz) caster sugar
2 eggs
20 g (¾ oz) cocoa powder
2 teaspoon ground
cinnamon
2 teaspoon ground cloves
1 teaspoon ground ginger
2 drops almond essence
375 g (1½ oz) plain flour

2 teaspoons baking
powder
65 g (2½ oz) crystallized
ginger
50 g (2 oz) plain chocolate
50 g (2 oz) raisins
200 g (7 oz) icing sugar
2-3 tablespoons cocoa
powder
Whole, chopped or flaked
almonds to finish

Melt the honey, butter and sugar in a pan over low heat. Gradually add the eggs, cocoa, cinnamon, cloves, ginger

and almond essence. Sift the flour and baking powder into a separate bowl, then gradually incorporate into the mixture.

Chop the crystallized ginger, break the chocolate into very small pieces and add them, together with the raisins, to the mixture while still over the heat.
Spread this mixture about 5 mm (½ in) thick over a greased baking sheet.

Bake in a preheated oven at 180-200° C (350-400° F, Gas Mark 4-6) for 25-30 minutes. Cut the cake into small squares or triangles.

For the icing: mix the icing sugar and cocoa powder with 2-3 tablespoons very hot water, beating until thick and creamy. Spread the icing over the cakes and sprinkle with the nuts before it sets. Press them in slightly so that they stick.

Opposite: Rhubarb tart

CHERRY RING

Serves 6-8

1 kg (2 lb) Morello cherries (or other sour cherries)
6 sponge fingers
225 g (7½ oz) butter, softened
4 eggs
200 g (7 oz) caster sugar
A pinch salt
Grated rind of 2 lemons
300 g (10 oz) plain flour
100 g (3½ oz) cornflour
2 teaspoons baking powder
100 g (3½ oz) semolina
3 tablespoons double cream
250 g (8 oz) icing sugar
1 egg white
3 tablespoons kirsch
100 g (3½ oz) almonds, cut into slivers

Wash, drain and stone the cherries. Crush the sponge fingers finely. Sift. Grease a savarin ring mould with 25 g (1 oz) softened butter. Dredge with 3 tablespoons crushed sponge fingers.

For the sponge mixture: cream the remaining butter in a bowl, then gradually add the eggs, the sugar, salt and grated lemon rind.
Sift the flour, cornflour and semolina into a separate bowl. Incorporate into the mixture, adding the cream.

Place one-third of the mixture in the mould. Spread it out evenly. Coat the cherries in the remaining crushed sponge fingers and arrange half of them over the sponge mixture.

Below: *Cherry ring*

Above: *Apricot cream torte*

Turn the second third of the mixture into the mould. Add the remaining cherries and cover with the remaining mixture. Bake in a preheated oven at 180° C (350° F, Gas Mark 4) for about 1 hour.

Place the cake upside down, still in the mould, on a wire rack. Leave for 10 minutes, then remove from the mould and leave to cool.

For the icing: combine the icing sugar with the egg white and the kirsch. Spread over the cake. Place the almonds in an un-greased frying pan and roast until golden, stirring constantly. Sprinkle over the icing.

APRICOT CREAM TORTE
Serves 6-8

350 g (11½ oz) butter
5-6 eggs
250 g (8 oz) caster sugar
1 sachet vanilla sugar
4-5 tablespoons brandy or
orange liqueur (Cointreau
or Grand Marnier)
350 g (11½ oz) plain flour

3 teaspoons baking
powder
2 tablespoons apricot jam
125 g (4 oz) icing sugar
2 tablespoons lemon juice
Whipped cream
Apricot strips to finish

Cream the butter, then incorporate the eggs, sugar, vanilla sugar and 2 tablespoons brandy or orange liqueur. Combine the flour and baking powder and gradually add to the mixture. Turn the mixture into a fluted, 26 cm (10½ in) round cake tin. Bake in a preheated oven at 180-200° C (350-400° F, Gas Mark 4-6) for 40-45 minutes.

For the icing: sieve the apricot jam and heat with the remaining brandy or orange liqueur and use to coat the cake. Leave to cool, then mix in the icing sugar and lemon juice, beating until smooth and creamy. Cover the cake. Transfer the whipped cream to an icing bag and decorate the rim of the cake. Decorate with apricot strips.

Above: *Coffee Madeleines*

COFFEE MADELEINES

Makes 16

*200 g (7 oz) butter,
softened
150 g (5 oz) caster sugar
3 eggs
5 teaspoons instant coffee
4 tablespoons rum
75 g (3 oz) plain flour*

*75 g (3 oz) cornflour
1 teaspoon baking powder
3 tablespoons apricot jam
100 g (3½ oz) chocolate
1 tablespoon icing sugar
Chocolate coffee beans*

Cream 150 g (5 oz) butter in a bowl, then gradually add the sugar, eggs and 3 teaspoons instant coffee dissolved in 1 tablespoon rum.

Sift the flour, cornflour and baking powder and gradually add to the coffee mixture. Turn the mixture into well-greased madeleine moulds. Spread it out evenly. Bake in a preheated oven at 180-200° C (350-400° F, Gas Mark 4-6) for about 15 minutes. Turn out of the tins and leave to cool.

For the icing: mix the jam with 1 tablespoon water and 2 tablespoons rum. Use to coat the sponges. Melt the chocolate and the remaining butter in a bowl over a pan of hot water, stirring until smooth and creamy. Mix the icing sugar and the remaining instant coffee with the remaining rum.

Incorporate into the chocolate cream and mix well until smooth, then beat using an electric mixer until creamy. Transfer this coffee cream to an icing bag. Pipe on to the madeleines and decorate with chocolate coffee beans.

PEANUT BUTTER LOAF

Serves 6

About 325 g (11 oz) peanut butter
175 g (6 oz) soft brown sugar
1 sachet vanilla sugar
4 eggs
Juice and rind of ½ orange

175 g (6 oz) plain flour
75 g (3 oz) cornflour
1 teaspoon baking powder
100 g (3½ oz) peanuts, chopped
100 g (3½ oz) chocolate
20 g (¾ oz) butter

Cream the peanut butter, brown sugar and vanilla sugar in a bowl. Gradually add the eggs, orange juice and rind.

Sift the flour, cornflour and baking powder into a bowl. Gradually incorporate into the mixture. Then add 50 g (2 oz) chopped peanuts. Turn the mixture into a greased and lined, 30 x 11 cm (12 x 4½ in) loaf tin. Spread it out evenly. Bake in a preheated oven at 180° C (350° F, Gas Mark 4) for about 1 hour. Turn out of the tin and leave to cool.

For the icing: melt the chocolate and butter in a bowl over a pan of hot water, stirring until smooth and creamy. Use to coat the cake and sprinkle with the remaining chopped peanuts.

CHOCOLATE LAYER CAKE

Serves 6

275 g (9 oz) butter
250 g (8 oz) caster sugar
1 sachet vanilla sugar
2 eggs
4 egg yolks
1-2 tablespoons rum
150 g (5 oz) plain flour

100 g (3½ oz) cornflour
3 teaspoons baking powder
4 egg whites
100 g (3½ oz) chocolate

Cream 250 g (8 oz) butter in a bowl, then add the sugar, vanilla sugar, eggs, egg yolks and rum.

Sift the flour, cornflour and baking powder. Gradually add to the mixture. Whisk the egg whites into stiff peaks and gently fold them in.
Grease and line a 30 x 11 cm (12 x 4½ in) loaf tin. Cover the base of the tin with 1-2 tablespoons mixture. Spread it out evenly using a brush. Place the tin about 20 cm (8 in) below a preheated grill for 2 minutes until golden. Add a layer of the mixture and cook for 2 minutes until golden. Repeat this procedure until all

the mixture is used up. Place the tin lower under the grill each time, so that the top layer of mixture is always 20 cm (8 in) below the grill.

Run a knife round the edges of the tin to loosen the cake and turn out on to a baking sheet. Peel off the paper. Return the cake to the hot oven for about 5 minutes.

For the icing: melt the chocolate with the remaining butter in a bowl over a pan of hot water, stirring until smooth and creamy. Coat the cake.

Below: *Chocolate layer cake*

Above: *Apple and cinnamon tart*

APPLE AND CINNAMON TART

Serves 8

200 g (7 oz) butter
225 g (7½ oz) caster sugar
1 sachet vanilla sugar
A pinch of salt
4 eggs
1 teaspoon ground cinnamon
½ teaspoon ground ginger
A pinch of cardamom

250 g (8 oz) plain flour
2 teaspoons baking powder
12-15 medium-sized apples
Mixed fruit jam
2 packets clear jelly glaze mix
3 tablespoons apple juice
250 ml (8 fl oz) white wine

Cream the butter in a bowl, then gradually incorporate 200 g (7 oz) sugar, the vanilla sugar, salt, eggs, cinnamon, ginger and cardamom.

Sift the flour and baking powder, then gradually add to the mixture. Turn the mixture on to a well-greased baking sheet.

Peel and core the apples using an apple corer. Cut into circular slices about 1 cm (½ in) thick. Arrange on the sponge mixture so that they overlap slightly. Fill the middle of the slices with jam. Bake in a preheated oven at 180-200° C (350-400° F, Gas Mark 4-6) for about 40 minutes.

For the icing: mix the glaze mix with the apple juice, the white wine, the remaining sugar and 250 ml (8 fl oz) water following the instructions on the packet. Use to glaze the tart.

PRALINE LAYER CAKE

Serves about 8

350 g (11½ oz) butter
200 g (7 oz) almond paste
140 g (4½ oz) caster sugar
4 eggs
100 g (3½ oz) plain flour
1 teaspoon baking powder
50 g (2 oz) ground
almonds
40 g (1½ oz) fresh
breadcrumbs
25 g (1 oz) cornflour
400 ml (14 fl oz) milk
200 g (7 oz) hazelnut
chocolate spread
25 g (1 oz) icing sugar
100 g (3½ oz) chocolate

Cream 125 g (4 oz) butter and 125 g (4 oz) almond paste in a bowl. Gradually add 125 g (4 oz) sugar and the eggs. Sift the flour and baking powder into a separate bowl. Gradually add the ground almonds and breadcrumbs. Add these ingredients to the creamed mixture.

Spread the mixture about 1 cm (½ in) thick on to a greased and lined baking sheet. Bake in a preheated oven at 180-200° C (350-400° F, Gas Mark 4-6) for about 20 minutes. Turn out immediately on to a sheet of greaseproof paper. Peel off the baked greaseproof paper.

For the filling: mix the cornflour and 1 tablespoon sugar with 3-4 tablespoons milk. Heat the remaining milk, incorporate the cornflour mixture, bring to the boil, remove from the heat.

Mix 175 g (6 oz) hazelnut chocolate spread into the hot creamy mixture. Leave to cool, stirring from time to time. Cream 200 g (7 oz) butter, then gradually incorporate into the hazelnut chocolate cream.

Cut the sponge into three strips. Spread two of them with hazelnut chocolate cream. Place them one on top of the other and top with the third strip of sponge.

Combine the remaining almond paste with the icing sugar. Roll it out into a rectangle the same size as the cake and cover the cake.

For the icing: melt the chocolate with the remaining butter in a bowl over a pan of hot water, stirring until smooth and creamy. Use to coat the cake.

Soften the remaining hazelnut chocolate spread in a bowl over a pan of hot water. Transfer to an icing bag (or funnel made of greaseproof paper). Pipe on to the cake. Leave to cool. When ready to serve, cut into pieces.

GINGERBREAD PONY

500 g (1 lb) honey
75 g (3 oz) lard
1 tablespoon mixed spices
for gingerbread
(mixture of ground
cinnamon, nutmeg,
aniseed, cloves, coriander
and ginger)
250 g (8 oz) wheat flour
2 teaspoons baking
powder
100 g (3½ oz) candied
lemon peel
100 g (3½ oz) whole
blanched almonds
3 egg whites
Icing sugar to finish

Cream the honey and the lard with 2 tablespoons water. Incorporate the spices. Sift the flour and baking powder. Sprinkle on to the honey-lard mixture, reserving a little to coat the candied lemon peel, and incorporate.

Roll out the dough until 1 cm (½ in) thick on a floured work surface. Transfer to a well-greased and lined baking sheet. Cut into the shape of a pony using a pointed knife.

Brush with water. Decorate with halved almonds using the photograph as an example. Coat with a beaten egg white. Bake in a preheated oven at 180° C (350° F, Gas Mark 4) for about 25 minutes.
Leave to cool.

For the icing: mix the icing sugar with the remaining egg whites until thick and creamy. Transfer to a funnel made of greaseproof paper. Use to decorate the pony.

Right: *Gingerbread pony*

ORANGE AND LEMON CAKE

Serves 8-10

350 g (11½ oz) butter
400 g (13 oz) caster sugar
1 sachet vanilla sugar
6 eggs
Grated rind of 2 oranges
Grated rind of 1 lemon
350 g (11½ oz) plain flour

50 g (2 oz) cornflour
2 teaspoons baking
powder
250 ml (8 fl oz) orange
juice
3 tablespoons lemon juice

Cream the butter in a bowl, then incorporate 300 g (10 oz) sugar, the vanilla sugar, eggs, grated rind of 1 orange and ½ lemon. Sift the flour, cornflour and baking powder separately and add to the mixture. Turn the mixture into a fluted ring mould.

Bake in a preheated oven at 180-200° C (350-400° F, Gas Mark 4-6) for about 1 hour. Turn out of the mould. Clean the mould, then replace the cake. Prick it in several places with a cocktail stick.

Combine the orange and lemon juice with the remaining sugar and lemon rind. Pour half of this mixture over the cake, then turn the cake out of the mould. Prick the cake again with the cocktail stick, then sprinkle the rest of the mixture over it.

APRICOT GÂTEAU

Serves 8-10

6 eggs
375 g (12 oz) granulated
sugar
2 sachets vanilla sugar
175 g (6 oz) plain flour
175 g (6 oz) cornflour
½ teaspoon baking
powder

375 g (12 oz) butter,
softened
3 tablespoons apricot jam
3 tablespoons apricot
liqueur
1 teaspoon rum
25 (1 oz) icing sugar

Break the eggs into a mixing bowl. Take out 2 teaspoons egg white and set to one side in a covered container. Beat the eggs using an electric mixer until thick and frothy. Incorporate the sugar and vanilla sugar and continue beating for 2 minutes. Add 2 tablespoons water.

Sift the flour, cornflour and baking powder into a separate bowl. Gradually add to the egg mixture. Melt the butter in a pan (do not allow to boil) and add to the mixture, stirring constantly.

Turn the mixture into a greased cake tin. Bake in the middle of a preheated oven at 150-180° C (300-350° F, Gas Mark 2-4) for 60-85 minutes. Turn the cake out on to a wire rack and leave to cool slightly.

For the coating: combine the apricot jam, liqueur and rum with 1 tablespoon water. Heat, stirring constantly. Use to coat the sponge cake.

To finish: mix the icing sugar with the reserved egg white, adding a little water if necessary. Transfer this mixture to a funnel made of greaseproof paper and use to decorate the cake.

LEMON LOAF

Serves 6

250 g (8 oz) butter
200 g (7 oz) caster sugar
1 sachet vanilla sugar
4 eggs
A pinch of salt
Grated rind of 1 lemon

Juice of 2½ lemons
200 g (7 oz) plain flour
50 g (2 oz) cornflour
2 teaspoons baking
powder
100 g (3½ oz) icing sugar

Slices of glacé lemons and oranges to finish (optional) Melt the butter in a pan. Leave to cool, then add the granulated sugar, vanilla sugar, eggs, salt, lemon rind and juice of 1 lemon.

Sift the flour, cornflour and baking powder into a bowl and gradually incorporate. Turn the mixture into a greased and lined loaf tin. Bake in a preheated oven at 180° C (350° F, Gas Mark 4) for about 1 hour. Leave the cake to cool in the tin for about 10 minutes before turning it out.

For the icing: combine the icing sugar and the remaining lemon juice until thick and creamy. Use to coat the cake, then decorate if desired with orange and lemon slices.

Above: *Orange and lemon cake and Apricot gâteau*

ORANGE AND COCONUT CUP CAKES

Serves 20

165 g (5½ oz) butter, softened
100 g (3½ oz) almond paste
100 g (3½ oz) granulated sugar
1 sachet vanilla sugar
4 eggs
A pinch of salt
Grated rind of ½ lemon or orange
25 g (1 oz) candied orange peel, finely chopped
125 g (4 oz) desiccated coconut
Icing sugar
Whipped cream
Glacé fruits
Chocolate vermicelli

Cream the butter and almond paste, then gradually add the sugar, vanilla sugar, eggs, salt and lemon or orange rind. Mix well, then incorporate the candied orange peel and the desiccated coconut.

Turn this mixture into well-greased bun tins or into twenty paper cases. Place on a baking sheet and bake in a preheated oven at 180° C (350° F, Gas Mark 4) for about 25 minutes. Remove from the tin and leave to cool.

Dredge with icing sugar and pipe with whipped cream, then decorate with glacé fruits or chocolate vermicelli.

Below: *Cherry crisps*

CHERRY CRISPS

Serves 8

1 kg (2 lb) Morello cherries
200 g (7 oz) whole blanched almonds
250 g (8 oz) butter, softened
400 g (13 oz) icing sugar
A pinch of salt
2 teaspoons grated lemon rind
6 eggs
300 g (10 oz) plain flour
100 g (3½ oz) cornflour
1 teaspoon baking powder
4 tablespoons double cream
3-4 tablespoons kirsch
Whipped cream

Above: *Orange and coconut cup cakes*

Wash, drain, hull and stone the cherries. Halve the almonds.

For the sponge mixture: cream the butter in a bowl, then gradually add 250 g (8 oz) icing sugar, the salt, grated lemon rind and eggs, reserving 2 teaspoons egg white in a covered container for the icing.

Sift the flour, cornflour and baking powder into a bowl, and gradually incorporate into the mixture. Add the cream.

Turn the mixture on to a greased and lined baking sheet. Spread it out evenly. Arrange the cherries and the almonds over the mixture. Bake in a preheated oven at 200° C (400° F, Gas Mark 6) for 30-35 minutes. Leave to cool for about 15 minutes.

For the icing: mix the remaining icing sugar with the kirsch and the reserved egg white until thick and creamy.

Use to coat the cake. Cut into equal slices. Serve with whipped cream.

FRANKFURT RING CAKE

Serves 6-8

300 g (10 oz) butter, softened
300 g (10 oz) caster sugar
1 sachet vanilla sugar
4 drops lemon essence or 1 tablespoon rum
3 eggs
150 g (5 oz) plain flour
50 g (2 oz) cornflour
2 teaspoons baking powder
1 packet vanilla blancmange mix
500 ml (18 fl oz) milk
125 g (4 oz) chopped blanched almonds
Cherry jam or other red fruit jam
Some glacé cherries to finish

Cream 100 g (3½ oz) butter in a bowl, then add 150 g (5 oz) sugar, the vanilla sugar, lemon essence or rum and the eggs.
Sift the flour, cornflour and baking powder into a bowl and gradually incorporate into the mixture.
Turn the mixture into a 24 cm (9½ in) savarin ring mould. Bake in a preheated oven at 180-200° C (350-400° F, Gas Mark 4-6) for 35-45 minutes.

For the butter cream: mix the blancmange mixture with 100 g (3½ oz) sugar and the milk, following the instructions on the packet. Heat, stirring constantly, then leave to cool. Stir from time to time. Cream the remaining 200 g (7 oz) butter (reserve a small knob) and gradually incorporate the blancmange mixture (the butter and the blancmange must both be at room temperature so that the mixture does not 'separate').

Below: *Frankfurt Ring Cake*

For the praline mixture: heat the almonds with the knob of butter and the remaining sugar until they are a dark golden colour. Turn on to a sheet of aluminium foil and leave to cool.

Cut the cake into three equal layers. Spread the bottom layer with jam. Then cover it with butter cream, followed by the middle layer. Spread this with jam and butter cream. Finally add the top of the ring and coat with butter cream. Reserve a little for piping. Cover the cake with praline and decorate with the remaining butter cream mixture. Add a few cherries or cherry or red fruit jam. Chill overnight.

Alternative: you can use a deep, 24 cm (9½ in) round sandwich tin instead of a savarin ring mould.

DEMERARA DREAMS

Makes 20

250 g (8 oz) butter	1 teaspoon baking powder
175 g (6 oz) granulated sugar	125 g (4 oz) currants
1 sachet vanilla sugar	100 g (3½ oz) chopped almonds
5 eggs	4 tablespoons demerara sugar
2 tablespoons rum	
250 g (8 oz) plain flour	

Cream the butter in a bowl, then add the granulated sugar, vanilla sugar, eggs and rum. Sift the flour and baking powder into a bowl, then gradually incorporate into the creamed mixture. Add the currants, mix well, then turn the mixture on to a well-greased baking sheet. Spread it out evenly.

For the filling: sprinkle the almonds and demerara sugar over the sponge mixture. Bake in a preheated oven at 180-200° C (350-400° F, Gas Mark 4-6) for about 25 minutes.

Cut the cake into diamond shapes while still hot. Serve immediately.

Tip: you can make these demerara dreams in advance, leave them to cool and then store them in an airtight container.

Left: *Demerara dreams*

SPICED CHOCOLATE BUNS

Makes 24

200 g (7 oz) honey or
treacle
125 g (4 oz) caster sugar
65 g (2½ oz) butter
2 tablespoons milk
2 eggs
½ bottle lemon flavouring
1 teaspoon cardamom
½ teaspoon ground
nutmeg
1 teaspoon ground
cinnamon

250 g (8 oz) plain flour
25 g (1 oz) cocoa powder
3 teaspoons baking
powder
65 g (2½ oz) currants
65 g (3½ oz) chopped
blanched almonds
65 g (2½ oz) candied
lemon peel, chopped
175 g (6 oz) apricot jam
200 g (7 oz) chocolate

Melt the honey or treacle, the sugar, butter and milk over a low heat, stirring constantly. Pour into a bowl and leave to cool. Then incorporate the eggs, lemon flavouring, cardamom, nutmeg and cinnamon.

Sift the flour, cocoa powder and baking powder into a bowl and gradually incorporate into the mixture. Add the currants, chopped almonds and candied lemon peel.

Using a tablespoon, transfer this mixture to small cake tins placed on a baking sheet. Bake in a preheated oven at 180-200° C (350-400° F, Gas Mark 4-6) for 10-15 minutes. Turn out of the tins immediately and leave to cool.

Below: *Spiced chocolate buns*

For the coating: sieve the jam, then bring it to boiling point together with 2 tablespoons water. Brush a thin layer over the buns.
Melt the chocolate in a bowl over a pan of hot water, stirring until smooth and creamy. Cover the cakes.

Tip: if you do not have small, round cake tins, fold a length of aluminium foil into twelve layers, measuring 15 x 30 cm (6 x 12 in). Draw two circles, 15 cm (6 in) in diameter, side by side on the top layer. Cut out the circles through all the layers at once, making 24 circles. Place the circles, one at a time, over an upturned, round glass and smooth down to form cake moulds.

PINEAPPLE AND MARZIPAN LOAF

Serves 6-8

200 g (7 oz) butter
200 g (7 oz) almond paste
175 g (6 oz) caster sugar
1 sachet vanilla sugar
3 eggs
300 g (10 oz) plain flour

2 teaspoons baking powder
250 g (8 oz) pineapple chunks
125 g (4 oz) chocolate

Cream 175 g (6 oz) butter and the almond paste in a bowl. Add the sugar, then the vanilla sugar and the eggs.

Sift the flour and baking powder into a bowl. Gradually incorporate into the creamed mixture. Drain the pineapple chunks well and add 200 g (7 oz) to the mixture. Turn it into a 30 x 11 cm (12 x 4½ in) loaf tin. Bake in a preheated oven at 180-200° C (350-400° F, Gas Mark 4-6) for 60-70 minutes. Leave to cool.

For the icing: break the chocolate into pieces and melt in a bowl over a pan of hot water together with the remaining butter, stirring until smooth and creamy.

Use to cover the cake and decorate with the remaining pineapple.

MADEIRA CAKE

Serves 6

300 g (10 oz) butter, softened
275 g (9 oz) icing sugar
4 eggs, separated
A pinch of salt

Pulp of 1 vanilla pod
2 tablespoons rum
275 g (9 oz) cornflour
A pinch of baking powder

Cream the butter, then incorporate first the icing sugar, then the egg yolks, salt, vanilla pulp and rum, taking care to mix well each time (5-6 minutes in total).

Sift the cornflour and baking powder into a bowl and gradually add to the mixture. Whisk the egg whites into stiff peaks and gently fold them in.

Turn the mixture into a well greased and floured, 30 x 11 cm (12 x 4½ in) loaf tin. Spread it out evenly. Bake in a preheated oven at 160-180° C (325-350° F, Gas Mark 3-4) for 70-80 minutes. Leave to cool in the tin.

Right: *Madeira cake*

CHOCOLATE CHERRY RING

Serves 8

250 g (8 oz) butter, softened
325 g (11 oz) caster sugar
4 eggs
4 egg yolks
2 teaspoons grated lemon rind
100 g (3½ oz) plain flour
150 g (5 oz) cornflour
1 teaspoon baking powder
50 g (2 oz) ground almonds
4 tablespoons cocoa powder

1 kg (2 lb) Morello cherries (or other sour cherries)
1 sachet powdered gelatine or 4 gelatine leaves
500 ml (18 fl oz) double cream
2 sachets vanilla sugar
3 tablespoons rum
100 g (3½ oz) milk superfine cooking chocolate
Icing sugar to finish

Cream the butter in a bowl, then add 200 g (7 oz) sugar, the whole eggs, egg yolks and lemon rind. Sift the flour, 100 g (3½ oz) cornflour and the baking powder into a bowl. Incorporate into the mixture, then add the ground almonds.

Set one third of the mixture to one side and incorporate the cocoa powder into the remaining two-thirds. Turn the chocolate mixture into a greased savarin ring mould. Spread it out evenly, then cover with the remaining mixture. Bake in a preheated oven at 180° C (350° F, Gas Mark 4) for 45-50 minutes. Leave the cake to cool in the tin for 10 minutes. Turn it out carefully, then leave to cool completely before cutting into three layers.

Below: *Chocolate cherry ring*
Opposite: *Cream waffles*

For the filling: wash the cherries and leave them to drain. Hull and stone them. Put them in a bowl and mix with the remaining sugar. Leave them for about 1 hour. Drain, saving the juice.

Mix the remaining cornflour with 3-4 tablespoons cherry juice. Add enough water to the remaining juice to make 250 ml (8 fl oz) liquid. Bring to the boil and stir in the cornflour mixture. Add the cherries. Bring back to the boil. Boil for 3-4 minutes, then remove from the heat and leave to cool.

Mix the gelatine with 4 tablespoons water. Leave for 10 minutes until it becomes translucent. Whip the cream until firm, adding the vanilla sugar. Heat the gelatine until it has completely dissolved. Add the rum and stir into the whipped cream.

Arrange half of the cherries over the first layer of sponge. Cover with a layer of whipped cream about 2 cm (¾ in) thick. Cover with the second layer of sponge, pressing down gently. Cover with the remaining cherries and another 2 cm (¾ in) thick layer of whipped cream. Add the top of the cake and cover the entire cake with the remaining whipped cream. Chill overnight.

To finish: grate the chocolate into fine curls using a potato peeler. Sprinkle all over the cake and dredge with icing sugar.

CREAM WAFFLES

Makes 12 waffles

150 ml (½ pint) double cream
3 eggs, separated
100 g (3½ oz) caster sugar

A pinch of salt
Grated rind of ½ lemon
250 g (8 oz) plain flour
1 teaspoon baking powder

Whip the cream with the egg yolks, sugar, salt and lemon rind. Sift the flour and baking powder into a bowl and stir into the cream mixture.
Whisk the egg whites into stiff peaks. Fold them in. Grease the waffle-iron. Heat it and pour in the mixture. Cook the waffles until they are golden on both sides. Leave to cool on a wire rack.

Suggestion: serve with whipped cream, vanilla ice-cream, redcurrants dredged in sugar, red fruit jam or jelly.

ALMOND AND ORANGE CUP CAKES

Makes 12-14 cakes

200 g (7 oz) almond paste
100 g (3½ oz) caster sugar
2 eggs
2 egg yolks
2 egg whites
100 g (3½ oz) plain flour
A pinch of baking powder

30 g (1½ oz) candied
orange peel
2-3 tablespoons flaked
almonds
3 tablespoons apricot jam
3 tablespoons run

Beat the almond paste well, then gradually incorporate 65 g (2½ oz) sugar and the whole eggs.

Beat the egg yolks using an electric mixer until thick and frothy. Whisk the egg whites into stiff peaks. Add the remaining sugar, beating constantly, then fold into the yolks.
Sift the flour and baking powder into a bowl and add gradually to the almond mixture, together with egg mixture. Stir in the candied orange peel. Turn the mixture into small, well-greased bun tins about 8 cm (3 in) deep, top with flaked almonds. Bake on a baking sheet in a preheated oven at 180-200° C (350-400° F, Gas Mark 4-6) for 20 minutes.

For the coating: mix the apricot jam with the rum and one tablespoon water. Brush the sponge cakes with this mixture. Serve immediately or store in an airtight container once they have dried slightly.

Below: *Almond and orange cup cakes*

HAZELNUT FLORENTINES

Makes about 25

300 g (10 oz) whole
hazelnuts
50 g (2 oz) honey
150 g (5 oz) caster sugar
250 ml (8 fl oz) double
cream
100 g (3½ oz) flaked
almonds

Grated rind of 1 lemon
A pinch of ground
cinnamon
25 g (1 oz) plain flour
Milk
200 g (7 oz) superfine
cooking chocolate

Spread 250 g (8 oz) hazelnuts over a baking sheet and roast in a preheated oven at 200-220° C (400-425° F, Gas Mark 6-7) for 8-12 minutes.

Above: *Hazelnut florentines*

Leave to cool slightly, then peel them by rubbing them together in your hands.

Put the honey, sugar and cream in a pan and bring to the boil. Boil for 5-6 minutes. Stir in the roasted hazelnuts, flaked almonds, lemon rind, cinnamon and flour. Bring back to the boil. Remove from the heat.

Using a tablespoon, place little mounds of this mixture on to a greased baking sheet, about 1½ tablespoons per florentine. Wet your fingers in the milk and smooth the mixture out evenly. Then top with the remaining whole hazelnuts, arranging them evenly.

Bake in a preheated oven at 180° C (350° F, Gas Mark 4) for 20 minutes. Leave to cool for about 10 minutes before removing them from the baking sheet. Then leave them to cool completely.

For the icing: melt the chocolate in a bowl over a pan of hot water. Leave to cool slightly until it is smooth and creamy. Coat the bases of the florentines, then make wavy lines using a fork. Leave to set.

HAZELNUT RUM LOAF

Serves 6

250 g (8 oz) whole
hazelnuts
275 g (9 oz) butter,
softened
175 g (6 oz) caster sugar
1 sachet vanilla sugar

4 eggs
200 g (7 oz) plain flour
1 teaspoon baking powder
5 tablespoons rum
4 tablespoons apricot jam
100 g (3½ oz) chocolate

Crush 150 g (5 oz) hazelnuts, then spread them over a baking sheet and toast them lightly. Grind the remaining 150 g (5 oz) hazelnuts. Cream the butter and add the ground hazelnuts. Then gradually add the sugar, vanilla sugar and eggs. Sift the flour and baking powder into a separate bowl, then gradually add to the mixture. Stir the toasted hazelnuts into the mixture and turn it into a

greased and lined, 30 x 11 cm (12 x 4½ in) loaf tin. Bake in a preheated oven at 180-200° C (350-400° F, Gas Mark 4-6) for 60-75 minutes. Turn out of the tin immediately, prick the base with a fork, then sprinkle the rum over all sides.

For the coating: sieve the apricot jam and mix with 3 tablespoons water. Bring to the boil and use to coat the cake. Leave to cool.

For the chocolate icing: break the chocolate into pieces and melt in a bowl over a pan of hot water, stirring constantly until smooth and creamy.
Use to coat the sides of the cake.

Richt: *Tyrolean ring cake*
Below: *Hazelnut rum loaf*

TYROLEAN RING CAKE

Serves 6-8

200 g (7 oz) butter,
softened
175 g (6 oz) caster sugar
3 eggs
3 egg yolks
Grated rind of ½ lemon
1 teaspoon ground
cinnamon
A pinch of salt

200 g (7 oz) ground
hazelnuts
125 g (4 oz) plain flour
1 teaspoon baking powder
3 egg whites
200 g (7 oz) bitter
chocolate
Icing sugar

Cream the butter, then gradually incorporate the sugar, whole eggs, egg yolks, the grated lemon rind, cinnamon, salt and ground hazelnuts. Sift the flour and baking powder into a bowl and gradually incorporate into the mixture.

Whisk the egg whites into stiff peaks. Gently fold them into the mixture. Cut the chocolate into small pieces and stir into the mixture.

Turn the mixture into a well greased, 24 cm (9½ in) diameter savarin ring mould. Bake in a preheated oven at 180° C (350° F, Gas Mark 4) for 70 minutes. Remove the cake from the tin and leave to cool. Dredge with icing sugar.

CHOCOLATE LOG

Serves 6

125 g (4 oz) butter
150 g (5 oz) caster sugar
4 eggs
100 g (3½ oz) chocolate
50 g (2 oz) plain flour
1 teaspoon baking powder
2 packets chocolate
blancmange mix

2 tablespoons milk
75 g (3 oz) ground
almonds or hazelnuts
125 g (4 oz) icing sugar
4 tablespoons cocoa
powder
40 g (1½ oz) almonds cut
into slithers

Cream 100 g (3½ oz) butter, then gradually add the sugar and eggs. Grate the chocolate and add to the butter. Sift the flour, baking powder and chocolate blancmange mixes into a bowl, then gradually incorporate into the mixture.

Add the milk (just enough to give the mixture a dropping, but not sloppy consistency). Add the ground almonds or hazelnuts. Turn into a suitable greased baking tin. Bake in a preheated oven at 180-200° C (350-400° F, Gas Mark 4-6) for 50-60 minutes.

For the icing: sift the icing sugar and cocoa powder. Mix with 1½ tablespoons hot water, beating until thick and creamy.
Melt the remaining butter, add to the chocolate mixture and mix well. Use to coat the chocolate log when it is cold. Insert the almond slithers all over the cake.

Below: *Chocolate log*

Above: *Apple cake*

APPLE CAKE

Serves 6

100-125 g (3½-4 oz) butter
125 g (4 oz) caster sugar
2-3 eggs
A pinch of salt
4 drops lemon flavouring
200 g (7 oz) plain flour

2 teaspoons baking
powder
1-4 tablespoons milk
500-700 g (1 lb-1 lb 6 oz)
apples
2 tablespoons apricot jam

Cream the butter in a bowl, then gradually incorporate the sugar, eggs, salt and lemon flavouring. Sift the flour and baking powder into a separate bowl, then gradually add to the mixture. Add the milk, a little at a time, making sure the mixture does not become too sloppy. Turn into a deep, 28 cm (11 in) round cake tin. Smooth the mixture out evenly.

For the filling: peel the apples, cut into quarters, remove the cores, then cut into thin slices lengthways. Arrange on the mixture. Bake in a preheated oven at 180-200° C (350-400° F, Gas Mark 4-6) for 40-50 minutes.

For the coating: sieve the jam, then mix it with 1 tablespoon water. Use to coat the cake as soon as it is out of the oven.

Alternative: you can use 750 g (1½ lb) Morello cherries instead of the apples. Wash, drain, hull and stone them, then spread over the top of the mixture.

WALNUT AND ORANGE CHOCOLATE RING

Serves 6

1 orange	50 g (2 oz) cornflour
175 g (6 oz) butter, softened	50 g (2 oz) cocoa powder
150 g (5 oz) caster sugar	1 teaspoon baking powder
6 eggs, separated	100 g (3½ oz) ground walnuts
2 tablespoons rum	50 g (2 oz) chopped walnuts
2 tablespoons orange liqueur (Grand Marnier or Cointreau)	25 g (1 oz) pistachio nuts, coarsely chopped
½ teaspoon ground ginger	140 g (4½ oz) apricot jam
1 teaspoon ground cinnamon	200 g (7 oz) milk superfine cooking chocolate
½ teaspoon ground nutmeg	250 g (8 oz) whole walnuts to finish
100 g (3½ oz) plain flour	

Wash the orange, dry it, then grate it finely.
Cream 125 g (4 oz) butter, then gradually add 100 g (3½ oz) sugar, the egg yolks, rum, orange liqueur, ginger, cinnamon and nutmeg. Whisk the egg whites into firm peaks, gradually incorporate the remaining sugar, beating constantly. Gently fold half the egg whites into the mixture.

Sift the flour, cornflour, cocoa and baking powder into a separate bowl. Gradually incorporate. Then add the ground walnuts, the chopped walnuts and pistachios, together with 1 tablespoon apricot jam. Mix well, then add the remaining egg whites.

Turn the mixture into a well-greased and floured savarin ring mould. Spread it out evenly. Bake in a preheated oven at 180° C (350° F, Gas Mark 4) for 60-70 minutes. Remove from the oven and leave to cool for 30 minutes in the tin.
Turn out on to a wire rack. Leave to cool completely.

For the icing: sieve the remaining apricot jam, then mix with one tablespoon water and bring to the boil. Use to coat the cake and leave to cool.

Melt the chocolate in a bowl over a pan of hot water with the remaining butter. Use to coat the cake. Decorate with whole walnuts, pressing them down slightly into the icing while it is still soft. Wrap the cake in aluminium foil and keep for several days before eating.

ENGLISH FRUIT CAKE

Serves 6-8

300 g (10 oz) raisins	½ teaspoon ground nutmeg
300 g (10 oz) grapes, well washed	7 eggs, separated
200 g (7 oz) chopped candied mixed peel	1 teaspoon bitter orange marmalade
125 ml (4 fl oz) whisky	350 g (11½ oz) plain flour
50 g (2 oz) almond paste	1 teaspoon baking powder
125 g (4 oz) soft brown sugar	200 g (7 oz) whole blanched almonds
1 teaspoon ground cinnamon	1 tablespoon milk

Soak the raisins, grapes and mixed peel in the whisky overnight.

Mix the almond paste, soft brown sugar, cinnamon and nutmeg in a bowl, then gradually incorporate 6 egg yolks and the marmalade. Mix well until creamy. Whisk the egg whites into stiff peaks. Fold half into the mixture.

Sift the flour and baking powder into a bowl, add the mixed fruit soaked in whisky. Gently fold in the remaining egg whites.
Turn the mixture into a well greased and floured deep, about 26 cm (10½ in) round cake tin. Spread it out evenly. Cover with halved almonds.

Mix the remaining egg yolk with the milk and brush over the almonds. Bake in a preheated oven at 150° C (300° F, Gas Mark 2) for 1½ hours. After about 45 minutes, cover the cake with a sheet of greased greaseproof paper. Leave to cool on a wire rack. Keep for several days in an airtight container before eating.

Suggestion: if you wish to make a gift of this cake, wrap it up in cellophane paper tied with a maroon ribbon.

Opposite: *English fruit cake and Walnut and orange chocolate ring*

COCONUT RING

Serves 6

4 eggs
200 g (7 oz) caster sugar
1 sachet vanilla sugar
100 g (3½ oz) plain flour
100 g (3½ oz) cornflour

1 teaspoon baking powder
150-165 g (5-5½ oz)
desiccated coconut
200 g (7 oz) butter
2 tablespoons apricot jam

Beat the eggs using an electric mixer at high speed for 2 minutes, then gradually incorporate the sugar and the vanilla sugar, beating constantly. Sift the flour, cornflour and baking powder into a separate bowl and gradually incorporate into the mixture, together with 125 g (4 oz) desiccated coconut.

Melt the butter and add to the mixture while still hot. Turn the mixture into a greased and floured savarin ring mould. Smooth it out evenly. Bake in a preheated oven at 180° C (350° F, Gas Mark 4) for about 55 minutes.

For the coating: sieve the apricot jam and mix it with 2 tablespoons water. Coat the cake as soon as it is out of the oven, then dredge with the remaining desiccated coconut.

MARBLE DELIGHT

Serves 8

300 g (10 oz) butter
300 g (10 oz) caster sugar
1 sachet vanilla sugar
5 eggs
A pinch of salt
1 tablespoon rum

500 g (1 lb) plain flour
2 teaspoons baking
powder
125 ml (4 fl oz) milk
4 tablespoons cocoa
powder

Cream the butter, then gradually incorporate 275 g (9 oz) sugar, the vanilla sugar, eggs, salt and rum. Sift the flour and baking powder into a bowl and add 2 tablespoons milk. Turn two-thirds of this mixture into a fluted 22 cm (8½ in) diameter ring mould.

Incorporate the cocoa powder into the rest of the mixture, together with the remaining sugar and milk, making sure that the mixture does not become too sloppy. Pour this mixture over the plain mixture and bring the plain mixture up over the top using a fork to create a marbling effect.
Bake in a preheated oven at 180-200° C (350-400° F, Gas Mark 4-6) for 50-65 minutes.

SHERRY CUP CAKES

Makes about 5 cakes

125 g (4 oz) butter
125 g (4 oz) caster sugar
Pulp of 1 vanilla pod

4 eggs
125 g (4 oz) plain flour
250 ml (8 fl oz) sherry

Melt the butter and leave to cool slightly. When it starts to coagulate, incorporate the sugar, then the vanilla pulp, eggs and flour. Turn the mixture into small, greased and floured moulds. Bake in a preheated oven at 220° C (425° F, Gas Mark 7) for 12-15 minutes. Leave in the moulds for about 5 minutes. Turn them out, then put them back and sprinkle them with sherry. Leave to absorb.

Suggestion: serve with unsweetened whipped cream and some sherry.

Left: *Coconut ring*

Above: *Sherry cup cakes*

FLORENTINE SLICES

Makes 10-15

200 g (7 oz) plain flour
½ teaspoon baking
powder
175 g (6 oz) caster sugar
2 sachets vanilla sugar
A pinch of salt
150 g (5 oz) butter
2 tablespoons honey
250 ml (8 fl oz) double

cream
100 g (3½ oz) flaked
almonds
100 g (3½ oz) chopped
hazelnuts
25 g (1 oz) diced glacé
cherries
75 g (3 oz) superfine
cooking chocolate

Combine the flour and baking powder on a work
surface. Make a well in the centre. Add 75 g (3 oz) sugar,
1 sachet vanilla sugar, the salt and 2 tablespoons water.
Work into a thick paste using some of the flour. Add
100 g (3½ oz) butter cut into pieces and cover with the
remaining flour.

Quickly knead all the ingredients into a smooth dough.
Roll out into a 28 x 36 cm (11 x 14 in) rectangle. Divide
the mixture into two 14 x 36 cm (5½ x 14 in) strips. Fold
over 1-2 cm (½-¾ in) along the long edges of the strips in
towards the centre. Place on a well-greased baking sheet
and bake in a preheated oven at 200° C (400° F, Gas Mark
6) for about 10 minutes.

For the filling: melt the remaining butter, then
incorporate the remaining sugar, vanilla sugar and the
honey. Stir until the mixture caramelizes.
Incorporate the cream and stir constantly until the sugar
has completely dissolved.

Add the almonds, hazelnuts and glacé cherries. Continue
stirring over the heat until the mixture forms a smooth
ball. Spread over the pastry strips once out of the oven.
Return to the oven and bake at the same temperature for
10-12 minutes. Leave to cool slightly, then cut into
2-3 cm (¾-1½ in) strips.

Melt the chocolate in a bowl over a pan of hot water.
Coat the edges and tops of the slices.

COTTAGE CHEESE CRUMBLE

Serves about 8

250 g (8 oz) plain flour
½ teaspoon baking
powder
300 g (10 oz) caster sugar
2 sachets vanilla sugar
A pinch of salt
1 egg
150 g (5 oz) butter

750 g (1½ lb) cottage
cheese
3 tablespoons lemon juice
50 g (2 oz) cornflour
3 eggs, separated
250 ml (8 fl oz) double
cream

Combine 150 g (5 oz) flour and the baking powder on a
work surface. Make a well in the centre and add
75 g (3 oz) sugar, 1 sachet vanilla sugar, the salt and
1 egg. Work into a thick paste using some of the flour.
Add 75 g (3 oz) butter cut into pieces. Cover with the
remaining flour and quickly knead into a smooth dough.

Leave to rest. Spread two-thirds of the mixture out over
the base of a deep, 28 cm (11 in) round cake tin. Roll the
remaining pastry into a 3 cm (1½ in) wide strip and use
to line the sides of the tin. Prick the pastry base with a
fork. Bake in a preheated oven at 200-220° C
(400-425° F, Gas Mark 6-7) for 10 minutes.

For the filling: incorporate 150 g (5 oz) sugar, the lemon
juice, cornflour and egg yolks into the cottage cheese.
Whisk the egg whites into stiff peaks.
Whip the cream. Gently fold these two ingredients into
the cottage cheese. Take the pastry out of the oven, cover
with the cottage cheese mixture and smooth down
evenly.

Combine the remaining flour with the remaining sugar,
vanilla sugar and butter. Quickly knead the ingredients
together, then sprinkle over the filling. Return to a
preheated oven at 180° C (350° F, Gas Mark 4) and bake
for 70-80 minutes. Turn the oven off and leave the cheese
crumble to cool with the door half-open.

CHERRY CREAM SLICES

Makes about 5

625 g (1½ lb) puff pastry
1.5 kg (3½ lb) Morello
cherries (or other sour
cherries)
200 g (7 oz) caster sugar
3 sachets vanilla sugar
2 cinnamon sticks
Rind of 1 lemon

About 875 g (1¾ lb)
Morello cherries in syrup
50 g (2 oz) cornflour
9 tablespoons kirsch
500 ml (18 fl oz) double
cream
140 g (4½ oz) icing sugar

Roll out the puff pastry and cut into 10 equal rectangles. Place five of them on a baking sheet sprinkled with water. Bake in a preheated oven at 220° C (425° F, Gas Mark 7) for about 12 minutes. Bake the remaining rectangles in the same way and leave to cool. Cut each rectangle into two layers with a bread knife.

Below: *Cherry cream slices*

For the filling: wash, drain, hull and stone the cherries. Put 125 ml (4 fl oz) water, the sugar, 2 sachets vanilla sugar, the cinnamon sticks and lemon rind into a pan. Bring to the boil, then cover and cook for about 8 minutes over a low heat.

Strain the cherries in syrup, saving the juice. Reserve 2 teaspoons and transfer 500 ml (18 fl oz) to a pan. Heat with the cornflour and 4 tablespoons kirsch. Bring to the boil, then take off the heat and add the cherries. Leave to cool. Taste and add a little sugar if necessary. Spread the cherries over half of the pastry rectangles.

Whip the cream until very firm. Incorporate 50 g (2 oz) icing sugar, the remaining vanilla sugar and 4 tablespoons kirsch. Fill an icing bag fitted with a fluted nozzle and pipe over the cherries.

For the icing: combine the remaining icing sugar with the reserved cherry juice and the remaining kirsch. Use to coat the remaining pastry rectangles. Leave to dry slightly, then place them on the cream. lace in the refrigerator until they are to be served.

HAZELNUT AND PEAR PIE

Serves 6

250 g (8 oz) plain flour
1-2 tablespoons caster
sugar
A pinch of salt
100 g (3½ oz) butter
75 g (3 oz) lard
1 kg (2 lb) pears
4 tablespoons lemon juice
A pinch of ground
cinnamon

A pinch of ground
nutmeg
65 g (2½ oz) brown sugar
50 g (2 oz) ground
hazelnuts
25 g (1 oz) flaked
hazelnuts
1 tablespoon fresh
breadcrumbs
Condensed milk

Sift the flour on to a work surface and make a well in the centre. Incorporate 3 tablespoons cold water, the sugar and salt. Combine into a paste using some of the flour. Add 75 g (3 oz) butter and the lard cut into small pieces. Cover with the remaining flour and knead into a smooth dough.
Leave to rest for about 1 hour.

For the filling: peel, quarter and core the pears, then cut into chunks. Sprinkle with the lemon juice. Combine the cinnamon and nutmeg with 50 g (2 oz) brown sugar, then with the ground and flaked hazelnuts and sprinkle over the pears. Stir gently to incorporate all the ingredients.

Above: *Hazelnut and pear pie*

Roll out half the pastry and line the base and sides of a
3 cm (1½ in) deep, 28 cm (11 in) round cake tin. Cover
with the breadcrumbs, then add the filling.

Brush the top edge of the pastry with condensed milk.
Roll out the remaining pastry into a slightly thicker layer
and cover the tart.
Press the edges together well to seal the tart. Cut off the
excess pastry.

You can use the pastry trimmings to decorate the pie.
Brush them with condensed milk on the undersides to
stick them to the pastry top. Soften the remaining butter,
sprinkle hazelnuts over the top and dredge with the
remaining brown sugar. Bake in a preheated oven at
200-220° C (400-420° F, Gas Mark 6-7) for about
45 minutes.
Serve with whipped cream.

RASPBERRY VOLS-AU-VENT

Makes about 4

300 g (10 oz) puff pastry
Condensed milk
250 g (8 oz) raspberries

125 ml (4 fl oz) double
cream
25 g (1 oz) icing sugar

Roll the pastry out into a 43 x 48 cm (17 x 18¾ in) rectangle. Using a 8.5 cm (3½ in) round pastry cutter, cut out ten circles. Then cut out a 5 cm (2 in) circle from each larger circle to make rings and tops. Set aside the ten rings and four tops.

Knead the remaining six tops together with the remaining pastry. Roll out again into a 25.5 x 18.5 cm

(10½ x 7½ in) rectangle and cut out a further six rings. Set them aside. Roll out the remaining pastry into a 4 x 8.5 cm (1½ x 3½ in) rectangle and cut out four bases.

Place the four bases on a baking sheet sprinkled with water and prick with a fork. Brush the condensed milk over the rim of the bases. Brush three rings with condensed milk. Place them on one of the bases, add a fourth ring, making sure that no excess milk runs on to the sides. Assemble three more pastry cases in the same way.

Using a fluted pastry cutter, cut out four circles from the remaining pastry. Lay them on the vols-au-vent, then

Right:
Raspberry vols-au-vent

brush the tops with condensed milk. Bake in a preheated oven at 200-220° C (400-425° F, Gas Mark 6-7) for 15-20 minutes. Take the tops out a little sooner. Leave to cool.

For the filling: put about 1 tablespoon raspberries into each pastry case. Reserve the best for decoration, then purée and sieve the rest. Set to one side.
Whip the cream for 30 seconds. Add the icing sugar. Incorporate and continue whipping until very firm. Add the raspberry purée. Top the pastry cases with the raspberry-flavoured whipped cream. Decorate with whole raspberries and the pastry tops, if desired. Serve immediately.

Alternative: instead of raspberries, you can use strawberries, redcurrants, blackberries or bilberries lightly cooked in a covered pan.

Above: *Cherry almond tart*

BRAIDS

Makes 30-40

500 g (1 lb) plain flour	2 tablespoons rum
1 teaspoon baking powder	3 eggs
100 g (3½ oz) caster sugar	4 tablespoons milk
A few drops of lemon	125 g (4 oz) butter
flavouring	Icing sugar to finish

Sift the flour and baking powder on to a work surface. Make a well in the centre. Add the sugar, lemon flavouring, rum, eggs and milk. Combine with some of the flour. Add the butter cut into pieces. Cover with the remaining flour and knead into a smooth dough.

Roll the pastry out thinly. Cut into strips using a pastry wheel. Cut the strips into sections, then cut them down the middle so as to be able to insert one of the two ends to make the 'braids'.

Heat a deep-fat fryer. Brown the braids on both sides. Remove them using a slotted spoon and leave to drain on a wire rack. Dredge with icing sugar.

CHERRY ALMOND TART

Serves 6

150 g (5 oz) plain flour	breadcrumbs
½ teaspoon baking	500 g (1 lb) stoned
powder	Morello cherries in syrup
125 g (4 oz) caster sugar	3 tablespoons double
2 sachets vanilla sugar	cream
1 egg, separated	15 g (½ oz) cornflour
100 g (3½ oz) butter	100 g (3½ oz) flaked
1 tablespoon fresh	almonds

Sift the flour and baking powder on to a work surface and make a well in the centre. Add 50 g (2 oz) sugar, 1 sachet vanilla sugar and the egg white. Mix with some of the flour.
Add the butter cut into pieces and cover with the remaining flour. Quickly knead into a smooth dough.

Roll out two-thirds of the pastry and cover the base of a greased, deep, 28 cm (11 in) round cake tin. Make a 2 cm (¾ in) wide strip using the remaining pastry and line the sides of the tin. Prick the pastry base with a fork and sprinkle with the breadcrumbs.

For the filling: drain the cherries and arrange over the pastry. Combine the egg yolk, the remaining sugar and vanilla sugar and the cornflour. Incorporate the almonds, then pour over the cherries. Bake in a preheated oven at 180-200° C (350-400° F, Gas Mark 4-6) for 45 minutes.

POPPY SEED SLAB CAKES

Serves 6-8

375 g (12 oz) plain flour
3 teaspoons baking
powder
75 g (3 oz) caster sugar
1 sachet vanilla sugar
4 eggs
225 g (7½ oz) butter
350-400 g (11½-13 oz)
plum jam
625 g (1½ lb) ground
poppy seeds

375 ml (12 fl oz) double
cream
5-6 tablespoons honey
1 teaspoon ground
cinnamon
3 drops bitter almond
essence
125 g (4 oz) raisins
15 medium-sized apples
Whipped cream

Sift the flour and baking powder on to a work surface
and make a well in the centre. Add the sugar, vanilla

sugar and 2 eggs. Combine with some of the flour, then
add 175 g (6 oz) butter cut into pieces.
Cover with the remaining flour and quickly knead into a
smooth dough. Roll out and place on a greased baking
sheet.

For the filling: spread the plum jam over the pastry.
Smooth it out evenly.

Combine the ground poppy seeds with 500 ml (18 fl oz)
water, 3-4 tablespoons honey, the cinnamon and bitter
almond essence. Bring to the boil, then take off the heat.
Incorporate the raisins and leave to cool slightly.
Add the remaining eggs, mix well and spread over the
layer of plum jam.

OLD ENGLISH APPLE TART

Serves 6-8

350 g (11½ oz) plain flour	fruit soaked in brandy
½ teaspoon salt	Grated rind of 1 lemon
150 g (5 oz) butter	1 egg
500 g (1 lb) apples	1 tablespoon caster sugar
425 g (14 oz) mixed dried	Whipped cream to serve

Sift the flour on to a work surface and make a well in the centre. Add 7 tablespoons cold water and the salt. Combine with some of the flour. Add the butter cut into pieces and cover with the remaining flour. Knead and leave to rest for 10 minutes.

Divide the pastry into two. Roll out one half and line a 2-3 cm (¾-1½ in) deep, 28 cm (11 in) round flan tin. Set aside the remaining half.

For the filling: peel, quarter and core the apples, then cut them into medium-sized pieces. Mix the lemon rind into the mixed dried fruit. Spread over the pastry. Roll out the remaining pastry and cut into 12 strips using a pastry wheel.
Arrange them over the filling, weaving them into a lattice. Press the ends down firmly at the edge of the tart. Beat the egg and use to coat the pastry strips and the rim of the tart. Dredge with the sugar and bake in a preheated oven at 200° C (400° F, Gas Mark 6) for 35 minutes. Serve warm with whipped cream.

Above: *Poppy seed slab cakes*
Right: *Old English apple tart*

Peel, halve, and core the apples, then slice them almost through and place on the filling.
Bake in a preheated oven at 180-200° C (350-400° F, Gas Mark 4-6) for 45-50 minutes.

About 15 minutes before the final cooking time, combine the remaining butter with the remaining honey. Spread this mixture over the apples.
Serve with whipped cream if desired.

FRUITS OF THE FOREST TARTLETS

Makes about 6

200 g (7 oz) plain flour
1 teaspoon baking powder
75 g (3 oz) caster sugar
1 sachet vanilla sugar
A pinch of salt
4 drops lemon flavouring
100 g (3½ oz) butter
Whipped cream
500-750 g (1-1½ lb) fruits

of the forest
(strawberries, cherries,
raspberries, blackberries,
bilberries)
1 sachet clear jelly glaze
mix
250 ml (8 fl oz) white wine
(optional)
Whipped cream

Sift the flour and baking powder on to a work surface and make a well in the centre. Add 65 g (2½ oz) sugar, the vanilla sugar, salt, lemon flavouring and 2 table-spoons water. Start to knead using some of the flour.

Cut the butter into pieces and add to the mixture. Cover with the remaining flour and knead quickly.

Roll the pastry out 3 mm (⅛ in) thick. Cut out pastry circles with a 10-12 cm (4-4½ in) round pastry cutter. Grease smooth-sided tartlet tins and line with the pastry. Prick the bases with a fork. Arrange the tins on a baking sheet and bake in a preheated oven at 180-200° C (350-400° F, Gas Mark 4-6) for 10-15 minutes. Leave to cool, then fill with whipped cream and cover with fruits of the forest, having reserved their juice.

For the glaze: make up the jelly glaze mix following the instructions on the packet using the juice from the fruits or the white wine and sweeten with the remaining sugar. Pour over the fruits.
Serve with whipped cream.

CHOCOLATE CREAM BISCUITS

Makes about 20

250 g (8 oz) plain flour
2 teaspoons baking
powder
100 g (3½ oz) caster sugar
1 sachet vanilla sugar
2 tablespoons double
cream

375 g (12 oz) butter
1 packet chocolate
blancmange mix
250 ml (8 fl oz) milk
75 g (3 oz) icing sugar
20 g (¾ oz) cocoa powder

Sift the flour and baking powder on to a work surface and make a well in the centre. Add 50 g (2 oz) sugar, the vanilla sugar and cream. Start to knead the ingredients using some of the flour. Then add 175 g (6 oz) butter cut into pieces and cover with the remaining flour. Quickly knead into a smooth dough. If it is too sticky, leave to rest for a while. Then roll out until 3 mm (⅓ in) thick. Cut out 40 rounds using a 7 cm (2¾ in) round pastry cutter. Arrange them on a baking sheet and bake in a preheated oven at 180-200° C (350-400° F, Gas Mark 4-6) for 12-15 minutes.

For the cream filling: make up the blancmange mix following the instructions on the packet, first combining it with 4 tablespoons cold milk and the remaining sugar, then adding the remaining milk. Leave to cool, stirring from time to time.

For the icing: combine the icing sugar with the cocoa powder. Sift, then mix with 1½ tablespoons hot water to form a thick cream. Incorporate 25 g (1 oz) melted butter. Mix well and coat half of the cold biscuits.

Cream 150 g (5 oz) butter and gradually incorporate into the blancmange mixture. The ingredients must not be too cold, or else the mixture will separate. Melt the remaining butter and incorporate into the mixture. Fill an icing bag, then pipe the cream into a spiral on the other half of the biscuits. Cover with the chocolate-coated biscuits. Decorate with the chocolate cream.

Opposite: *Fruits of the forest tartlets*
Below: *Chocolate cream tarts*

GOOSEBERRY SLICES

Serves about 8

200 g (7 oz) plain flour
1 teaspoon baking powder
350 g (11½ oz) caster
sugar
1 sachet vanilla sugar
1 egg
125 g (4 oz) butter
Raspberry jam
750 g (1½ lb) gooseberries
2 tablespoons white wine

(optional)
1 packet clear jelly glaze
mix
25 g (1 oz) chopped
almonds
4 gelatine leaves
500 ml (18 fl oz) double
cream
4 tablespoons lemon juice

Sift the flour and baking powder on to a work surface and make a well in the centre. Add 75 g (3 oz) sugar, the vanilla sugar and egg. Combine with some of the flour. Add the butter (reserving a knob) cut into pieces and cover with flour. Quickly knead into a smooth dough. If it is sticky, leave to rest for a short while.

Roll out the pastry into a 30 x 30 cm (12 x 12 in) square. Place on a greased baking sheet. Bake in a preheated oven at 200-220° C (400-425° F, Gas Mark 6-7) for 20 minutes. Remove from the oven and cut into two layers, then leave to cool. Cover half of them with raspberry jam.

For the filling: wash and drain the gooseberries. Cook over a low heat with 200 g (7 oz) sugar and 2 tablespoons water or white wine, stirring until soft (they must not disintegrate). Make the glaze by mixing the glaze mix with 1 tablespoon sugar and the gooseberry juice and following the instructions on the packet. Add the gooseberries.

For the praline: heat the reserved knob of butter and 15 g (½ oz) sugar until it starts to brown. Incorporate the chopped almonds, continue to heat while stirring until the praline is deep golden. Leave to cool on a greased baking sheet. Crush. Arrange a layer of gooseberries over the jam pastry layer and top with the remaining pastry layer. Press down firmly.

Put the gelatine in a small pan with 3 tablespoons cold water. Leave to soak for 10 minutes. Heat the gelatine until dissolved, then incorporate the lemon juice. Whip the cream with the remaining sugar for 30 seconds. Incorporate the gelatine mixture. Spread over the cake. Sprinkle with the praline. Leave to set, then cut into slices.

Below: *Gooseberry slices*

Above: *Bitter almond essence doughnuts*

ALMOND DOUGHNUTS

Makes 20-30

500 g (1 lb) plain flour
2 teaspoons baking
powder
150 g (5 oz) caster sugar
3-4 drops bitter almond
essence

2 tablespoons rum
3 eggs
150 g (5 oz) butter
Frying oil
Icing sugar

Leave to rise and fry in a deep-fat fryer until golden on both sides. Remove the doughnuts with a slotted spoon and leave to drain on a wire rack. Dredge with icing sugar while still hot.

Sift the flour and baking powder on to a work surface and make a well in the centre. Add the sugar, bitter almond essence, rum and eggs. Combine with some of the flour. Add the butter cut into pieces and cover with the remaining flour. Quickly knead into a smooth dough. If it is sticky, leave to rest for a short while. Then roll out until 1 cm (½ in) thick and cut into almond-shaped pieces.

Above: *Pineapple pie*

PINEAPPLE PIE

Serves 6

225 g (7½ oz) plain flour
1 tablespoon icing sugar
A pinch of salt
250 g (8 oz) butter
500 g (1 lb) pineapple chunks in syrup
100 g (3½ oz) caster sugar

1 sachet vanilla sugar
3 eggs, separated
50 g (2 oz) ground almonds
125 ml (4 fl oz) double cream

Sift 175 g (6 oz) flour on to a work surface and make a well in the centre. Add the icing sugar, salt and 3 tablespoons cold water. Combine with some of the flour. Cut half the butter into pieces, cover with the remaining flour and quickly knead into a smooth dough. Leave to rest for 1-2 hours.

Line a 2-3 cm (¾-1½ in) deep, 28 cm (11 in) round flan or cake tin. Prick the base with a fork.

For the filling: drain the pineapple well and arrange over the pastry. In a mixing bowl, cream the remaining butter, then gradually add the caster sugar, vanilla sugar and egg yolks and mix well.
Incorporate the ground almonds into the remaining flour and gradually add to the mixture.
Whip the cream until firm and fold into the mixture.
Whisk the egg whites into peaks and gently fold them in.
Pour the mixture over the pineapple chunks.
Bake in a preheated oven at 180-200° C (350-400° F, Gas Mark 4-6) for 40-45 minutes.

STRAWBERRY AND RHUBARB TARTLETS

Makes 20-30

175 g (6 oz) plain flour
250 g (8 oz) caster sugar
2 eggs
A pinch of salt
2 teaspoons grated lemon rind
Pulp of 1 vanilla pod
200 g (7 oz) butter
100 g (3½ oz) hazelnuts, finely chopped

100 g (3½ oz) crunchy rolled oats
750 g (1½ lb) strawberries
1.5 kg (3½ lb) rhubarb
125 ml (4 fl oz) white wine
450 g (15 oz) redcurrant jelly
1 sachet powdered gelatine or 4 gelatine leaves

Sift the flour on to a work surface and make a well in the centre. Add 100 g (3½ oz) sugar, the eggs, salt, lemon rind and vanilla. Work into a thick paste using some of the flour. Cut the butter into pieces and add to the flour mixture, together with the chopped hazelnuts and rolled oats. Quickly knead into a smooth dough. Make into a ball and leave to rest for 2 hours.

For the filling: wash, drain, hull and halve the strawberries. Wash the rhubarb and cut into 5 cm (2 in) long chunks.

Bring the white wine and the remaining sugar to the boil. Add the rhubarb and cook until tender (it must not disintegrate). Drain (saving the juice). Divide the ball of pastry into two and roll out each half into a 40 x 14 cm (16 x 5½ in) rectangle.

Transfer these pastry strips to a greased baking sheet. Make a 2 cm (¾ in) deep rim along the long sides of the strips. Bake in a preheated oven at 200° C (400° F, Gas Mark 6) for 20-25 minutes. Remove from the oven and brush immediately with redcurrant jelly. Fill with strawberry and rhubarb pieces.

For the glaze: soak the gelatine in 4 tablespoons cold water in a small pan for 10 minutes. Mix the remaining jelly with the rhubarb juice and bring to the boil. Allow to reduce for 8-10 minutes until only 400 ml (14 fl oz) is left. Add the gelatine. Mix well. Leave to cool slightly, then coat the fruits. Cut each strip into ten slices

Below: *Strawberry and rhubarb tartlets*

STRAWBERRY MOUSSE TARTLETS

Makes 10-11

150 g (5 oz) plain flour
½ teaspoon baking
powder
175 g (6 oz) caster sugar
1 sachet vanilla sugar
1 egg
65 g (2½ oz) butter

2 sachets powdered
gelatine
500-700 g (1 lb-1 lb 6 oz)
strawberries
Juice of ½ lemon
500-600 ml (18 fl oz-1
pint) double cream

Sift the flour and baking powder on to a work surface. Make a well in the centre. Add 65 g (2½ oz) sugar, the vanilla sugar and egg. Incorporate the butter cut into pieces. Cover

Below:
Strawberry mousse tartlets

with flour and quickly knead into a smooth dough. Roll out until 3 mm (⅓ in) thick. Cut out circles using a fluted 10 cm (4 in) round pastry cutter. Transfer to a greased baking sheet and prick with a fork. Bake in a preheated oven at 180-200° C (350-400° F, Gas Mark 4-6) for 10-15 minutes. Leave to cool.

For the individual mousses: soak the gelatine in a pan in 6 tablespoons cold water for 10 minutes. Wash and drain the strawberries, reserving a few, then purée them, adding 100 g (3½ oz) sugar and the lemon juice.

Heat the gelatine, stirring constantly, until it has dissolved, then add to the strawberry purée. When the mixture starts to set, whip 375 ml (12 fl oz) cream until firm and gently fold into the purée. Mix well and pour into oiled, fluted, 7 cm (2¾ in) round jelly moulds. Smooth out evenly and place in a refrigerator.

When the mousses have set, quickly plunge the moulds into hot water and turn them out on to the biscuits.

Whip the remaining cream with the remaining sugar. Fill an icing bag and decorate the tarts. Add the halved strawberries just before serving.

COTTAGE CHEESE PARCELS

Makes about 10

150 g (5 oz) plain flour	into pieces
2 sachets vanilla sugar	250 g (8 oz) cornflour
A pinch of salt	50 g (2 oz) caster sugar
150 g (5 oz) cottage cheese	1 egg, separated
	25 g (1 oz) raisins
150 g (5 oz) butter, cut	1 ½ tablespoons milk

Sift the flour on to a work surface, make a well in the centre, then add 1 sachet vanilla sugar, the salt, cottage cheese and butter. Quickly knead into a smooth dough. It must not be too soft. If so, add a little more flour. Leave to rest in a refrigerator for 1 hour.

For the filling: combine the cornflour, sugar, the remaining vanilla sugar and the egg white. Incorporate the raisins.

Roll out half the pastry into a 30 x 30 cm (12 x 12 in) square, then cut into 10 x 10 cm (4 x 4 in) squares. Place some filling in the middle of each square. Beat the egg yolk and milk together and brush over the edges of the pastry. Fold over the pastry squares to make parcels.

Roll out the remaining pastry and cut into thin strips. Arrange two strips on each parcel, intertwining them to form a cross. Brush with the egg-milk mixture. Bake in a preheated oven at 200-220° C (400-425° F, Gas Mark 6-7) for 25 minutes.

MARZIPAN FINGERS

Makes 30-40

500 g (1 lb) plain flour
1 teaspoon baking powder
175 g (6 oz) caster sugar
2 sachets vanilla sugar
3 eggs

250 g (8 oz) butter
4 tablespoons jam
125 g (4 oz) almond paste
Grated rind of ½ lemon

Sift 250 g (8 oz) flour and ½ teaspoon baking powder on to a work surface and make a well in the centre. Add 75 g (3 oz) sugar, 1 sachet vanilla sugar and 1 egg. Combine with some of the flour. Add 125 g (4 oz) butter cut into pieces and cover with the remaining flour. Quickly knead into a smooth dough. If it is sticky, leave to rest for a short while.

Roll out the pastry into a 40 x 32 cm (16 x 12¾ in) rectangle. Place on a greased baking sheet. Prick with a fork. Bake in a preheated oven at 180-200° C (350-400° F, Gas Mark 4-6) for 15 minutes. Coat with the jam as soon as it is out of the oven.

For the filling: using an electric mixer fitted with a kneading attachment, combine the almond paste with the remaining butter. Then gradually incorporate the remaining sugar and vanilla sugar, eggs and lemon rind. Mix the remaining flour and baking powder together. Gradually incorporate into the almond butter mixture.

Fill an icing bag fitted with a fluted nozzle and pipe this mixture on to the cooked strips. Return to the oven at the same temperature and bake for 20 minutes. Cut into small fingers immediately.

Opposite: *Marzipan fingers*
Right: *Gooseberry crumble*

GOOSEBERRY CRUMBLE

Serves 8-10

625 g (1½ lb)
gooseberries
400 ml (14 fl oz) white
wine
325 g (11 oz) caster sugar
1 cinnamon stick

A twist of lemon rind
125 g (4 oz) plain flour
125 g (4 oz) ground
almonds
Ground cinnamon
150 g (5 oz) butter

Hull, wash and drain the gooseberries. Prick each one several times with a darning needle. Place in a pan with the white wine, 200 g (7 oz) sugar, the cinnamon stick and lemon rind. Bring to the boil and cook over a low heat for 8 minutes. Drain.

Put the flour in a bowl together with the ground almonds, the remaining sugar and some ground cinnamon. Melt the butter, allow to cool before adding to the pan, mixing well with two forks to break up the mixture.
Place the drained gooseberries in a well-greased flan dish, cover with the crumble mixture, spreading it out evenly. Bake in a preheated oven at 200° C (400° F, Gas Mark 6) for 20-25 minutes.

APFELSTRUDEL

Serves 6

200 g (7 oz) strong (bread) flour
A pinch of salt
150 g (5 oz) butter, softened
1-1.5 kg (2-3½ lb) apples
2 tablespoons rum

50 g (2 oz) sultanas
50 g (2 oz) fresh breadcrumbs
100 g (3½ oz) caster sugar
1 sachet vanilla sugar
50 g (2 oz) chopped almonds

Sift the flour on to a work surface and make a well in the centre. Add the salt, 75 ml (2½ fl oz) warm water and 50 g (2 oz) softened butter. Combine with some of the flour, then cover with the remaining flour and knead quickly into a smooth dough. Knead into a ball and leave to rest for 30 minutes in a large, covered pan in which water has previously been boiled. The pan must still be hot, but absolutely dry. Line the bottom of the pan with greaseproof paper.

For the filling: peel, quarter and core the apples, then cut into thin slices. Sprinkle with rum and mix in the sultanas.

Melt the remaining butter. Smooth out the dough on a floured cloth and coat with a thin layer of melted butter. Then, using the hands, stretch it out into a 50 x 70 cm (20 x 28 in) rectangle.
The dough should be so thin that it is transparent.
Cut off any thick pieces of pastry there may be at the edges. Coat the pastry with melted butter.

Sprinkle two-thirds of the pastry with breadcrumbs, starting with the widest sides and leaving a 3 cm (1½ in) margin along the short sides. Cover with the apples and sultanas, sugar, vanilla sugar and chopped almonds. Fold the short sides which have no breadcrumbs over the filling and roll up the pastry and the filling lengthways. Press the two pastry edges firmly together.

Place the strudel on a greased baking sheet and coat the pastry with melted butter. Bake in a preheated oven at 180-200° C (350-400° F, Gas Mark 4-6) for 45-55 minutes. Coat with the remaining butter during the cooking time.

Above right: *Almond and apple pie*
Below: *Apfelstrudel*

ALMOND AND APPLE PIE

Serves 6

275 g (9 oz) plain flour	1.25 kg (3 lb) apples
1 teaspoon baking powder	Ground cinnamon
140 g (4½ oz) caster sugar	3 tablespoons ground
1 sachet vanilla sugar	almonds
A pinch of salt	2 tablespoons fresh
1 egg, separated	breadcrumbs
175 g (6 oz) butter	40 g (1½ oz) almonds, cut
250 ml (8 fl oz) double	into slivers
cream	

Sift the flour and baking powder on to a work surface. Make a well in the centre. Add 50 g (2 oz) sugar, the vanilla sugar, salt and egg white. Combine with some of the flour, then add the butter cut into pieces and half the cream. Cover with flour and knead into a smooth dough. Leave to rest for 2-3 hours in a refrigerator.

For the filling: peel, quarter, core and slice the apples. Sprinkle with ground cinnamon and 65 g (2½ oz) sugar. Roll out two-thirds of the pastry and line a greased, 28-30 cm (11-12 in) diameter flan dish.
In a bowl, combine the ground almonds with the breadcrumbs and sprinkle over the pastry. Arrange the apple slices on top.
Roll out the remaining pastry and cut to the size of the flan dish. Dampen the edge of the pastry and place the pastry top over the fruit. Seal the edges together and prick the top with a fork. Bake in a preheated oven at 200° C (400° F, Gas Mark 6) for 50 minutes. After 20 minutes, beat the remaining cream with the egg yolk. Spread this mixture over the pie. Combine the cinnamon with the remaining sugar and sprinkle over the pie, together with the almond slivers.

TWO MELON TARTLETS

Makes 16

200 g (7 oz) plain flour
140 g (4½ oz) caster sugar
1 egg yolk
A pinch of salt
2 teaspoons grated lemon rind
1 tablespoon brandy
25 g (1 oz) butter
250 g (8 oz) apricot jam

2 melons, about 1.5 kg (3½ lb) in total
4 tablespoons lemon juice
1 sachet powdered gelatine or 4 gelatine leaves
4 egg whites
½ watermelon

Sift the flour on to a work surface and make a well in the centre. Add 65 g (2½ oz) sugar, the egg yolk, salt, 1 teaspoon grated lemon rind and the brandy. Combine with some of the flour. Add the butter cut into pieces. Cover with the remaining flour and quickly knead into a smooth dough.

Leave to rest for 30 minutes in a refrigerator. Roll out the pastry and cut into 8 cm (3 in) circles. Line greased tartlet tins with the pastry. Prick the bases with a fork and bake in a preheated oven at 200° C (400° F, Gas Mark 6) for 15-18 minutes. Leave to cool, then remove from the tins.

For the filling: coat the tartlets with apricot jam. Cut up 1 melon, remove the seeds and scrape out the flesh using a large spoon. Liquidize into a purée, together with the remaining lemon rind and the juice. Place in a refrigerator.

Soak the gelatine in 4 tablespoons cold water in a small pan for 10 minutes, then heat until completely dissolved. Incorporate in the melon purée. Heat the remaining sugar with 4 tablespoons water until it forms a syrup. Whisk the egg whites into stiff peaks, then mix with the syrup and incorporate into the melon purée.

Halve the remaining melon, remove the seeds, cut into eight pieces and peel the slices. Finely dice half the flesh,

Below: *Two melon tartlets*

slicing the remaining half finely. Add the dice to the melon purée and place in the refrigerator until firm. Use to fill the tartlets. Return to the refrigerator for 30 minutes before adding the melon slices and some watermelon balls and slices.

HAZELNUT TARTLETS

Makes 16-18

200 g (7 oz) whole hazelnuts
225 g (7½ oz) plain flour
475 g (15½ oz) caster sugar
1 egg yolk
2 pinches of salt
150 g (5 oz) butter
Grated rind of 1 lemon
½ teaspoon ground cinnamon
8 egg whites

Above: *Hazelnut tartlets*

Spread the hazelnuts over a baking sheet and roast for 8-12 minutes in a preheated oven at 200-220° C (400-425° F, Gas Mark 6-7). When cool, rub the hazelnuts between your hands to remove the skins. Grind.

For the pastry: sift the flour on to a work surface and make a well in the centre, reserving 1 tablespoon for the filling. Add 75 g (3 oz) sugar, the egg yolk and a pinch of salt and combine with some of the flour.

Add the butter cut into pieces, cover with the remaining flour and quickly knead all the ingredients into a smooth dough. Leave to rest for about 30 minutes in a refrigerator.

Grease the base of 16-18, 9 cm (3½ in) round tartlet tins. Arrange the tins so that they touch each other. Roll out the pastry the same size as all the tins together. Drape the pastry over the rolling pin, then place over the tins. Roll the rolling pin over the pastry, pressing down firmly to cut it. Press the pastry down into the tins, then prick with a fork. Bake in a preheated oven at 180° C (350° F, Gas Mark 4) for 8-10 minutes.

For the filling: place the ground hazelnuts, the remaining sugar and salt, the grated lemon rind, ground cinnamon and 8 egg whites in a pan. Heat, stirring constantly, for 8-10 minutes until they form a smooth ball. The sugar should have dissolved. Take off the heat and incorporate the reserved flour.

Spoon this mixture into the blind-baked tartlets. Return to the oven at the same temperature and cook for a further 30-35 minutes. Leave to cool for 10 minutes before turning out of the tins.

PEACH AND ALMOND TARTLETS

Makes 16

350 g (11½ oz) plain flour
175 g (6 oz) caster sugar
2 eggs
A pinch of salt
½ teaspoon ground cinnamon
200 g (7 oz) butter
8 large, ripe peaches
1 sachet powdered gelatine or 4 gelatine leaves
4 egg yolks

400 ml (14 fl oz) apricot juice
2 tablespoons lemon juice
3 tablespoons apricot brandy
400 g (13 oz) plain almond paste
200 ml (7 fl oz) double cream
250 g (8 oz) apricot jam
100-150 g (3½-5 oz) flaked almonds

Sift the flour on to a work surface and make a well in the centre. Add 100 g (3½ oz) sugar, the eggs, salt and cinnamon. Combine with some of the flour. Add the butter cut into pieces, then cover with the remaining flour and knead into a smooth dough. Leave to rest for 30 minutes in a refrigerator.

Grease 16, 10 cm (4 in) round tart tins. Arrange the tins so that they touch each other. Roll out the pastry, then drape over the rolling pin and lay it over the tins. Roll the rolling pin over the pastry, pressing down firmly to cut it. Press the pastry into the tins, then prick with a fork.
Bake in a preheated oven at 220° C (425° F, Gas Mark 7)

Below: *Peach and almond tartlets*

for 12-15 minutes. Leave to cool slightly before removing from the tins.

For the filling: quickly plunge the peaches into boiling water, then soak in cold water. Peel and halve them and remove the stones. Slice almost through to the flat, cut side of the peaches.

Soak the gelatine in 4 tablespoons cold water in a pan for 10 minutes. Then heat, stirring constantly, until it has dissolved.
Beat the egg yolks and the remaining sugar using an electric mixer until thick and pale yellow.

Bring the apricot juice and lemon juice to the boil. Add a little to the egg yolk mixture. Take the fruit juice off the heat and add the warm gelatine. Mix into the egg yolk mixture and leave to cool, stirring occasionally.

Incorporate the apricot brandy in the almond paste and mix well. Transfer to an icing bag and fill the middle of the tartlets with this mixture, leaving a 1 cm (½ in) gap around the edges.

Whip the cream until firm and fold into the cooled egg yolk mixture. Transfer this mixture to another icing bag fitted with a medium-sized nozzle and cover the almond paste with a small mound of cream. Leave to cool for 15 minutes. Toast the almonds in an ungreased frying pan.

Place a peach half in each tartlet. Sieve the apricot jam, bring to the boil and take off the heat. Leave until warm and coat each peach and the sides of the tartlets. Press flaked almonds around the peaches.

HAZELNUT ROULADE RING

Serves 8

300 g (10 oz) plain flour
2 teaspoons baking powder
200 g (7 oz) caster sugar
1 sachet vanilla sugar
A pinch of salt
1 egg
3 tablespoons milk

125 g (4 oz) butter, softened
200 g (7 oz) ground hazelnuts
4-5 drops bitter almond essence
1 egg, separated

Combine the flour and baking powder. Make a well and add 100 g (3½ oz) sugar, the vanilla sugar, salt, egg and 2 tablespoons milk or water. Work these ingredients into a thick paste using some of the flour. Cut the butter into pieces and add to the mixture. Cover with the remaining

Above: *Hazelnut roulade ring*

flour and knead quickly. If it is sticky, leave to rest in a refrigerator.

For the filling: combine the ground hazelnuts with the remaining sugar, the bitter almond essence, half an egg yolk, the egg white and 3-4 tablespoons water to form a smooth cream.
Roll the pastry into a 36 x 46 cm (14 x 18 in) rectangle. Cover with a layer of hazelnut cream. Roll it up, starting from the longest side, and make into a ring. Place on a greased baking sheet.

Beat the remaining egg yolk with the remaining milk and brush over the pastry. Make incisions in the top of the ring to form a star. Bake in a preheated oven at 180-200° C (350-400° F, Gas Mark 4-6) for 45 minutes.

BLACKBERRY MERINGUE BOATS

Makes 12

125 g (4 oz) plain flour
A pinch of baking powder
150 g (5 oz) caster sugar
2 sachets vanilla sugar
1 egg yolk
½ tablespoon milk
65 g (2½ oz) butter
40 g (1½ oz) chocolate
2 teaspoons cornflour

250 ml (8 fl oz) double
cream
1 egg
3 tablespoons kirsch
250 g (8 oz) blackberries
1 tablespoon blackberry
or redcurrant jelly
1 egg white

Sift the flour and baking powder on to a work surface and make a well in the centre. Add 25 g (1 oz) sugar, 1 sachet vanilla sugar, the egg yolk and milk. Combine with some of the flour. Add the butter (reserving 1 teaspoon) cut into pieces, cover with the remaining flour and quickly knead into a smooth paste. Leave to rest for 1 hour in a refrigerator.

Roll the pastry out. Cut into 12 rounds and line greased boat-shaped tins, cutting away any excess pastry. Bake

in a preheated oven at 200°C (400°F, Gas Mark 6) for 12 minutes. Remove from the tins immediately and leave to cool. Melt the chocolate with the reserved butter in a bowl over a pan of hot water. Coat the inside of the pastry cases.

For the filling: mix the cornflour with 1 tablespoon sugar, the remaining vanilla sugar and the cream in a small pan. Add the egg. Bring to the boil, beating constantly. When the mixture is smooth, remove from the heat. Incorporate the kirsch. Leave to cool, then spoon into the pastry cases. Smooth out evenly.

Wash and drain the blackberries, then dredge with 2 tablespoons sugar (save the juice). Place in a pan with the jelly and bring to the boil. Boil for a short while, then arrange on the pastry cases. Coat the edges with melted jelly.

Whisk the egg white into peaks, then gradually incorporate the remaining sugar, whisking constantly. Fill an icing bag fitted with a large, fluted nozzle and decorate the tartlets.
Place under a preheated grill for 1-2 minutes until golden.

HAZELNUT CROISSANTS

Makes 10-12

300 g (10 oz) puff pastry
Condensed milk
100 g (3½ oz) ground
hazelnuts

50 g (2 oz) caster sugar
3-4 drops bitter almond
essence
Icing sugar to finish

Remove the pastry from the refrigerator to bring it up to room temperature. Roll it out into a 70 x 14 cm (27 x 5½ in) rectangle. Cut into triangles using a pastry wheel. The base of the triangles should measure 10 cm (4 in). Brush condensed milk over the edges of the triangles.

For the filling: combine the ground hazelnuts with the sugar, bitter almond essence and 3 tablespoons water.

Spread over the pastry triangles and roll them up into croissants. Place on a baking sheet sprinkled with cold water. Brush with condensed milk and bake in a preheated oven at 200-220° C (400-425° F, Gas Mark 6-7) for 15 minutes. Dredge with icing sugar.

Alternative: you can coat the croissants with 300 g (10 oz) icing sugar combined with 1 egg white and a few drops of lemon juice.

APPLE TURNOVERS

Makes about 6

2 tablespoons raisins
4 tablespoons rum
375 g (12 oz) plain flour
125 g (4 oz) caster sugar
2 sachets vanilla sugar
1 egg
175 g (6 oz) butter

150 g (5 oz) almond paste
75 g (3 oz) icing sugar
6 apples, about 1 kg (2 lb)
1 egg yolk
1 tablespoon milk
75 g (3 oz) chopped
blanched almonds

Soak the raisins in 3 tablespoons rum overnight.

sift the flour on to a work surface and make a well in the centre. Add 75 g (3 oz) sugar, the vanilla sugar and the egg. Combine with some of the flour. Add the butter cut into pieces and cover with the remaining flour. Quickly knead into a smooth dough. Leave to rest for 30 minutes in a refrigerator.

For the filling: combine the almond paste and icing sugar with the remaining rum. Cover and set aside. Peel the apples and core them using an apple-corer.

Above: *Apple turnovers*
Opposite: *Blackberry apple boats*

Use a knife to enlarge the hole. Divide the almond paste in two. Cut one half into six pieces. Use to fill the base of the apples. Cut six more pieces from the remaining almond paste and seal each hole. Roll the apples in the remaining sugar.

On a floured surface, roll out the pastry to 33 x 50 cm (13 x 20 in) and cut out 4, 15 x 15 cm (6 x 6 in) squares. Place an apple on each square. Lift up the 4 corners to wrap over the apples, pressing the edges together to seal them. Cut out 4, 4 cm (1½ in) diameter circles from the remaining pastry and place on the top. Press down slightly to ensure they stick.

Beat the egg yolk and the milk together and brush over the pastry. Sprinkle with the chopped almonds and place on a greased baking sheet in a preheated oven at 200° C (400° F, Gas Mark 6) for 30 minutes.

APPLE AND WHITE WINE CREAM TARTLETS

Makes 10-15

150 g (5 oz) plain flour
½ teaspoon baking powder
125 g (4 oz) caster sugar
2 sachets vanilla sugar
1 egg
65 g (2½ oz) butter
6 small apples

125 ml (4 fl oz) white wine
1 cinnamon stick
1 packet vanilla blancmange mix
1 packet clear jelly glaze mix
50 g (2 oz) flaked almonds

Sift the flour and baking powder on to a work surface, then make a well in the centre. Add 65 g (2½ oz) sugar, 1 sachet vanilla sugar and the egg. Combine with some of the flour. Add the butter cut into pieces and cover with flour, then knead into a smooth dough. Roll out thinly. Cut into 10 cm (4 in) diameter circles. Place on a greased baking sheet and bake in a preheated oven at 180-200° C (350-400° F, Gas Mark 4-6) for 10-15 minutes.

For the filling: peel, halve and core the apples. Bring 125 ml (4 fl oz) water, the white wine, the remaining sugar and vanilla sugar and the cinnamon stick to the boil. Add the apple halves, cover and poach over a low heat (they must stay firm). Drain (saving the juice) and leave to cool.

Using 250 ml (8 fl oz) of the reserved juice, make up the blancmange following the instructions on the packet (but with no water). Pour into the cooled tartlets. Place an apple half in each tartlet. Make up the tart glaze using 250 ml (8 fl oz) of the apple cooking liquid. Pour over the apples. Sprinkle with toasted flaked almonds.

KIWI TARTLETS

Makes about 4

300 g (10 oz) cream cheese
3 small glasses advocat

3 sachets vanilla sugar
4 tartlet pastry cases
2 kiwi fruits

Beat the cream cheese with the advocat and vanilla sugar in a bowl. Transfer the mixture to an icing bag fitted with a large nozzle and fill the pastry cases. Peel and quarter the kiwi fruits lengthways, then cut into slices. Arrange decoratively over the cream cheese.

POPPY SEED STRUDEL

Serves 6

250 g (8 oz) strong (bread) flour
A pinch of salt
2 eggs
1 tablespoon frying oil
500 g (1 lb) ground poppy seeds
100 g (3½ oz) caster sugar

3 tablespoons honey
Grated rind of 1 lemon
100 g (3½ oz) raisins
250 g (8 oz) cooking apples
50 g (2 oz) butter, softened
Icing sugar to finish

Sift the flour on to a work surface and make a well in the centre. Add the salt, 100 ml (3½ oz) hot water, 1 egg and the oil. Combine with some of the flour, then quickly knead into a smooth dough. Knead into a ball and leave to rest for 30 minutes in a large, covered, hot, absolutely dry pan in which water has previously been boiled, the base being covered with greaseproof paper.

For the filling: Sprinkle 375-500 ml (12-18 fl oz) boiling water over the poppy seeds. Leave to soak, stirring until a smooth paste is formed. Combine the sugar, honey, the remaining egg, the lemon rind and raisins. Peel, core and coarsely grate the apples.

Roll the pastry out into a thin layer on a floured tea towel. Using the hands, stretch it out into a 50 x 70 cm (20 x 28 in) rectangle. The pastry should be transparent. Make the edges even by cutting off any pastry which is too thick. Spread the filling over two-thirds of the pastry, leaving a 3 cm (1½ in) margin on the short sides.

Below: *Kiwi tartlets*

Above: *Poppy seed strudel*

Roll up the cake using the tea towel. Smooth down the
long edge of the pastry using your finger so that the cake
does not unroll. Place on a greased baking sheet and
coat with the softened butter. Bake in a preheated oven
at 200-220° C (400-425° F, Gas Mark 6-7) for 50 minutes.
Leave to cool, then dredge with icing sugar.

APRICOT WINDMILLS

Makes 5-6

300 g (10 oz) puff pastry
400 g (13 oz) apricot
halves in syrup
Blanched almonds

1 egg yolk
1 tablespoon milk
2 tablespoons apricot jam

Roll out the pastry to 46 x 20 cm (18 x 8 in). Cut into rectangles and circles and 10 x 10 cm (4 x 4 in) squares for the windmill-shaped tarts.

Drain the apricot halves well, place in the pastry pieces. Shape into windmills, oval and round Flemish and Danish pastries. Place on a baking sheet sprinkled with water. Decorate with blanched almonds and pastry shapes. Beat the egg yolk with the milk. Brush over the pastry. Do not let it run down on to the baking sheet. Bake in a preheated oven at 200-220° C (400-425° F, Gas Mark 6-7) for 15 minutes.

For the glaze: sieve the jam, then heat with 1 tablespoon water. Brush over the pastries as soon as they are out of the oven.

MIXED FRUIT AND NUT SQUARES

Makes 10-15

150 g (5 oz) mixed dried
fruit and nuts (almonds,
figs, hazelnuts, raisins)
2 tablespoons rum
300 g (10 oz) puff pastry
250 g (8 oz) black grapes
250 g (8 oz) white grapes
500 g (1 lb) apples
500 g (1 lb) pears
Rind of 1 large lemon
5 tablespoons lemon juice
250 g (8 oz) butter,

softened
400 g (13 oz) icing sugar
A pinch of salt
6 eggs
625 g (1½ lb) plain flour
2 teaspoons baking
powder
150 g (5 oz) crushed
hazelnuts
1 egg, separated
Whipped cream to serve

Soak the dried fruit and nuts in the rum for 1-2 hours. Take the puff pastry out of the refrigerator. Wash and drain the black and white grapes, halve them and remove the pips. Peel, quarter and core the apples and pears. Cut into moderately thin slices. Mix the fresh and dried fruits and nuts, adding the lemon rind and 2 tablespoons lemon juice.

For the fruit mixture: in a mixing bowl, cream the butter, then gradually add 250 g (8 oz) icing sugar, the salt

and 6 eggs. Sift the flour and baking powder into a separate bowl, then gradually incorporate into the creamed butter. Add the fresh and dried fruit and nut mixture, then the crushed hazelnuts. Spread over a greased baking sheet. Smooth out evenly.

Roll out the puff pastry on a work surface, drape it over the rolling pin, then carefully lay it over the fruit mixture. Press it down lightly over the edges. Beat the egg yolk with a little water and brush over the pastry. Prick with a fork. Bake in a preheated oven at 180-200° C (350-400° F, Gas Mark 6-7) for 35 minutes.

For the icing: mix the remaining icing sugar and lemon juice together with a little egg white. Coat the cake while still hot. Leave to cool slightly, then cut into squares. Serve warm with whipped cream.

Opposite: *Apricot windmills*
Below: *Mixed fruit and nut squares*

COTTAGE CHEESE GÂTEAU

Serves 6

50 g (2 oz) raisins
4 tablespoons rum
75 g (3 oz) blanched almonds
75 g (3 oz) rusks
125 g (4 oz) butter, softened
200 g (7 oz) caster sugar
1 sachet vanilla sugar
5 eggs, separated
Grated rind of 1 lemon
3 tablespoons lemon juice
A pinch of salt
1 kg (2 lb) cottage cheese
1 packet vanilla blancmange mix
1 tablespoon semolina
Icing sugar to finish
Whipped cream to serve

Soak the raisins in the rum for 3-4 hours. Grind the blanched almonds finely. Place the rusks on a clean tea towel and crush with a rolling pin. Mix with the ground almonds. Spread over the base of a greased, deep, 28 cm (11 in) round cake tin. Smooth out evenly.

Cream the butter, then gradually add the sugar, vanilla sugar, egg yolks, lemon rind, lemon juice and salt. Stir until the sugar has dissolved.

Combine the rum-soaked raisins and the cottage cheese. Make up the vanilla blancmange mix following the instructions on the packet and incorporate it, together with the semolina, into the cottage cheese mixture. Whisk the egg whites into stiff peaks. Gently fold them in. Pour this mixture over the almond-crumb mixture. Smooth it out evenly and bake in a preheated oven at 180° C (350° F, Gas Mark 4) for 75-90 minutes. Cover the cake with greaseproof paper if it is becoming too brown on top. Leave to cool in the oven with the door ajar, then carefully remove from the tin and dredge with icing sugar. Serve with whipped cream.

MILANESE MARZIPAN DISCS

Makes 10-15

200 g (7 oz) plain flour
65 g (2½ oz) caster sugar
Grated rind of ½ lemon
125 g (4 oz) butter
200 g (7 oz) almond paste
25 g (1 oz) icing sugar
1 egg yolk
1 tablespoon lemon juice
1-2 tablespoons rum
2-3 tablespoons apricot jam
3-4 glacé cherries
Whipped cream to serve

Sift the flour on to a work surface and make a well in the centre. Add the caster sugar, lemon rind and butter cut into pieces. Cover with a little flour and quickly knead into a smooth dough, gradually incorporating the remaining flour.

Roll the pastry out to 3 mm (⅓ in). Cut out 8 cm (3 in) diameter circles. Place on a greased baking sheet lined with greaseproof paper.

For the filling: knead 125 g (4 oz) almond paste using an electric mixer fitted with a kneading attachment. Then incorporate the icing sugar, egg yolk and lemon juice. Mix well until creamy. Fill an icing bag fitted with a small nozzle and pipe a small mound on to half the pastry circles. Bake in a preheated oven at 180-200°C (350-400°F, Gas Mark 4-6) for 15 minutes. Leave to cool.

Knead the remaining almond paste, using the mixer. Incorporate the rum and 1 tablespoon apricot jam. Spread over the remaining half of the pastry circles. Cover with the circles which have already been decorated. Quarter the glacé cherries and place a piece on each biscuit.

For the glaze: mix the remaining apricot jam with 2 tablespoons water. Sieve and bring to the boil. Brush over the discs. Decorate with whipped cream if desired.

Left: *Cottage cheese gâteau*

Above: *Milanese marzipan discs*

APPLE LATTICE

Serves 6-8

250 g (8 oz) plain flour
2 sachets vanilla sugar
A pinch of salt
250 g (8 oz) cornflour
250 g (8 oz) butter

2 kg (4½ lb) apples
75-100 g (3-3½ oz) caster
sugar
125 g (4 oz) sultanas
Condensed milk

Sift the flour on to a work surface and make a well in the centre. Add 1 sachet vanilla sugar, the salt, cornflour and butter cut into pieces. Cover the ingredients with flour and quickly knead into a smooth dough. If it is too soft, add a little more flour and leave to rest for 1 hour in a refrigerator.

For the filling: peel, quarter and core the apples. Cook in a covered pan over a low heat with the sugar and the remaining vanilla sugar until soft. Leave to cool, then incorporate the sultanas.

Roll out two-thirds of the pastry and line a greased baking sheet. Cover with the apple-sultana mixture. Roll out the remaining pastry thinly, then cut into 1 cm (½ in) wide strips. Intertwine the strips over the cake to form a lattice. Brush with condensed milk and bake in a preheated oven at 200-220° C (400-425° F, Gas Mark 6-7) for 30-35 minutes.

PASTRY HEARTS

Makes about 10

300 g (10 oz) puff pastry
25 g (1 oz) warm, melted
butter

50 g (2 oz) caster sugar
1 sachet vanilla sugar

Take the pastry out of the refrigerator a few hours beforehand. Then roll it out into a 55 x 22 cm (22 x 8½ in) rectangle. Brush with the butter. Mix the sugar and vanilla sugar together and sprinkle over the pastry.

Fold the left side two-thirds of the way towards the right, then the right side one-third towards the left, then roll it out to 30 x 30 cm (12 x 12 in). Fold the left and right edges into the centre again, leaving a 2 cm (¾ in) gap in the middle. Fold the left side over the right side again and leave to rest in the refrigerator until firm enough to be cut. Using a sharp knife, cut the pastry into 5 mm (⅕ in) thick slices.

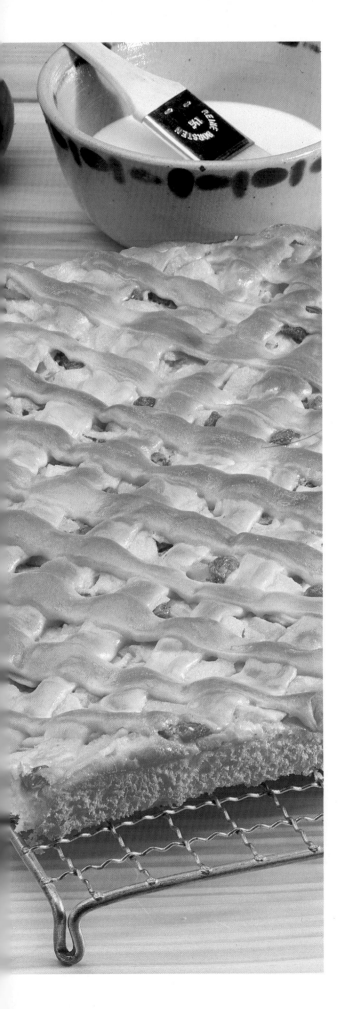

Above: *Pastry hearts*
Opposite: *Apple lattice*

Dredge the tops of the pastry hearts with icing sugar if desired, then place on a baking sheet sprinkled with cold water. Bake in a preheated oven at 180-200° C (350-400° F, Gas Mark 6-7) for 15-20 minutes.

CREAM CHEESE AND CUMIN PUFFS

Makes 10-15

250 g (8 oz) plain flour	250 g (8 oz) butter
3 tablespoons baking powder	Condensed milk to glaze the pastry
250 g (8 oz) cream cheese	1 tablespoon cumin

Sift the flour and baking powder on to a work surface and make a well in the centre. Incorporate the well-drained cream cheese. Add the butter cut into pieces. Cover with flour and, working from the centre, quickly knead the ingredients into a smooth dough.

Roll the pastry out until 5 mm (½ in) thick. Fold over several times. Roll again. Repeat this procedure once or twice. Leave the pastry to rest for 24 hours in a refrigerator.

Roll the pastry out to 5 mm (½ in) and cut into strips and triangles. Brush with the condensed milk and sprinkle with cumin. Place on a baking sheet sprinkled with cold water and bake in a preheated oven at 200-220°C (400-425°F, Gas Mark 6-7) for 10 minutes.

CHERRY STRUDEL

Serves 6

300 g (10 oz) strong
(bread) flour
1 egg
75 g (3 oz) caster sugar
A pinch of salt
1 tablespoon frying oil
1.5 g (3½ lb) Morello
cherries

225 g (7½ oz) rusks
150 g (5 oz) butter
125 g (4 oz) blanched
almonds
½ teaspoon ground
cinnamon
1 teaspoon grated lemon
rind

Sift the flour on to a work surface and make a well in the centre. Add 100 ml (3½ fl oz) water, the egg, a pinch of sugar, the salt and oil. Combine with some of the flour, then quickly knead into a smooth dough. Leave to rest for 30 minutes on greaseproof paper in a large, hot, absolutely dry, covered pan in which water has previously been boiled.

For the filling: wash and drain the cherries, then remove the stalks and stones. Cut the rusks into small cubes. Melt 100 g (3½ oz) butter and quickly brown the rusk croutons, stirring constantly. Toast the almonds in an ungreased frying pan.

Roll the pastry out thinly on a floured tea towel, then stretch it out with the hands to 50 x 70 cm (20 x 28 in). It should be transparent. Smooth off the edges, removing any pastry which is too thick. Mix the cherries, rusks and almonds, then add the remaining sugar, the cinnamon and lemon rind. Spread the filling over two-thirds of the pastry, leaving a 3 cm (1½ in) margin along the edges.

Roll up the strudel using the tea towel. Using your fingers, smooth down along the pastry edge to prevent the strudel from unrolling. Keeping the strudel tightly rolled, place it on a greased baking sheet and bake in a preheated oven at 200° C (400° F, Gas Mark 6) for 40-45 minutes. Brush the strudel with the remaining butter during the cooking time.

Suggestion: serve warm with custard or whipped cream.

Left:
Cherry strudel

Above: *Cherry pie with mulled wine sauce*

CHERRY PIE WITH MULLED WINE SAUCE

Serves 6

250 g (8 oz) plain flour
5-6 tablespoons caster sugar
A pinch of salt
175 g (6 oz) butter
75 g (3 oz) sponge fingers
75 g (3 oz) ground almonds
500 g (1 lb) stoned Morello cherries in syrup
250 g (8 oz) apples
Condensed milk
1 teaspoon ground cinnamon
100-125 ml (3½-4 fl oz) red wine
2 pieces lemon rind
1 cinnamon stick
2 cloves
2 tablespoons cornflour
Whipped cream to serve

Sift the flour on to a work surface, then make a well in the centre. Add 2 tablespoons sugar, the salt and 6 tablespoons water. Combine with some of the flour. Add the butter cut into pieces and cover with the remaining flour. Knead quickly into a smooth dough. Leave to rest for 1-2 hours in a refrigerator.

For the filling: place the sponge fingers in a plastic bag. Seal the bag, lay it flat on the work surface and crush the biscuits with a rolling pin.

In a mixing bowl, combine the crushed biscuits and the ground almonds. Drain the cherries (saving the juice).

Peel, quarter and core the apples and grate them coarsely.

Roll out a good half of the pastry and line a deep, 26 cm (10½ in) round cake tin.
Sprinkle with the sponge finger-almond mixture. Cover with the cherries and grated apples.

Roll out the remaining pastry the same size as the tin. Coat the edges of the pie with condensed milk, then cover with the rolled-out pastry. Press down well around the edges, then cut off the excess pastry. If there is enough pastry left over, cut out decorative shapes (flowers or characters). Coat the undersides with water to make them stick, then press them firmly on to the pastry. Brush the top of the pie with water and prick with a fork.

Mix 2 tablespoons sugar with the ground cinnamon. Sprinkle over the pie. Bake in a preheated oven at 200-220° C (400-425°F, Gas Mark 6-7) for 45 minutes.

Mulled wine sauce: mix the cherry juice with the red wine to make 500 ml (18 fl oz) sauce.
Add the lemon rind, cinnamon stick, cloves and 1-2 tablespoons sugar, then bring to the boil. Combine the cornflour with 2 tablespoons cold water, then stir into the sauce to thicken it.
Strain and sweeten to taste.

Serve this sauce hot, even boiling, with the pie. Serve with whipped cream.

REDCURRANT MERINGUE PIE

Serves 6

250 g (8 oz) plain flour
200 g (7 oz) caster sugar
1 egg
1 teaspoon ground cinnamon
125 g (4 oz) butter

40 g (1½ oz) almonds, cut into slivers
500 g (1 lb) redcurrants
3 egg whites
Whipped cream to serve

Sift the flour on to a work surface. Make a well in the centre and add 65 g (2½ oz) sugar, the egg and ground cinnamon. Work into a thick paste using some of the flour. Incorporate the butter cut into pieces and cover with the remaining flour. Knead quickly into a smooth dough, gradually incorporate the remaining flour, then leave to rest for 30 minutes in a refrigerator.

Grease a deep, 28 cm (11 in) round cake tin. Roll out the pastry so that it is slightly larger than the tin. Line the tin, making the sides about 2 cm (¾ in) high. Prick with a fork. Bake blind in a preheated oven at 200° C (400° F, Gas Mark 6) for 20 minutes. Leave to cool.

For the filling: toast the almonds in an ungreased frying pan. Sprinkle over the base of the tart. Wash the redcurrants. Drain and hull them. Whisk the egg whites into very stiff peaks (a cut made with a knife should remain visible).

Below: Redcurrant meringue pie

Incorporate the remaining sugar. Transfer 3 tablespoons of this mixture to an icing bag. Gently fold in the redcurrant to the remaining meringue mixture. Fill the tart. Smooth down evenly.

Using the icing bag, pipe meringue rosettes around the rim of the pie. Bake in a preheated oven at 150-180° C (300-350°F, Gas Mark 2-4) for 20-25 minutes. If the meringue starts to brown too much, cover with greaseproof paper 10 minutes before the end of the cooking time. Serve with whipped cream.

APPLE DOME

Serves 6

350 g (11½ oz) plain flour
175 g (6 oz) caster sugar
1 sachet vanilla sugar
1 egg
A pinch of salt
Grated rind of 2-3 lemons
200 g (7 oz) butter

50 g (2 oz) almond paste
2.5 kg (5½ lb) apples
Juice of 1-2 lemons
100 g (3½ oz) raisins
65 g (2½ oz) sponge fingers
1 egg yolk

Sift the flour on to a work surface. Make a well in the centre, then add 100 g (3½ oz) sugar, the vanilla sugar, the egg, salt and grated rind of 1 lemon. Add the butter and almond paste cut into small pieces. Cover with the remaining flour and quickly knead into a smooth dough. Leave to rest overnight.

For the filling: peel and core the apples, then cut into 1 cm (½ in) thick pieces. Place in a pan together with the lemon juice, the remaining lemon rind and sugar. Bring to the boil, cover and cook over a low heat for 10 minutes, stirring gently occasionally (the apples must not disintegrate). Incorporate the raisins. Take off the heat and drain.

Roll out half the pastry to 3 mm (⅛ in). Cut out the base of the tart using a deep, sliding-based, 24 cm (9½ in) round cake tin as a template. Reassemble the tin and place the pastry base on the base of the cake tin. Prick the base with a fork, then bake blind in a preheated oven at 200° C (400° F, Gas Mark 6) for about 15 minutes. Leave the tart base to cool slightly in the tin.

Using some of the remaining pastry, roll out an 80 x 5 cm (32 x 2 in) strip. Line the sides of the tin. Crush the sponge fingers very finely and dredge over the baked tart base. Add the filling, piling it into a dome shape. Mix the egg yolk with 1 tablespoon water and brush over the sides of the pie, reserving a little for the top.

Roll out the remaining pastry to 3 mm (⅓ in) thick and cover the filling. Seal the edges well. Cut off any excess pastry and use to make flowers or other decorative shapes. Brush the top of the pie with the egg mixture. Prick with a fork. Arrange the pastry shapes over the top and brush with egg yolk.

Bake in a preheated oven at 200° C (400° F, Gas Mark 6) for 30 minutes. Leave to cool for 5-6 hours in the tin. Then turn out of the tin carefully, loosening the sides of the pie with a knife if necessary.

Suggestion: serve with whipped cream flavoured with calvados or custard.

Above: *Almond and poppy seed delight*

ALMOND AND POPPY SEED DELIGHT

Serves 6

200 g (7 oz) plain flour	50 g (2 oz) raisins
75 g (3 oz) caster sugar	100 g (3½ oz) candied
4 eggs	lemon peel
A pinch of salt	1-2 teaspoons ground
Grated rind of 2 lemons	cinnamon
50 g (2 oz) ground	1-2 teaspoons ground
hazelnuts	cloves
100 g (3½ oz) butter	50 g (2 oz) ground
250 ml (8 fl oz) milk	almonds
250 g (8 oz) ground poppy	4 rusks
seeds	2 tablespoons rum
200 g (7 oz) almond paste	4 tablespoons apricot jam
50 g (2 oz) honey	50 g (2 oz) flaked almonds

Sift the flour on to a work surface. Make a well in the centre and add the sugar, 1 egg, the salt, grated rind of 1 lemon and the ground hazelnuts. Combine with some of the flour. Incorporate the butter cut into pieces. Cover with the remaining flour and quickly knead into a smooth dough. Leave to rest for 30 minutes in a refrigerator.

For the filling: bring the milk to the boil, then pour it over the poppy seeds. Leave to soak, stirring constantly until a thick paste is formed. Add the almond paste cut into small cubes. Mix well until the almond paste and poppy seeds form a smooth dough. Incorporate the honey, raisins, finely chopped candied lemon rind, the remaining lemon rind, the cinnamon, cloves and ground almonds. Crush the rusks finely and add to the mixture, together with the remaining eggs and the rum.

Roll out two-thirds of the pastry thinly and line a loaf tin. Add the filling. Cover with the remaining pastry. Seal the edges well using pieces of pastry. Bake in a preheated oven at 180° C (350° F, Gas Mark 4) for 8 minutes. Leave to cool.

For the apricot glaze: sieve the apricot jam, then thin it down with 4 tablespoons water and bring to the boil. Coat the cake with this mixture and cover with flaked almonds.

LEMON SQUARES

Makes 10-15

300 g (10 oz) puff pastry	Grated rind of 4 lemons
400 g (13 oz) butter,	250 ml (8 fl oz) lemon
softened	juice
550 g (1 lb 2 oz) icing	200 g (7 oz) plain flour
sugar	200 g (7 oz) cornflour
A pinch of salt	1 teaspoon baking powder
6 eggs	

Take the puff pastry out of the refrigerator a few hours before you wish to use it. Then roll it out until it is the same size as a baking sheet.
Sprinkle the baking sheet with water before laying on the pastry. Lift the pastry up at the edges. If necessary, wrap several layers of aluminium foil around the edges so that the pastry keeps its shape.
Prick with a fork.

Cream the butter, then incorporate first 350 g (11½ oz) icing sugar, then the salt, eggs (reserving a little egg white for the icing), the grated rind of 3 lemons and half the lemon juice.

Mix the flour, cornflour and baking powder together and gradually incorporate into the mixture. Spread this filling over the puff pastry and bake in a preheated oven at 200° C (400° F, Gas Mark 6) for 25-30 minutes. Leave to cool slightly.

For the icing: thoroughly combine the remaining icing sugar, lemon juice and lemon rind with a little egg white. Coat the cake. When completely cold, cut into squares using a knife dipped in hot water.

Right: *Lemon squares*

HAZELNUT STRUDEL

Serves 6

250 g (8 oz) strong (bread) flour	hazelnuts
A pinch of salt	2 eggs, separated
1 egg	1 teaspoon ground cinnamon
1 tablespoon frying oil	100 g (3½ oz) raisins
250 g (8 oz) honey	1 tablespoon milk
400 g (13 oz) ground	Icing sugar to finish

Sift the flour on to a work surface. Make a well in the centre, then incorporate the salt, 100 ml (3½ fl oz) warm water, the egg and oil. Knead quickly into a smooth dough, gradually incorporating the flour into the other ingredients.

Leave this pastry to rest for 30 minutes on greaseproof paper in a large, covered, hot and absolutely dry pan in which water has previously been boiled.

For the filling: combine the honey, ground hazelnuts, 1 egg yolk and the egg whites with 6-8 tablespoons water, the ground cinnamon and raisins to form a smooth ball.

Roll the pastry out thinly on a floured tea towel. Then stretch it out using the hands into a 50 x 70 cm (20 x 28 in) rectangle. It should be transparent. Level off the edges, cutting off any pastry which is too thick.
Spread the filling over the pastry, leaving a 3 cm (1½ in) margin along the short sides of the rectangle.

Fold these edges over the filling, then roll up the strudel using the tea towel. Smooth down all along the outer edge of the pastry so that the strudel does not unroll. Place on a greased baking sheet.

Mix the remaining egg yolk into the milk, then brush over the strudel. Bake in a preheated oven at 200-220° C (400-425° F, Gas Mark 6-7) for 35 minutes. Dredge with icing sugar 5 minutes before the end of the cooking time.

RHUBARB TARTLETS

Makes 7-8

150 g (5 oz) plain flour	cooking chocolate
1 teaspoon baking powder	750 g (1½ lb) rhubarb
225 g (7½ oz) caster sugar	1 packet jelly glaze mix (red)
2 sachets vanilla sugar	250 ml (8 fl oz) double cream
1 egg	
75 g (3 oz) butter	
25 g (1 oz) superfine	

Sift the flour and baking powder on to a work surface and make a well in the centre. Add 75 g (3 oz) sugar, 1 sachet vanilla sugar and the egg. Combine with some of the flour. Add the butter cut into pieces, then quickly knead with the remaining flour to form a smooth dough. If the dough is sticky, leave it to rest for a short while in a refrigerator.

Roll out the pastry to 3 mm (⅓ in), then cut into 10 cm (4 in) diameter circles using a pastry cutter. Transfer to a greased baking sheet and prick with a fork. Bake blind in a preheated oven at 180-200° C (350-400° F, Gas Mark 4-6) for 10-15 minutes. Leave to cool.

For the chocolate coating: melt the chocolate in a bowl over a pan of hot water, stirring until smooth and creamy. Coat a 1 cm (½ in) wide strip along the sides of the biscuits.

For the filling: wash and dry the rhubarb, then cut into 2 cm (¾ in) long chunks. Do not peel. Dredge with the remaining sugar. As soon as the rhubarb has produced some juice, bring it to the boil, then cook over a low heat until tender. It must not disintegrate. Leave to cool slightly, then drain, saving 250 ml (8 fl oz) juice.

Make up the jelly glaze with this juice, following the instructions on the packet. Sweeten to taste. Arrange the rhubarb pieces in the centre of the biscuits, then cover with the glaze.

Whip the cream for 30 seconds with the remaining vanilla sugar. Fill an icing bag and decorate the edges of the tartlets.

Left:
Rhubarb tartlets

LEMON LOG

Serves 6

4 eggs
125 g (4 oz) caster sugar
1 sachet vanilla sugar
75 g (3 oz) plain flour
50 g (2 oz) cornflour
A pinch of baking powder

2 gelatine leaves
5 tablespoons lemon juice
500 ml (18 fl oz) double cream
100 g (3½ oz) icing sugar

Using an electric mixer at high speed, beat the eggs in a mixing bowl with 3-4 tablespoons very hot water for 1 minute until thick and creamy. Combine the caster and vanilla sugars, then gradually incorporate (taking 1 minute). Beat for a further 2 minutes.

Sift the flour, cornflour and baking powder together, then gradually incorporate half into the egg-sugar mixture, with the mixer at low speed. Add the remaining half in the same way. Turn this mixture on to a greased and lined baking sheet, surrounding it with a strip of aluminium foil folded over several times if necessary to prevent the mixture from running. Bake in a preheated oven at 200-220° C (400-425° F, Gas Mark 6-7) for 10-15 minutes.

Turn out of the tin immediately on to a tea towel dusted with sugar. Sprinkle the greaseproof paper with cold water and peel off carefully and quickly. Roll up the sponge in the tea towel and place in a refrigerator.

For the filling: mix the gelatine with 2 tablespoons cold water in a small pan and heat, stirring constantly, until completely dissolved. Add the lemon juice. Whip the cream until very firm, then gently fold in the gelatine, while beating constantly. Gradually add 75 g (3 oz) icing sugar.

Carefully unroll the sponge and fill with the lemon cream; then roll it up again and dredge with the remaining icing sugar.

Alternative: set aside one-third of the lemon cream and use to ice the Swiss roll, making ridges using a fork.

CHOCOLATE TRUFFLE LOG

Serves 6

4 eggs
150 g (5 oz) caster sugar
1 sachet vanilla sugar
75 g (3 oz) plain flour
50 g (2 oz) cornflour
20 g (¾ oz) cocoa powder
1 teaspoon baking powder
125 g (4 oz) butter

400 g (13 oz) superfine milk cooking chocolate
250 ml (8 fl oz) double cream
6 tablespoons Cointreau or Grand Marnier
Grated rind of ½ orange

Using an electric mixer at high speed, beat the eggs in a mixing bowl with 3 tablespoons very hot water for 1 minute. Combine 125 g (4 oz) caster sugar and the vanilla sugar and gradually incorporate, beating constantly for 1 minute. Beat for a further 2 minutes. Mix the flour, cornflour, cocoa (reserving 1 teaspoon) and baking powder together. Sift half over the egg-sugar mixture, with the mixer at low speed. Then, when a smooth consistency has been achieved, incorporate the remaining flour mixture in the same way.

Melt 50 g (2 oz) butter, leave to cool, then gradually add to the mixture. Turn this mixture on to a greased baking sheet lined with greaseproof paper. If necessary, fold the paper up at the front edge of the baking sheet to prevent the mixture from running. Bake in a preheated oven at 200-220° C (400-425° F, Gas Mark 6-7) for 10-15 minutes.

Turn out of the tin immediately on to a tea towel dusted with sugar. Sprinkle the greaseproof paper with cold water, then peel it off carefully and quickly. Roll the sponge up using the tea towel and place in a refrigerator.

For the filling: cut the chocolate into small pieces. Bring the cream to the boil, then remove from the heat and add the chocolate. Beat using a whisk until smooth and creamy. Leave to cool, stirring constantly.

Bring the remaining sugar to the boil with 6 tablespoons water, stirring until the sugar has completely dissolved. Leave to cool. Add the liqueur. Unroll the sponge and sprinkle with the liqueur syrup.

Whisk the chocolate cream to make it lighter, smoother and glossier. Cream the remaining butter, adding the orange rind. Add to the chocolate cream. Spread two-thirds over the sponge (remove any brown crust there may be on the sponge). Transfer 2 tablespoons of this mixture to an icing bag.

Coat the sponge with the remaining cream, then decorate using the icing bag.
Dredge with the reserved cocoa powder.

Above: *Chocolate truffle log*
Pages 317 and 317: *Lemon log*

FIG AND SULTANA LOAF

Serves 6

125 g (4 oz) whole
hazelnuts
125 g (4 oz) dried figs
3 eggs
125 g (4 oz) caster sugar
1 sachet vanilla sugar
½ tablespoon rum
A pinch of ground
cinnamon

125 g (4 oz) plain flour
50 g (2 oz) cornflour
1 teaspoon baking powder
65 g (2½ oz) chopped
almonds
125 g (4 oz) candied
lemon peel
250 g (8 oz) sultanas

Chop the hazelnuts in two and dice the figs. In a mixing bowl, beat the eggs until thick and creamy using an electric mixer at high speed. Mix the caster and vanilla sugar together, then gradually incorporate, beating constantly for 1 minute. Beat for a further 3 minutes. Add the rum and cinnamon.

Sift the flour, cornflour and baking powder together, then gradually incorporate with the egg-sugar mixture,

Below: *Fig and sultana loaf*

together with the almonds, chopped candied lemon peel, hazelnuts, figs and sultanas.
Turn this mixture into a greased, lined, 30 x 11 cm (12 x 4½ in) loaf tin. Smooth it out evenly. Bake in a preheated oven at 180-200° C (350-400° F, Gas Mark 4-6) for 70-90 minutes.

BRAZILIAN CREAMS

Makes 16-17

6 egg whites
150 g (5 oz) caster sugar
1 sachet vanilla sugar
A pinch of ground
cinnamon
150 g (5 oz) ground
hazelnuts
65 g (2½ oz) plain flour
20 g (¾ oz) cornflour
1 tablespoon milk

2-3 teaspoons instant
coffee
100 g (3½ oz) hazelnut
chocolate spread
125 g (4 oz) butter,
softened
Cocoa powder
16-17 chocolate coffee
beans to finish

In a mixing bowl, whisk the egg whites into stiff peaks, then, beating constantly, gradually incorporate the sugar (reserving 1 teaspoon) and vanilla sugar. Add the cinnamon and ground hazelnuts. Incorporate the flour carefully. Line a greased baking sheet with greaseproof paper. Mark out 34 circles, 6 cm (2½ in) in diameter. Fill the circles with the hazelnut mixture and bake in a preheated oven at 150° C (300° F, Gas Mark 2) for 30 minutes.

For the filling: mix the cornflour and reserved sugar with the milk. Bring to the boil, stirring constantly. Add the coffee. Add the hazelnut chocolate spread to the hot mixture. Remove from the heat and leave to cool, stirring occasionally.

Cream the butter, then gradually incorporate into the mixture. Fill an icing bag with this coffee cream and pipe on to half of the sponge biscuits (reserving some to decorate the tops).
Cover the cream with a second sponge biscuit. Dredge the edges with cocoa (placing a paper circle in the middle of the biscuit for a perfect result).

Decorate with coffee cream whirls topped with coffee beans. Serve with a glass of sherry.

Opposite: *Brazilian creams*

Above: *Orange brandy delights*

ORANGE BRANDY DELIGHTS

Makes 12

2 eggs
125 g (4 oz) caster sugar
1 sachet vanilla sugar
75 g (3 oz) plain flour
50 g (2 oz) cornflour
1 teaspoon baking powder
50 g (2 oz) ground almonds
2 oranges
3 sugar lumps
125 ml (4 fl oz) orange juice
2-3 tablespoons orange

liqueur (Cointreau or Grand Marnier)
375 ml (12 fl oz) double cream
40-50 g (1½-2 oz) icing sugar
2 tablespoons brandy
75 g (3 oz) chopped toasted almonds
Almond paste, glacé cherries and other fruits to finish

Make the moulds using a 30 cm (12 in) wide piece of aluminium foil. Fold over every 15 cm (6 in), making six folds. Cut two circles, 15 cm (6 in) in diameter, through all thicknesses, making twelve identical circles. Place each circle under the base of a 8 cm (3 in) can and pull the foil up to make the sides of the mould, 4 cm (1½ in) high.

For the sponge mixture: Using an electric mixer at high speed, beat the eggs with 3-4 tablespoons very hot water for 1 minute until thick and frothy. In a bowl, mix 100 g (3½ oz) caster sugar and the vanilla sugar together and gradually incorporate using the mixer (1 minute). Beat for a further 2 minutes.

On a work surface, thoroughly mix the flour, cornflour and baking powder together. Sift half over the egg mixture, with the mixer at low speed. Incorporate the remaining flour mixture in the same way. Add the ground almonds. Turn this mixture into the little, greased foil moulds arranged on a baking sheet. Bake in a preheated oven at 180-200° C (350-400° F, Gas Mark 4-6) for 25 minutes. Remove from the moulds immediately and leave to cool.

To make the orange cakes: boil 2 tablespoons water with the remaining sugar. Wash and dry 1 orange, grate

the rind on to the syrup using the edges and corners of the sugar lumps. Add the orange juice and the orange liqueur. Sprinkle over six cakes. Whip the cream for 30 seconds, then add the icing sugar. Transfer to an icing bag and decorate the orange cakes.
Peel the remaining orange and cut two segments into quarters. Place on the whipped cream whirls.

For the brandy cakes: incorporate the brandy in the remaining whipped cream. Cut six cakes into two layers and fill with the brandy cream. Coat the cakes with the cream all over, then sprinkle with chopped toasted almonds. Finish with the almond paste and glacé fruit decorations.

CHOCOLATE AND RASPBERRY CREAM CAKES

Makes about 8

4 eggs	150 g (5 oz) butter
125 g (4 oz) caster sugar	200 g (7 oz) raspberries
1 sachet vanilla sugar	250 ml (8 fl oz) double
75 g (3 oz) plain flour	cream
50 g (2 oz) cornflour	100 g (3½ oz) icing sugar
1 teaspoon baking powder	Raspberry jam
20 g (¾ oz) cocoa powder	

*U*sing an electric mixer at high speed, beat the eggs in a mixing bowl with 2 tablespoons very hot water for 1 minute until thick and frothy. Then gradually incorporate the sugar and vanilla sugar (1 minute) and continue beating for a further 2 minutes.

Combine the flour, cornflour, baking powder and cocoa in a mixing bowl. Sift and gradually incorporate half into the egg-sugar mixture, with the mixer at low speed. When incorporated, repeat the procedure with the remaining flour mixture.
Add 50 g (2 oz) cooled, melted butter.

Pour the mixture on to a well-greased and lined baking sheet. If necessary, fold the greaseproof paper up at the edges to prevent the mixture from running. Bake in a preheated oven at 200-220° C (400-425° F, Gas Mark 6-7) for 10-15 minutes. Turn the sponge out immediately on to a sheet of paper dusted with sugar. Sprinkle the baking paper with cold water and peel off quickly but carefully. Leave the sponge to cool.

For the filling: wash and then purée the raspberries. Whip the cream until very firm.

Cream the remaining butter, then gradually incorporate the icing sugar. Add to the raspberry purée and gently fold in the whipped cream.

Cut two 9 cm (3½ in) wide strips of sponge. Brush with jam. Spread three-quarters of the raspberry cream over the remaining sponge, then cut into strips about 6 cm (2½ in) wide. Lay these strips one on top of the other, then place them upright on one of the jam-covered strips of sponge. Cover with the remaining jam-covered strip. Cover completely with the remaining raspberry cream and decorate with plain whipped cream. Place in a refrigerator. Cut into slices when ready to serve.

Tip: if the cake is being made the night before, completely cover the raspberry cream with plain whipped cream so that it does not turn brown.

Below: *Chocolate and raspberry cream cakes*

Above: *Royal fruit cake*

ROYAL FRUIT CAKE

Serves 6-8

500 g plain flour
2 teaspoons baking
powder
275 g (9 oz) caster sugar
2 sachets vanilla sugar
2 tablespoons milk
250 g (8 oz) butter

6 eggs
1 tablespoon rum
100 g (3½ oz) chopped
almonds
150-200 g (5-7 oz) raisins
100 g (3½ oz) candied
lemon peel

Combine half the flour and half the baking powder on a work surface. Make a well in the centre and add 75 g (3 oz) sugar, 1 sachet vanilla sugar and the milk. Incorporate using some of the flour. Add half the butter cut into pieces and cover with the remaining flour. Knead the dough. If it is too sticky, place in a refrigerator. Roll out one-third and use to cover the base of a deep, 28 cm (11 in) round cake tin. Roll out half of the remaining pastry the same size as the tin. Cut into 16-20 strips using a pastry wheel. Roll the remaining pastry into a sausage shape and use to line the sides of the tin, 3 cm (1½ in) deep.

For the sponge filling: beat the eggs for 1 minute until thick and frothy using, an electric mixer at high speed. In a separate bowl, mix the remaining sugar and vanilla sugar together, gradually incorporate, taking 1 minute, then continue beating for 2 minutes. Add the rum.

Combine the remaining flour and baking powder. Sift half over the egg-sugar mixture and incorporate with the mixer at low speed. As soon as the mixture is smooth, incorporate the remaining flour mixture in the same way. Add the almonds, raisins and chopped candied lemon peel. Mix well, then incorporate the remaining cooled, melted butter.

Pour this mixture over the pastry. Smooth it out evenly. Weave the pastry strips into a lattice on top. Bake in a preheated oven at 180-200° C (350-400° F, Gas Mark 4-6) for 65-80 minutes.

CHERRY AND ALMOND PIE

Serves 6

4 eggs
200 g (7 oz) caster sugar
1 sachet vanilla sugar
A pinch of ground
cinnamon
A pinch of ground cloves
Grated rind of ½ lemon
200 g (7 oz) ground
almonds
4 tablespoons fresh
breadcrumbs
1 teaspoon baking powder
875 g (1¾ lb) stoned
Morello cherries in syrup
Icing sugar to finish
(optional)

Beat the eggs for 1 minute until thick and frothy, using an electric mixer at high speed. Gradually add the sugar, vanilla sugar, cinnamon, cloves and lemon rind, beating with the mixer for 1 minute. Continue beating for a further 2 minutes.

In a mixing bowl, combine the ground almonds, breadcrumbs and baking powder. Gradually sift half over the egg-sugar mixture, then incorporate with the mixer at low speed. When smooth, incorporate the remaining ground almond mixture in the same way. Transfer half this mixture to a greased and lined, deep, 28 cm (11 in) round cake tin.

Drain the cherries. Arrange half over the mixture, cover with the remaining mixture, then add the remaining cherries. Bake in a preheated oven at 180° C (350° F, Gas Mark 4) for 1 hour. Leave the cake to cool in the tin. Dredge with icing sugar if desired.

Below: *Cherry and almond pie*

KIWI CREAM CAKES

Makes about 15

3 eggs
100 g (3½ oz) caster sugar
1 sachet vanilla sugar
50 g (2 oz) plain flour
50 g (2 oz) cornflour
A pinch of baking powder
100 g (3½ oz) butter, melted
7 small kiwi fruits

250 ml (8 fl oz) double cream
150 g (5 oz) natural yoghurt
2 tablespoons lemon juice
2 tablespoons toasted flaked almonds
Icing sugar to finish

Cut out fourteen 15 cm (6 in) diameter circles from a sheet of aluminium foil to make the moulds. Place over a 10 cm (4 in) diameter can and smooth down the sides to make a 2 cm (¾ in) deep rim.

For the sponge mixture: place the eggs, 65 g (2½ oz) sugar and the vanilla sugar in a bowl over a pan of hot water and beat using a whisk until thick and creamy. Remove the bowl from the pan and continue beating until cold. Combine the flour, cornflour and baking powder. Fold into the eggs gently and gradually, without beating. Gradually add the cooled, melted butter.

Arrange the greased foil moulds on a baking sheet, pour

Below: *Kiwi cream cakes*

in the sponge mixture and bake in a preheated oven at 200-220° C (400-425° F, Gas Mark 6-7) for 10 minutes. Turn out of the moulds immediately and leave to cool.

For the filling: peel and slice the kiwi fruits, then arrange them over half the sponges.
Whip the cream for 30 seconds, then gradually incorporate the remaining sugar. Whip until firm. Add the yoghurt and lemon juice. Mix well, then spread over the kiwi slices. Top with the remaining sponges. Decorate with the toasted flaked almonds. Dredge with icing sugar. Place in a refrigerator.

JAM SWISS ROLL

Serves 6

3 eggs
150 g (5 oz) sugar
1 sachet vanilla sugar
100 g (3½ oz) plain flour

50 g (2 oz) cornflour
1 teaspoon baking powder
250-375 g (8-12 oz) jam
Icing sugar to finish

Using an electric mixer at high speed, beat the eggs in a mixing bowl with 5-6 tablespoons very hot water for 1 minute until thick and frothy. Combine the sugar and vanilla sugar in a separate bowl, then gradually incorporate, taking 1 minute. Continue beating for a further 2 minutes.

Sift the flour, cornflour and baking powder together. Gradually incorporate half of the flour mixture into the eggs with the mixer at low speed. When smooth, incorporate the remaining flour mixture in the same way.

Turn this mixture on to a greased and lined baking sheet. If necessary, fold the paper up to prevent the mixture from running. Bake in a preheated oven at 200-220° C (400-425° F, Gas Mark 6-7) for 10-15 minutes. Turn the sponge out immediately on to a clean tea towel dusted with sugar. Sprinkle cold water over the greaseproof paper, then peel off quickly but carefully.

Spread the sponge with the jam of your choice, then roll it up and dredge with icing sugar.

Above: *Raspberry mousse slice*

RASPBERRY MOUSSE SLICES

Makes 6

3 eggs
150 g (5 oz) caster sugar
2 sachets vanilla sugar
100 g (3½ oz) plain flour
50 g (2 oz) cornflour
1 teaspoon baking powder
500 g (1 lb) raspberries

4 gelatine leaves
500 ml (18 fl oz) double cream
125 g (4 oz) icing sugar
A little grated chocolate to finish

*U*sing an electric mixer at high speed, beat the eggs in a mixing bowl with 5-6 tablespoons very hot water for 1 minute until thick and frothy. Mix the sugar and 1 sachet vanilla sugar together, then gradually incorporate into the egg mixture, taking 1 minute. Then beat for a further 2 minutes.

In a separate bowl, combine the flour, cornflour and baking powder.
Gradually incorporate half of the flour mixture into the egg-sugar mixture until smooth, then incorporate the remaining flour in the same way. Pour this mixture on to a greased and lined baking sheet. If necessary, fold up the paper to prevent the mixture from running. Bake in a preheated oven at 200-220° C (400-425° F, Gas Mark 6-7) for 10-15 minutes. Turn out immediately on to a clean tea towel dusted with sugar. Sprinkle the greaseproof paper with cold water, then peel off quickly and carefully.

For the filling: wash, drain and hull the raspberries, reserving some for decoration. Liquidize and sieve them. Put the gelatine in a small pan with 3 tablespoons cold water. Leave to soak for 10 minutes.

Whip the cream for 30 seconds, then incorporate the icing sugar and the remaining vanilla sugar, beating constantly until very firm. Heat the gelatine until dissolved, then incorporate in the raspberry purée and fold gently into the whipped cream.
Cut the sponge into 2 layers. Spread two-thirds of the cream over the bottom layer. Top with the remaining layer of sponge, then coat with the remaining cream. Sprinkle with the grated chocolate. Cut this sponge cake into equal portions and decorate with raspberries tossed in sugar.

MANDARIN CREAM CAKES

Makes 14

2 eggs
75 g (3 oz) caster sugar
1 sachet vanilla sugar
50 g (2 oz) plain flour
50 g (2 oz) cornflour
100 g (3½ oz) butter, melted
1 tablespoon icing sugar

300 g (10 oz) mandarin segments (in syrup)
Rind of ½ lemon
1 sugar lump
3 gelatine leaves
375 ml (12 fl oz) double cream

Cut out fourteen 15 cm (6 in) diameter circles from a sheet of aluminium foil. Place over a 10 cm (4 in) diameter can and smooth down to make moulds with 2 cm (¾ in) deep sides.

For the sponge mixture: put the eggs, 65 g (2½ oz) caster sugar and the vanilla sugar in a bowl over a pan of hot water and beat until frothy and pale yellow using an electric mixer. Remove the bowl from the pan and continue beating for 5 minutes or until the mixture is cool.

Sift the flour and cornflour together. Gradually incorporate into the egg-sugar mixture with the mixer at low speed. Gradually add the cooled, melted butter. Arrange the moulds on a baking sheet and pour in the sponge mixture.

Bake in a preheated oven at 200-220° C (400-425° F, Gas Mark 6-7) for 8-12 minutes. Turn out of the moulds immediately and curve into a banana shape. Leave to cool, then dredge with icing sugar.

For the filling: drain the mandarin segments, saving the juice. Grate the lemon rind using the corners and edges of the sugar lump. Put the gelatine in a small pan with 3 tablespoons cold water. Leave to soak for 10 minutes. Put the cream in a bowl. Add the mandarin juice and sugar lump and mix well until the sugar has dissolved. Add the remaining sugar and whip the cream until very firm. Heat the gelatine until dissolved, then incorporate in the whipped cream. Transfer to an icing bag and pipe into the sponges.
Decorate with mandarin segments.

Below: *Mandarin cream cakes*

CHOCOLATE PYRAMID

Serves 4

4 eggs
200 g (7 oz) caster sugar
50 g (2 oz) plain flour
50 g (2 oz) cornflour
1 teaspoon baking powder
40 g (1½ oz) cocoa

powder
500 ml (18 fl oz) milk
1 packet chocolate blancmange mix
275 g (9 oz) butter
Grated chocolate to finish

Using an electric mixer at high speed, beat the eggs in a mixing bowl with 4 tablespoons very hot water for 1 minute. Incorporate 125 g (4 oz) sugar and continue beating for 2 minutes.

Sift the flour, cornflour, baking powder and 4 tablespoons cocoa powder together. Incorporate half into the egg-sugar mixture, with the mixer at low speed. When smooth, incorporate the remaining flour mixture in the same way.

Transfer this mixture to a greased and lined baking sheet. If necessary, fold up the paper at the edges to prevent the mixture from running. Bake in a preheated oven at 200-220° F (400-425° F, Gas Mark 6-7) for 12-15 minutes.

Turn the sponge out of the tin immediately on to a clean tea towel dusted with sugar. Sprinkle the greaseproof paper with cold water and peel off quickly but carefully. Leave to cool.

Above: *Chocolate pyramid*

For the filling: make up the blancmange mix using the milk and the remaining sugar and cocoa, following the instructions on the packet.

Incorporate 25 g (1 oz) butter into the hot blancmange mixture. Leave to cool, stirring occasionally; then cream the remaining butter and gradually incorporate into the blancmange.

Cut the sponge into 8 cm (3 in) wide strips. Arrange them side by side. Set aside one-third of the chocolate cream mixture, then cover the sponge strips with the remaining two-thirds. Lay them one on top of the other, then leave to cool.

Cut the cake in half diagonally, then place the two straight, layered sides together in the centre to make a pyramid (the slices of cake should be triangular). Cover and decorate with the remaining cream and sprinkle with grated chocolate.

Above: *Coffee praline log*

COFFEE PRALINE LOG

Serves 4

250 g (8 oz) hazelnuts
4 eggs
125 g (4 oz) caster sugar
A pinch of salt
1 teaspoon grated lemon rind
65 g (2½ oz) plain flour
65 g (2½ oz) cornflour

4 gelatine leaves
4 egg yolks
225 g (7½ oz) icing sugar
1 tablespoon instant coffee
1-3 tablespoons brandy
500 ml (18 fl oz) double cream

*T*oast the hazelnuts in an ungreased frying pan, stirring constantly. Leave to cool slightly when golden, then rub between your hands to remove the skins. Finely grind 75 g (3 oz) hazelnuts and reserve the rest.

For the sponge mixture: put the whole eggs in a bowl with 3-4 tablespoons very hot water and beat for 1 minute using an electric mixer at high speed until thick and frothy. Mix the sugar, salt and lemon rind together in a separate bowl, then gradually incorporate into the egg mixture, beating for 1 minute, then for a further 2 minutes. Mix the flour and cornflour together in a separate bowl. Sift half on to the mixture and gradually incorporate with the mixer at low speed. Repeat this procedure with the remaining flour mixture and the ground hazelnuts. Transfer this mixture on to a greased and lined baking sheet. If necessary, fold up the paper at the edges to prevent the mixture from running. Bake in a preheated oven at 220-240° F (425-475° F, Gas Mark 7-9) for 10 minutes.

Turn the sponge out immediately on to a clean tea towel dredged with sugar. Sprinkle cold water over the greaseproof paper, then peel off quickly but carefully. Roll the sponge up tightly in the tea towel. Leave to cool.

For the filling: put the gelatine in a small pan with 3 tablespoons cold water. Leave to soak for 10 minutes. Using an electric mixer, beat the egg yolks with 75 g (3 oz) icing sugar until creamy. Dissolve the instant coffee in the brandy, then incorporate in the egg-sugar mixture.

Whip 400 ml (14 fl oz) cream until very firm. Heat the gelatine until dissolved, then incorporate it in the egg-sugar mixture as soon as it starts to thicken, together with the crean. Unroll the sponge and spread with the coffee cream. Roll it up again, then transfer to a dish. Leave to cool for 30 minutes.

For the praline: heat the remaining icing sugar, stirring constantly, until it turns light brown. Incorporate the remaining hazelnuts. Stir until the mixture is golden. Pour over a greased baking sheet. Leave to cool, then crush with a rolling pin.

Whip the remaining cream, spread over the sponge cake, then cover completely with the praline.

HAZELNUT CHOCOLATE CUP CAKES

Makes 20

2 eggs	powder
100 g (3½ oz) caster sugar	20 paper cases
1 sachet vanilla sugar	200 g (7 oz) hazelnut
125 g (4 oz) plain flour	chocolate spread
4 tablespoons cornflour	Grated chocolate and
½ teaspoon baking	chocolate coffee beans

Using an electric mixer at high speed, beat the eggs in a mixing bowl with 2 tablespoons very hot water for 1 minute until thick and frothy. Mix the sugar and vanilla sugar together. Gradually incorporate, taking 1 minute, then continue beating for a further 2 minutes.
In a separate bowl, mix the flour, cornflour and baking powder together. With the mixer at low speed, incorporate half the flour mixture into the egg-sugar mixture. Then incorporate the remaining flour mixture in the same way.

Using a teaspoon, fill paper cases with the mixture. Transfer them to a baking sheet and bake in a preheated oven at 180-200° C (350-400° F, Gas Mark 4-6) for 25 minutes. Leave to cool.

Put the hazelnut chocolate spread in a bowl over a pan of hot water and melt, stirring constantly until it forms a runny paste. Fill an icing bag and decorate the cakes. Top with the grated chocolate and coffee beans.

Right:
Hazelnut chocolate cup cakes

Above: *Chocolate brandy log*

CHOCOLATE BRANDY LOG

Serves 6

4 eggs
200-225 g (7-8 oz) caster
sugar
1 sachet vanilla sugar
75 g (3 oz) plain flour
50 g (2 oz) cornflour

A pinch of baking powder
1 packet chocolate
blancmange mix
500 ml (18 fl oz) milk
175-200 g (6-7 oz) butter

*U*sing an electric mixer at high speed, beat the eggs in a mixing bowl with 3-4 tablespoons very hot water for 1 minute until thick and frothy. Combine 125 g (4 oz) sugar and the vanilla sugar. Gradually incorporate, taking 1 minute, then continue beating for 2 minutes.

Sift the flour, cornflour and baking powder together in a separate bowl. Incorporate into the egg-sugar mixture with the mixer at low speed. When smooth, incorporate the remaining flour mixture in the same way.

Pour this mixture on to a greased, lined baking sheet. Fold the paper up at the edges if necessary to prevent the mixture from running. Bake in a preheated oven at 200-220° C (400-425° F, Gas Mark 6-7) for 10-15 minutes. Turn the sponge out of the tin immediately on to greaseproof paper dredged with sugar. Sprinkle the baking paper with cold water, then peel off quickly but carefully. Roll the sponge up and leave to cool.

For the filling: make up the blancmange mix using the remaining sugar and the milk, following the instructions on the packet. Then leave to cool, stirring occasionally.

Cream the butter, then gradually incorporate into the chocolate blancmange (both the butter and the blancmange should be at room temperature).

Unroll the sponge carefully and cover with the chocolate cream, reserving some to cover the top of the log. Roll the sponge up again. Cut off any over-cooked crusts at the ends. Cover with the remaining chocolate cream. Make a wavy pattern using a fork.

WHITE WINE AND STRAWBERRY RING

Serves 6

2 eggs
250 g (8 oz) sugar
2 sachets vanilla sugar
125 g (4 oz) plain flour
4 tablespoons cornflour
½ teaspoon baking
powder

375 ml (12 fl oz) white
wine
750 g (1½ lb) strawberries
1 packet jelly glaze mix
(red)
125 ml (4 fl oz) double
cream

*B*eat the eggs with 2 tablespoons very hot water for 1 minute using an electric mixer at high speed. Mix 100 g (3½ oz) sugar and 1 sachet vanilla sugar together. Incorporate gradually, using the mixer for 1 minute, then continue beating for a further 2 minutes.

Sift the flour, cornflour and baking powder together. Gradually incorporate half into the egg-sugar mixture, with the mixer at low speed. Incorporate the remaining flour mixture in the same way. Pour this mixture into a savarin ring mould. Bake in a preheated oven at 180-200° C (350-400° F, Gas Mark 4-6) for 35 minutes.

For the glaze: 3 hours before serving, bring 125 ml (4 fl oz) water to the boil with the remaining sugar and vanilla sugar. Remove from the heat and add the white

Right: *White wine and strawberry ring*

wine. Remove the cake from the tin, pour one-third of this mixture into the tin, return the cake to the tin and sprinkle with the remaining liquid. Leave to cool.

For the filling: wash, drain and hull the strawberries. Pass 250 g (8 oz) strawberries through a very fine sieve and collect the juice. Make up the juice to 250 ml (8 fl oz) with a little water if necessary. Make the glaze using this juice and 25 g (1 oz) sugar, following the instructions on the packet. Pour over the sponge ring, but do not cover completely. Leave to cool.

Mix the remaining drained, whole strawberries with the remaining sugar. Pile up in the centre of the cake.

Whip the double cream until very firm.
Transfer to an icing bag and decorate the cake.

Alternatives: a liqueur or other spirit can be used instead of the white wine and other fruits can be used instead of the strawberries.

WALNUT AND HAZELNUT SLICES

Makes about 4

6 eggs	walnuts
150 g (5 oz) caster sugar	4 gelatine leaves
2 sachets vanilla sugar	750 ml (1½ pints) double
A pinch of salt	cream
½ teaspoon ground	100 g (3½ oz) plain
cinnamon	chocolate
1 tablespoon plain flour	Chocolate flakes and
1 teaspoon baking	whole hazelnuts or
powder	walnuts to finish
250 g (8 oz) chopped	

Beat the eggs for 1 minute until thick and frothy using an electric mixer at high speed.
Mix the sugar (reserving 1 teaspoon), 1 sachet vanilla sugar, the salt and ground cinnamon together. Gradually incorporate into the eggs, taking 1 minute, then beat for a further 2 minutes.

Sift the flour and baking powder together. Add the chopped walnuts. Incorporate half into the egg-sugar mixture with the mixer at low speed. Repeat the procedure with the remaining flour mixture.

Pour the mixture on to a greased, lined baking sheet. If necessary, fold up the paper at the edges to prevent the mixture from running. Bake in a preheated oven at 200° C (400° F, Gas Mark 6) for 12-15 minutes. Turn the sponge out of the tin immediately on to paper dredged with sugar. Sprinkle the baking paper with cold water

and peel off carefully but quickly. Leave to cool and cut into two layers.

For the filling: Put the gelatine in a small pan with 3 tablespoons cold water. Leave to soak for 10 minutes. Whip the cream for 30 seconds. Add the remaining vanilla sugar and reserved sugar, beating constantly until the cream is very firm. Heat the gelatine until dissolved, then incorporate in the cream. Coarsely grate the chocolate and incorporate into three-quarters of the cream. Spread this cream over one of the layers of sponge. Cover with the other layer. Mark out the portions on the top of the cake with the point of a knife. Fill an icing bag with the remaining cream and decorate the top of the cake. Cut into slices, then add the chocolate flakes and whole hazelnuts or walnuts.

Above: *Walnut and hazelnut slices*

APRICOT JAM AND HAZELNUT ROULADE

Serves about 4

4 eggs
100 g (3½ oz) caster sugar
1 sachet vanilla sugar
Grated rind of ½ lemon
50 g (2 oz) plain flour
1 teaspoon baking powder
100 g (3½ oz) ground

hazelnuts
300 g (10 oz) apricot jam
3 tablespoons apricot liqueur
Icing sugar to finish
Whipped cream to serve

*U*sing an electric mixer at high speed, beat the eggs with 3-4 tablespoons very hot water for 1 minute until thick and frothy. Combine the caster sugar, vanilla sugar and lemon rind in a separate bowl and gradually incorporate, taking 1 minute. Beat for a further 2 minutes.

Sift the flour and baking powder together, then add the ground hazelnuts. Incorporate half into the egg-sugar mixture, with the mixer at low speed. Transfer this mixture to a greased and lined baking sheet. Bake in a preheated oven at 200-220° C (400-425° F, Gas Mark 6-7) for 10-15 minutes.

Turn out of the tin on to a tea towel dredged with sugar. Sprinkle cold water over the baking paper and peel off quickly.

For the filling: thin the jam down with the apricot liqueur and spread over the sponge while still hot. Roll the sponge up. Cut off the ends of the cake. Dredge with icing sugar and serve with whipped cream.

CHERRY ROULADE

Serves 6

750 g (1½ lb) Morello cherries	4 gelatine leaves
350 g (11½ oz) caster sugar	3 limes
	250 ml (8 fl oz) dry white wine
4 eggs	4 egg yolks
A pinch of salt	250 ml (8 fl oz) double cream
2 teaspoons grated lemon rind	50 g (2 oz) toasted flaked almonds
75 g (3 oz) plain flour	Icing sugar to finish
65 g (2½ oz) cornflour	

*T*he evening before, wash, drain, hull and stone the cherries. Save the juice and the stones and bring to the boil with 100 g (3½ oz) sugar. Boil until the sugar has dissolved. Pour through a sieve on to the cherries. Leave to rest overnight.

For the sponge mixture: using an electric mixer at high speed, beat the eggs with 3-4 tablespoons very hot water for 1 minute until thick and frothy. Combine 125 g (4 oz) sugar, the salt and grated lemon rind and gradually incorporate, taking 1 minute, then beat for a further 2 minutes.

Sift the flour and cornflour together. Incorporate half into the egg-sugar mixture with the mixer at low speed. When smooth, follow the same procedure for the remaining flour mixture.

Pour this mixture on to a greased and lined baking sheet. If necessary, fold up the paper at the edges to prevent the mixture from running. Bake in a preheated oven at 220-240° C (425-475° F, Gas Mark 7-9) for 10 minutes.

Turn the sponge out of the tin immediately on to a clean tea towel dredged with sugar. Sprinkle the baking paper with cold water and peel off carefully but quickly. Roll the sponge up in the tea towel and place in a refrigerator.

For the lime cream: put the gelatine in a small pan with 4 tablespoons cold water and leave to soak for 10 minutes. Wash and dry the limes, finely grate the rind, then squeeze them, saving the juice. Heat the white wine and lemon rind.
Beat the egg yolks with the remaining sugar for 4-5 minutes until pale yellow and creamy, with the mixer at high speed. Incorporate into the hot white wine and continue beating until thick and creamy. Remove from the heat. Add the gelatine and stir until it has completely dissolved. Leave to cool, stirring occasionally.

For the filling: whip the cream until firm and incorporate into the mixture. Unroll the sponge and cover with two-thirds of the lime cream. Add the cherries. Wait for 4-5 minutes, then roll the sponge up again. Transfer to a plate and cover with the remaining cream. Sprinkle with the flaked almonds and dredge with icing sugar.

Left: *Cherry roulade*

Above: *Chocolate almond squares*

CHOCOLATE ALMOND SQUARES

Makes 10

4 eggs
100 g (3½ oz) caster sugar
1 sachet vanilla sugar
3 tablespoons rum
2 drops bitter almond
essence
50 g (2 oz) ground
almonds
50 g (2 oz) cornflour

50 g (2 oz) fresh
breadcrumbs
1 teaspoon baking powder
50 g (2 oz) grated
chocolate
4 tablespoons apricot jam
100 g (3½ oz) chocolate
15 g (½ oz) butter
Flaked almonds to finish

Using an electric mixer at high speed, beat the eggs in a mixing bowl with 2-3 tablespoons very hot water for 1 minute.
When thick and frothy, incorporate the sugar and vanilla sugar, taking 1 minute, then beat for a further 2 minutes. Add 1 tablespoon rum and the bitter almond essence.

Mix the ground almonds, cornflour, breadcrumbs, baking powder and grated chocolate together. Sift and incorporate half into the mixture with the mixer at low speed. When smooth, repeat the procedure with the remaining almond mixture.

Transfer this mixture on to a greased and lined baking sheet, folding the paper up at the edges if necessary to prevent the mixture from running. Bake in a preheated oven at 200-220° C (400-425° F, Gas Mark 6-7) for 10-15 minutes.
Turn the sponge out of the tin immediately on to greaseproof paper dredged with sugar. Sprinkle cold water over the baking paper and peel off quickly. Leave to cool.

Sieve the jam, then thin it down with the remaining rum and 2 tablespoons water. Bring to the boil, then use to coat the sponge. Leave to cool.

For the chocolate icing: cut the chocolate into pieces and melt with the butter in a bowl over a pan of hot water, stirring until smooth and creamy.
Spread over the jam. Leave to cool slightly, then, with the point of a knife, mark out 5 x 5 cm (2 x 2 in) squares on the sponge. Cut the sponge cake as soon as the chocolate sets.

Above: *Marzipan purses*

MARZIPAN PURSES

Makes 10

1 egg	*blancmange mix*
100 g (3½ oz) caster sugar	*125 ml (4 fl oz) cold milk*
1 sachet vanilla sugar	*65 g (2½ oz) butter*
100 g (3½ oz) plain flour	*100 g (3½ oz) icing sugar*
1 teaspoon baking powder	*200 g (7 oz) almond paste*
1 packet chocolate	*Cocoa powder to finish*

Cut out ten 15 cm (6 in) diameter circles from a sheet of aluminium foil (folded in two if possible). Smooth these circles over yoghurt pots to make 10 small cake moulds.

Using an electric mixer at high speed, beat the egg in a mixing bowl with 3 tablespoons very hot water for 1 minute until thick and frothy. Combine 75 g (3 oz) sugar and vanilla sugar and gradually incorporate, taking 1 minute, then beat for a further 2 minutes.
Sift the flour and baking powder together. Incorporate

half into the mixture with the mixer at low speed. Incorporate the remaining half in the same way. Place 2 heaped teaspoons of this mixture in each of the greased moulds.

Transfer the moulds to a baking sheet and bake in a preheated oven at 180-200° C (350-400° F, Gas Mark 4-6) for 15 minutes.
Loosen the sponges from the moulds immediately, running round the edges with the blade of a knife. Peel off the moulds carefully and leave to cool.

For the filling: make up the chocolate blancmange mixture, mixing the powder with the remaining sugar and 3 tablespoons milk. Bring the remaining milk to the boil, pour over the powder mixture, then return to the boil, stirring constantly. Remove from the heat and leave to cool, stirring occasionally. Cream the butter and gradually incorporate into the chocolate blancmange. Cut each little cake into two layers. Cover the bottom layer with chocolate cream. Place the second layer on top. Spread the cream over the sides of the cakes. Incorporate 75 g (3 oz) icing sugar into the almond paste. Roll the almond paste out on a work surface dusted with the remaining icing sugar. Cut into strips 9 cm (3½ in) wide and 18 cm (7 in) long.

Lay each cake on its side on a strip, leaving 2 cm (¾ in) at the bottom and 3 cm (1½ in) at the top. Wrap up each cake and seal the edges of the strip, dampening them. Fold the almond paste under the base of the cake, set the cake upright and gently pinch the excess paste at the top into even folds to make the cakes look like little purses. Dredge with cocoa powder and place in a refrigerator.

KIRSCH CREAM DOME

Serves 6

2 eggs	fruit jam (cherry,
150 g (5 oz) caster sugar	strawberry or redcurrant)
2 sachets vanilla sugar	500 ml (18 fl oz) double
75 g (3 oz) plain flour	cream
40 g (1½ oz) cornflour	2 tablespoons kirsch
1 teaspoon baking powder	Some fresh cherries to
200-250 g (7-8 oz) red	finish

*U*sing an electric mixer at high speed, beat the eggs with 3-4 tablespoons very hot water, depending on the size of the eggs, for 1 minute until thick and frothy. Mix 100 g (3½ oz) sugar and 1 sachet vanilla sugar together and gradually incorporate into the egg mixture, taking 1 minute, then beat for a further 2 minutes.

Sift the flour, cornflour and baking powder together. Incorporate half into the mixture with the mixer at low speed. When smooth, repeat the procedure the remaining half. Pour the mixture on to a greased baking sheet lined with greaseproof paper, folding the paper up at the edges to prevent the mixture from running. Bake in a preheated oven at 200-220° C (400-425° F, Gas Mark 6-7) for 10-15 minutes.

Turn the sponge out immediately on to a tea towel dredged with sugar. Sprinkle cold water over the baking paper and peel it off. Spread the sponge with jam and roll it up. Leave to cool, then cut into 1 cm (½ in) thick slices. Use to line a 2.5 litre (4½ pint) capacity, 23 cm (9 in) round fruit bowl. Reserve a few slices.

For the filling: whip the cream for 30 seconds, then add the remaining sugar and vanilla sugar. Beat until firm.

Flavour with the kirsch.
Turn this cream into the fruit bowl lined with the sponge slices and cover with the remaining slices. Place in a refrigerator until ready to serve, then turn it out on to a flat dish. Decorate with cherries.

Below: *Kirsch cream dome*

JAM DOUGHNUTS

Makes about 20

500 g (1 lb) strong (bread) flour
1 sachet powdered easy-blend yeast
25 g (1 oz) caster sugar
1 sachet vanilla sugar
3 drops bitter almond essence
1 teaspoon salt
100 g (3½ oz) butter, melted and cooled
3 eggs, 1 separated
125 ml (4 fl oz) warm milk
Jam
Oil for frying
Icing sugar to finish

*C*ombine the flour and yeast thoroughly in a bowl. Add the sugar, vanilla sugar, almond essence, salt, butter, 2 whole eggs, 1 egg yolk and milk. Knead using an electric mixer fitted with a kneading attachment, first at low, then at high speed for 5 minutes until smooth. If the dough is sticky, add a little more flour, but not too much as it must still be elastic.

Leave to rise in a warm place until it has doubled in bulk. Then knead again.

Roll the dough out to 5 mm (¼ in). Using a pastry cutter, mark out 5-6 cm (2-2½ in) diameter circles over half of the dough. Brush the egg white over the edges of the circles. Fill the centres with the jam of your choice. Place the other half of dough on top. Cut through both thicknesses of dough using a pastry cutter. Press the edges of the two circles firmly together.
Place on a baking sheet and leave to prove in a warm place until doubled in bulk.
Heat the oil in a deep-fat fryer. When very hot, add the doughnuts. Cook on both sides, remove from the pan using a slotted spoon and place on a wire rack. Dredge with icing sugar.

Alternative: instead of dredging the doughnuts with icing sugar, toss them in granulated sugar or coat them with glacé icing.

PLUM BAKE

Serves 8-10

500 g (1 lb) strong (bread) flour
1 sachet powdered easy-blend yeast
75 g (3 oz) caster sugar
1 sachet vanilla sugar
A pinch of salt
75 g (3 oz) butter, melted and cooled
250 ml (8 fl oz) warm milk
3 kg (7 lb) plums

Pages 340 and 341: *Jam doughnuts*

Above: *Plum bake*

Combine the yeast and flour thoroughly. Add the sugar, vanilla sugar, salt, butter and milk. Knead all these ingredients together for 5 minutes using an electric mixer fitted with a kneading attachment at low, then at high speed.

Leave to rise in a warm place until doubled in bulk. Knead again. Stretch the dough out over a greased baking sheet, placing a strip of aluminium foil around the edges to hold it in shape if necessary.

For the filling: wash, drain and dry the plums. Remove the stones, cut the plums into quarters and arrange over the dough.

Leave to rise again in a warm place until the dough has doubled in bulk again.

Bake in a preheated oven at 200-220° C (400-425° F, Gas Mark 6-7) for 20-30 minutes. Leave the tart to cool slightly, then dredge with icing sugar if desired.

PINEAPPLE BRIOCHE

Serves 6-8

65 g (2½ oz) fresh yeast
175 g (6 oz) caster sugar
65 g (2½ oz) strong
(bread) flour
250 g (8 oz) butter,
softened
2 eggs
7 egg yolks
1 teaspoon salt
500 g (1 lb) tinned
pineapple (8 slices)

100 ml (3½ fl oz)
maraschino
1 tablespoon apricot jam
4 tablespoons cornflour
4 eggs, separated
500 ml (18 fl oz) cold milk
Pulp of 1 vanilla pod
250 g (8 oz) pineapple
chunks in syrup
100 g (3½ oz) glacé fruits

Mix the crumbled yeast with 4 tablespoons warm water until completely dissolved.

Incorporate 1 teaspoon sugar and the flour. Knead into an elastic dough. Leave in a warm place for 30 minutes to rise.

Cream the butter, then add 50 g (2 oz) sugar, followed by the whole eggs, egg yolks and salt. Gradually incorporate the flour-yeast mixture using an electric mixer fitted with a kneading attachment for 5 minutes. Turn the dough into a greased and floured, 24 cm (9½ in) round, 12 cm (4½ in) deep, fluted ring mould. Leave to prove in a warm place for 40-45 minutes, then bake in a preheated oven at 180° C (350° F, Gas Mark 4) for 30-35 minutes. Remove from the mould carefully. Leave the brioche to cool, then cut into three equal layers. Drain the pineapple slices.

For the syrup: bring 100 g (3½ oz) sugar and 125 ml (4 fl oz) water to the boil. Boil for 5 minutes, then remove from the heat. Incorporate the maraschino and apricot jam. Leave to cool.

Separate the three layers of brioche and place them side by side on a baking sheet. Dredge with 15 g (½ oz) sugar. Place under a preheated grill for 2-3 minutes. Place the brioche base on a plate, sprinkle with a little syrup. Cover with 4 pineapple slices. Place the middle layer of brioche on top. Press down lightly. Sprinkle with syrup and cover with the remaining pineapple slices. Add the top layer of brioche. Press down lightly. Sprinkle with the remaining syrup. Place in a refrigerator.

For the vanilla cream: mix the cornflour with 4 table-spoons milk. Add the 4 remaining egg yolks. Bring the remaining milk and the vanilla to the boil. Add the cornflour-egg yolk mixture, stirring well. Remove from the heat.

Whisk the egg whites into peaks. Bring the egg-cream mixture back to the boil. Gently fold in the whisked egg whites and remove from the heat.

Add the pineapple chunks. Fill the centre of the brioche with this cream and serve the rest separately. Decorate with glacé fruits.

Left: Pineapple brioche

Above: Jam rolls

JAM ROLLS

Makes about 12

400 g (13 oz) strong
(bread) flour
1 sachet powdered easy-
blend yeast
50 g (2 oz) caster sugar
1 sachet vanilla sugar
A pinch of salt
Grated rind of 1 lemon

3 eggs, separated
200 ml (7 fl oz) warm milk
200 g (7 oz) butter, melted
and cooled
Apricot, plum or bilberry
jam
Icing sugar to finish

Combine the flour and yeast thoroughly. Incorporate the sugar, vanilla sugar, salt, lemon rind, egg yolks, milk and half the butter. Knead for 5 minutes using an electric mixer fitted with a kneading attachment, first at low, then at high speed.

Leave in a warm place until the dough has clearly risen. Knead again. Roll out until 1 cm (½ in) thick and cut into 6 x 8 cm (2½ x 3 in) rectangles.

Spread 1 teaspoon jam over each rectangle of dough, then roll them up. Brush the rolls with the remaining butter, then place on a baking sheet, leaving sufficient space between them. Leave to prove in a warm place until they have clearly risen again. Bake in a preheated oven at 200° C (400° F, Gas Mark 6) for 30 minutes. Dredge with icing sugar and serve hot or cold.

Suggestion: serve with vanilla sauce.

CREAM-FILLED CROISSANTS

Makes about 12

300 g (10 oz) strong
(bread) flour
1 sachet powdered easy-
blend yeast
50 g (2 oz) caster sugar
1 sachet vanilla sugar
3 drops lemon flavouring
A pinch of salt

200 g (7 oz) butter
1 egg
450 ml (¾ pint) warm milk
Oil for frying
1 packet vanilla
blancmange mix
Icing sugar to finish

Combine the flour and yeast thoroughly in a bowl. Add the sugar, vanilla sugar, lemon flavouring, salt, 50 g (2 oz) cooled, melted butter, the egg and 150 ml (¼ pint) warm milk. Knead for 5 minutes using an electric mixer fitted with a kneading attachment first at low, then at high speed. If the dough is too sticky, add a little flour, but not too much as the dough must still be elastic.

Leave to rise in a warm place until doubled in bulk. Knead again with the mixer at high speed.

Roll out until 1 cm (½ in) thick. Using a pastry cutter, cut out six 10 cm (4 in) diameter circles. Cut these in half to make 12 semi-circles.

Transfer them to a floured baking sheet, then leave to prove in a warm place until the dough has doubled in bulk. Heat the oil in a deep-fat fryer and brown the semi-circles on both sides.

For the filling: make up the blancmange mix using the remaining milk, following the instructions on the packet. Then incorporate the remaining butter. Slice the croissants across almost to the middle and fill with the blancmange mixture. Dredge with icing sugar.

VANILLA CREAM CRUMBLES

Makes about 15

800 g (1 lb 10 oz) strong
(bread) flour
1 sachet powdered easy-
blend yeast
350 g (11½ oz) caster
sugar
2 sachets vanilla sugar
A pinch of salt

3 eggs
1.2 litres (2 pints) milk
375 g (12 oz) butter
50 g (2 oz) ground
almonds
2 packets vanilla
blancmange mix

Combine 500 g (1 lb) flour and the yeast thoroughly. Incorporate 100 g (3½ oz) sugar, 1 sachet vanilla sugar, the salt, 1 egg, 200 ml (7 fl oz) warm milk and 100 g (3½ oz) cooled, melted butter. Knead these ingredients together for 5 minutes using an electric mixer fitted with a kneading attachment, first at low, then at high speed. If the dough is too sticky, add a little flour, but not too much, as it must still be elastic.

Leave in a warm place until the dough has clearly risen. Knead again. Roll the dough out and transfer to a greased baking sheet. If necessary, wrap several thicknesses of aluminium foil around the edges so that the dough keeps its shape.

For the crumble: in a bowl, combine the remaining flour with 150 g (5 oz) sugar and the remaining vanilla sugar. Incorporate 200 g (7 oz) softened butter and the ground almonds. Knead these ingredients together using an electric mixer fitted with a kneading attachment until the mixture resembles lumpy breadcrumbs. Spread over the dough.

Leave to prove in a warm place until clearly risen. Then bake in a preheated oven at 200-220° C (400-425° F, Gas Mark 6-7) for 20-25 minutes. Leave to cool.

For the filling: make up the vanilla blancmange mixes using the remaining milk. Add the remaining sugar and eggs. Cook following the instructions on the packet.

Cut the remaining butter into two or three pieces and incorporate into the hot blancmange mixture. Leave to cool, stirring occasionally.
Cut the cake into two layers and fill with this cream.

Above: *Vanilla cream crumbles*

Above: *Mini almond Danish pastries*

MINI ALMOND DANISH PASTRIES

Makes 10-15

500 g (1 lb) strong (bread) flour
1 sachet powdered easy-blend yeast
125 g (4 oz) caster sugar
1 sachet vanilla sugar
A pinch of salt
175 g (6 oz) butter
2 eggs
125 ml (4 fl oz) warm milk
200 g (7 oz) almond paste
125 g (4 oz) chopped, blanched almonds
4 tablespoons apricot jam

Combine the flour and yeast thoroughly in a bowl. Add 50 g (2 oz) sugar, the vanilla sugar, salt, 100 g (3½ oz) cooled, melted butter, the eggs and warm milk. Knead for 5 minutes using an electric mixer fitted with a kneading attachment, first at low, then at high speed.

Leave to rise in a warm place until doubled in bulk. Knead again, then roll out on a floured work surface into a 40 x 60 cm (16 x 24 in) rectangle. Spread with the remaining softened butter.

For the filling: dice the almond paste, then knead together with the almonds and the remaining sugar. Roll out over the rectangle of dough, pressing down lightly. Then roll up both layers together and cut into 2 cm (¾ in) thick slices.

Leave to prove in a warm place until doubled in bulk. Bake in a preheated oven at 200-220° C (400-425° F, Gas Mark 6-7) for 10-15 minutes).

For the glaze: sieve the jam, then thin it down with 3 tablespoons water and bring to the boil. Brush over the pastries immediately.

HAZELNUT PUFFS

Makes about 10

375 g (12 oz) strong (bread) flour
1 sachet powdered easy-blend yeast
150 g (5 oz) caster sugar
1 sachet vanilla sugar
175 g (6 oz) butter
1 egg
150 ml (¼ pint) warm milk
200 g (7 oz) ground hazelnuts
4 drops bitter almond essence
6 tablespoons rum (optional)
1 egg, separated
2 tablespoons apricot jam
65 g (2½ oz) icing sugar

Combine the flour and yeast thoroughly in a bowl. Make a well in the centre. Add 50 g (2 oz) sugar, the vanilla sugar, 50 g (2 oz) cooled, melted butter, the whole egg and 125 ml (4 fl oz) milk. Knead for 5 minutes using an electric mixer fitted with a kneading attachment, first at low, then at high speed.

Roll the dough out on a floured surface into a 50 x 40 cm (20 x 16 in) rectangle.
Coat half the rectangle with the remaining softened butter. Then bring the left side of the rectangle two-thirds of the way towards the right. Bring the right side one-third of the way towards the left, overlapping the two sides slightly. Then fold the pastry over in the other direction. Place in a refrigerator for 15 minutes.

Fold the pastry again following the three stages of the above procedure. Return to the refrigerator for 15 minutes, then divide the pastry into two. Roll out each half into a 36 x 36 cm (14 x 14 in) square. Cut into 12 x 12 cm (4½ x 4½ in) squares.

For the filling: combine the ground hazelnuts and the remaining sugar thoroughly. Add the almond essence. Add 4 tablespoons rum (or water). Spread this mixture in the middle of each square. Brush the edges of the squares with the beaten egg white and fold them up into triangles. Arrange on a well-greased baking sheet and leave to prove for 30 minutes at room temperature.

Beat the egg yolk with the remaining milk and brush over the pastry. Bake in a preheated oven at 200° C (400° F, Gas Mark 6) for 15 minutes.

For the coating and icing: sieve the jam, then bring to the boil with 2 tablespoons water. Brush over the pastries immediately.
Mix the icing sugar with the remaining rum (or water) and use to coat the pastries.

Below: *Hazelnut puffs*

SUGAR TWISTS

Makes about 8

40 g (1½ oz) fresh yeast
1 tablespoon warm milk
50 g (2 oz) caster sugar
250 g butter, softened
1 sachet vanilla sugar

A pinch of salt
Grated rind of 1 lemon
2 eggs
500 g (1 lb) strong (bread)
flour

Mix the yeast with the milk and 1 teaspoon sugar. Leave for 15 minutes at room temperature. Cream the butter in a mixing bowl, then add the remaining sugar (reserving 1-2 teaspoons), the vanilla sugar, salt, lemon rind and eggs.

Gradually incorporate the flour using an electric mixer fitted with a kneading attached at low speed. Add the yeast mixture, then knead for 5 minutes at high speed.

Roll the dough into a long sausage shape. Divide into 16 equal portions. Stretch each piece out until 36 cm (15 in) long. Coat in the reserved sugar. Make into a horseshoe shape, then hold the two ends together and twist into shape. Place on a greased baking sheet. Leave to prove for 30 minutes in a warm place until they have clearly risen. Bake in a preheated oven at 200° C (400° F, Gas Mark 6) for 15-20 minutes).

APPLE FRITTERS

Makes 35-40

625 g (1¼ lb) strong
(bread) flour
40 g (1½ oz) fresh yeast
225 g (7½ oz) caster sugar
250 ml (8 fl oz) warm milk
A pinch of salt
Grated rind of 1 lemon

3 eggs
2 egg yolks
1.5 kg (3½ lb) apples
2 teaspoons ground
cinnamon
Lard or oil for frying

Sift the flour into a bowl. Make a well in the centre. Crumble the yeast into a bowl and mix with 1 teaspoon sugar and 3 tablespoons milk. When the yeast has dissolved, mix into a thick paste with a little flour.

Leave in a warm place for 10-15 minutes. When the paste begins to crack on the surface, add 25 g (1 oz) sugar and the remaining milk. Mix together, then pour into the flour, adding the salt, lemon rind, whole eggs and egg yolks.

Knead for 5 minutes using an electric mixer fitted with a kneading attachment, first at low, then at high speed. Leave to rise in a warm place until doubled in bulk, then knead well by hand on a work surface.

Peel, quarter and core the apples. Dice them and incorporate into the dough.

Leave to prove for a further 10-15 minutes. Place 5-6 tablespoons of the mixture into the heated deep-fat fryer and cook on both sides (5-7 minutes in total). Remove the fritters with a slotted spoon and leave to drain on kitchen paper.

Then repeat the procedure until all the mixture has been used up.
Combine the remaining sugar with the cinnamon and toss the fritters in this mixture.

Below: Apple fritters

Opposite: *Sugar twists*

Above: *Apple crumble bake*

APPLE CRUMBLE BAKE

Serves 8-10

750 g (1½ lb) strong
(bread) flour
1 sachet powdered easy-
blend yeast
250 g (8 oz) caster sugar
2 sachets vanilla sugar

A pinch of salt
1 egg
300 g (10 oz) butter
125 ml (4 fl oz) warm milk
500 g (1 lb) apples
A pinch of cinnamon

*T*horoughly combine 400 g (13 oz) flour with the yeast in
a bowl. Add 50 g (2 oz) sugar, 1 sachet vanilla sugar, the
salt, egg, 50 g (2 oz) cooled, melted butter and the milk.

Knead for 5 minutes using an electric mixer fitted with a
kneading attachment, first at low, then at high speed.
Leave to rise in a warm place until doubled in bulk.

Knead well by hand on a work surface.
Roll out, then place on a greased baking sheet. If necessary, place a strip of aluminium foil folded over several
times around the edges so that the dough keeps its
shape.

For the filling: peel, quarter and core the apples. Cut into thick slices. Spread out evenly over the dough.

For the crumble: sift the remaining flour into a bowl. Add the remaining sugar and vanilla sugar and the cinnamon. Mix well. Add the remaining butter cut into pieces. Combine all the ingredients until the mixture resembles lumpy breadcrumbs. Spread over the apples.

Leave to prove in a warm place until the dough has doubled in volume; then bake in a preheated oven at 200-220° C (400-425° F, Gas Mark 6-7) for 30 minutes.

ALMOND AND RAISIN RING

Serves 6-8

375 g (12 oz) strong (bread) flour	200 g (7 oz) almond paste
1 sachet powdered easy-blend yeast	2-3 tablespoons rum
	175 g (6 oz) raisins
50 g (2 oz) caster sugar	50 g (2 oz) chopped, blanched almonds
1 sachet vanilla sugar	1 tablespoon apricot jam
225 g (7½ oz) butter	50 g (2 oz) icing sugar
1 egg	Toasted, flaked almonds
125 ml (4 fl oz) warm milk	to finish

Above: *Almond and raisin ring*

*T*horoughly combine the flour and yeast in a mixing bowl. Add the sugar, vanilla sugar, 50 g (2 oz) cooled, melted butter, the egg and warm milk. Knead for 5 minutes using an electric mixer fitted with a kneading attachment, first a low, then at high speed.

Roll out on a floured surface into a 50 x 40 cm (20 x 16 in) rectangle. Spread half with 125 g (4 oz) softened butter. Fold the rectangle two-thirds of the way over from the left to the right, then fold over the remaining third from the right to the left, slightly overlapping the two short sides of the rectangle in the middle. Fold the dough in half the other way. Place in a refrigerator for 15 minutes. Roll out into a 40 x 50 cm (16 x 20 in) rectangle.

For the filling: knead the almond paste with the remaining butter using an electric mixer fitted with a kneading attachment. Incorporate 1 tablespoon rum. Spread over the rectangle of dough. Mix the raisins and chopped almonds together and sprinkle over the filling.

Divide the dough into two halves lengthways. Roll the two halves up, starting from the longer side. Twist them and assemble into a ring. Place on a greased baking sheet and leave to rest for 30 minutes at room temperature.
Bake in a preheated oven at 180-200° C (350-400° F, Gas Mark 4-6) for 35-40 minutes.

For the coating and icing: sieve the jam, then bring to the boil with 1 tablespoon water. Brush over the ring immediately. Leave to cool slightly. Sift the icing sugar and mix with the remaining rum to form a runny paste. Brush over the ring and sprinkle with flaked almonds immediately.

Above: *Hazelnut pretzels*

HAZELNUT PRETZELS

Makes 20-30

500 g (1 lb) strong (bread)
flour
1 sachet powdered easy-
blend yeast
25 g (1 oz) sugar
1 sachet vanilla sugar
1 teaspoon salt
Grated rind of ½ lemon
100 g (3½ oz) butter,
melted

2 eggs
1 egg yolk
1 egg white
125 ml (4 fl oz) warm milk
100 g (3½ oz) ground
hazelnuts
Oil for frying
Sugar and cinnamon
mixed together

ALMOND SQUARES

Makes about 20

500 g (1 lb) strong (bread) flour	250 ml (8 fl oz) warm milk
1 sachet powdered easy-blend yeast	200 g (7 oz) almond paste
150 g (5 oz) caster sugar	100 ml (3½ fl oz) double cream
A pinch of salt	1 sachet vanilla sugar
225 g (7½ oz) butter	40 g (1½ oz) flaked almonds

*T*horoughly combine the flour and yeast in a bowl. Add 100 g (3½ oz) sugar, the salt, 100 g (3½ oz) cooled, melted butter and the milk.
Knead for 5 minutes using an electric mixer fitted with a kneading attachment, first at low, then at high speed. Leave to rise in a warm place until doubled in bulk, then knead again. Roll out and spread over a greased baking sheet.

For the filling: knead together the remaining butter and the almond paste. Fill an icing bag fitted with a wide nozzle. Using the fingers, make grooves in the dough every 2-3 cm (¾-1¼ in) and fill each one with almond paste. Leave to prove in a warm place until doubled in bulk.
Whip the cream, transfer to an icing bag and pipe into the remaining hollows on the top of the cake.

Below: *Almond squares*

Combine the flour and yeast. Add the sugar, vanilla sugar, salt, lemon rind, melted butter, whole eggs, egg yolk, half the egg white and the milk. Knead for minutes using an electric mixer fitted with a kneading attachment, first at low, then at high speed. Incorporate the ground hazelnuts. Leave to rise in a warm place until doubled in bulk, then knead well.

Roll out into a 42 x 36 cm (16½ x 14 in) rectangle. Cut into 5 mm (⅓ in) wide strips. Make into pretzel shapes, attaching the ends with the remaining beaten egg white. Cover with a tea towel and leave to prove in a warm place.

Heat a deep-fat fryer and brown the pretzels on both sides. Remove with a slotted spoon and toss in the sugar-cinnamon mixture. Leave to cool on a wire rack.

Above: *Brioches*

Combine the remaining sugar with the vanilla sugar, dredge over the cake, then sprinkle with the flaked almonds.

Bake in a preheated oven at 200-220° C (400-425° F, Gas Mark 6-7) for 20 minutes.

BRIOCHES

Makes 6-8

500 g (1 lb) strong (bread) flour
50 g (2 oz) fresh yeast
50 g (2 oz) caster sugar
7 g (¼ oz) salt

40 g (1½ oz) butter, softened
6 eggs
Fresh breadcrumbs

Sift 100 g (3½ oz) flour into a bowl. Mix the yeast with 6 tablespoons warm water and add 1 tablespoon sugar. Leave until dissolved. Add to the flour. Mix well, adding a little water if necessary. Leave to rise in a warm place until doubled in bulk.

Sift the remaining flour into a bowl, add the salt and the remaining sugar. Cream the butter, incorporate the eggs one at a time, then mix into the flour. Add the yeast dough.

Knead for 5 minutes using an electric mixer fitted with a kneading attachment, first at low, then at high speed.

Grease a 33 x 10 cm (13 x 4 in) loaf tin or a 1 litre (1¾ pint) capacity, fluted, ring mould or even small, 8 cm (3 in) round fluted moulds. Sprinkle breadcrumbs over the inside. Add the dough and leave to prove in a warm place for 30 minutes until doubled in bulk.

Bake in a preheated oven at 200° C (400° F, Gas Mark 6) for 40 minutes, if using a large tin, or 20 minutes for the small moulds.

Gift-wrapping suggestions: spray an old bread basket with gold paint. Line with lace and arrange the brioches in it carefully. Wrap in pretty paper.

If you have baked a single, large brioche, return it to the cleaned tin, then wrap it in pretty paper, attaching the hand-written recipe with gift-wrap ribbon.

PLUM AND CINNAMON BAKE

Serves 6-8

400 g (13 oz) strong (bread) flour
20 g (¾ oz) fresh yeast
4 tablespoons warm milk
165 g (5½ oz) caster sugar
1 sachet vanilla sugar
3 small eggs
175 g (6 oz) butter
Grated rind of 2 lemons
1 kg (2 lb) plums
125 ml (4 fl oz) double cream
Ground cinnamon
Whipped cream
Plum brandy

Sift 250 g (8 oz) flour into a bowl. Make a well in the centre. Mix the crumbled yeast with the milk and 2 teaspoons sugar. Work into a thick paste with some of the flour. Leave for 10-15 minutes until the surface of the paste begins to crack, then add 50 g (2 oz) sugar, the vanilla sugar, 1 egg, 75 g (3 oz) softened butter and half the lemon rind.

Knead for 5 minutes using an electric mixer fitted with a kneading attachment, first at low, then at high speed. Leave to rise in a warm place until doubled in bulk, then knead by hand on a work surface.

For the filling: wash, dry, halve and stone the plums. Grease a 3 cm (1¼ in) deep, 28 cm (11 in) round cake tin

and line with the dough. Prick the base with a fork. Arrange the plums over the base, overlapping them slightly. Leave to prove for 15 minutes. Bake in a preheated oven at 200° C (400° F, Gas Mark 6) for 15 minutes.

Beat the remaining eggs with 75 g (3 oz) sugar until creamy. Whip the cream, adding a pinch of cinnamon. Incorporate into the egg-sugar mixture and pour over the plums.
Bake for 10 minutes at the same temperature until the egg cream mixture is firm.

Sift the remaining flour into a bowl, then incorporate a little cinnamon, the remaining sugar and lemon rind. Rub in the remaining butter cut into small pieces until a lumpy mixture is formed. Spread over the tart and return to the oven for a further 15-20 minutes at the same temperature.

Suggestion: serve with whipped cream flavoured with plum brandy.

Below: *Plum and cinnamon bake*

WHITE WINE CREAM DOUGHNUTS

Makes about 20

350 g (11½ oz) strong (bread) flour
1 sachet powdered easy-blend yeast
40 g (1½ oz) caster sugar
1 sachet vanilla sugar
2 drops bitter almond essence
A pinch of salt
65 g (2½ oz) butter, melted

2 eggs
100 ml (3½ fl oz) warm milk
Oil for frying
250 ml (8 fl oz) double cream
1 packet vanilla blancmange mix
100 ml (3½ fl oz) white wine
Icing sugar to finish

Thoroughly combine the flour and yeast in a bowl. Add the caster sugar, vanilla sugar, almond essence, salt, melted butter, eggs and warm milk. Knead for 5 minutes using an electric mixer fitted with a kneading attachment, first at low, then at high speed. If the dough is too sticky, add a little flour, but not too much as it must still be elastic.

Leave in a warm place until it has clearly risen, then knead by hand on a work surface. Roll out until 2 cm (¾ in) thick. Cut out circles using a 7 cm (2¾ in) round pastry cutter. Place on a clean, floured tea towel. Cover and leave until the dough has risen again.

Heat a deep-fat fryer and add the circles of dough. Cook on both sides, then remove with a slotted spoon, place on a wire rack and leave to cool.

For the filling: whip the cream until very firm.

In a separate bowl, make up the blancmange mix using the white wine, following the instructions on the packet. Fold into the whipped cream. Transfer to an icing bag fitted with a large, fluted nozzle. Pipe on to half the doughnuts and cover with the rest.

CHOCOLATE HAZELNUT BRIOCHE

Serves 6-8

500 g (1 lb) strong (bread) flour
1 sachet powdered easy-blend yeast
200 g (7 oz) caster sugar
1 sachet vanilla sugar
250 g (8 oz) butter, melted
50 g (2 oz) hazelnut spread (from health food

shops)
6 eggs
8 tablespoons warm milk
Fresh breadcrumbs
25 g (1 oz) cocoa powder
65 g (2½ oz) grated cooking chocolate
Icing sugar to finish

Above: *Chocolate hazelnut brioche*

Thoroughly combine the flour and yeast in a bowl. Add 175 g (6 oz) sugar, the vanilla sugar, 200 g (7 oz) melted butter, the hazelnut spread, eggs and 5 tablespoons milk. Knead well for 5 minutes using an electric mixer fitted with a kneading attachment, first at low, then at high speed.

Leave to rise in a warm place until doubled in bulk. Knead by hand on a work surface.

Place two-thirds of the dough in a greased, fluted, ring mould dusted with breadcrumbs. Incorporate the cocoa powder, the remaining sugar, the grated chocolate and the remaining milk into the remaining dough. Add to the mould, bringing the plain dough up to the top by making spiral movements. Leave in a warm place until it has risen by a third. Bake in a preheated oven at 180-200° C (350-400° F, Gas Mark 4-6) for 50 minutes. Brush the remaining melted butter over the cake and dredge with icing sugar.

APPLE BAKE

Serves 8-10

500 g (1 lb) strong (bread)
flour
1 sachet powdered easy-
blend yeast
75 g (3 oz) caster sugar
1 sachet vanilla sugar
A pinch of salt
250 ml (8 fl oz) warm milk

75 g (3 oz) butter, melted
and cooled
1.5 kg (3½ lb) apples
20 g (¾ oz) sultanas
25 g (1 oz) blanched
almonds, cut into slivers
3 rounded tablespoons
apricot jam

Thoroughly combine the flour and yeast in a bowl. Add the sugar, vanilla sugar, salt, warm milk and melted butter. Knead for 5 minutes using an electric mixer fitted with a kneading attachment, first at low, then at high speed. If the dough is too sticky, add a little flour, but not too much as it must still be elastic.

Leave the dough in a warm place until it has clearly risen; then knead by hand on a work surface. Roll out and place on a greased baking sheet. If necessary, surround with a strip of aluminium foil folded over several times so that the dough keeps its shape.

For the filling: peel, quarter, core and slice the apples. Arrange them evenly over the dough. Add the almonds and raisins. Leave to prove in a warm place until it has clearly risen. Bake in a preheated oven at 200-220° C (400-425° F, Gas Mark 6-7) for 20-30 minutes.

For the glaze: thin down the jam with 1 tablespoon water. Bring to the boil and brush over the tart as soon as it is out of the oven.

Below:
Apple bake

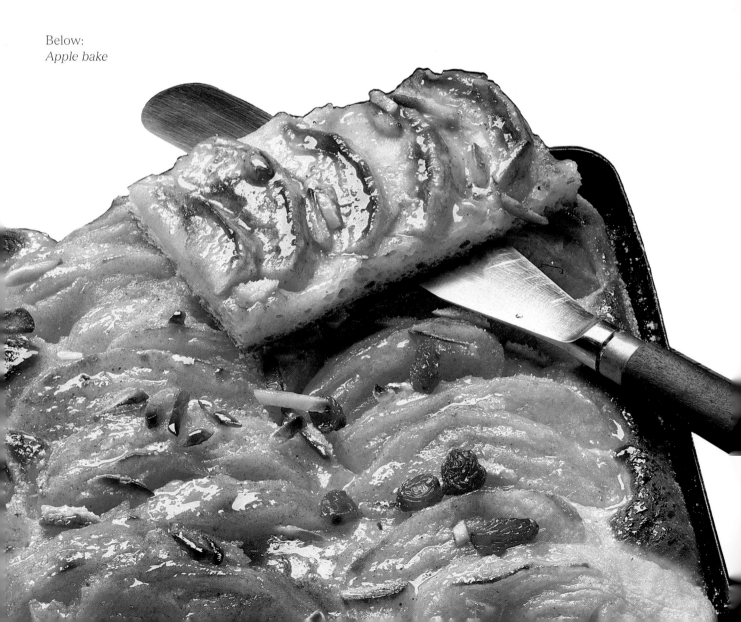

Above: *Date ring*

DATE RING

Serves about 8

500 g (1 lb) strong (bread) flour
20 g (¾ oz) fresh yeast
50 g (2 oz) caster sugar
125 ml (4 fl oz) warm milk
2 small eggs
A pinch of salt
175 g (6 oz) butter
150 g (5 oz) stoned dates
200 g (7 oz) almond paste
2 heaped tablespoons plum jam
Grated nutmeg

Sift the flour into a bowl. Make a well in the centre and add the crumbled yeast, 1 teaspoon sugar and 4 tablespoons warm milk, then work into a paste with some of the flour. Leave in a warm place for 10-15 minutes until the surface begins to crack.
Add the remaining sugar and milk, the eggs, salt and 100 g (3½ oz) softened butter. Knead the ingredients together for 5 minutes using an electric mixer fitted with a kneading attachment, first at low, then at high speed.
Leave the dough to rise in a warm place until doubled in bulk, then knead by hand on a work surface. Roll out into a 30 x 50 cm (12 x 20 in) rectangle.

Melt the remaining butter. Chop the dates coarsely. Knead the almond paste in a mixing bowl, adding the jam and nutmeg. Incorporate the butter and dates. Spread this mixture over the dough, then roll it up, starting from the longest side of the rectangle. Then cut the rolled cake into 5 cm (2 in) thick slices.

Arrange the slices in a deep, 28 cm (11 in) round cake tin, leaving a little space between them. Leave to prove in a warm place for 30 minutes. Bake in a preheated oven at 200° C (400° F, Gas Mark 6) for 40 minutes.

APRICOT NESTS

Makes about 16

500 g (1 lb) strong (bread) flour
40 g (1½ oz) fresh yeast
100 g (3½ oz) caster sugar
500 ml (18 fl oz) milk
150 g (5 oz) butter
2 pinches of salt
1 egg
A little grated lemon rind
½ packet vanilla blancmange mix
1 egg yolk
8 apricots
100 g (3½ oz) raisins

Sift the flour into a bowl. Make a well in the centre. Add the crumbled yeast, 1 teaspoon sugar and a little warm milk; then mix into a thick paste with a little flour. Leave to rest for 10-15 minutes until the surface of the paste begins to crack. Add 20 g (¾ oz) sugar, 250 ml (8 fl oz) milk, 75 g (3 oz) softened butter, a pinch of salt, the whole egg and the grated lemon rind.

Knead for 5 minutes using an electric mixer fitted with a kneading attachment, first at low, then at high speed. Leave to rise in a warm place until doubled in bulk, then knead by hand on a work surface. Leave to prove for 15 minutes.

For the filling: make up the blancmange mix using 75 g (3 oz) sugar and the remaining salt and milk, following the instructions on the packet. Incorporate the egg yolk. Leave to cool, stirring occasionally.

Quickly blanch the apricots in a pan of simmering water, then refresh in cold water. Peel, halve and stone them.

Roll the dough out into a 30 x 46 cm (12 x 18 in) rectangle and brush with 50 g (2 oz) melted butter. Scatter the raisins over the dough. Roll up, starting from the longest side of the rectangle.

Cut the roll of dough into about 16 slices. Arrange on a greased baking sheet. Make a hollow in the centre of each slice and fill with the well-stirred blancmange mixture. Top with an apricot half.

Bake in a preheated oven at 200-220° C (400-425° F, Gas Mark 6-7) for 20 minutes. Brush with the remaining melted butter as soon as the pastries are out of the oven.

COCKSCOMBS

Makes 10-12

375 g (12 oz) strong (bread) flour
1 sachet powdered easy-blend yeast
50 g (2 oz) caster sugar
1 sachet vanilla sugar
225 g (7½ oz) butter
2 eggs
150 ml (¼ pint) warm milk
200 g (7 oz) almond paste
1 egg white
1 egg yolk
2 tablespoons apricot jam
65 g (2½ oz) icing sugar
2 tablespoons lemon juice

Thoroughly combine the flour and yeast in a bowl. Add the sugar, vanilla sugar, 50 g (2 oz) cooled, melted butter, 1 egg and 125 ml (4 fl oz) warm milk. Knead for 5 minutes using an electric mixer fitted with a kneading attachment, first at low, then at high speed.

Roll the dough out into a 50 x 40 cm (16 x 20 in) rectangle. Fold the left side of the rectangle two-thirds of the way to the right, then fold the right side one-third towards the left, overlapping the edges slightly. Then fold the dough in half the other way. Place in a refrigerator for 15 minutes.

Fold the dough again following the same procedure and return to the refrigerator for 15 minutes. Divide into two halves and roll out to form two 36 x 36 cm (14 x 14 in) squares. Cut into 12 x 12 cm (4½ x 4½ in) squares.

For the filling: cream the almond paste with the remaining butter and 1 egg. Spread this filling in the centre of the squares of dough. Brush the edges of the pastry with the egg white and fold the squares over to form parcels. Make incisions on the outside edge of the parcels every 15 mm (⅓ in).
Place on a greased baking sheet and leave to rise for 30 minutes at room temperature.

Beat the egg yolk with the remaining milk and brush over the parcels. Bake in a preheated oven at 200° C (400° F, Gas Mark 6) for 15 minutes.

Left: *Apricot nests*

Above: *Cockscombs*

For the apricot coating: sieve the apricot jam, thin it
down with 2 tablespoons water and bring to the boil.
Remove from the heat and brush over the parcels.

For the glacé icing: mix the icing sugar and lemon juice
together and use to coat the parcels.

Above: *Easter bunnies*

EASTER BUNNIES

Makes about 2

500 g (1 lb) rye flour
250 g (8 oz) strong
wholewheat (bread) flour
65 g (2½ oz) fresh yeast
1 teaspoon caster sugar
125 ml (4 fl oz) vegetable

oil
2 teaspoons salt
1 black olive
Sesame, cumin or poppy
seeds

Mix the rye and wholewheat flours together. Make a well in the centre. Add the crumbled yeast to the flour with the sugar and 100 ml (3½ fl oz) warm water. Mix into a thick paste using some of the flour, then leave to rest in a warm place for 10-15 minutes. When the surface of the paste begins to crack, add 500 ml (18 fl oz) warm water, the vegetable oil and salt. Leave the dough to rise in a warm place until doubled in bulk, then knead by

hand on a work surface. Make into a thick roll. Break off four 200 g (7 oz) portions and roll into balls, then break off a further six 100 g (3½ oz) portions and roll into oval-shaped balls. Make the remaining dough into a small ball.

Assemble three round balls to make the body of the rabbit and place on a greased baking sheet. Brush the balls of dough with water where they touch. Stretch the fourth ball out slightly and put in place to form the head. Stick an olive into the dough to make the eye, then add the oval balls to make the paws and ears. Finally add the small ball for the tail. Brush the whole rabbit with water and sprinkle with sesame, poppy or cumin seeds as desired. Bake in a preheated oven at 240° C (475° F, Gas Mark 9) for 35-45 minutes.

NEW YEAR PRETZEL

Serves 6-8

1 sachet dried yeast
125 ml (4 fl oz) warm milk
50 g (2 oz) caster sugar
500 g (1 lb) strong (bread)
flour
1 sachet vanilla sugar

A pinch of salt
1 egg
250 g (8 oz) butter,
softened
Condensed milk

Combine the yeast with the milk and 1 teaspoon sugar. Leave to rest for 15 minutes. Put the flour into a bowl and make a well in the centre. Put the remaining sugar, the vanilla sugar, salt, egg and butter cut into pieces around the edge of the well. Pour the yeast mixture into the centre.
Knead for 5 minutes using an electric mixer fitted with a kneading attachment, first at low, then at high speed. Reserve a little dough for decoration, then divide the rest into three equal portions. Roll each into a sausage shape, plait them and make them into a pretzel shape. Make a flower and leaves with the remaining dough using suitable moulds.

Brush the whole pretzel with condensed milk and leave to rise in a warm place for 30 minutes. Bake in a preheated oven at 200° C (400° F, Gas Mark 6) for 40 minutes.

Gift suggestion: place the pretzel on a wooden board, wrapped in a cloth loosely tied with a ribbon.

Below: *New Year pretzel*

Above: *Easter lamb*

EASTER LAMB

Serves 8-10

*375 g (12 oz) strong
(bread) wheat flour
125 g (4 oz) rye flour
1 sachet powdered easy-
blend yeast
1 teaspoon caster sugar*

*2 teaspoons salt
2 eggs, beaten
50 g (2 oz) butter, melted
Almonds, cut into slivers
2 currants*

Mix the flours together in a bowl, then incorporate the yeast. Add the sugar, salt, 1½ eggs, the melted butter and 250 ml (8 fl oz) warm water. Knead for 5 minutes using an electric mixer fitted with a kneading attachment, first at low, then at high speed. Leave the dough to rise in a warm place until doubled in bulk, then knead by hand on a work surface.

Use a quarter of the dough to make the lamb's head, ears and legs. Roll the remaining dough into small balls. Assemble on a greased baking sheet to make the body. Add the head, ears and legs. Leave to rise in a warm place until doubled in bulk. Brush with the remaining beaten egg and sprinkle with almonds. Use 2 currants to make the eyes. Bake in a preheated oven at 200-220° C (400-425° F, Gas Mark 6-7) for 25 minutes.

Gift suggestions: place the lamb on a wooden board (or in a shallow box) covered with a thick layer of shredded green tissue paper scattered with daisies. You could, if you wish, attach a little glass or golden metal bell for decoration. Wrap in cellophane paper, or, if the box has a lid, it could be decorated with Easter motifs.

DAMSON AND POPPY SEED TART

Serves 8

500 g (1 lb) strong (bread)
flour
40 g (1½ oz) fresh yeast
100 g (3½ oz) caster sugar
250 ml (8 fl oz) double
cream, warmed
375 g (12 oz) butter,
softened
A pinch of salt
2 egg yolks
250 g (8 oz) poppy seeds
50 g (2 oz) honey

Grated rind of 1 lemon
Ground cinnamon
50 g (2 oz) raisins
2 tablespoons rum
3 eggs
3 tablespoons fresh
breadcrumbs
1 kg (2 lb) damsons
2 tablespoons milk
125 g (4 oz) icing sugar
2 tablespoons lemon juice

Sift the flour into a bowl and make a well in the centre. Add the crumbled yeast and 1 teaspoon sugar. Heat 3 tablespoons cream and add 1 tablespoonful to the flour. Knead into a thick paste with a little flour. Leave to rest in a warm place for 10-15 minutes. When the surface of the paste begins to crack, add 50 g (2 oz) sugar and the remaining warm cream. Add the butter cut into pieces, the salt and 1 egg yolk. Knead for 5 minutes using an electric mixer fitted with a kneading attachment, first at low, then at high speed. Cover the dough and leave to rise in a cool place for 6 hours. Do not place in a refrigerator.

For the filling: grind the poppy seeds to a powder and bring to the boil with the remaining cream and sugar, and the honey. Remove from the heat and incorporate the lemon rind and cinnamon. Mix well. Incorporate the raisins and leave to cool. Then add the rum, 3 eggs and the breadcrumbs.

Wash, dry, halve and stone the damsons. Flour the work surface and roll the dough out into a 46 x 39 cm (18 x 15½ in) rectangle. Cut into 12 cm (4½ in) wide strips. Place on a well-greased baking sheet. Spread the filling in the centre of each strip and cover with the plums. Fold the long sides of the strips towards the centre to prevent the filling from running. Beat the remaining egg yolk with the milk and brush over the dough. Bake in a preheated oven at 200-220° C (400-425° F, Gas Mark 4-6) for 25 minutes.

For the glacé icing: mix the icing sugar with the lemon juice and use to coat the tart while still hot.

RHUM BABA

Serves 8

200 ml (7 fl oz) milk
20 g (¾ oz) fresh yeast
300 g (10 oz) strong
(bread) flour
200 g (7 oz) caster sugar
65 g (2½ oz) butter,

softened
4 eggs
4 tablespoons rum
200 ml (7 fl oz) double
cream

Pour the warm milk over the yeast and leave for 10 minutes until the mixture begins to froth. Incorporate in the flour, then add half the sugar, the softened butter and the eggs. Combine gently, then leave to rise until doubled in bulk.

Knead the dough, then put into a savarin ring mould and bake in a preheated oven at 200° C (400° F, Gas Mark 6) for 25 minutes.

Boil 125 ml (4 fl oz) water with the remaining sugar for 6 minutes. Remove from the heat and add the rum.

Slowly pour this syrup over the cake when out of the tin so that it absorbs all the liquid.

Serve with whipped cream.

Below: *Damson and poppy seed tart*

BUTTER DELIGHT

Serves 8

500 g (1 lb) strong (bread) flour
1 sachet powdered easy-blend yeast
150 g (5 oz) caster sugar
2 sachets vanilla sugar
A pinch of salt
250 ml (8 fl oz) warm milk
200 g (7 oz) butter
50 g (2 oz) flaked almonds

Thoroughly combine the flour and yeast in a bowl. Add 75 g (3 oz) sugar, 1 sachet vanilla sugar, the salt, warm milk and 75 g (3 oz) cooled, melted butter. Knead for 5 minutes using an electric mixer fitted with a kneading attachment, first at low, then at high speed. If the dough is too sticky, add a little flour, but not too much, as the dough must still be elastic. Leave in a warm place until the dough has clearly risen, then knead again by hand on a work surface. Roll the dough out and line a well-greased baking sheet. If necessary, wrap a strip of aluminium foil folded into several layers around the dough so that it keeps its shape.

Below: *Butter delight*

Mix the remaining sugar and vanilla sugar together. Dredge over the cake. Sprinkle with flaked almonds. Leave to prove in a warm place until it has clearly risen. Bake in a preheated oven at 200-220° C (400-425° F, Gas Mark 6-7) for 15 minutes.

Alternative: whip 250 ml (8 fl oz) double cream until very firm. Spread over the cake as soon as it is out of the oven.

BRIOCHE PLAIT

Serves 6

500 g (1 lb) strong (bread) flour
1 sachet powdered easy-blend yeast
50 g (2 oz) caster sugar
1 sachet vanilla sugar
A pinch of salt
2 eggs
1 egg white
250 ml (8 fl oz) double cream
150 g (5 oz) sultanas
1 egg yolk
1 tablespoon milk

Combine the flour and yeast in a bowl. Add the sugar, vanilla sugar, salt, whole eggs, egg white and cream. Knead for 5 minutes using an electric mixer fitted with a kneading attachment first at low, then at high speed. Leave to rise in a warm place until doubled in bulk. Incorporate the raisins.

Roll two-thirds of the dough into two 40 cm (16 in) long sausage shapes. Plait them and place on a greased baking sheet. Make a hollow in the centre by pressing down with a rolling pin. Beat the egg yolk and milk together and brush over the dough, reserving a little.

Roll the remaining dough into two 34 cm (13½ in) sausage shapes. Plait them and place on top of the first plait. Leave to prove in a warm place until doubled in bulk (in height and width). Brush with the remaining milk-egg yolk mixture. Bake in a preheated oven at 180-200° C (350-400° F, Gas Mark 4-6) for 35 minutes.

Opposite: *Brioche plait*

POPPY SEED CRUMBLE BAKE

Serves 8-10

700 g (1 lb 6 oz) strong (bread) flour
3 sachets powdered easy-blend yeast
300 g (10 oz) caster sugar
3 sachets vanilla sugar
A pinch of salt
250 g (8 oz) butter
400 ml (14 fl oz) milk

500 g (1 lb) ground poppy seeds
4 drops lemon flavouring
½ teaspoon ground cinnamon
1 tablespoon honey (optional)
75 g (3 oz) raisins

Combine 500 g (1 lb) flour and the yeast in a bowl. Add 75 g (3 oz) sugar, 1 sachet vanilla sugar, 75 g (3 oz) cooled, melted butter and 250 ml (8 fl oz) warm milk. Knead for 5 minutes using an electric mixer fitted with a kneading attachment, first at low, then at high speed. Leave to rise in a warm place until doubled in bulk, then knead by hand on a work surface. Roll out and line a well-greased baking sheet. If necessary, wrap a strip of aluminium foil folded into several layers around the dough so that it keeps its shape.

For the filling: mix the poppy seeds with a little very hot water and leave to soak. Add 125 g (4 oz) sugar, 1 sachet vanilla sugar, the lemon flavouring, ground cinnamon (reserving a pinch), 75 g (3 oz) melted butter and the remaining warm milk (or 1 tablespoon honey). Mix well until smooth. Incorporate the raisins. Leave to cool, then spread over the dough.

Mix together the remaining flour and sugar, vanilla sugar, pinch of cinnamon and butter (cut into pieces). Knead roughly until the mixture resembles lumpy breadcrumbs. Sprinkle over the filling. Bake in a preheated oven at 180-200° C (350-400° F, Gas Mark 4-6) for 25-30 minutes.

Below: *Poppy seed crumble*

Above: *Bread of angels*

BREAD OF ANGELS

Serves 6

1 kg (2 lb) strong (bread) flour
40 g (1½ oz) fresh yeast
250 ml (8 fl oz) warm milk
200 g (7 oz) icing sugar
250 g (8 oz) butter, softened
1 sachet vanilla sugar

A pinch of salt
½ teaspoon ground saffron
4 tablespoons rum
100 g (3½ oz) chopped almonds
5 egg yolks
Icing sugar to finish

Sift the flour into a bowl. Make a well in the centre and add the crumbled yeast mixed with 3 tablespoons warm milk and 1 teaspoon icing sugar. Knead into a thick paste with some of the flour. Leave in a warm place for 10-15 minutes until the surface of the paste begins to crack. Add the remaining milk and icing sugar, the butter cut into pieces, the vanilla sugar, salt, saffron, rum, almonds and egg yolks.

Knead for 5 minutes using an electric mixer fitted with a kneading attachment, first at low, then at high speed. Leave to rise in a warm place until doubled in bulk, then knead again by hand on a work surface. Roll into a 1.2 m (46 in) long sausage shape. Make into a pretzel shape.

Leave to prove in a warm place until doubled in bulk. Place on a greased baking sheet and bake in a preheated oven at 200° C (400° F, Gas Mark 6) for 20-30 minutes. Dredge with pretzel with icing sugar as soon as it is out of the oven.

Above: *Bilberry crumble squares*

BILBERRY CRUMBLE SQUARES

Makes about 10

800 g (1 lb 10 oz) strong (bread) flour	*1.5 kg (3½ lb) bilberries*
40 g (1½ oz) fresh yeast	*4 rusks*
250 ml (8 fl oz) warm milk	*2 teaspoons ground cinnamon*
200 g (7 oz) caster sugar	*200 g (7 oz) butter*
150 g (5 oz) lard	*Icing sugar to finish*
A pinch of salt	

Sift 500 g (1 lb) flour into a bowl and make a well in the centre. Add the crumbled yeast and mix with a little warm milk and 1 teaspoon sugar. Knead into a thick paste with a little flour. Leave for 10-15 minutes until the paste begins to crack. Then add 65 g (2½ oz) sugar and the remaining milk, the lard cut into pieces and the salt.

Knead for 5 minutes using an electric mixer fitted with a kneading attachment first at low, then at high speed. Leave to rise in a warm place until doubled in bulk, then knead again by hand. Roll out and place on a greased baking sheet. If necessary, wrap a strip of aluminium foil folded into several layers around the dough so that it keeps its shape.

For the filling: wash the bilberries carefully, then drain them. Crush the rusks finely and sprinkle over the dough. Add the bilberries.

Combine the remaining flour and sugar and the cinnamon. Add the butter cut into pieces and quickly knead until the mixture resembles lumpy breadcrumbs. Sprinkle over the bilberries. Leave to prove in a warm place until doubled in bulk.

Roll out and line a greased baking sheet. Bake in a preheated oven at 200° C (400° F, Gas Mark 6) for 30-40 minutes. Leave to cool, then lightly dredge with icing sugar.

BOHEMIAN POPPY SEED STRUDEL

Serves 6

500 g (1 lb) strong (bread) flour
25 g (1 oz) fresh yeast
175 g (6 oz) caster sugar
750 ml (1¼ pints) warm milk
A pinch of salt
Grated rind of 1 lemon
3 eggs
125 g (4 oz) butter, softened
500 g (1 lb) ground poppy seeds
200 g (7 oz) candied lemon peel
2 tablespoons honey
1 sachet vanilla sugar
100 g (3½ oz) raisins
125 g (4 oz) icing sugar
2 tablespoons lemon juice
1 tablespoon rum
50 g (2 oz) hazelnuts, coarsely chopped

Sift the flour into a bowl. Make a well in the centre and add the crumbled yeast, 1 teaspoon sugar and 50 ml (2 fl oz) warm milk. Knead into a thick paste using a little flour, then leave for 10-15 minutes in a warm place until the surface begins to crack. Then add 75 g (3 oz) sugar and 200 ml (7 fl oz) warm milk, the salt, lemon rind, 1 egg and the butter cut into pieces.

Knead for 5 minutes using an electric mixer fitted with a kneading attachment, first at low, then at high speed. Leave to rise in a warm place until doubled in bulk, then knead again by hand on a work surface.

For the filling: heat the remaining milk. Pour it over the poppy seeds and leave to soak. Incorporate the chopped candied lemon peel, the remaining sugar and eggs, the honey, vanilla sugar and raisins.

Roll out the dough into a 55 x 40 cm (22 x 16 in) rectangle. Coat with a layer of the poppy seed mixture, leaving a

2 cm (¾ in) border at the edges. Fold up the short sides of the rectangle towards the middle, then roll up the filled pastry and place on a greased baking tray. Cut crosses into the pastry every 10 cm (4 in). Leave to rest in a warm place for 15 minutes. Bake in a preheated oven at 180-200° C (350-400° F, Gas Mark 4-6) for 35 minutes.

For the glacé icing: combine the icing sugar, lemon juice and rum and use to coat the strudel as soon as it is out of the oven. Sprinkle with lightly toasted hazelnuts.

Below: *Bohemian poppy seed strudel*

Above: *Cream-filled pastries*

mix with 125 ml (4 fl oz) cold milk and the egg yolks. Heat the remaining milk with the remaining salt and butter and 50 g (2 oz) sugar. Incorporate this mixture into the blancmange mix. Bring back to the boil. Remove from the heat and leave to cool, stirring occasionally.

Shape the dough into a roll. Divide it into two halves and roll each half into a ball. Leave to rest for 8 minutes, then roll out each ball into a 28 x 15 cm (11 x 6 in) oval shape. Place on a greased baking sheet and leave to rest for 15-20 minutes.

For the almond topping: heat 125 ml (4 fl oz) cream with the honey, the remaining sugar and the lemon rind. Boil for 2-3 minutes. Incorporate the almonds and 1 tablespoon flour. Leave to cool, then coat the oval dough shapes. Smooth out evenly. Bake in a preheated oven at 200° C (400° F, Gas Mark 6) for 20-25 minutes. Leave to cool.

Sieve the vanilla cream mixture. Whip the remaining cream until firm. Gently fold into the vanilla cream. Cut the pastries into two layers and fill with this cream. Place in a refrigerator for 1-1½ hours. Cut into fingers.

CREAM-FILLED PASTRIES

Makes about 2

300 g (10 oz) strong (bread) flour	blancmange mix
25 g (1 oz) fresh yeast	2 egg yolks
125 g (4 oz) caster sugar	375 ml (12 fl oz) double cream
600 ml (1 pint) milk	40 g (1½ oz) honey
100 g (3½ oz) butter	1 teaspoon grated lemon rind
2 pinches of salt	
1 egg	300 g (10 oz) almonds, cut into slivers
1½ packets vanilla	

Sift the flour and make a well in the centre, reserving 1 tablespoonful. Add the crumbled yeast, 1 teaspoon sugar and a little warm milk. Knead into a thick paste with a little flour. Leave for 10-15 minutes in a warm place until the surface of the paste begins to crack, then add 40 g (1½ oz) sugar, 125 ml (4 fl oz) warm milk, 65 g (2½ oz) butter cut into pieces, a pinch of salt and the whole egg.

Knead for 5 minutes using an electric mixer fitted with a kneading attachment, first at low, then at high speed. Leave to rise in a warm place until doubled in bulk, then knead again by hand.
For the vanilla cream filling: combine the blancmange

CHELSEA BUNS

Makes 8-10

500 g (1 lb) strong (bread) flour	2 eggs
1 sachet powdered easy-blend yeast	125 ml (4 fl oz) warm milk
100 g (3½ oz) caster sugar	100 g (3½ oz) raisins
2 sachets vanilla sugar	50 g (2 oz) chopped, blanched almonds
A pinch of salt	175 g (6 oz) icing sugar
125 g (4 oz) butter	2 tablespoons lemon juice

Mix the flour and yeast together in a bowl. Add half the sugar, 1 sachet vanilla sugar, the salt, 100 g (3½ oz) cooled, melted butter, the eggs and warm milk. Knead for 5 minutes using an electric mixer fitted with a kneading attachment, first at low, then at high speed. Leave the dough to rise in a warm place until doubled in bulk, then knead by hand on a work surface.

Roll out into a 46 x 34 cm (18 x 13½) rectangle. Coat with 25 g (1 oz) softened butter.

For the filling: mix the raisins with the remaining sugar and vanilla sugar and the chopped almonds. Sprinkle over the dough. Roll it up and cut into 15 mm (⅓ in) thick

slices. Place on a greased baking sheet. Press down
lightly with your hand.
Leave to prove until doubled in bulk. Bake in a preheated
oven at 180-200° C (350-400° F, Gas Mark 4-6) for
15-20 minutes.

For the glacé icing: combine the icing sugar with the
lemon juice and use to coat the Chelsea buns.

Below: *Chelsea buns*

CREAM CHEESE PASTRY

CREAM CHEESE AND POPPY SEED TART

Serves 6

150 g (5 oz) cream cheese
125 ml (4 fl oz) milk
6 tablespoons oil
275 g (9 oz) caster sugar
1 sachet vanilla sugar
A pinch of salt
300 g (10 oz) plain flour
2 teaspoons baking

powder
375 g (12 oz) ground
poppy seeds
2 packets vanilla
blancmange mix
50 g (2 oz) semolina
100 g (3½ oz) raisins
2 eggs, separated

Combine the cream cheese with 6 tablespoons milk, the oil, 75 g (3 oz) sugar, the vanilla sugar and salt in a mixing bowl.

Sift the flour and baking powder together. Incorporate half into the cream cheese mixture; then knead in the remaining half. Roll the pastry out and line a greased baking sheet.

For the filling: mix the poppy seeds with 500 ml (18 fl oz) water. Bring to the boil, then leave to soak.

Make up the vanilla blancmange mixes, adding the semolina, the remaining sugar and 125 ml (4 fl oz) milk. Heat the remaining milk and add it to the blancmange mixture, stirring constantly. Bring back to the boil briefly. Add the poppy seeds and raisins and leave to cool.

Spread half of this mixture over the pastry. Whisk the egg whites into peaks and incorporate into the remaining mixture with the egg yolks. Spread over the filling. Bake in a preheated oven at 180-200° C (350-400° F, Gas Mark 4-6) for 30 minutes. Serve with whipped cream.

ORANGE AND MARZIPAN PLAITS

Makes 3

200 g (7 oz) almond paste
50 g (2 oz) butter,
softened
2 tablespoons orange
marmalade
Grated rind of ½ orange
150 g (5 oz) cream cheese
7 tablespoons milk
6 tablespoons oil
75 g (3 oz) caster sugar

1 sachet vanilla sugar
A pinch of salt
300 g (10 oz) plain flour
2 teaspoons baking
powder
1 egg, separated
100 g (3½ oz) icing sugar
2-3 tablespoons orange
juice

Pages 376 and 377: *Cream cheese and poppy seed tart*

Above: *Orange and marzipan plaits*

Combine the almond paste with the butter, orange marmalade and orange rind in a bowl.

For the pastry: combine the cream cheese, 6 table-spoons milk, the oil, sugar, vanilla sugar and salt in a bowl. Sift the flour and baking powder together. Stir half into the cheese mixture, then knead in the second half. Roll the dough out into a 36 x 48 cm (14 x 19 in) rectangle; then cut into 12 x 12 cm (4½ x 4½ in) squares. Spread the filling over half the squares, leaving a 5 mm-1 cm (¼-½ in) border around the edge. Brush the edges of the squares with the beaten egg white. Place the plain pastry squares on top of the filled ones. Crimp the

pastry around the edges. Starting 1 cm (½ in) down from one of the short sides, cut the 'parcels' into three equal strips, then plait the three strips, starting from the uncut short side. Press together at the ends. Place the plaits on a greased, lined baking sheet. Beat the egg yolk with the remaining milk and coat the pastry.
Bake in a preheated oven at 180-200° C (350-400° F, Gas Mark 4-6) for 15-20 minutes.

For the glaze: combine the icing sugar and orange juice. Brush over the plaits as soon as they are out of the oven.

CHERRY PARCELS

Makes 8-10

150 g (5 oz) cream cheese
6 tablespoons milk
6 tablespoons oil
75 g (3 oz) caster sugar
1 sachet vanilla sugar
A pinch of salt
300 g (10 oz) plain flour
2 teaspoons baking
powder
450 g (15 oz) stoned
Morello cherries in syrup
Condensed milk
A pinch of ground
cinnamon
1 heaped tablespoon
almonds, cut into slivers

Combine the cream cheese with the milk, oil, sugar (reserving 1 tablespoon), vanilla sugar and salt in a mixing bowl.

Sift the flour and baking powder together. Stir half into the cheese mixture, then knead in the remaining half. Roll out the pastry. Cut into 12 x 12 cm (4½ x 4½ in) squares and place on a greased, floured baking sheet.

Drain the cherries well, then arrange in the centre of the pastry squares. Brush the edges of the squares with some condensed milk, then pull up each corner towards the centre.

Below: *Cherry parcels*

Coat the parcels with the condensed milk. Mix the reserved sugar and the cinnamon together and dredge over the pastries. Sprinkle with the almonds and bake in a preheated oven at 180-200° C (350-400° F, Gas Mark 4-6) for 20 minutes.

GERMAN CHRISTMAS CAKE

Serves 6-8

500 g (1 lb) plain flour
2 teaspoons baking
powder
150-175 g (5-6 oz) caster
sugar
1 sachet vanilla sugar
A pinch of salt
4 drops bitter almond
essence
2 tablespoons rum
4 drops lemon flavouring
A pinch of cardamom
A pinch of nutmeg
2 eggs
225 g (7½ oz) butter
50 g (2 oz) lard
250 g (8 oz) cream cheese
250-375 g (8-12 oz) raisins
125-150 g (4-5 oz) ground
almonds
50 g (2 oz) candied lemon
peel
50 g (2 oz) icing sugar

Preheat the oven to 240° C (475° F, Gas Mark 9).

Mix the flour and baking powder together in a bowl. Make a well in the centre. Add the sugar, vanilla sugar, salt, flavourings, spices and eggs. Combine into a smooth paste using some of the flour.

Cut 125 g (4 oz) butter and the lard into pieces and combine in a mixing bowl with the cream cheese and raisins. Add the ground almonds and chopped candied lemon peel. Spread this mixture over the paste. Cover with the remaining flour and knead quickly into a smooth dough. If it is too sticky, add a little flour.

Roll the dough into a log shape and transfer to a baking sheet lined with aluminium foil. Turn the oven down to 160-180° C (325-350° F, Gas Mark 3-4) and bake the cake for 50-60 minutes.

Coat with the remaining melted butter as soon as the cake is out of the oven and dredge with icing sugar.

RICH APPLE TART

Serves 6

150 g (5 oz) cream cheese
600 ml (1 pint) milk
150 g (5 oz) caster sugar
1 sachet vanilla sugar
6 tablespoons oil
A pinch of salt
300 g (10 oz) plain flour
2 teaspoons baking powder
20 g (¾ oz) cornflour

1 packet vanilla blancmange mix
125 ml (4 fl oz) double cream
1 egg, separated
1.25 kg (3 lb) apples
2 tablespoons apricot jam
1-2 tablespoons apricot liqueur

Combine the cream cheese with 6 tablespoons milk, 75 g (3 oz) sugar, the vanilla sugar, oil and salt in a mixing bowl. Sift the flour and baking powder together. Stir half into the cheese mixture, then knead in the remaining half. Roll the pastry out and line a greased baking sheet.

For the filling: make up the blancmange mix, combining it with the cornflour, the remaining sugar and 6 tablespoons milk. Bring the remaining milk to the boil, then remove from the heat. Incorporate the blancmange mix, bring back to the boil and boil for a moment. Remove from the heat and leave to cool, stirring occasionally. Incorporate the cream and egg yolk. Whisk the egg white into very stiff peaks (a cut with a knife should remain visible). Fold gently into the blancmange-cream mixture. Spread over the pastry.

Peel, quarter, core and slice the apples. Arrange over the pastry. If necessary, surround it with a strip of aluminium folded over several times so that the pastry keeps its shape. Bake in a preheated oven at 180-200°C (350-400° F, Gas Mark 4-6) for 35 minutes.

For the glaze: sieve the jam, mix with the apricot liqueur. Coat the tart as soon as it is out of the oven.

BANANA TURNOVERS

Makes about 10

150 g (5 oz) cottage
cheese
7 tablespoons milk
6 tablespoons oil
75 g (3 oz) caster sugar
1 sachet vanilla sugar
A pinch of salt
300 g (10 oz) plain flour

2 teaspoons baking
powder
4-5 bananas
Apricot jam
1 egg, separated
Some flaked almonds
3 sugar lumps

Combine the cheese with 6 tablespoons milk, the oil,
sugar, vanilla sugar and salt in a mixing bowl. Sift the
flour and baking powder together. Stir half the flour
mixture into the cream cheese, then knead in the
remaining half. Roll the pastry out; then cut into ten
12 x 12 cm (4½ x 4½ in) squares.

For the filling: peel the bananas and cut into two or
three pieces, depending on the length. Coat each pastry
square with apricot jam. Place a piece of banana in the
centre. Coat it with jam. Brush the edges of the squares
with the egg white; then fold two corners together
towards the centre. Press the corners together to seal
them well. Place on a greased baking sheet.

Beat the egg yolk with the remaining milk and brush
over the pastry. Sprinkle with the flaked almonds. Wrap
the sugar lumps in a tea towel and crush with a rolling
pin. Sprinkle the crushed sugar lumps over the pastry.

Bake in a preheated oven at 180-200° C (350-400° F, Gas
Mark 4-6) for 15-20 minutes. Serve hot with whipped
cream or custard.

Alternative: kiwi fruit jam can be used instead of
apricot jam.

Below: *Banana turnovers*

Above: *Cottage cheese, fruit and nut ring*

COTTAGE CHEESE, FRUIT AND NUT RING

Serves 8-10

150 g (5 oz) butter
165 g (5½ oz) caster sugar
2 sachets vanilla sugar
1 teaspoon salt
Grated rind of 1 lemon
3 eggs
400 g (13 oz) cottage

cheese
375 g (12 oz) plain flour
4 teaspoons baking powder
100 g (3½ oz) chopped almonds, hazelnuts and raisins

Cream 125 g (4 oz) butter, then gradually incorporate 125 g (4 oz) sugar, 1 sachet vanilla sugar, the salt, half the lemon rind, 2 eggs and 150 g (5 oz) cottage cheese. Sift 350 g (11½ oz) flour and the baking powder together. Stir half into the cheese mixture, then knead in the remaining half. Shape the dough into a roll and place in a fluted ring mould. Press the mixture down slightly.

For the filling: combine the remaining cottage cheese, sugar, vanilla sugar, lemon rind, flour, egg and melted butter. Fill an icing bag and pipe the mixture over the dough.

Sprinkle with the nuts and raisins. Bake in a preheated oven at 180-200° C (350-400° F, Gas Mark 4-6) for 50 minutes.

Above: *Fruit loaf*

FRUIT LOAF

Serves 6

175 g (6 oz) butter
125 g (4 oz) caster sugar
2 eggs
1 teaspoon salt
Grated rind of ½ lemon
150 g (5 oz) cottage
cheese
350 g (11½ oz) plain flour
4 teaspoons baking
powder
125 g (4 oz) sultanas
Sugar-cinnamon mixture

Cream 125 g (4 oz) butter in a bowl, then gradually add the sugar, eggs, salt and lemon rind. Incorporate the cottage cheese.
Sift the flour and baking powder together. Gradually incorporate two-thirds of the flour mixture into the cheese mixture.

Combine the remaining flour with the sultanas and incorporate, kneading well. Roll into a ball, then make into an oval shape.

Flatten one side of the dough slightly using a rolling pin, then fold the other side on top.

Place on a greased, lined baking sheet. Bake in a preheated oven at 180-200° C (350-400° F, Gas Mark 4-6) for 50 minutes.

Coat with the remaining melted butter as soon as the loaf is out of the oven and dredge with the sugar-cinnamon mixture.

from the heat. Add the poppy seeds, cinnamon, egg, cream or condensed milk, brandy, rosewater and raisins. Mix well and leave to cool.

For the pastry: combine the cream cheese with the reserved milk, the oil, 65 g (2½ oz) sugar, the vanilla sugar and salt in a mixing bowl. Sift the flour and baking powder together. Stir half into the cheese mixture, then knead in the remaining half.

Shape the pastry into a roll. Divide into five equal pieces. Set one piece aside. Roll three pieces out into 28 cm (11 in) circles. Place one pastry circle on the lined base of a 28 cm (11 in) sliding-based cake tin. Roll the fourth piece into a sausage shape and press around the sides of the tin to a depth of 2 cm (¾ in).

Spread one-third of the poppy seed filling over the pastry base. Cover with a pastry circle. Add a further third of the filling and cover with the remaining pastry circle. Add the remaining filling. Roll out the reserved pastry and cut into strips using a pastry wheel. Place them over the filling, making a lattice. Brush the pastry with a little milk. Bake in a preheated oven at 180-200° C (350-400° F, Gas Mark 4-6) for 50-55 minutes.

For the sugar icing: mix the remaining sugar with 1 tablespoon water and brush over the cake as soon as it is out of the oven.

Below: *Rosewater tart*

ROSEWATER TART

Serves 6

300 ml (½ pint) milk
250 g (8 oz) caster sugar
100 g (3½ oz) butter
400 g (13 oz) ground
poppy seeds
1 teaspoon ground
cinnamon
1 egg
2 teaspoons double cream
or condensed milk

5 tablespoons brandy
5 tablespoons rosewater
100 g (3½ oz) raisins
125 g (4 oz) cream cheese
5 tablespoons oil
1 sachet vanilla sugar
A pinch of salt
300 g (10 oz) plain flour
2 teaspoons baking
powder

Bring the milk (reserving 5 tablespoons) to the boil in a pan with 140 g (4½ oz) sugar and the butter. Remove

APPLE AND
POPPY SEED SPIRALS

Makes about 5

500-625 g (l-1¼ lb) apples
(Boskoop, for example)
150 g (5 oz) caster sugar
A twist of lemon rind
1 cinnamon stick
250 g (8 oz) ground poppy
seeds
75 g (3 oz) butter,
softened
2 tablespoons honey
2 eggs
75 g (3 oz) raisins
2-3 drops bitter almond
essence
200 g (7 oz) cream cheese
6 tablespoons milk
8 tablespoons oil
1 sachet vanilla sugar
A pinch of salt
400 g (13 oz) plain flour
3 teaspoons baking
powder
150-175 g (5-6 oz) icing
sugar
6 tablespoons rum

Peel, quarter and core the apples. Cut into pieces. Put
50 g (2 oz) sugar, the lemon rind and cinnamon stick in a
pan containing 250 ml (8 fl oz) water and bring to the boil.
Cover and cook over a low heat. The apples must not
disintegrate. Remove the apples with a slotted spoon and
leave to cool.

Add the poppy seeds to the apple cooking juice
immediately. Bring to the boil, stirring constantly, then
remove from the heat. Incorporate the butter, honey and
1 egg. Leave to soak, then add the raisins and bitter
almond essence.

For the pastry: combine the cream cheese, milk, oil, the
remaining egg and sugar, the vanilla sugar and salt.
Sift the flour and baking powder together. Stir half into
the cheese mixture, then knead in the rest.

Roll the pastry out until it measures 50 x 40 cm
(20 x 16 in). Spread the filling over the pastry. Scatter the
apple pieces over. Roll up the filled pastry. Cut into
15 mm-2 cm (⅓-¾ in) slices. Place on a greased baking
sheet and bake in a preheated oven at
180-200° C (350-400° F, Gas Mark 4-6) for 15-20 minutes.

For the glacé icing: combine the icing sugar with the
rum and spread over the buns.

FRUIT AND
COTTAGE CHEESE CRUMBLE

Serves 8-10

875 g (1¾ lb) cottage
cheese
6 tablespoons milk
6 tablespoons oil
325 g (11 oz) granulated
sugar
2 sachets vanilla sugar
A pinch of salt
625 g (1¼ lb) plain flour
2 teaspoons baking
powder
325-350 g (11-11½ oz)
butter
2 eggs
75 g (3 oz) cornflour
1.5 kg (3½ lb) damsons or
1.5 kg (3½ lb) tinned fruit
in syrup (Morello
cherries, peaches,
apricots)
Ground cinnamon

Combine 150 g (5 oz) cottage cheese with the milk, oil,
75 g (3 oz) sugar, 1 sachet vanilla sugar and salt in a
mixing bowl. Sift 300 g (10 oz) flour and the baking
powder together. Gradually stir half into the cheese
mixture, then knead in the remaining half. Roll the
pastry out and line a well-greased baking sheet.

For the filling: cream 150 g (5 oz) butter and gradually
add 150 g (5 oz) sugar, the remaining vanilla sugar, the
eggs, the remaining cottage cheese and the cornflour.

Wash, drain, halve and stone the damsons. Incorporate
in the filling mixture. Spread over the pastry.

Alternatively, the cream mixture can be spread over the
pastry and covered with well-drained tinned fruit,
pressed down slightly into the pastry.

For the crumble: melt the remaining butter in a pan.
Leave to cool. Sift the remaining flour into a bowl. Make
a well in the centre. Add the remaining sugar and the
cinnamon. Mix together first with a fork, then using the
hands until the mixture becomes lumpy. Sprinkle over
the filling. Bake in a preheated oven at
180-200° C (350-400° F, Gas Mark 4-6) for 45 minutes.

Opposite: *Apple and poppy seed spirals*

CHOUX PASTRY

PINEAPPLE PUFFS

Makes about 10

50 g (2 oz) butter
150 g (5 oz) plain flour
4 tablespoons cornflour
4-6 eggs
1 teaspoon baking powder
350 g (11½ oz) pineapple
chunks (in syrup)

500 ml (18 fl oz) double
cream
2 teaspoons caster sugar
1 sachet vanilla sugar
2-3 teaspoons kirsch
Icing sugar to finish

Bring 250 ml (8 fl oz) water and the butter to the boil in a pan. Remove from the heat. Sift the flour and cornflour together, then add to the butter mixture. Return to the heat, stirring quickly for 1 minute, until the dough comes away from the sides and base of the pan. Transfer the mixture to a bowl and incorporate the eggs, one at a time, using an electric mixer fitted with a kneading attachment at high speed. Leave to cool; then incorporate the baking powder.

Transfer the mixture to an icing bag and pipe mounds the size of small mandarin oranges on to a greased and floured baking sheet. Bake in a preheated oven at 200-220° C (400-425° F, Gas Mark 6-7) for 25-30 minutes. Do not open the oven door during the first 15 minutes as the pastry will sink immediately. Cut off the tops of the pastries as soon as they are out of the oven.

For the filling: drain the pineapple chunks. Add the sugar and vanilla sugar to the cream, then whip until firm. Incorporate the kirsch and pineapple chunks in the cream. Transfer this mixture to an icing bag and fill the pastries. Replace the tops. Dredge with icing sugar. Serve immediately.

Alternative: pineapple juice can be used instead of kirsch to flavour the whipped cream.

CHERRY CREAM PUFF

Serves 4-6

50 g (2 oz) butter
150 g (5 oz) plain flour
50 g (2 oz) cornflour
4-6 eggs
1 teaspoon baking powder
500 g (1 lb) Morello
cherries (or other sour
cherries) or

400 g (13 oz) stoned
Morello cherries in syrup
50 g (2 oz) caster sugar
2 sachets vanilla sugar
500 ml (18 fl oz) double
cream
25 g (1 oz) icing sugar

Put the butter in a pan containing 250 ml (8 fl oz) water and bring to the boil; then remove from the heat. Sift the flour and 4 tablespoons cornflour together and add to the melted butter. Return to the heat and beat for 1 minute until the mixture comes away cleanly from the sides and base of the pan. Transfer the mixture to a bowl and incorporate the eggs, one at a time, using an electric mixer fitted with a kneading attachment at high speed. Leave to cool, then incorporate the baking powder. Transfer this mixture to a piping bag fitted with a wide nozzle and pipe a fat sausage shape on to a greased and floured baking sheet. Bake in a preheated oven at 200-220° C (400-425° F, Gas Mark 6-7) for 25-30 minutes. Do not open the oven during the first 15 minutes, as the pastry will sink immediately.
Cut off the top of the pastry as soon as it is out of the oven to form a lid.

For the filling: wash, hull and stone the cherries. Put them in a pan with the sugar and 1 sachet vanilla sugar. Mix together and leave until the cherries have produced some juice; then bring quickly to the boil. If using tinned cherries, drain them and save 250 ml (8 fl oz) juice to mix with the remaining cornflour. Bring to the boil, stirring constantly. Add the cherries. Leave to cool. Add some extra sugar if necessary.

Whip the cream for 30 seconds, then add the icing sugar, reserving 1 tablespoon, and the remaining vanilla sugar. Continue beating until the cream is very firm. Transfer to an icing bag. Fill the pastry puff with the cherries and cover with whipped cream. Dredge with the reserved icing sugar. Serve immediately.

Pages 388 and 389: *Pineapple puffs*

Above: *Cherry cream puff*

Above: *Fruit cream éclairs*

FRUIT CREAM ÉCLAIRS

Makes 5-6

50 g (2 oz) butter or lard
150 g (5 oz) plain flour
4 tablespoons cornflour
4-6 eggs
1 teaspoon baking powder
1 sachet powdered gelatine or 4 gelatine leaves

3 sugar lumps
Rind of ½ orange
6 tablespoons orange juice
500 ml (18 fl oz) double cream
375 g (12 oz) mandarin segments (in syrup)

Put the butter or lard in a pan containing 250 ml (8 fl oz) water and bring to the boil; then remove from the heat. Sift the flour and cornflour together and incorporate into the melted butter. Return to the heat and beat for 1 minute until the mixture comes away cleanly from the sides and base of the pan. Transfer the mixture to a bowl and incorporate the eggs, one at a time, using an electric mixer fitted with a kneading attachment at high speed. Leave to cool, then carefully incorporate the baking powder.

Transfer the mixture to an icing bag and pipe fingers on to a greased and floured baking sheet. Bake in a pre-heated oven at 200-220° C (400-425° F, Gas Mark 6-7) for 20 minutes. Cut a lid out of each pastry puff as soon as they are out of the oven.

For the filling: mix the gelatine with 2 tablespoons cold water and leave to soak for 10 minutes.
Grate the orange rind using the corners and edges of the sugar lumps. Add to the melted gelatine and heat until completely dissolved.

Whip the cream until firm, then gradually incorporate the orange-flavoured gelatine. Whip the cream again so that it is very firm.

Spread some of the cream over the base of the éclairs, then place the lid on top and cover with a layer of cream. Drain the mandarin segments and arrange on top of the cream.

CREAM GÂTEAU

Serves 6

175 g (6 oz) plain flour	powder
25 g (1 oz) granulated sugar	500 g (1 lb) stoned Morello cherries in syrup
2 sachets vanilla sugar	500 ml (18 fl oz) double cream
100 g (3½ oz) butter	
50 g (2 oz) cornflour	25 g (1 oz) icing sugar
2-3 eggs	Redcurrant jelly
1½ teaspoons baking	Icing sugar to finish

Sift 100 g (3½ oz) flour into a mixing bowl and make a well in the centre. Add the sugar and vanilla sugar, followed by 75 g (3 oz) butter cut into pieces. Cover with flour and quickly knead into a smooth dough.

Place in a refrigerator for a short while; then roll the pastry out and line a greased, deep, 28 cm (11 in) round springform cake tin. Prick the base with a fork.

Bake in a preheated oven at 200-220° C (400-425° F, Gas Mark 6-7) for 15 minutes. Remove the base of the tin with the pastry as soon as it is out of the oven. Leave to cool, then transfer the pastry from the base on to a plate.

For the choux pastry: put the remaining butter in a pan containing 125 ml (4 fl oz) water and bring to the boil; then remove from the heat. Sift the remaining flour and 15 g (½ oz) cornflour together and incorporate into the melted butter.

Return to the heat and beat for 1 minute until the mixture comes away cleanly from the sides and base of the pan. Transfer the mixture to a bowl and incorporate the eggs, one at a time, using an electric mixer fitted with a kneading attachment at high speed. Leave to cool, then carefully incorporate the baking powder.

Roll the pastry out into three 28 cm (11 in) diameter circles. Place each circle on the base of a greased and floured, 28 cm (11 in) round cake tin, making sure that the pastry is not too thin at the edges so that it does not brown too much. Bake in a preheated oven at 200-220° C (400-425° F, Gas Mark 6-7) for 20-25 minutes until the pastry is golden.

Remove the cake tin bases as soon as the pastry circles are out of the oven and leave to cool on a wire rack so that they stay crispy.

For the filling: drain the cherries and reserve 250 ml (8 fl oz) juice. Add a little water if there is insufficient

juice. Mix the remaining cornflour with 4 tablespoons juice. Bring the remaining juice to the boil. Remove from the heat and add the cornflour mixture. Bring back to the boil for a moment, then add the cherries. Sweeten to taste, leave to cool, then place in a refrigerator.

Whip the cream for 30 seconds, then incorporate the icing sugar and the remaining vanilla sugar. Continue beating until firm.

Spread a thin layer of redcurrant jelly over the shortcrust pastry and cover with the first choux pastry layer. Spread with the cherry cream, followed by one-third of the whipped cream. Add the second pastry layer. Fill with the remaining whipped cream, then crush the third choux pastry layer and sprinkle over the gâteau. Dredge with icing sugar. Serve immediately.

Below: *Cream gâteau*

Above: *Swans*

SWANS

Makes about 2

50 g (2 oz) butter	gelatine
150 g (5 oz) plain flour	500 ml (18 fl oz) double
25 g (1 oz) cornflour	cream
4-5 eggs	25 g (1 oz) caster sugar
1 teaspoon baking powder	1 sachet vanilla sugar
2 teaspoons powdered	Icing sugar to finish

Put the butter in a pan containing 250 ml (8 fl oz) water and bring to the boil; then remove from the heat. Sift the flour and cornflour together and incorporate into the melted butter. Return to the heat and beat for 1 minute until the mixture comes away cleanly from the sides and base of the pan. Transfer the mixture to a bowl and incorporate the eggs, one at a time, using an electric mixer fitted with a kneading attachment at high speed. Leave to cool, then incorporate the baking powder.

Spoon small mounds of the choux pastry (reserving 2 tablespoons) on to a greased and floured baking sheet. Bake in a preheated oven at 200-220° C (400-425° F, Gas Mark 6-7) for 25-30 minutes. Do not open the oven during the first 15 minutes as the pastry will sink immediately. Cut out lids from the pastry puffs as soon as they are out of the oven.

Make a funnel out of greaseproof paper and fill with the reserved pastry mixture. Pipe one figure '2' for each pastry puff on to a greased and floured baking sheet. Bake in a preheated oven at 200-220° C (400-425° F, Gas Mark 6-7) for 15 minutes.

For the filling: mix the gelatine with 2 tablespoons cold water. Leave to soak for 10 minutes; then heat, stirring constantly until completely dissolved.

Whip the cream until firm, then incorporate the cooled gelatine and whip again until firm, adding the sugar and vanilla sugar. Fill the pastry puffs. Remove the bases of the '2'-shapes to make the tails, then insert the curved sections to make the necks. Cut the lids in half to make the wings. Add the tails. Dredge with icing sugar.

LITTLE RINGS

Makes 10-12

50 g (2 oz) butter	4-6 eggs
150 g (5 oz) plain flour	1 teaspoon baking powder
4 tablespoons cornflour	Oil for frying
25 g (1 oz) caster sugar	200 g (7 oz) icing sugar
1 sachet vanilla sugar	2 teaspoons lemon juice

Put the butter in a pan containing 250 ml (8 fl oz) water and bring to the boil; then remove from the heat. Sift the flour and cornflour together and incorporate into the melted butter. Return to the heat and beat for 1 minute until the mixture comes away from the sides and base of the pan. Transfer the mixture to a bowl, then gradually incorporate the sugar, vanilla sugar and eggs, one at a time, using an electric mixer fitted with a kneading attachment at high speed.
Leave to cool, then incorporate the baking powder.

Transfer the mixture to an icing bag and pipe small rings on to 10 x 10 cm (4 x 4 in) sheets of greaseproof paper. Place in a hot deep-fat fryer. Remove the greaseproof paper as soon as the pastry rings come away from it. Cook on both sides until golden. Remove using a slotted spoon and drain well on a wire rack.

For the glacé icing: combine the icing sugar with the lemon juice and 2 tablespoons very hot water. Coat the rings with this mixture.

Below: *Little rings*

Left:
Éclairs

ÉCLAIRS

Makes 7-8

25 g (1 oz) butter
75 g (3 oz) plain flour
15 g (½ oz) cornflour
2-3 eggs
A pinch of baking powder

Apricot jam
75 g (3 oz) hazelnut
chocolate spread
250 ml (8 fl oz) double
cream

Put the butter in a pan containing 125 ml (4 fl oz) water and bring to the boil. Remove from the heat. Sift the flour and cornflour together and incorporate into the melted butter. Return to the heat and beat quickly for 1 minute until the mixture comes away from the sides and base of the pan. Transfer the mixture to a bowl and incorporate the eggs, one at a time, using an electric mixer fitted with a kneading attachment at high speed. Leave to cool and incorporate the baking powder.

Transfer this mixture to a piping bag fitted with a wide nozzle and pipe 6 cm (2½ in) long fingers on to a greased and floured baking sheet. Bake in a preheated oven at 200-220° C (400-425° F, Gas Mark 6-7) for 20 minutes. Cut lids out of the pastry puffs as soon as they are out of the oven.

For the glaze: heat a little sieved apricot jam and brush over the lids.

For the filling: melt the hazelnut chocolate spread in a bowl over a pan of hot water, stirring until smooth and creamy. Leave to cool slightly.

Whip the cream until firm. Fold in the hazelnut chocolate spread and whip again. Transfer this cream to an icing bag and fill the éclairs.

Opposite: *All the ingredients for a good cake*

CHERRY CORN CAKE

Serves 6

100 g (3½ oz) butter, softened	100 g (3½ oz) cornflour
75 g (3 oz) clear honey	150 g (5 oz) wholewheat flour
A pinch of salt	2 teaspoons baking powder
1 teaspoon ground cinnamon	3 egg whites
A pinch of ground cloves or 1 crushed clove	750 g (1½ lb) Morello cherries, stoned
3 egg yolks	

Cream the butter in a mixing bowl for 30 seconds using an electric mixer, first at low, then at high speed. Gradually incorporate the honey, salt, cinnamon and ground cloves. Beat until smooth. Add the egg yolks one at a time, beating each for 30 seconds.

Sift the cornflour, wholewheat flour and baking powder together and gradually incorporate in the mixture. Leave to rest for 40 minutes.

Whisk the egg whites into stiff peaks and gently fold them into the mixture. Turn two-thirds of this mixture into a greased, 28 cm (11 in) round, springform cake tin. Arrange the cherries 5 mm (¼ in) from the edge, then carefully top with the remaining mixture using a dessertspoon. Bake in a preheated oven at 180-200° C (350-400° F, Gas Mark 4-6) for 40-50 minutes.

HONEY CAKE

Serves 6

425 g (14 oz) plain wheat flour	175 g (6 oz) honey
100 g (3½ oz) spelt flour (available from health food shops)	A pinch of salt
	1 egg
	250 ml (8 fl oz) warm milk
1 sachet powdered easy-blend yeast	200 g (7 oz) butter
	200 g (7 oz) flaked almonds

Thoroughly combine 400 g (13 oz) wheat flour, the spelt flour and yeast in a mixing bowl. Incorporate 75 g (3 oz) honey, the salt, egg, milk and 100 g (3½ oz) melted butter. Work the dough for 5 minutes using an electric mixer, first at low, then at high speed. Cover and leave to rise in a warm place until it has clearly increased in bulk.

For the filling: heat the remaining butter and honey in a pan, stirring constantly. Incorporate the almonds and the remaining flour and bring to the boil. Remove the pan from the heat and leave to cool, stirring occasionally.

Knead the dough again with the electric mixer at high speed, then roll the dough out on to a greased baking sheet and prick with a fork. Spread the filling over the dough and leave in a warm place to prove. Bake in a preheated oven at 200° C (400° F, Gas Mark 6) for 15-20 minutes.

Tip: this cake freezes very well. If warmed for a few minutes in a preheated oven at 200° C (400° F, Gas Mark 6), it will lose none of its moistness.

HAZELNUT RING

Serves 4

400 g (13 oz) plain flour	125 g (4 oz) hazelnut spread
2 teaspoons baking powder	4 tablespoons maple syrup
200 g (7 oz) cottage cheese	½ teaspoon ground cinnamon
6 tablespoons milk	150 g (5 oz) sultanas
100 ml (3½ fl oz) oil	150 g (5 oz) nibbed hazelnuts
100 g (3½ oz) honey	
A pinch of salt	1 tablespoon condensed milk
1 egg	
75 g (3 oz) butter	

Sift the flour and baking powder together. Incorporate the cottage cheese, milk, oil, honey, salt and egg. Knead the dough using an electric mixer at high speed for 1 minute, then roll out into a 40 x 50 cm (16 x 20 in) rectangle.

Combine the butter, hazelnut spread, maple syrup and cinnamon in a separate bowl. Spread over the dough and cut into two pieces lengthways (photograph no. 1). Sprinkle with the sultanas and nibbed hazelnuts. Fold the two halves of dough together again lengthways and twist them (photograph no. 2).

Place the ring on a greased baking sheet and make 1 cm (½ in) deep incisions in it (photograph no. 3). Brush with the condensed milk and bake in a preheated oven at 180° C (350° F, Gas Mark 4) for 35-40 minutes.

Tip: hazelnut spread is available from health food shops and caterers.

Page 398: *Cherry corn cake*
Page 399: *Irish fruit cake (recipe p. 402)*

Opposite: *Hazelnut ring*

2

3

FIG AND HAZELNUT ROLL

Serves 6

450 g (15 oz) wholewheat
flour
1 sachet powdered easy-
blend yeast
100 g (3½ oz) clear honey
200 ml (7 fl oz) warm milk
50 g (2 oz) butter
1 egg

250 g (8 oz) dried figs
125 g (4 oz) blanched
hazelnuts
Juice of ½ lemon
1 teaspoon ground
aniseed
1 egg yolk

Thoroughly combine the flour and yeast in a bowl.
Incorporate 50 g (2 oz) honey, the milk, butter and egg.
Work the mixture for 5 minutes using an electric mixer,
first at low, then at high speed. Leave to rise in a warm
place until increased in bulk.

For the cream filling: wash and dice the figs. Crush the
hazelnuts coarsely. Combine both these ingredients with
the remaining honey, the lemon juice and ground
aniseed.

Knead the dough again with the mixer at high speed.
Roll out into a 36 x 40 cm (14 x 16 in) rectangle. Spread
the filling over the dough, leaving 2 cm (¾ in) at the
edges. Roll up the dough, place it on a greased baking
sheet and leave to prove in a warm place until well risen.

Beat the egg yolk with a little water and brush over the
cake. Bake in a preheated oven at 180° C (350° F, Gas
Mark 4) for 40 minutes.

IRISH FRUIT CAKE

Serves 6-8

100-150 ml (3½ fl oz-¼
pint) whisky
200 g (7 oz) sultanas
125 g (4 oz) currants
100 g (3½ oz) grapes
200 g (7 oz) chopped
candied mixed peel
300 g (10 oz) butter,
softened
250 g (8 oz) honey
A pinch of salt

6 eggs
300 g (10 oz) plain flour
3 teaspoons baking
powder
100 g (3½ oz) nibbed
almonds
65 g (2½ oz) flaked
almonds
3 tablespoons peach and
apricot jam

Sprinkle the whisky over the dried fruit, fresh grapes
and candied peel. Cover and leave to soak overnight.

For the mixture: beat the butter in a mixing bowl for
30 seconds using an electric mixer at high speed.
Gradually incorporate the honey and salt, beating until
smooth.
Add the eggs one at a time. Combine the flour, baking
powder and nibbed almonds together in a separate bowl
and incorporate them in the mixture. Beat at medium
speed, then add the soaked dried fruit.
Transfer the mixture to a greased, 22 cm (8½ in), round,
springform cake tin with the sides lined with aluminium
foil. Sprinkle over the flaked almonds. Bake in a
preheated oven at 150-160° C (300-325° F, Gas Mark 2-3)
for 2¼ hours. Turn out of the tin carefully. Heat the jam
and brush over the cake while still hot.

APRICOT BAKE

Serves 6

150 g (5 oz) butter,
softened
125 g (4 oz) maple syrup
Grated rind of ½ lemon
4 egg yolks
200 g (7 oz) spelt flour
(available from health

food shops)
1 teaspoon baking powder
1 teaspoon lemon juice
4 egg whites
750 g (1½ lb) apricots
2-3 tablespoons apricot
jelly

Cream the butter in a mixing bowl for 30 seconds, using
an electric mixer at high speed. Gradually incorporate
100 g (3½ oz) maple syrup and the lemon rind. Stir until
smooth, then add the egg yolks, one at a time.

Sift the spelt flour and baking powder together, add the
lemon juice and the remaining maple syrup. Incorporate

Above: *Apricot bake*

in the mixture, beating constantly at medium speed. Whisk the egg whites into stiff peaks and gently fold into the mixture. Transfer to a greased, 28 cm (11 in) round cake tin.

For the filling: wash, halve and stone the apricots. Arrange them on the mixture and bake in a preheated oven at 180-200° C (350-400° F, Gas Mark 4-6) for 40-45 minutes. Heat the apricot jelly in a pan and brush over the cake as soon as it is out of the oven.

Tips: dredging the base of the tart with ground almonds or coating it with beaten egg white prevents the pastry from becoming soggy due to the juices from the apricots.

Morello cherries or quartered apples can be used instead of apricots, in which case the cake should be brushed with hot cherry or apple jelly.

DAMSON PIE

Serves 6

250 g (8 oz) wholewheat flour
A pinch of salt
200 g (7 oz) butter, softened
1 kg (2 lb) damsons
200 g (7 oz) almond paste
1 egg, separated
1 tablespoon fresh breadcrumbs
1-2 tablespoons milk
2 tablespoons brown sugar

Combine the flour and salt with 2-3 tablespoons cold water in a mixing bowl. Incorporate the butter. Work the mixture using an electric mixer, first at low, then at high speed. Then knead the dough into a smooth ball by hand. Place the dough in a refrigerator if it is too sticky.

For the filling: wash, drain, halve and stone the damsons. Combine the almond paste with the egg white. Add the damsons.

Roll out half the pastry and line a 28 cm (11 in) round flan dish. Dredge with the breadcrumbs and arrange the damsons. Beat the egg yolk with the milk and brush half of this mixture over the edges of the pastry.

Roll out the remaining pastry, drape it over the damsons and cut to size. Cut out small shapes from the surplus pastry, brush with egg yolk and arrange over the pie. Brush with the remaining egg yolk, prick with a fork and dredge with the brown sugar. Bake in a preheated oven at 200-230° C (400-450° F, Gas Mark 6-8) for 45 minutes. Serve the pie hot with whipped cream or vanilla sauce.

APPLE PIE

Serves 6

250 g (8 oz) plain flour
A pinch of salt
250 g (8 oz) butter, softened
1½ tablespoons honey
1 tablespoon milk
75 g (3 oz) flaked almonds
1.5 kg (3½ lb) apples
(Boskop, for example)
100 g (3½ oz) sultanas
2 tablespoons fresh breadcrumbs
Whipped cream sweetened with maple syrup or honey (optional)

Combine the flour, salt and 2-3 tablespoons cold water in a mixing bowl. Incorporate 200 g (7 oz) butter. Beat using an electric mixer first at low, then at high speed, then work the mixture into a smooth ball. Place in a refrigerator for 2 hours.

For the coating: heat the honey, milk and the remaining butter in a pan, stirring until smooth. Incorporate the almonds and leave to cool.

For the filling: peel, halve, core and thinly slice the apples. Combine them with the sultanas.

Roll out half of the pastry and line a greased, 28 cm (11 in) round flan dish.
Dredge with the breadcrumbs, add the apples, press down the sides of the pastry and brush with cold water.

Roll out the remaining pastry. Drape it over the apples and crimp the edges to seal them. Coat with the almond sauce and prick the base with a fork.
Bake in a preheated oven at 180-200° C (350-400° F, Gas Mark 4-6) for 50 minutes. If the almonds seem to be browning too much during the cooking time, cover the pie with greaseproof paper or aluminium foil. Serve warm with the whipped cream sweetened with maple syrup or honey.

Opposite: *Damson pie*

Roll out the dough.

Arrange the damsons.

Decorate the pie with small pastry shapes.

Above: *Canadian apple cake*

CANADIAN APPLE CAKE

Serves 6-8

200 g (7 oz) butter
75-100 g (3-3½ oz) maple
syrup
1 vanilla pod
or grated rind of ½ lemon
A pinch of salt
3 eggs
50 g (2 oz) spelt flour
(available from health
food shops)

or plain wheat flour
1 teaspoon baking powder
125 g (4 oz) rolled oats
625-750 g (1¼-1½ lb)
apples
50 g (2 oz) raisins and
sultanas
40 g (1½ oz) flaked
almonds

Cream 150 g (5 oz) softened butter in a mixing bowl for 30 seconds using an electric mixer at high speed. Gradually incorporate the maple syrup, salt and the seeds removed from the vanilla pod or the lemon rind. Combine until incorporated. Add the eggs one at a time, beating each one for 30 seconds.

Mix the flour, baking powder and rolled oats together in a bowl. Incorporate in the mixture at low speed. Turn two-thirds of the mixture into a 28 cm (11 in) round cake tin.

For the filling: peel, quarter and core the apples. Cut them into small pieces and arrange over the flour mixture. Sprinkle with the raisins and sultanas and the remaining crumbled pastry. Cut the remaining butter into slivers and arrange over the cake together with the flaked almonds. Bake in a preheated oven at 160° C (325° F, Gas Mark 3) for 50-60 minutes. Serve with whipped cream sweetened with maple syrup.

BILBERRY ROULADE

Serves 6

4 eggs	1 teaspoon baking powder
125 g (4 oz) honey	8 gelatine leaves
50 g (2 oz) buckwheat flour	250 g (8 oz) bilberries
100 g (3½ oz) nibbed hazelnuts or blanched almonds	500 ml (18 fl oz) double cream
	2-3 tablespoons lemon juice

Beat the eggs with 3-4 tablespoons hot water in a mixing bowl for 1 minute, using an electric mixer at high speed. Gradually incorporate 100 g (3½ oz) honey and beat for a further 2 minutes.

Combine the buckwheat flour, baking powder and nibbed hazelnut or almonds in a separate bowl. Quickly incorporate half in the egg mixture, with the mixer at low speed, then incorporate the remaining flour mixture. Turn the mixture on to a greased baking sheet lined with greaseproof paper and bake in a preheated oven at 200° C (400° F, Gas Mark 6) for 15 minutes.

Turn the sponge out immediately on to a tea towel. Sprinkle the greaseproof paper with cold water and peel off quickly but carefully. Roll the sponge up in the tea towel and leave to cool.

For the cream filling: soak the gelatine leaves in a small pan with 3 tablespoons cold water. Wash and purée 200 g (7 oz) bilberries. Sweeten with the remaining honey. Heat the carefully drained gelatine until dissolved and incorporate in the bilberry purée. Whip the cream as soon as the mixture starts to set. Transfer 3 tablespoons to an icing bag fitted with a star-shaped nozzle, and incorporate the rest in the fruit purée, adding the lemon juice.

Carefully unroll the sponge and spread with two-thirds of the filling. Roll the cake up again and cover with the remaining filling. Decorate using the cream in the icing bag and the remaining bilberries. Place in a refrigerator.

Alternative: raspberries, blackberries, strawberries or redcurrants can be used instead of bilberries.

APRICOT SEMOLINA GÂTEAU

Serves 8

300 g (10 oz) plain wheat flour	milk
100 g (3½ oz) buckwheat flour	150 g (5 oz) butter, melted
1 sachet powdered easy-blend yeast	Rind of 3-4 lemons
225 g (7½ oz) honey	75 g (3 oz) semolina
2 pinches of salt	4 eggs, separated
1 litre (1¾ pints) warm	1.5 kg (3½ lb) ripe apricots
	3 tablespoons fresh breadcrumbs

Combine the wheat flour, buckwheat flour and yeast in a mixing bowl. Add 75 g (3 oz) honey, a pinch of salt, 200 ml (7 fl oz) warm milk and 75 g (3 oz) cooled, melted butter. Work the ingredients together for 5 minutes using an electric mixer, first at low, then at high speed. Cover and leave to rise in a warm place until clearly increased in bulk.

For the semolina: bring 750 ml (1¼ pints) milk, the lemon rind and the remaining butter, honey and salt to the boil in a pan. Stir in the semolina, simmer for 5 minutes, then remove from the heat.
Beat the egg yolks in a bowl with the remaining milk, incorporate in the semolina and leave to cool.

Wash, halve and stone the apricots. Beat the dough again with the mixer at high speed and roll it out on to a greased baking sheet. Dredge with the breadcrumbs and arrange the apricots. Leave the dough to prove in a warm place until well risen.

Whisk the egg whites into stiff peaks and gently fold into the semolina. Spread the mixture over the apricots and bake in a preheated oven at 180-200° C (350-400° F, Gas Mark 4-6) for 40-45 minutes.

CARROT AND HAZELNUT GÂTEAU

Serves 8

500 g (1 lb) carrots
500 g (1 lb) nibbed hazelnuts
4 teaspoons baking powder
8 eggs, separated
3 tablespoons orange juice
Grated rind of 1 unwaxed orange
300 g (10 oz) honey
2 tablespoons peach and apricot jam
150 g (5 oz) bitter chocolate
Almond paste carrot shapes to finish

Peel, wash and grate the carrots. Mix the nibbed hazelnuts and baking powder together. Beat the egg yolks in a bowl with the orange juice and orange rind, using an electric mixer at high speed. Incorporate 150 g (5 oz) honey. Whisk the egg whites into stiff peaks, then gradually incorporate the remaining honey. Fold into the egg yolk mixture and add the grated carrots.

Turn into a greased, lined, 28 cm (11 in) round, springform cake tin. Bake in a preheated oven at 180-200° C (350-400° F, Gas Mark 4-6) for 55-60 minutes. Turn the cake out of the tin, carefully peel off the greaseproof paper and leave to cool.

For the icing: bring the jam to the boil with 2 tablespoons water and brush over the cake.

Melt the chocolate in a bowl over a pan of hot water and use to coat the cake. Decorate with almond paste carrot shapes and serve with whipped cream sweetened with honey.

FRUIT TART

Serves 6

100 g (3½ oz) plain wheat flour
100 g (3½ oz) buckwheat flour
A pinch of salt
1 tablespoon honey
100 ml (3½ fl oz) double cream
100 g (3½ oz) butter,
softened
625-700 g (1¼-1½ lb) fruit (strawberries, raspberries, black-berries or poached and stoned apricots)
3 rounded tablespoons jelly (flavour depends on the fruits used)

Sift the wheat flour, buckwheat flour and salt into a mixing bowl. Add the honey, cream and butter. Combine thoroughly using an electric mixer, first at low, then at high speed until the mixture forms a smooth ball. Place the dough in a refrigerator if it is too sticky.

Roll the pastry out and line a well greased, 28 cm (11 in) round cake tin. Prick the base with a fork and bake in a preheated oven at 180-200° C (350-400° F, Gas Mark 4-6) for 20-25 minutes.

For the filling: wash the fruit carefully and arrange over the base of the cooled tart.
Heat the jelly and brush over the fruit. Serve with whipped cream sweetened with maple syrup.

Suggestion: if using apricots, poach and stone them before arranging on the base of the tart.

BUCKWHEAT GÂTEAU

Serves 10

6 eggs
125 g (4 oz) honey
Grated rind of ½ lemon
175 g (6 oz) buckwheat flour
1 sachet powdered gelatine
2-3 tablespoons lemon
juice
750 ml (1¼ pints) double cream
6 tablespoons maple syrup
About 350 g (11½ oz) cranberry jam

Beat the eggs with 2 tablespoons hot water for 1 minute using an electric mixer at high speed. Gradually add the honey and lemon rind, beating for 3 minutes. Incorporate a third of the buckwheat flour. Beat for a short while at low speed, then repeat the procedure with the remaining flour. Transfer to a greased, lined,

28 cm (11 in) round, springform cake tin and bake in a preheated oven at 180-200° C (350-400° F, Gas Mark 4-6) for 30-35 minutes.

Turn out of the tin immediately on to a wire rack. Peel off the greaseproof paper, leave the cake to cool, then cut into three layers.

For the filling: soak the gelatine in a pan with 3 table-spoons cold water for 10 minutes, then heat, stirring until dissolved. Add the lemon juice. Whip the cream, incorporate the gelatine and the maple syrup.

Transfer a quarter of the cream to an icing bag fitted with a star-shaped nozzle.

Spread half the cranberry jam over the base of the cake, followed by a third of the remaining whipped cream. Place the second layer of cake on top, pressing down gently. Spread with the remaining jam (reserving ½ tablespoon for decoration), and half the remaining cream. Place the third layer of cake on top, pressing down gently, and cover all the cake with the remaining whipped cream.

Decorate with the whipped cream in the icing bag. When ready to serve, decorate with the remaining jam or some fresh cranberries.

Below: *Buckwheat gâteau*

Gradually incorporate the honey.

Add the toasted hazelnuts

Pipe into paper cases.

FRUIT AND NUT CUP CAKES

Makes 26-28

200 g (7 oz) nibbed
hazelnuts
300 g (10 oz) butter,
softened
300 g (10 oz) honey
4 tablespoons rum
5 eggs
300 g (10 oz) plain flour
2 teaspoons baking
powder
Fruit (raspberries,
blackberries, kiwi fruits,
pineapples)
Whipped cream
Dark bitter chocolate
Hazelnuts, almonds,
mixed dried fruit, bananas

Toast the nibbed hazelnuts in an ungreased frying pan, then leave to cool.

For the mixture: cream the butter in a mixing bowl for 30 seconds using an electric mixer at high speed. Gradually incorporate the honey and rum, stirring until smooth. Add the eggs one at a time, beating each one for 30 seconds.

Sift the flour and baking powder together and incorporate in the mixture with the mixer at medium speed; then add the toasted hazelnuts. Transfer this mixture to an icing bag and pipe into 26-28 paper cases. Bake in a preheated oven at 180° C (350° F, Gas Mark 4) for 30-35 minutes. When cold, decorate the cup cakes with the fruit and whipped cream or the chocolate and walnuts, hazelnuts and mixed dried fruit.

CHOCOLATE NUT CAKE

Serves 6

300 g (10 oz) dark bitter
chocolate
9 large eggs
100 g (3½ oz) honey
25 g (1 oz) buckwheat
flour
1 teaspoon baking powder
150 g (5 oz) nibbed
hazelnuts
200 g (7 oz) butter,
softened
25 g (1 oz) toasted, flaked
almonds

Melt 150 g (5 oz) chocolate in a bowl over a pan of hot water, then leave to cool. Beat 7 eggs for 1 minute, using an electric mixer at high speed. Gradually incorporate the honey (reserving 1 tablespoon) and beat for 1 more minute.

Sift the buckwheat flour and baking powder together and incorporate in the egg mixture, beating at low speed for a moment; then add the melted chocolate and the nibbed hazelnuts in the same way.

Turn the mixture into a greased, lined, 28 cm (11 in) round, springform cake tin. Bake in a preheated oven at 150-160° C (300-325° F, Gas Mark 2-3) for 55 minutes. Turn the cake out immediately on to a wire rack and peel off the greaseproof paper. Leave to cool, then cut into two layers.

For the filling: melt the remaining chocolate in a bowl over a pan of hot water. Leave to cool, then, using a balloon whisk, beat in 200 g (7 oz) butter. Add the reserved honey and the remaining eggs. Transfer a little of this mixture to an icing bag fitted with a star-shaped nozzle. Spread some of the mixture over the bottom layer of the cake, place the second layer on top, then cover the whole cake with the remaining mixture. Decorate the sides with the toasted, flaked almonds and the sides with the chocolate cream in the icing bag.

APPLE AND POPPY SEED CAKE

Serves 6

700 g (1 lb 6 oz) apples
10 eggs, separated
300 g (10 oz) set honey
Grated rind of 1 lemon
200 g (7 oz) nibbed
hazelnuts
250 g (8 oz) poppy seeds,
crushed
50 g (2 oz) buckwheat
flour
1 teaspoon baking powder
150 g (5 oz) dark bitter
chocolate
200 g (7 oz) butter,
softened

Peel, quarter, core and dice the apples. Whisk the egg whites into peaks in a mixing bowl with 5 tablespoons cold water and gradually incorporate the honey.

Combine the lemon rind with the egg yolks and gently fold into the egg whites. Add the hazelnuts, poppy seeds, buckwheat flour and baking powder, followed by the diced apples.

Turn the mixture into a greased or lined, 28 cm (11 in) round cake tin. Bake in a preheated oven at 180° C (350° F, Gas Mark 4) for 55-60 minutes.

Opposite: *Fruit and nut cup cakes*

BANANA AND ALMOND TART

Serves 6

250 g (8 oz) wholewheat
flour
1 teaspoon baking powder
150 g (5 oz) clear honey
A pinch of salt
1 egg
1 vanilla pod
100 g (3½ oz) butter

1.5 kg (3½ lb) bananas
Juice of 2 lemons
200 g (7 oz) raspberries
3 egg whites
75 g (3 oz) nibbed
almonds
125 g (4 oz) desiccated
coconut

Sft the flour and baking powder into a bowl. Add
75 g (3 oz) honey, the egg, salt, vanilla pod and softened
butter. Combine the ingredients using an electric mixer
fitted with a kneading attachment, first at low, then at
high speed. Make the dough into a smooth ball and, if it
is too sticky, place it in a refrigerator for a short while.
Roll out two-thirds of the dough, line a greased,
28 cm (11 in) round, springform cake tin, then prick the
base with a fork. Bake in a preheated oven at
180-200° C (350-400° F, Gas Mark 4-6) for 20-25 minutes.

For the filling: peel the bananas and cut into
3 cm (1¾ in) thick chunks. Sprinkle with lemon juice and
arrange close together over the base of the tart.
Wash the raspberries and use to decorate the tart. Beat
the egg whites into peaks, incorporate the remaining
honey, followed by the nibbed almonds and desiccated
coconut. Cover the fruits. Bake in a preheated oven at
200° C (400° F, Gas Mark 6) for 12-15 minutes.

PLUM AND HAZELNUT TART

Serves 6

200 g (7 oz) plain flour
½ sachet powdered easy-
blend yeast
100 g (3½ oz) honey
A pinch of salt
100-150 ml (3½ fl oz-¼
pint) warm milk

100 g (3½ oz) butter
50 g (2 oz) fresh
breadcrumbs
50 g (2 oz) nibbed
hazelnuts
1 kg (2 lb) plums
3 tablespoons apricot jelly

Combine the flour and yeast in a mixing bowl, then
incorporate 50 g (2 oz) honey, the salt, milk and
50 g (2 oz) melted butter. Knead for 5 minutes using an
electric mixer fitted with a kneading attachment, first at
low, then at high speed. Leave the dough to rise in a
warm place until increased in bulk.

For the filling: melt the remaining butter and honey in a
frying pan, then add the breadcrumbs and nibbed
hazelnuts. Stir until browned, then leave to cool. Crush
using a spoon.

Wash, dry, halve, stone and slice the plums.

Knead the dough again with the mixer at high speed.
Roll it out and line a greased, 28 cm (11 in) round cake tin.
Cover with half the hazelnut mixture, arrange the plums
to create a fish-scale effect. Leave the dough in a warm
place to prove. Bake in a preheated oven at
200° C (400° F, Gas Mark 6) for 30 minutes.

Heat the jelly, then brush over the tart as soon as it is out
of the oven. Sprinkle with the remaining hazelnut
mixture.
Serve with whipped cream sweetened with maple syrup.

Below: *Plum and hazelnut tart*

Above: *Fruit baskets*

FRUIT BASKETS

Makes 6

200 g (7 oz) plain wheat
flour
200 g (7 oz) cottage
cheese
200 g (7 oz) butter
1 egg, separated

A pinch of salt
6 tablespoons honey
625 g (1¼ lb) berries
3 tablespoons orange
juice

Combine the flour, drained cottage cheese, softened butter, egg yolk and salt for 1 minute using an electric mixer fitted with a kneading attachment. Make the dough into a ball, wrap it in a sheet of aluminium foil and leave to rest overnight in a refrigerator. Roll the pastry out until 5 mm (¼ in) thick. Cut into six, 10 cm (4 in) diameter rounds and place on a greased baking sheet. Roll out the remaining pastry into a 40 cm (16 in) long strip. Cut into twelve, 15 mm (⅓ in) wide strips. Twist the strips and join the ends together to form twelve, 10 cm (4 in) diameter circles. Place two circles on top of each other on each tartlet base.
Bake in a preheated oven at 180° C (350° F, Gas Mark 4) for 30 minutes. Leave to cool. Coat the pastry with the hot honey.

For the filling: wash and drain the berries. Fill the baskets. Combine the remaining honey with the orange juice and pour over the fruits.

MARZIPAN BONBONS

Makes 50

300 g (10 oz) almond paste
About 25 g (1 oz) blanched pine kernels or flaked almonds
75 g (3 oz) dark bitter chocolate
50 g (2 oz) dried apricots, diced
25 g (1 oz) candied orange peel, finely chopped
Cocoa powder to finish

Divide 100 g (3½ oz) almond paste into fourteen pieces. Roll into balls and insert the pine kernels or almonds to form prickles. Melt 40 g (1½ oz) chocolate in a bowl over a pan of hot water. Spoon the chocolate over the hedgehogs, holding them with a fork; then place in a refrigerator.

Apricot marzipan fingers: combine 100 g (3½ oz) almond paste with the diced, dried apricots. Make into sixteen fingers. Melt the remaining chocolate in a bowl over a pan of hot water and coat the fingers as soon as the icing starts to set. Make a pattern using a fork, then place in a refrigerator.

Orange marzipan fingers: combine the remaining almond paste with the candied orange peel. Make into 20 balls, then toss them in the cocoa powder. Place in paper cases.

BERLIN DOUGHNUTS

Serves 6

500 g (1 lb) plain flour
1 sachet powdered easy-blend yeast
100 g (3½ oz) honey
A pinch of salt
Grated rind of ½ lemon
2 eggs
1 egg yolk
100-150 ml (3½ fl oz-¼
pint) warm milk
75 g (3 oz) butter, melted and cooled
1 egg white
Morello cherry jam or stewed plums
Oil for frying
Demerara sugar to finish

Thoroughly combine the flour and yeast in a mixing bowl. Incorporate the honey, salt, lemon rind, eggs, egg yolk, milk and butter. Knead for 5 minutes using an electric mixer fitted with a kneading attachment, first at low, then at high speed. Leave to rise in a warm place until increased in bulk, then quickly knead again at high speed.

Roll the dough out until 5 mm (¼ in) thick, and cut into 8 cm (3 in) diameter circles. Brush half the circles with the egg white and spoon the cherry jam or stewed plums on to the centre. Cover with the remaining circles, crimp the edges together to seal, then leave the dough in a warm place to prove.

Fry the doughnuts on both sides, remove from the oil using a slotted spoon, leave to drain on a wire rack, then toss in the demerara sugar.

HONEY AND SESAME PANCAKES

Serves 6

250 g (8 oz) plain flour
2 teaspoons baking powder
250 g (8 oz) honey
1 tablespoon milk
1 teaspoon ground cinnamon
A pinch of ground cloves
or 1 crushed clove
A pinch of nutmeg
100 g (3½ oz) chopped candied mixed peel
Milk or single cream to coat
Sesame seeds to finish

Sift the flour and baking powder into a mixing bowl; then incorporate the honey, milk, cinnamon, cloves, nutmeg and candied peel.
Quickly knead using an electric mixer fitted with a kneading attachment, first at low, then at high speed. Make the dough into a smooth ball, placing it in a refrigerator if too sticky.

Roll the dough out thinly, then cut out the shapes of your choice. Place on a baking sheet lined with greaseproof paper. Brush with the milk or cream, dredge with the sesame seeds and bake in a preheated oven at 180-200° C (350-400° F, Gas Mark 4-6) for 12 minutes.

Opposite: *Berlin doughnuts*

Above: *Cream puffs*

CREAM PUFFS

Serves 4

75 g (3 oz) butter
A pinch of salt
100 g (3½ oz) plain wheat flour
50 g (2 oz) buckwheat flour
4-5 eggs
A pinch of baking powder

3 gelatine leaves
375-500 g (12 oz-1 lb) strawberries
375-500 ml (12-18 fl oz) double cream
4 tablespoons maple syrup

Bring 250 ml (8 fl oz) water, the butter and salt to the boil. Remove from the heat. Quickly add the sifted wheat and buckwheat flours and stir until a smooth dough is formed. Return to the heat for 1 minute, stirring constantly, then transfer immediately to a mixing bowl. Incorporate the eggs one at a time using an electric mixer fitted with a kneading attachment at high speed, adding the fifth egg only if the dough has become shiny and sticky. Leave to cool, then add the baking powder and make into small balls on a floured baking sheet.
Bake in a preheated oven at 200-230° C (400-450° F, Gas Mark 6-8) for 30-35 minutes. Do not open the door for the first 15 minutes, as the choux pastry will sink immediately. When out of the oven, cut a lid in each puff and leave to cool.

For the cream filling: soak the gelatine in cold water, drain, then heat, stirring constantly until dissolved. Cut the strawberries into two or four pieces. Whip the cream lightly, incorporate the gelatine and maple syrup, then whip until firm. Fill an icing bag. Pipe half the cream into the puffs, insert the strawberries, then cover with the remaining cream and top with the pastry lids.

Tip: to prevent the puffs from going soft, it is advisable to fill them just before serving.

FRUIT AND NUT SPIRALS

Serves 6-8

500 g (1 lb) plain flour
1 sachet powdered easy-blend yeast
175 g (6 oz) honey
2 eggs
A pinch of salt
100-150 ml (3½ fl oz-¼ pint) warm milk

150 g (5 oz) butter
75 g (3 oz) sultanas
75 g (3 oz) currants
75 g (3 oz) nibbed almonds
1 tablespoon condensed milk

Combine the flour and yeast in a mixing bowl; then incorporate 75 g (3 oz) honey, the eggs, salt, milk and 100 g (3½ oz) cooled, melted butter. Knead the dough for 5 minutes using an electric mixer fitted with a kneading attachment, first at low, then at high speed. Leave to rise in a warm place until increased in bulk, then beat again thoroughly with the mixer at high speed. Roll out into a 40 x 50 cm (16 x 20 in) rectangle.

For the filling: combine the remaining softened butter and honey and spread over the dough. Mix the dried fruit and the almonds together and scatter over the dough. Roll the dough up lengthways and cut into 15 mm-2 cm (⅓-¾ in) thick slices. Arrange the slices on a greased baking sheet and brush with condensed milk.

Leave the dough in a warm place to prove. Bake in a preheated oven at 180-200° C (350-400° F, Gas Mark 4-6) for 20 minutes. Serve warm.

Below: *Fruit and nut spirals*

Spread the apricot jelly over the pastry.

Cover with the filling

Cut into triangles.

Below: *Hazelnut triangles*

HAZELNUT TRIANGLES

Makes about 20

125 g (4 oz) plain wheat
flour
½ teaspoon baking
powder
50 g (2 oz) buckwheat
flour
150 g (5 oz) honey
1 small egg

175 g (6 oz) butter
2 tablespoons apricot jelly
75 g (3 oz) nibbed
hazelnuts
125 g (4 oz) flaked
hazelnuts
50 g (2 oz) dark bitter
chocolate

Sift the wheat flour, baking powder and
50 g (2 oz) buckwheat flour into a mixing bowl, then
incorporate 50 g (2 oz) honey, the egg and
75 g (3 oz) softened butter. Quickly knead using an
electric mixer fitted with a kneading attachment, first at
low, then at high speed, to form a smooth dough. If the
dough is too sticky, place it in a refrigerator for a short
while. Roll the dough out on to a greased baking sheet
and spread with the apricot jelly.

For the filling: melt the remaining butter and honey,
then incorporate all the hazelnuts and the remaining
buckwheat flour. Combine thoroughly and leave to cool
before spreading over the dough.

Bake in a preheated oven at 180° C (350° F, Gas Mark 4)
for 25-30 minutes. Leave to cool, then cut into triangles.
Melt the chocolate in a bowl over a pan of hot water and
dip in the corners of the triangles.

SESAME SQUARES

Makes 30-40

200 g (7 oz) sesame seeds
75 g (3 oz) butter,
softened
150 g (5 oz) clear honey
Grated rind of 1 lemon
½ teaspoon ground
cinnamon

A pinch of salt
½ teaspoon cardamom
1 egg
50 g (2 oz) barley flour
100 g (3½ oz) wholewheat
flour

Toast 150 g (5 oz) sesame seeds in an ungreased frying
pan, then leave to cool. Cream the butter using an
electric mixer at high speed. Combine the honey, lemon
rind, cinnamon, salt, cardamom, egg, barley flour and
wholewheat flour, then gradually incorporate in the
butter, beating at medium speed. Finally add the toasted
sesame seeds. Cover and leave to rest for 1 hour.

Roll out into a square on a greased baking sheet, dredge
with the remaining sesame seeds and bake in a
preheated oven at 180-200° C (350-400° F, Gas Mark 4-6)
for 15 minutes. Cut into 3 x 5 cm (1¼ x 2 in) slabs.

Suggestion: a sprinkling of freshly ground pepper can
be used instead of the cardamom.

APRICOT AND HAZELNUT FRITTERS

Makes 10-12

125 g (4 oz) butter,
softened
100 g (3½ oz) demerara
sugar
Grated rind of 1 lemon
A pinch of salt
2 eggs
200 g (7 oz) cottage
cheese
250 g (8 oz) plain wheat

flour
125 g (4 oz) buckwheat
flour
2 teaspoons baking
powder
100 g (3½ oz) dried
apricots, diced
100 g (3½ oz) nibbed
hazelnuts
Oil for frying

Cream the butter in a mixing bowl for 30 seconds using
an electric mixer at high speed, then gradually
incorporate the sugar, lemon rind and salt, beating until
smooth. Add the eggs one at a time, beating each one for
30 seconds. Incorporate the cottage cheese.

Sift the wheat and buckwheat flours and baking powder
together. Incorporate in the mixture, beating at medium
speed. Add the diced, dried apricots and nibbed
hazelnuts.

Make into small balls of dough using two teaspoons, then
fry on both sides in the very hot oil for 4-5 minutes.

STUFFED DATES

Makes 10-15

250 g (8 oz) dates, with stones
100 g (3½ oz) almond paste

40 g (1½ oz) dark bitter chocolate

Stone the dates. Cut the almond paste into as many pieces as there are dates. Shape into small rolls and stuff the dates.

Melt the chocolate in a bowl over a pan of hot water. Dip both ends of the stuffed dates in the chocolate and place in a refrigerator.

HAZELNUT COOKIES

Makes 15-20

50 g (2 oz) butter, softened
200 g (7 oz) hazelnut spread
A pinch of salt
150 g (5 oz) demerara sugar
2 eggs

125 g (4 oz) buckwheat flour
125 g (4 oz) spelt flour (available from health food shops)
1 teaspoon baking powder
25 g (1 oz) flaked almonds

Cream the butter in a mixing bowl for 30 seconds, using an electric mixer fitted with a kneading attachment at high speed. Gradually incorporate the hazelnut spread, salt and sugar, then beat until smooth. Add the eggs one at a time, beating each one for 30 seconds.
Sift the buckwheat flour, spelt flour and baking powder together and gradually incorporate in the mixture. Make small mounds of the mixture using two teaspoons and arrange on a baking sheet lined with greaseproof paper. Insert the almonds and bake in a preheated oven at 180-200° C (350-400° F, Gas Mark 4-6) for 15 minutes.

Below: *Stuffed dates*

RUM BUTTER CRISPS

Above: *Hazelnut cookies*
Below: *Rum butter crisps*

Makes 15-20

250 g (8 oz) plain wheat flour
125 g (4 oz) spelt flour (available from health food shops)
50 g (2 oz) nibbed almonds
75 g (3 oz) brown sugar

A pinch of salt
Grated rind of ½ lemon
2 tablespoons rum
1 egg yolk
250 g (8 oz) butter, softened
50 g (2 oz) dark bitter chocolate

Sift the wheat four and spelt flour together, then add the almonds, brown sugar, salt, lemon rind, rum, egg yolk and butter. Combine thoroughly using an electric mixer fitted with a kneading attachment, first at low, then at high speed. Make into a smooth ball. If the dough is too sticky, place it in a refrigerator for a short while.

Roll the dough out until 3 mm (⅓ in) thick. Cut out shapes of your choice and arrange them on a baking sheet lined with greaseproof paper. Bake in a preheated oven at 180-200° C (350-400° F, Gas Mark 4-6) for 12-15 minutes. Melt the chocolate in a bowl over a pan of hot water and drizzle over the biscuits.

ALMOND ROUNDS

Makes 20-30

300 g (10 oz) plain wheat flour	A pinch of salt
75 g (3 oz) buckwheat flour	1 egg yolk
1 teaspoon baking powder	250 g (8 oz) butter, softened
75 g (3 oz) brown sugar	200 g (7 oz) whole almonds
5 drops of vanilla extract	

Sift the wheat flour, buckwheat flour and baking powder into a mixing bowl, then incorporate the sugar, vanilla extract, salt, egg yolk and butter. Work the mixture using an electric mixer fitted with a kneading attachment, first at low, then at high sped. Incorporate the almonds and beat quickly at medium speed.

Make into a smooth ball, then shape into 2.5-3 cm (1-1¼ in) diameter rolls and place in a refrigerator until firm. Cut the rolls into 5 mm (¼ in) thick slices, place on a lightly greased baking sheet and bake in a preheated oven at 180-200° C (350-400° F, Gas Mark 4-6) for 12-15 minutes.

ALMOND BUTTER BISCUITS

Makes 20-30

375 g (12 oz) butter, softened	A pinch of salt
200 ml (7 fl oz) maple syrup	500 g (1 lb) plain flour
5 drops of vanilla extract	125 g (4 oz) blanched almonds

Cream the butter for 30 seconds using an electric mixer at high speed, then gradually incorporate the maple syrup, vanilla extract and salt. Beat until smooth. Gradually incorporate two-thirds of the flour with the mixer at medium speed, then knead the remaining flour and the almonds into the mixture by hand.

Leave to rest for a short while in a refrigerator, then make into shapes of your choice (fingers, rings, 'S'-shapes). Transfer to a greased baking sheet and bake in a preheated oven at 180-200° C (350-400° F, Gas Mark 4-6) for 15 minutes.

POPPY SEED TARTLETS

Makes 20

400 g (13 oz) plain flour	20 g (¼ oz) potato flour or arrowroot
2 teaspoons baking powder	1 tablespoon fresh breadcrumbs
500 g (1 lb) cottage cheese	200 g (7 oz) poppy seeds
300 ml (½ pint) milk	8 tablespoons stewed plums
100 ml (3½ fl oz) oil	4 tablespoons apricot jelly
225 g (7½ oz) honey	40 g (1½ oz) toasted, flaked almonds
A pinch of salt	
2 eggs	
50 g (2 oz) butter, softened	

Sift the flour and baking powder into a mixing bowl. Incorporate 200 g (7 oz) cottage cheese, 100 ml (3½ fl oz) milk, the oil, 75 g (3 oz) honey, the salt and 1 egg. Beat for 1 minute using an electric mixer fitted with a kneading attachment at high speed, then shape into a roll of dough.

For filling no. 1: combine the remaining cottage cheese with 75 g (3 oz) honey, the butter, potato flour or arrowroot and the remaining egg. Put to one side.

For filling no. 2: bring 200 ml (7 fl oz) milk to the boil. Crush the poppy seeds in a coffee grinder and incorporate in the milk with the remaining honey and the breadcrumbs; then leave to cool.

For filling no. 3: stir the stewed plums. Set to one side.

Cut the roll of dough into twenty slices. Roll into balls and flatten with your hand, so that the edges are slightly raised.

Arrange the rounds on a greased baking sheet and place 1 teaspoon of stewed plums in the centre. Place 1 teaspoon of filling no. 2 and 1 teaspoon of filling no. 1 around the stewed plums. Bake in a preheated oven at 200° C (400° F, Gas Mark 6) for 18-20 minutes, then leave to cool.

For the glaze: bring the apricot jelly to the boil with 4 tablespoons water. Brush over the tartlets and decorate the edges with the toasted, flaked almonds.

Opposite: *Poppy seed tartlets*

Make the tartlets.

Place the stewed plums in the centre.

Add the fillings.

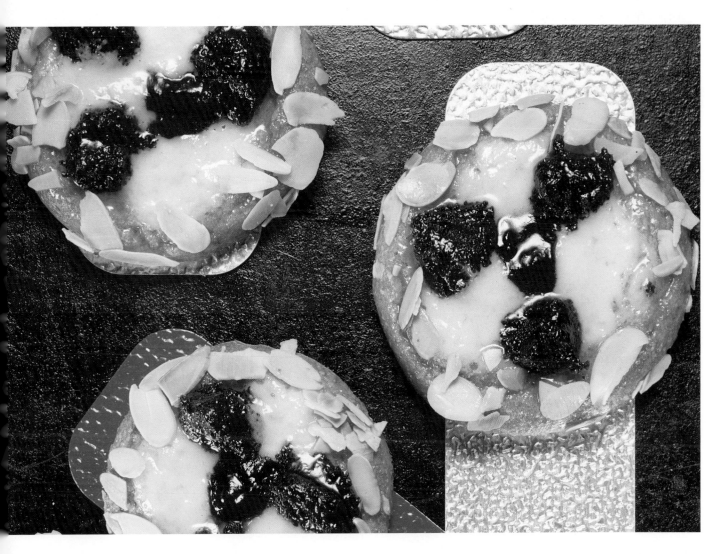

Above: *Bread plait*

STUFFED BREAD

Serves 6-8

375 g (12 oz) bread mix	thinly sliced and braised
250 ml (8 fl oz) warm	Salt
water	Freshly ground white
1 bread roll	pepper
1 onion	1 teaspoon mustard
1 tablespoon oil	1 teaspoon concentrated
1 bunch parsley, chopped	tomato purée
500 g (1 lb) meat, minced	Flour for kneading and
(half beef, half pork)	dusting
1 egg	75 g (3 oz) cheese
100 g (3½ oz) mushrooms,	(Gruyère, Edam, Gouda)

Combine the bread mix with the water in a mixing bowl, following the instructions on the packet. Leave to rise.

For the stuffing: soak the bread roll in some cold water. Peel and chop the onion, then brown in the hot oil. Squeeze the bread roll to remove the water and add to the onion with the parsley, minced meat, egg and sliced mushrooms. Season with the salt, pepper, mustard and tomato purée. Roll the stuffing into a 15 cm (6 in) diameter ball.

Put the dough on a work surface, dust with flour and knead quickly; then roll out on a floured work surface into a 30 cm (12 in) diameter circle. Any surplus dough can be used to decorate the loaf.

Place the ball of stuffing on the dough. Dice the cheese and scatter over the stuffing. Wrap the dough around the stuffing, place on a greased baking sheet, decorate with any surplus dough and leave to prove in a warm place. When risen, make a cut in the top of the dough, brush with water, dust with flour and bake in a preheated oven at 200-230° C (400-450° F, Gas Mark 6-8) for 1 hour.

BREAD PLAIT

Serves about 10

750 g (1½ lb) bread mix	Flour for kneading and
500 ml (18 fl oz) warm	dusting
water	

Combine the bread mix with the water, following the instructions on the packet. Leave to rest, dust with flour and knead for a short while.

Shape two-thirds of the dough into three, 40 cm (16 in) long rolls. Plait together and place on a greased baking sheet. Divide the remaining dough into three, shape into three 36 cm (14 in) long rolls, plait together and place on the first plait. Leave to rise in a warm place, brush with water, dust with flour and bake in a preheated oven at 200-230° C (400-450° F, Gas Mark 6-8) for 50 minutes.

Pages 424 and 425: *Cottage cheese and yoghurt rolls (recipe p. 444)*

HAM CROISSANTS

Makes 12

375 g (12 oz) bread mix
Flour for kneading and
dusting

125 g (4 oz) smoked ham,
thinly sliced

Combine the bread mix with 250 ml (8 fl oz) warm water, following the instructions on the packet. Leave the dough to rise, dust with flour, knead quickly and roll out into a 40 cm (16 in) diameter circle on a floured work surface.

Cut the circle into twelve segments and place a little ham on each one. Stretch out the curved edge slightly and roll up the dough towards the pointed end to make the croissants.

Arrange the croissants (pointed edge down) on a greased baking sheet, leave to prove in a warm place, then brush with water, dust lightly with flour and bake in a preheated oven at 200-230° C (400-450° F, Gas Mark 6-8) for 25 minutes.

SALAMI RYE BREAD

Serves 10-15

250 g (8 oz) rye, crushed
250 g (8 oz) strong (bread)
wheat flour
1 sachet powdered easy-
blend yeast

1 teaspoon caster sugar
1 teaspoon salt
150 g (5 oz) salami, finely
sliced

Combine the crushed rye, wheat flour and baking powder in a mixing bowl. Incorporate the sugar, salt and 250 ml (8 fl oz) warm water. Work into a smooth dough using an electric mixer fitted with a kneading attachment for 5 minutes, first at low, then at high speed. Add the salami and leave to rise in a warm place.

Knead the dough again and make into two long loaves. Place on a greased baking sheet, brush the tops with water and dust with flour. Bake in a preheated oven at 200° C (400° F, Gas Mark 6) for 40 minutes.

Below: *Salami rye bread*

ALMOND BREAD

Serves 6-8

500 g (1 lb) strong (bread) flour
1 sachet powdered easy-blend yeast
50 g (2 oz) caster sugar
1 sachet vanilla sugar
A pinch of salt
2 eggs
100 g (3½ oz) butter
100-150 ml (3½ fl oz-¼ pint) milk

125 g (4 oz) sultanas
100 g (3½ oz) currants
50 g (2 oz) chopped candied lemon peel
65 g (2½ oz) nibbed almonds
1 tablespoon condensed milk
1 tablespoon demerara sugar

Sift the flour and baking powder into a mixing bowl. Incorporate the sugar, vanilla sugar, salt, eggs, cooled, melted butter and warm milk. Knead for 5 minutes using an electric mixer fitted with a kneading attachment, first

Above: *Rye bread sandwiches*

at low, then at high speed. Leave to rise in a warm place until doubled in bulk. Add the sultanas, currants, candied lemon peel and 50 g (2 oz) nibbed almonds. Make the dough into a ball and leave to prove in a warm place until doubled in bulk again. Brush with condensed milk and dredge with the demerara sugar and the remaining nibbed almonds. Bake in a preheated oven at 180-200° C (350-400° F, Gas Mark 4-6) for 50 minutes.

Left: *Almond bread*

RYE BREAD SANDWICHES

Makes 6

6 round rye bread rolls
1 onion
250 g (8 oz) minced meat
2 tablespoons chopped
fresh parsley
125 g (4 oz) mushrooms,
finely sliced and braised
1 egg
Salt
Freshly ground pepper
12 slices of tomato
6 slices of Gouda cheese

Cut the rolls in two, remove the soft bread part and soak it in some water.

For the filling: peel and finely chop the onion. Squeeze the bread to remove the water and add to the onion, together with the minced meat, parsley, mushrooms and egg. Season with salt and pepper. Put the filling in the bread rolls. Place on a baking sheet lined with aluminium foil.

Bake in a preheated oven at 200-230° C (400-450° F, Gas Mark 6-8) for 30 minutes. After 20 minutes, place two slices of tomato and a slice of Gouda on the filling in each roll and replace the top.

CHEESE AND HAM CROISSANTS

Makes 10

125 g (4 oz) cream cheese
4 tablespoons milk
1 egg
4 tablespoons oil
1 teaspoon salt
300 g (10 oz) plain flour
2 teaspoons baking
powder
10 slices boiled ham
10 slices Gouda cheese
1 tablespoon condensed
milk

Mix the cream cheese, milk, egg, oil and salt together. Sift the flour and baking powder together and gradually incorporate in the cream cheese mixture. Roll the dough out and cut into five 12 x 12 cm (4½ x 4½ in) squares. Cut them in two diagonally.

Place a slice of Gouda and a slice of ham on each triangle. Roll up into croissants, place on a greased baking sheet, brush with the condensed milk and bake in a preheated oven at 180-200° C (350-400° F, Gas Mark 4-6) for 20 minutes.

Below: *Cheese and ham croissants*

PROVENÇAL FRENCH STICK

Serves 8-10

1 French stick, 50 cm (20 in) long, 8 cm (3 in) wide	Some stuffed green olives
250 g (8 oz) butter	Salt
1 heaped teaspoon green peppercorns	Freshly ground pepper
1-2 teaspoons capers	Worcester sauce
	250 g (8 oz) boiled ham
	2 eggs, hard-boiled

Cut the French stick open lengthways and remove some of the soft bread.

For the filling: cream the butter in a mixing bowl. Incorporate the green peppercorns, capers and some olives. Add the crumbled bread; season with salt, pepper and Worcester sauce. Dice the ham, peel and chop the eggs, then add to the butter mixture.

Fill the French stick, wrap in aluminium foil and place in a refrigerator. Cut into slices and serve with olives, green pepper and lamb's lettuce salad.

CURRANT BUNS

Makes 15

250 g (8 oz) strong (bread) wheat flour	50 g (2 oz) butter, melted and cooled
½ sachet powdered easy-blend yeast	1 egg
25 g (1 oz) caster sugar	1 tablespoon warm milk
1 sachet vanilla sugar	75 g (3 oz) currants
A pinch of salt	1 tablespoon condensed milk

Combine the flour and yeast in a mixing bowl. Incorporate the sugar, vanilla sugar, salt, butter, egg and milk. Work for 5 minutes using an electric mixer, first at low, then at high speed. Add the currants and leave the dough to rise in a warm place until doubled in bulk.

Knead again at high speed and make into a 30 cm (12 in) long roll. Cut into fifteen 2 cm (¾ in) thick slices, roll into small balls, place on a greased baking sheet and leave to prove until doubled in bulk. Brush with the condensed milk and bake in a preheated oven at 200-230° C (400-450° F, Gas Mark 6-8) for 15 minutes.

Below: *Provençal French stick*

Above: *Croissants*

CROISSANTS

Makes 16

500 g (1 lb) strong (bread) flour
1 sachet powdered easy-blend yeast
75 g (3 oz) caster sugar
1 sachet vanilla sugar
2 drops bitter almond essence
A pinch of salt
1 egg white
65 g (2½ oz) butter, melted and cooled
250 ml (8 fl oz) milk
1 egg yolk

Combine the flour and yeast in a mixing bowl. Incorporate the sugar, vanilla sugar, bitter almond essence, salt, egg white, butter and 200 ml (7 fl oz) warm milk. Work for 5 minutes using an electric mixer fitted with a kneading attachment, first at low, then at high speed. Leave the dough to rise in a warm place until doubled in bulk, then quickly knead again at high speed.

Divide the dough in four and roll out four 25 cm (10 in) diameter circles. Cut each circle into four segments. Roll up into croissants, place on a greased baking sheet and leave to prove in a warm place until doubled in bulk.

Combine the egg yolk with the remaining milk, brush over the croissants, then bake in a preheated oven at 200-230° C (400-450° F, Gas Mark 6-8) for 10-15 minutes.

CHEESE ROLLS

Makes 10

425 g (14 oz) strong
(bread) wheat flour
1 sachet powdered easy-
blend yeast
1 teaspoon caster sugar

1 teaspoon salt
Freshly ground pepper
200 g (7 oz) Gouda
cheese, coarsely grated
1 egg yolk

Combine the flour and yeast in a mixing bowl.
Incorporate the sugar, salt, pepper and 250 ml
(8 fl oz) warm water, then work into a smooth dough
using an electric mixer fitted with a kneading attachment
for 5 minutes, first at low, then at high speed. Add
150 g (5 oz) Gouda cheese and leave the dough to rise in a
warm place until doubled in bulk.

Knead again thoroughly and shape into 10 oval rolls.
Place on a greased baking sheet and leave to prove in a
warm place. Combine the egg yolk with 1 tablespoon
water, brush over the rolls and sprinkle with the
remaining cheese. Bake in a preheated oven at
180-200° C (350-400° F, Gas Mark 4-6) for 25 minutes.

Below: *Cheese rolls*

SESAME BREAD

Serves 8-10

500 g (1 lb) strong (bread)
wheat flour
1 sachet powdered easy-
blend yeast
1 teaspoon caster sugar

1 rounded teaspoon salt
5 tablespoons sesame
seeds, toasted
1 tablespoon milk

Combine the flour and yeast in a mixing bowl.
Incorporate the sugar, salt and 250 ml (8 fl oz) warm
water. Work into a smooth dough using an electric mixer
fitted with a kneading attachment for 5 minutes, first at
low, then at high speed. Add 3 tablespoons toasted
sesame seeds. Leave the dough to rise in a warm place
until doubled in bulk.

Knead again thoroughly, then turn into a greased loaf tin
and leave in a warm place to prove. Brush with the milk,
sprinkle with the remaining sesame seeds and bake in a
preheated oven at 200° C (400° F, Gas Mark 6) for
45 minutes.

SESAME ROLLS

Makes 24

375 g (12 oz) strong
(bread) wheat flour
1 sachet powdered easy-
blend yeast
1 teaspoon caster sugar

1 teaspoon salt
50 g (2 oz) butter, melted
and cooled
Sesame seeds to finish

Combine the flour and yeast in a mixing bowl.
Incorporate the sugar, salt, butter and 200 ml
(7 fl oz) warm water. Work into a smooth dough using an
electric mixer fitted with a kneading attachment for
5 minutes, first at low, then at high speed. Leave the
dough to rise in a warm place until doubled in bulk.

Make into 24 oval rolls, place on a greased baking sheet
and leave in a warm place to prove. Brush with water,
sprinkle with the sesame seeds and bake in a preheated
oven at 180-200° C (350-400° F, Gas Mark 4-6) for
30 minutes.

Opposite: *Sesame bread*

Above: *Cheese and herb bread*

CHEESE AND HERB BREAD

Serves 8-10

*500 g (1 lb) strong (bread)
wheat flour
1 sachet powdered easy-
blend yeast
1 teaspoon caster sugar
1 teaspoon salt
Freshly ground pepper
2-3 onions*

*2 knobs of butter
1 egg
100 g (3½ oz) Gouda
cheese, grated
5-6 tablespoons fresh
mixed herbs
1 egg yolk*

Combine the flour and yeast in a mixing bowl.
Incorporate the sugar, salt, pepper and 250 ml
(8 fl oz) warm water. Work into a smooth dough using an
electric mixer fitted with a kneading attachment for
5 minutes . Leave the dough to rise in a warm place until
doubled in bulk.

For the filling: peel and chop the onions. Brown in a
knob of butter. Incorporate the egg, cheese and mixed
herbs.

Knead the dough thoroughly, then roll out on a floured
work surface into a 30 x 40 cm (12 x 16 in) rectangle.
Spread with the remaining butter and the filling, then
fold over 4 cm (1½ in) along the long sides towards the
centre. Roll the dough up, folding the short sides over
towards the centre. Place in a greased loaf tin and leave
in a warm place to prove. Combine the egg yolk with
1 tablespoon water and brush over the bread. Bake in a
preheated oven at 180-200° C (350-400° F, Gas Mark 4-6)
for 40-45 minutes.

COUNTRY LOAF

Serves about 6

125 g (4 oz) strong (bread) wheat flour
250 g (8 oz) rye flour
125 g (4 oz) bulgar (cracked wheat)
1 sachet powdered easy-blend yeast
1 teaspoon caster sugar
2 teaspoons salt
Freshly ground pepper
4 tablespoons oil
125 g (4 oz) sour dough

Combine the wheat and rye flours, bulgar and yeast in a mixing bowl. Incorporate the sugar, salt, pepper, oil and 250 ml (8 fl oz) warm water. Work the mixture into a smooth dough using an electric mixer fitted with a kneading attachment, first at low, then at high speed. Add the sour dough and knead for 5 minutes to form a smooth dough. Leave the dough to rise in a warm place until doubled in bulk.

Knead again and shape into a ball. Place on a greased baking sheet. Leave to prove in a warm place. Cut a 1 cm (½ in) deep cross in the top of the dough, brush with water and dredge with flour. Bake in a preheated oven at 200° C (400° F, Gas Mark 6) for 50 minutes.

Tip: if you cannot buy sour dough direct from your baker, use 125 g (4 oz) of frozen sour dough mixture as described on page 442.

CHEESE LOAF

Serves 8-10

500 g (1 lb) strong (bread) wheat flour
1 sachet powdered easy-blend yeast
1 teaspoon caster sugar
1 teaspoon salt
Freshly ground pepper
3 tablespoons oil
250 g (8 oz) Emmental cheese
1 egg yolk

Combine the flour and yeast in a mixing bowl. Incorporate the sugar, salt, pepper, oil and 250 ml (8 fl oz) warm water. Work into a smooth dough using an electric mixer fitted with a kneading attachment for 5 minutes, first at low, then at high speed. Leave to rise in a warm place until doubled in bulk.

Add 175 g (6 oz) Emmental cheese cut into medium-sized cubes. Knead thoroughly, then turn into a greased,

20 cm (8 in) soufflé dish. Dice the remaining Emmental, insert into the dough and leave in a warm place to prove.

Combine the egg yolk with 1 tablespoon water, brush over the loaf and bake in a preheated oven at 200° C (400° F, Gas Mark 4) for 50 minutes. Turn out of the dish and serve hot or cold.

HAZELNUT LOAF

Serves 10-12

375 g (12 oz) bread mix
150 g (5 oz) blanched hazelnuts
Flour for kneading
Nibbed hazelnuts to finish

Combine the bread mix with 250 ml (8 fl oz) warm water, following the instructions on the packet. Incorporate the hazelnuts, knead, then leave to rise.

Dredge with flour, knead quickly and shape into a 30 cm (12 in) long loaf. Place on a greased baking sheet, leave to prove for 15 minutes. Make several 1 cm (½ in) deep incisions in the dough, pressing down very gently. Brush with water, sprinkle with the nibbed hazelnuts and bake in a preheated oven at 200-230°F (400-450° F, Gas Mark 6-8) for 35 minutes.

Below: *Cheese loaf*

HERB ROLLS

Makes 12

500 g (1 lb) strong (bread) flour
1 sachet powdered easy-blend yeast
1 teaspoon caster sugar
2 teaspoons salt
Freshly ground pepper
3 tablespoons oil

2 tablespoons fresh parsley, chopped
2 tablespoons leek, finely sliced
1 tablespoon dill, finely chopped (optional)
1 egg yolk

Combine the flour and yeast. Incorporate the sugar, salt, pepper, oil and 250 ml (8 fl oz) warm water. Work into a smooth dough using an electric mixer fitted with a kneading attachment for 5 minutes, first at low, then at high speed. Add the parsley, leek and dill.

Leave the dough to rise in a warm place until doubled in bulk. Knead thoroughly and make into 12 round rolls. Place on a greased baking sheet and leave in a warm place to prove. Cut a 1 cm (½ in) deep cross in each roll, pressing down very gently. Beat the egg yolk with 1 tablespoon water and brush over the rolls. Bake in a preheated oven at 180-200° C (350-400° F, Gas Mark 4-6) for 45 minutes.

Above: *Herb rolls*

CREAM CHEESE ROLLS

Makes 10-12

500 g (1 lb) strong (bread) flour
1 sachet powdered easy-blend yeast
1 teaspoon caster sugar
½ teaspoon salt

250 g (8 oz) cream cheese
50 g (2 oz) butter, melted and cooled
1 tablespoon milk
1 tablespoon cumin, sesame or poppy seeds

Combine the flour and yeast. Incorporate the sugar, salt, cream cheese, butter and 200 ml (7 fl oz) warm water. Work for 5 minutes using an electric mixer fitted with a kneading attachment, first at low, then at high speed. Leave the dough to rise in a warm place until doubled in bulk. Knead thoroughly and make into 10-12 round rolls. Place on a greased baking sheet and leave in a warm place to prove.

Brush with the milk, sprinkle with the cumin, sesame or poppy seeds and bake in a preheated oven at 180-200° C (350-400° F, Gas Mark 4-6) for 20-25 minutes.

ROLLS

Makes 10

375 g (12 oz) bread mix   Flour for kneading

Combine the bread mix with 250 ml (8 fl oz) warm water, following the instructions on the packet, then leave the dough to rise. Dust with flour, knead and make into 10 smooth balls. Place on a greased baking sheet and leave to prove for 15 minutes. Cut a 1 cm (½ in) deep cross in each roll.
Brush with water and bake in a preheated oven at 180-200° C (350-400° F, Gas Mark 4-6) for 35-40 minutes.

WHITE LOAF

Serves 15-20

500 g (1 lb) strong (bread) flour	*1 egg yolk*
1 sachet powdered easy-blend yeast	*100 ml (3½ fl oz) warm milk*
1 teaspoon caster sugar	*150 ml (5 fl oz) double cream*
1 teaspoon salt	*Fresh breadcrumbs to coat the tin*
2 eggs	

Combine the flour and yeast in a mixing bowl. Incorporate the sugar, salt, eggs, egg yolk, milk and cream. Work into a smooth dough using an electric mixer with a kneading attachment for 5 minutes, first at low, then at high speed.

Leave the dough to rise in a warm place until doubled in bulk.

Turn into a greased, 30 x 10 cm (12 x 4 in) loaf tin coated with breadcrumbs. Leave in a warm place to prove. Make a 1 cm (½ in) deep, lengthways cut in the dough, pressing down very gently. Brush with water and bake in a preheated oven at 180-200° C (350-400° F, Gas Mark 4-6) for 40-50 minutes.

Above: *Bacon loaf*

BACON LOAF

Serves 8-10

150 g (4 oz) streaky bacon, in one piece	*375 g (12 oz) bread mix*
	Flour for kneading

Below: *White loaf*

Dice the bacon, fry until brown and leave to cool. Combine the bread mix with 250 ml (8 fl oz) in a mixing bowl, following the instructions on the packet. Incorporate the bacon and leave the dough to rise.

Dust with flour, knead quickly, then shape into a smooth ball. Place on a greased baking sheet and leave to prove. Make a 1 cm (½ in) deep cut, pressing down very gently; then brush with water, dust with flour and bake in a preheated oven at 200-230° C (400-450° F, Gas Mark 6-8) for 40-50 minutes.

Above: *Pork brioche*

MEAT CRUST

Serves 8-10

375 g (12 oz) bread mix
100 g (3½ oz) Gouda cheese
200 g (7 oz) roast meat

125 g (4 oz) smoked ham
Flour for kneading
1 teaspoon sesame seeds to finish

Combine the bread mix with 250 ml (8 fl oz) warm water in a mixing bowl, following the instructions on the packet. Leave to rise. Grate the cheese coarsely, dice the roast meat and ham and incorporate all these ingredients in the dough. Dust with flour, quickly knead and shape into a smooth ball.

Place on a greased baking sheet and leave in a warm place to prove. Make 1 cm (½ in) deep incisions to form a lattice, pressing down very gently. Brush with water, sprinkle with the sesame seeds and bake in a preheated oven at 200-230° C (400-450° F, Gas Mark 6-8) for 50-60 minutes.

LINSEED LOAF

Serves 8-10

100 g (3½ oz) linseed
250 g (8 oz) cracked rye
250 g (8 oz) strong (bread) wheat flour
1 sachet powdered easy-blend yeast

1 heaped teaspoon caster sugar
1 heaped teaspoon salt
3 tablespoons oil
250 ml (8 fl oz) milk

Soak the linseed in 100 ml (3½ fl oz) hot water for 30 minutes. Combine the cracked rye, flour and yeast in a mixing bowl. Incorporate the sugar, salt, oil and milk, then work into a smooth dough using an electric mixer fitted with a kneading attachment for 5 minutes, first at low, then at high speed.

Add the linseed and leave the dough to rise in a warm place until clearly increased in bulk. Knead again thoroughly, then shape into an oval loaf. Place on a greased baking sheet and leave in a warm place to prove. Make a 1 cm (½ in) deep cut, pressing down gently. Brush with water and bake in a preheated oven at 200° C (400° F, Gas Mark 6) for 1 hour.

Note: linseed and cracked rye can be obtained from health food shops.

PORK BRIOCHE

Serves 8-10

375 g (12 oz) bread mix
Flour for kneading

1 kg (2 lb) boned pork loin, lightly salted

Combine the bread mix with 250 ml (8 fl oz) warm water in a mixing bowl, following the instructions on the packet. Leave the dough to rise, dust with flour, knead quickly and roll out on a floured surface into a strip twice the size of the pork joint, reserving any surplus dough.

Place the meat on the dough, brush the edges with water, bring the dough up over the meat and seal the edges. Place on a greased baking sheet. Plait the remaining dough and attach along the top of the bread case. Carefully make holes the size of a five-pence piece, then leave the dough in a warm place to prove. Brush with water and bake in a preheated oven at 200° C (400° F, Gas Mark 6) for 40-50 minutes.
Alternative: a boiled ham joint can be used instead of the pork loin.

PROVENÇAL HERB GRANARY BREAD

Serves 8-10

175 g (6 oz) bulgar
(cracked wheat)
250 g (8 oz) strong (bread)
flour
1 sachet powdered easy-
blend yeast

1 teaspoon icing sugar
2 teaspoons salt
3 tablespoons oil
2 teaspoons dried herbes
de Provence

Combine the bulgar, flour and baking powder in a mixing bowl. Incorporate the icing sugar, salt, oil and 200 ml (7 fl oz) warm water. Work into a smooth dough using an electric mixer for 5 minutes, first at low, then at high speed. Add the herbes de Provence.
Leave the dough to rise in a warm place until clearly increased in bulk. Knead again thoroughly.

Shape into a ball and place on a greased baking sheet. Leave in a warm place to prove. Make a 1 cm (½ in) deep cut in the dough, pressing down gently. Brush with water and bake in a preheated oven at
200° C (400°F (Gas Mark 6) for 50 minutes.

Below: *Provençal herb granary bread*

and 250 ml (8 fl oz) warm water in a mixing bowl, following the instructions on the packet. Incorporate the remaining butter, then leave the dough to rise. Dust with flour, quickly knead and roll out on a floured surface into a 36 x 36 cm (14 x 14 in) square.

Place half the sauerkraut mixture on the dough, arrange the sausages on top, then cover with the remaining sauerkraut. Fold over one side of the dough, brush with water, then fold over the other side. Press the edges of the dough together to seal them and crimp at both ends.

Place on a greased baking sheet, leave to prove in a warm place, brush with water and bake in a preheated oven at 200-230° C (400-450° F, Gas Mark 6-8) for 50 minutes.

Above: *Sauerkraut brioche*

SAUERKRAUT BRIOCHE

Serves 12-15

500 g (1 lb) tinned sauerkraut	*5 cloves*
2 knobs of butter	*375 g (12 oz) bread mix*
1 onion	*1-2 tablespoons cumin*
1 bay leaf	*4 smoked sausages*

Brown the sauerkraut in a knob of butter. Peel the onion, prick the bay leaf and cloves and add to the sauerkraut. Simmer for 15 minutes, remove the onion and leave the sauerkraut to cool.
For the dough: combine the dough mix with the cumin

RYE BREAD

Serves 12-15

250 g (8 oz) strong (bread) wheat flour	*1 sachet powdered easy-blend yeast*
125 g (4 oz) bulgar (cracked wheat)	*1 teaspoon caster sugar*
200 g (7 oz) cracked rye	*1-2 teaspoons salt*
	200 g (7 oz) sour dough

Combine the wheat flour, bulgar, cracked rye and yeast in a mixing bowl. Incorporate the sugar, salt and 300 ml (½ pint) warm water. Add the sour dough and knead using an electric mixer for 5 minutes, first at low, then at high speed.

Leave the dough to rise in a warm place until clearly increased in bulk. Knead thoroughly, then shape into an oval loaf. Place on a greased baking sheet and leave in a warm place to prove.

Brush with water and bake in a preheated oven at 200° C (400° F, Gas Mark 6) for 50-60 minutes, brushing with water occasionally while it is cooking to achieve a good crust.

Tip: if you cannot buy sour dough direct from your baker, use 200 g (7 oz) of the frozen sour dough mixture as described on page 442.

PARTY BREAD

Serves 12-15

1 500 g (1 lb) bloomer loaf
1 green pepper
1-2 tomatoes
1 tablespoon chopped
parsley

750 g (1½ lb) sausage
meat
40 g (1½ oz) butter,
melted

Cut the bread open at one end, reserving the heel. Remove the soft bread.

For the filling: halve, seed, core and wash the green pepper. Pour boiling water over the tomatoes, refresh in cold water, peel and remove the seeds. Chop the green pepper and tomatoes and combine with the parsley and sausage meat in a mixing bowl. Fill the bread, replace the heel, securing it with 2 cocktail sticks.

Place the loaf on a sheet of aluminium foil, cover with butter and fold up the foil. Bake in a preheated oven at 200° C (400° F, Gas Mark 6) for 1¼ hours. Serve hot or cold with a salad.

Below: *Party bread*

Above: *Sausage rolls*

SAUSAGE ROLLS

Makes 12

625 g (1¼ lb) frozen puff
pastry
12 sausages, about 15 cm

(6 in) long
1 tablespoon condensed
milk

Defrost the puff pastry at room temperature. Do not knead. Roll out into two 15 x 36 cm (6 x 14 in) rectangles. Cut each large rectangle into six 15 x 6 (6 x 2½ in) rectangles.

Place a sausage on each rectangle and brush the edges of the pastry with the condensed milk. Wrap the sausages in the pastry, place on a greased baking sheet, brush with condensed milk, then bake in a preheated oven at 200-230° C (400-450° F, Gas Mark 6-8) for 30 minutes.

SOUR DOUGH BREAD

Serves 10-12

400 g (13 oz) rye flour
300 g (10 oz) cracked rye
300 g (10 oz) bulgar
(cracked wheat)

200 g (7 oz) wholewheat
flour
1 tablespoon salt
20 g (¾ oz) fresh yeast

Combine 100 g (3½ oz) rye flour with 100 ml (3½ fl oz) warm water in a mixing bowl. Cover with a cloth, wrap in cling film and leave to rise in a warm place (20° C, 68° F) for 24 hours. Repeat the procedure and leave to prove for a further 24 hours; then add the remaining rye flour and 200 ml (7 fl oz) warm water and leave for 24 hours to rise for a third time.

Combine 500 g (1 lb) of this sour dough with the cracked rye, bulgar, wholewheat flour and salt. Mix the yeast with 250 ml (8 fl oz) warm water, incorporate gradually in the dough and knead into a stiff dough, adding a little water if necessary. Shape into a ball, dust with flour, cover with a cloth and leave to rise in a very warm place (30° C, 86° F) for 1 hour.

Place the dough in a floured wicker basket and leave to rest at room temperature for 2 hours until the surface begins to crack. Place the dough on a greased baking sheet and bake in a preheated oven at 240° C (475° F, Gas Mark 9) for the first 10 minutes, then at 230° C (450° F, Gas Mark 8) for 50 minutes.

Tip: you can either freeze the remaining sour dough or add enough flour to make a crumbly dough, which will keep in a refrigerator for 1 month. When ready to use, add enough water to restore it to its original consistency.

AUTUMN LOAF

Makes 2 rectangular loaves

500 g (1 lb) potatoes
500 g (1 lb) wholewheat
flour
40 g (1½ oz) fresh yeast
200 ml (7 fl oz) milk
3 knobs of butter,

softened
1 teaspoon salt
1 apple (Boskop, for
example)
200 g (7 oz) sunflower
seeds

Boil the potatoes, peel while still hot, then purée. Combine the potato purée and flour in a mixing bowl. Mix the yeast with 2-3 tablespoons warm water, then incorporate the milk, butter, salt and 200 ml (7 fl oz) warm water. Knead into an elastic dough.

Peel and finely grate the apple. Toast 150 g (5 oz) sunflower seeds in an ungreased frying pan for 5 minutes. Add to the dough, together with the grated apple. Leave to rise in a warm place for 1½ hours. Transfer to two greased loaf tins.

Sprinkle with the remaining sunflower seeds, leave to prove for 40 minutes and bake in a preheated oven at 230° C (450° F, Gas Mark 8) for 50-60 minutes. Turn the loaves out on to a wire rack and leave to cool.

Note: sunflower seeds are available from health food shops.

Opposite: *Autumn loaf*

COTTAGE CHEESE
AND YOGHURT ROLLS

Makes 12

40 g (1½ oz) fresh yeast
500 g (1 lb) wholewheat
flour
400 g (13 oz) cottage

cheese
1 teaspoon salt
1 egg yolk
3 tablespoons yoghurt

Mix the yeast with 3 tablespoons warm water and leave to rest in a warm place for 15 minutes. Incorporate the flour (reserving 2 tablespoons), cottage cheese, salt and 150 ml (¼ pint) warm water. Knead into an elastic dough. Dust with the reserved flour, cover and leave to rise for 1 hour until doubled in bulk.

Knead again, flour your hands and divide the dough into twelve small balls. Place on a greased baking sheet. Mix the egg yolk with the yoghurt and brush over the rolls. Leave to prove for 15 minutes and bake in a preheated oven at 200° C (400° F, Gas Mark 6) for 20 minutes.

CHESTNUT ROLLS

Makes 10

20 g (¾ oz) fresh yeast
300 g (10 oz) wholewheat
flour
100-150 ml (3½ fl oz-¼
pint) warm milk

50 g (2 oz) caster sugar
⅓ teaspoon salt
75 g (3 oz) butter
250 g (8 oz) chestnuts

Mix the yeast with 2 tablespoons warm water and leave to rest in a warm place for 15 minutes. Incorporate the flour, milk, sugar, salt and 50 g (2 oz) butter, then knead into a smooth dough. Cover and leave to rise for 1 hour until doubled in bulk.

Cut a cross in the chestnuts, place in boiling water for 5-10 minutes until the skin peels back. Peel, quarter and brown the chestnuts for 5 minutes in the remaining butter. Leave to cool, then incorporate in the dough.

Make 10 small balls of dough. Place on a floured baking sheet. Cut a cross in the tops and leave to prove for 15 minutes. Bake in a preheated oven at 180-200° C (350-400° F, Gas Mark 4-6) for 20-25 minutes.

CABBAGE LEAF RYE BREAD

Makes 2 round loaves

20 g (¾ oz) fresh yeast
500 g (1 lb) rye flour
200 g (7 oz) wholewheat
flour
200 g (7 oz) cottage
cheese

1 tablespoon salt
1 tablespoon cumin
1 tablespoon aniseed
12 large leaves from a
Savoy or white cabbage

Mix the yeast with 3 tablespoons warm water and leave to rest in a warm place for 15 minutes. Incorporate the rye flour, wholewheat flour, cottage cheese, salt, cumin, aniseed and 400 ml (14 fl oz) warm water. Knead into a stiff dough. Dust with flour, cover and leave to rise in a warm place for 1 hour until doubled in bulk. Shape into two balls.

Wash and drain the cabbage leaves. Wrap around the balls of dough, then place on a greased baking sheet. Leave in a warm place for 1 hour to prove. Bake in a preheated oven at 230° C (450° F, Gas Mark 8) for 1 hour. Peel off the cabbage leaves and leave the bread to cool.

Opposite: *Cottage cheese and yoghurt rolls*

BREAD ROLL CLUSTER

Makes 16 rolls

20 g (¾ oz) fresh yeast
500 g (1 lb) wholewheat flour
250 ml (8 fl oz) warm milk

1 teaspoon salt
8 tablespoons nibbed and flaked almonds and sesame seeds

Mix the yeast with 2 tablespoons warm water. Leave to rest in a warm place for 15 minutes. Incorporate the wholewheat flour, milk and salt, then knead into an elastic dough. Leave to rise for 1-2 hours, knead again and make into 16 small balls.

Sprinkle each roll with the almonds or sesame seeds. Place the rolls in a cluster on a greased baking sheet so that they touch. Leave to prove for 30 minutes. Bake in a preheated oven at 230° C (450° F, Gas Mark 8) for 20 minutes.

BARLEY BREAD

Serves about 8

30 g (1¼ oz) fresh yeast
1 tablespoon honey
300 g (10 oz) wholewheat flour

300 g (10 oz) barley flour
300 ml (½ pint) warm milk
2 250 ml (8 fl oz) cups sprouted barley

Mix the yeast with 3 tablespoons warm water. Incorporate the honey and leave to rest in a warm place for 15 minutes. Add the wholewheat and barley flours, milk and sprouted barley. Knead into an elastic dough. Leave to rise in a warm place for 1 hour.

Knead again, make into a ball and place on a floured baking sheet. Cut a cross in the top, brush with water, dust with flour and leave to prove for 1 hour. Bake in a preheated oven at 240° C (475° F, Gas Mark 9) for the first 10 minutes, then at 230° C (450° F, Gas Mark 8) for 50 minutes.

Note: barley flour and sprouted barley are available from food shops.

Opposite: *Bread roll cluster*

MUFFINS

Makes 6-8

250 g (8 oz) cornflour
1 teaspoon baking powder
300 ml (½ pint) warm
yoghurt
2 eggs

40 g (1½ oz) butter,
melted
1 teaspoon honey
½ teaspoon salt
50 g (2 oz) pumpkin seeds

Sift the cornflour and baking powder together. Combine the yoghurt, eggs, butter, honey and salt, then stir into the flour to form a smooth dough. Coarsely crush the pumpkin seeds and incorporate in the mixture. Turn the mixture into 6-8 greased, fluted tartlet tins and bake in a preheated oven at 200° C (400° F, Gas Mark 6) for 30 minutes. Leave to cool slightly before removing the tins. Serve warm with butter.

OAT BREAD

Serves 8-10

20 g (¾ oz) fresh yeast
400 g (13 oz) wholewheat
flour
250 ml (8 fl oz) beer

1-2 teaspoons salt
4 onions
3 knobs of butter
200 g (7 oz) rolled oats

Mix the yeast with 3 tablespoons warm water and leave to rest in a warm place for 15 minutes. Incorporate the flour, beer and salt, then knead into a stiff dough. Dust with flour, cover and leave to rise for 1 hour until doubled in bulk.

Peel and chop the onions, then brown in 2 knobs of butter. Fry the rolled oats in the remaining butter for 5 minutes until golden, then incorporate the onions.

Grease a loaf tin. Divide the dough into 20 portions, roll them out to the same length as the tin and spread a little onion-oat mixture over each one. Place them one on top of the other in the tin, leave to prove for 1 hour, then bake in a preheated oven at 200° C (400° F, Gas Mark 6) for 1 hour. Leave to cool in the tin.

MUSHROOM BREAD

Makes 2 loaves

50 g (2 oz) dried
mushrooms
20 g (¾ oz) fresh yeast
500 g (1 lb) wholewheat
flour

500 g (1 lb) bulgar
(cracked wheat)
1 teaspoon salt
2 tablespoons walnut oil

Soak the mushrooms in 500 ml (18 fl oz) boiling water for 2 hours. Drain, reserving the liquid. Add water to make the liquid up to 500 ml (18 fl oz). Chop the mushrooms.

Mix the yeast with 2-3 tablespoons warm water, then leave to rest in a warm place for 15 minutes. Incorporate the mushrooms, mushroom juice, flour, bulgar and salt. Knead into an elastic dough.

Dust the dough with flour, cover and leave to rise for 1 hour until doubled in bulk. Knead again, make into two long, thin rolls of dough, then place on a floured baking sheet. Leave to prove for 1 hour. Brush with the walnut oil and bake in a preheated oven at 230° C (450° F, Gas Mark 8) for 45 minutes.

Opposite: *Muffins*

VEGETARIAN
WHOLEMEAL STOTTIES

Makes 4

1 250 ml (8 fl oz) cup
sprouted wheat
1 250 ml (8 fl oz) cup
sprouted rye
1 250 ml (8 fl oz) cup
sprouted barley
1 teaspoon walnut oil

½ teaspoon salt flavoured
with herbs
A pinch of freshly ground
white pepper
3 tablespoons sesame
seeds

Chop the sprouted wheat, rye and barley finely. Add the walnut oil, flavoured salt and pepper, then make into four small, flat cakes. Sprinkle with the sesame seeds.

Place on a baking sheet lined with oiled greaseproof paper and bake in a preheated oven at 150° C (300° F, Gas Mark 2) for 1 hour with the oven door ajar, turning the stotties over half-way through cooking.

Suggestion: the pancakes can also be sprinkled with sunflower or marrow seeds, walnuts, small sprouted seeds (alfalfa, cress, etc.), cumin or aniseed, for example.

FILLED PANCAKES

Makes 4

15 g (½ oz) fresh yeast
250 g (8 oz) wholewheat
flour
½ teaspoon salt
100 g (3½ oz) butter

1 onion, peeled
1 clove garlic, peeled
½ teaspoon cumin
½ teaspoon coriander
½ teaspoon nutmeg

Combine the yeast with 2-3 tablespoons warm water in a mixing bowl. Incorporate the flour, salt and 6-8 tablespoons warm water. Knead into a smooth dough. Dust with flour, cover and leave to rise in a warm place for 1 hour until doubled in bulk. Divide the dough into four and roll out into four 15 x 36 cm (6 x 14 in) rectangles.

For the filling: reduce the butter, onion, garlic, cumin, coriander and nutmeg to a purée in a frying pan.

Spoon this filling on to the centres of the four rectangles of dough. Fold up the edges. Roll the rectangles out again to their original size. Fold them in three and leave

Above: *Vegetarian wholemeal stotties*

to prove for 1 hour. Prick both sides of the pancakes with a fork. Fry in an ungreased frying pan over medium heat for 10 minutes each side. Serve immediately.

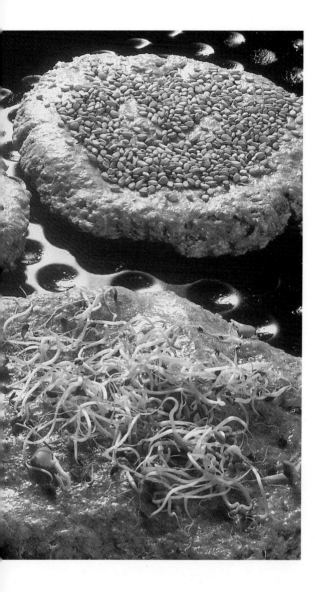

PAN-FRIED MILLET BREAD

Serves 5-6

200 g (7 oz) millet meal
30 g (1¼ oz) fresh yeast
7 teaspoons honey
200 g (7 oz) wholewheat flour
100-150 ml (3½ fl oz-¼ pint) warm milk

1 teaspoon salt
1 teaspoon cardamom seeds
2 teaspoons sunflower or corn oil
4 tablespoons millet seeds

Soak the millet meal in 300 ml (½ pint) water overnight, then drain.

Mix the yeast with 3 tablespoons warm water. Incorporate 1 teaspoon honey and leave to rest in a warm place for 15 minutes. Incorporate the millet meal and wheat flour, milk, salt, cardamom seeds and the remaining honey. Knead into an elastic dough. Cover and leave to rise in a warm place for 1 hour.

Put 1 teaspoon sunflower or corn oil and 2 teaspoons millet seeds in a frying pan.

Roll out a circle of dough the size of the frying pan and leave to prove in the pan for 30 minutes. Cover and cook each side over medium heat for 15 minutes. When turning the bread over, add the remaining oil and millet seeds. When cooked, sprinkle any remaining toasted seeds from the bottom of the pan over the bread. Serve hot or cold.

Note: millet meal and seeds are available from health food shops.

PITTA BREAD

Serves 8-10

30 g (1¼ oz) fresh yeast
1 tablespoon honey
500 g (1 lb) wholewheat flour

3 tablespoons olive oil
A pinch of salt
2 tablespoons sesame seeds

Mix the yeast with 3 tablespoons warm water. Incorporate the honey and leave to rest in a warm place for 15 minutes. Add the flour, olive oil, salt and 250 ml (8 fl oz) warm water, then knead into an elastic dough. Dust with flour, cover and leave to rise for 1 hour until doubled in bulk. Shape into a 30 cm (12 in) round cake and place on a greased baking sheet. Sprinkle with the sesame seeds and leave to prove for 30 minutes. Bake in a preheated oven at 230° C (450° F, Gas Mark 8) for 20 minutes.

PIZZAS AND PANCAKES

MINI-PIZZAS

Makes 12

20 g (¾ oz) fresh yeast
300 g (10 oz) wholewheat
flour
6 tablespoons corn oil
Salt
1 bunch parsley
1 bunch sorrel
2 cloves garlic
300 g (10 oz) carrots
300 g (10 oz) small, firm

tomatoes
300 g (10 oz) small
courgettes
300 g (10 oz) Mozzarella
cheese
Freshly ground black
pepper
1 tablespoon chopped
basil

Combine the yeast with 2-3 tablespoons warm water in a mixing bowl. Incorporate the flour, 200 ml (7 fl oz) warm water, 1 tablespoon corn oil, ½ teaspoon salt and the finely chopped parsley, sorrel and garlic. Knead the dough, then leave to rise in a warm place for 1 hour. Flour your hands, divide the dough into twelve and make twelve thin pizza bases.

For the topping: peel and wash the carrots. Cut into 5 mm (¼ in) thick slices. Brown in 1 tablespoon corn oil, add a little salt, then cook gently over a low heat for 10 minutes. Wash the tomatoes and cut into 8 mm (⅓ in) thick slices. Wash the courgettes, remove the ends and cut into 5 mm (¼ in) thick slices. Drain and dice the Mozzarella cheese.

Place the courgettes on top of four pizzas, the carrots on another four and the tomatoes on the remaining four. Scatter the cheese over all of them and season with salt and pepper. Place the pizzas on two greased baking sheets and bake separately in a preheated oven at 180-200° C (350-400° F, Gas Mark 4-6) for 25-30 minutes. Brush with the remaining corn oil, sprinkle with the chopped basil, and serve very hot.

SPROUTED PEA PIZZAS

Makes 4

30 g (1¼ oz) fresh yeast
400 g (13 oz) wholewheat
flour
7 tablespoons walnut oil
2 onions
1 clove garlic, crushed
Salt
Freshly ground pepper
1 kg (2 lb) tomatoes
1 250 ml (8 fl oz) cup

sprouted peas
1 250 ml (8 fl oz) cup
sprouted chick peas
1 250 ml (8 fl oz) cup
sprouted red lentils
1 250 ml (8 fl oz) cup
sprouted yellow lentils
4 tablespoons Parmesan
cheese, grated

Combine the yeast with 3-4 tablespoons warm water in a mixing bowl. Incorporate the flour, 200 ml (7 fl oz) warm water and 2 tablespoons walnut oil. Knead into an elastic dough.

Peel and chop the onions. Brown in 1 tablespoon walnut oil. Add the crushed garlic, salt and pepper, then knead into the dough. Leave to rise in a warm place for 30 minutes. Divide into four and roll out four 25 cm (10 in) diameter pizza bases. Place on two greased baking sheets.

For the topping: wash and slice the tomatoes and place on the pizza bases. Season with salt and pepper and place a different variety of sprouted peas on each quarter of each pizza. Leave to rise for 15 minutes, then bake in a preheated oven at 180-200° C (350-400° F, Gas Mark 4-6) for 25 minutes. Brush the pizzas with the remaining walnut oil, sprinkle with Parmesan and serve very hot.

Note: pea seeds are available from health food shops.

Opposite: *Sprouted pea pizzas*
Pages 452 and 453: *Mini-pizzas*

EMPANADAS
(Small, Spanish pasties)

Makes about 12

200 g (7 oz) wholewheat flour	250 ml (8 fl oz) sprouted kidney beans
100 g (3½ oz) cornflour	2 tablespoons tomato purée
100 g (3½ oz) butter	
1 egg	100 g (3½ oz) Parmesan cheese, grated
1 teaspoon salt	
1 onion	1 small green pepper, chopped
2 cloves garlic	
250 g (8 oz) tomatoes	2 tablespoons chopped parsley
10 black olives	
2 tablespoons olive oil	Freshly ground pepper

Combine the flour, cornflour, butter, egg, 1-3 tablespoons water and ¼ teaspoon salt in a mixing bowl. Knead into a stiff dough. Leave to rest for 1 hour at room temperature.

For the filling: peel and chop the onion and garlic. Pour boiling water over the tomatoes, refresh under cold water, peel and dice. Stone and finely chop the black olives.

Heat the olive oil in a frying pan, brown the onion, add the garlic, tomatoes, olives, sprouted beans and tomato purée. Leave this sauce to simmer for 10 minutes. Quickly blend it together using an electric mixer. Incorporate the grated Parmesan cheese, chopped green pepper and parsley. Season with salt and pepper to taste.

Roll the dough out until 5 mm (¼ in) thick, then cut into 12 cm (4½ in) diameter circles. Place a little filling in the centre of each circle and fold in half. Crimp the edges to seal them. Place the pasties on a greased baking sheet and bake in a preheated oven at 230° C (450° F, Gas Mark 8) for 15-20 minutes.

Note: kidney beans are available from health food shops.

Above: *Sauerkraut boats*

SAUERKRAUT BOATS

Makes 6-8

200 g (7 oz) rye flour	300 g (10 oz) tinned sauerkraut
200 g (7 oz) wholewheat flour	
	1 cooking apple
20 g (¾ oz) fresh yeast	50 g (2 oz) whole walnuts
1 teaspoon honey	Freshly ground pepper
2 onions	2-3 tablespoons walnut oil
1 tablespoon corn oil	

Combine the rye and wheat flours in a mixing bowl. Make a well in the centre. Mix the yeast with 3-4 tablespoons warm water and the honey in a separate bowl. Pour into the well and mix with a little flour.

CHEESE SAMOSAS
(Small, Indian pasties)

Makes 10-15

1 tablespoon chopped parsley	12 tablespoons sunflower oil
100 g (3½ oz) Gorgonzola cheese	200 g (7 oz) potatoes
250 g (8 oz) wholewheat flour	200 g (7 oz) onions
½ teaspoon salt	1 clove garlic
	1 teaspoon mustard seeds
	1 teaspoon curry powder

Combine the flour, salt, 2 tablespoons sunflower oil and 150 ml (¼ pint) cold water in a mixing bowl. Knead into an elastic dough. Make into a ball, brush with 1 tablespoon sunflower oil, wrap in a tea towel and leave to rest for 2 hours at room temperature.

For the filling: boil the potatoes in a pan, peel, then dice them. Peel and coarsely chop the onions and garlic. Heat 1 tablespoon sunflower oil to brown the onion and garlic. Incorporate the mustard seeds and curry powder and cook gently over a low heat for 7 minutes. Add the potatoes and the chopped parsley and continue cooking gently for a few minutes. Leave to cool. Crumble the Gorgonzola cheese with a fork and add to the filling.

Remove the dough from the tea towel and make into 3 cm (1¼ in) diameter balls. Roll out into small circles of dough, cut in half, place 1 teaspoon of the filling in each, brush the edges with water, fold up the dough to make semi-circles, then crimp the edges.

Heat the remaining sunflower oil and fry the samosas on both sides until golden. Serve very hot.

Cover and leave to rest in a warm place for 15 minutes. Incorporate 250 ml (8 fl oz) warm water, knead thoroughly and leave to rise for 30 minutes.

For the filling: peel and dice the onions, then brown them in the corn oil in a large frying pan. Add the sauerkraut. Peel the apple and chop into small pieces. Crush the walnuts coarsely. Add the apple and walnuts to the sauerkraut, together with the pepper.

Shape the dough into long, high-sided boats, fill with sauerkraut, place on a greased baking sheet and leave to prove for 30 minutes. Bake in a preheated oven at 200-230° C (400-450° F, Gas Mark 6-8) for 25 minutes. Drizzle with walnut oil as soon as they are out of the oven.

OLIVE-FILLED ROLLS

Makes 30

40 g (1½ oz) fresh yeast
625 g (1¼ lb) wholewheat flour
3 tablespoons olive oil
4 teaspoons dried herbes de Provence
1 teaspoon salt
150 g (5 oz) green olives stuffed with pimento
150 g (5 oz) blanched almonds
200 g (7 oz) Ricotta or cream cheese
200 g (7 oz) cottage cheese
1 red pepper

Combine the yeast with 100-150 ml (3½ fl oz-¼ pint) water in a mixing bowl. Incorporate the flour, salt, 300 ml (½ pint) warm water and 3 teaspoons herbes de Provence. Knead into an elastic dough. Leave to rise in a warm place for 1 hour until doubled in bulk.

For the filling: purée the olives and almonds in a bowl, add the Ricotta or cream cheese, the cottage cheese and the remaining herbes de Provence.

Make thirty small balls of dough. Make a hole in each with your thumb, then place on a greased baking sheet. Place 1 teaspoon filling in each hole. Leave to rise for 15 minutes, then bake in a preheated oven at 180-200° C (350-400° F, Gas Mark 4-6) for 25 minutes.

Wash, halve and core the red pepper. Cut into very thin strips, garnish the rolls and serve them very hot.

Opposite: *Olive-filled rolls*

TORTILLAS AU GRATIN

Makes 6

100 g (3½ oz) wholewheat flour
100 g (3½ oz) cornflour
2 teaspoons salt
11 tablespoons corn oil
1 aubergine
1 onion
200 g (7 oz) tomatoes

1 clove garlic
1 tablespoon green peppercorns
½ teaspoon chopped basil
Freshly ground pepper
150 g (5 oz) Mozzarella cheese

Combine the flour, cornflour, 300 ml (½ pint) water and 1 teaspoon salt in a mixing bowl. Heat 10 tablespoons oil in a frying pan over a high heat and make six 15 cm (6 in) diameter pancakes, cooking them on both sides. Keep warm.

For the filling: wash the aubergine and cut into 1 cm (½ in) thick slices. Sprinkle with the remaining salt and set aside for 15 minutes. Wipe and dice the slices. Heat the remaining oil and brown the diced aubergine.

Peel and chop the onion, then brown with the aubergine.

Wash and slice the tomatoes, add to the aubergine and onion, then cook gently over a low heat for 10 minutes.

Peel and crush the garlic, then add to the sauce. Season with the green peppercorns, basil and pepper. Drain the Mozzarella cheese, then cut into thin strips.

Fill the tortillas with the vegetables and cheese, then arrange them at an angle in a baking tin.
Cook in a preheated oven at 180° C (350° F, Gas Mark 4) for 20 minutes.

MUSHROOM PIROSHKI

Makes about 8

250 g (8 oz) wholewheat flour
150 ml (¼ pint) crème fraîche
1 egg
3 knobs of butter
1 teaspoon salt
1 onion

100 g (3½ oz) tinned sauerkraut
500 g (1 lb) mushrooms
Freshly ground pepper
A pinch of nutmeg
A pinch of sweet paprika
2 tablespoons chopped parsley

Combine the flour, egg, 100 ml (3½ fl oz) crème fraîche, 1 knob butter and ½ teaspoon salt in a mixing bowl. Knead into a stiff dough. Wrap in cling film and leave to rest in a refrigerator overnight.

For the filling: peel and dice the onion. Finely chop the sauerkraut. Wash and coarsely chop the mushrooms. Heat the remaining butter, brown the onion, followed by the sauerkraut and mushrooms. Season with the remaining salt, the pepper, nutmeg and paprika. Bring to the boil, then simmer for 10 minutes, stirring occasionally. Incorporate the parsley and the remaining crème fraîche.

Roll the dough out as thinly as possible, then cut out 10 cm (4 in) diameter circles. Place the filling in the centre, dampen the edges, and fold up the dough. Place on a greased baking sheet. Bake in a preheated oven at 230° C (450° F, Gas Mark 8) for 15 minutes. Serve hot with vegetable stock or crème fraîche.

Opposite: *Tortillas au gratin*

FLORENTINE PANCAKES

Serves 8-10

300 g (10 oz) wholewheat flour	1 clove garlic
1 teaspoon salt	Freshly ground pepper
1 teaspoon lemon juice	150 g (5 oz) Parmesan cheese
14 tablespoons olive oil	500 g (1 lb) tomatoes
2 kg (4½ lb) spinach, with stems	65 g (2½ oz) pine kernels

Combine the flour, salt, lemon juice and 6 tablespoons oil in a mixing bowl. Knead into a stiff dough, gradually adding 250 ml (8 fl oz) water. Brush with 2 tablespoons oil, cover and leave to rest in a warm place for 1 hour.

Divide the dough into six, roll out six 25 cm (10 in) diameter circles on a floured tea towel, then wrap in cling film to keep them moist.

For the filling: wash the spinach, then cook in 1 tablespoon oil, stirring occasionally. Peel and finely chop the garlic, then add to the spinach. Season with salt and pepper. Grate 100 g (3½ oz) Parmesan cheese. Wash the tomatoes and cut into thin slices. Crush 50 g (2 oz) pine kernels.

Place a circle of dough on the base of a cake tin, brush with 1 tablespoon oil, sprinkle with 25 g (1 oz) grated Parmesan and 7 g (¼ oz) crushed pine kernels, then cover with spinach and sliced tomato.

Brush another dough circle with 1 tablespoon oil and place on top of the first one, oiled side down. Bake in a preheated oven at 240° C (475° F, Gas Mark 9) for 10 minutes.

Take out of the oven, brush with 1 tablespoon oil and place the ingredients on top, as above. Cover with a third dough circle, bake, then repeat the procedure until all the dough circles have been used. Sprinkle the remaining Parmesan and pine kernels over the final dough circle before baking. Serve hot.

Above: *Florentine pancakes*

KASHMIR NAAN BREAD
(Filled bread pockets from Kashmir)

Makes 6

30 g (1¼ oz) fresh yeast	seeds
750 g (1½ lb) wholewheat flour	75 g (3 oz) walnuts
	75 g (3 oz) cashew nuts
150 ml (¼ pint) yoghurt	75 g (3 oz) almonds
200 ml (7 fl oz) milk	75 g (3 oz) dried apricots
2 eggs	75 g (3 oz) raisins
1 teaspoon salt	5 tablespoons walnut oil
4 knobs of butter	1 teaspoon cinnamon
1 piece root ginger, walnut-sized	1 teaspoon grated lemon rind
1 teaspoon cardamom	

FETA PASTY

Serves 8-10

500 g (1 lb) wholewheat flour	300 g (10 oz) Feta cheese
250 g (8 oz) butter	100 g (3½ oz) green olives stuffed with pimento
750 g (1½ lb) cream cheese	1 egg yolk
4 eggs	50 g (2 oz) pine kernels

Combine the flour, butter, 250 g (8 oz) cream cheese and 2 eggs in a mixing bowl. Knead into an elastic dough. Cover and leave to rest at room temperature for 1 hour.

For the filling: combine the remaining cream cheese, the Feta cheese, sliced olives and 2 eggs in a mixing bowl.

Roll out into a 60 x 20 cm (24 x 8 in) strip of dough very thinly on a floured tea towel. Stretch it out a further 5 cm (2 in) along a 15 cm (6 in) section of one of the ends. Spread the filling over the dough, leaving a 15 cm (6 in) strip of dough clear on the narrow end. Fold this strip over the filling, then completely cover the filling, crimping the edges of the dough to seal.

Place on a greased sheet of aluminium foil with slightly raised sides. Brush with the egg yolk, sprinkle with the pine kernels and bake in a preheated oven at 200° C (400° F, Gas Mark 6) for 1 hour. Cut into slices as soon as it is out of the oven. Serve hot or cold.

Mix the yeast with 2 tablespoons warm water. Incorporate the flour, yoghurt, warm milk, eggs, salt and 2 knobs of butter. Knead, then leave to rise for 1 hour.

For the filling: peel and finely chop the ginger. Add the cardamom seeds. Crush the walnuts and almonds. Dice the apricots, then combine them with the walnuts, almonds, raisins, walnut oil, cinnamon, lemon rind, ginger and cardamom.

Divide the dough into six and roll out into six oval shapes. Add the filling, fold over the dough to form pointed oval shapes, then place on a greased baking sheet.
Brush with the remaining butter, leave to prove for 15 minutes, then bake in a preheated oven at 230° C (450° F, Gas Mark 8) for 15 minutes.

USEFUL TIPS

Cakes and biscuits are often baked for special occasions. Cakes are perfect for celebrations, such as weddings, christenings, birthdays or anniversaries. Baking biscuits is especially important when preparing for the high point of the culinary year: Christmas.

The art of baking
Traditionally, cakes are usually round. Originally, round pancakes were eaten at the winter solstice to represent the sun.

There are many different types of cake tin: smooth-sided, sliding-based cake tins, fluted ring moulds and sandwich tins. Springform cake tins are made of tin or aluminium (ideal for gas ovens) or steel, which is perfect for electric ovens.

With Teflon-coated cake tins, your cakes are guaranteed not to stick. But whatever tin you use, all you have to do to prevent the cake from sticking is to grease it thoroughly, then coat it with breadcrumbs or line it with greaseproof paper. Fluted flan dishes are used for fruit flans. They are often ceramic, sometimes even porcelain or ovenproof glass, the advantage of these being that the flan can be served at the table straight from the oven. There are also small, individual tins for baking delicious tartlets using all sorts of fruits.

The base of the cake
Let's start with the main part of the cake. It is frequently a Genoese sponge cut into two or more layers. Pastry, such as sweet pastry, is often used as a tart base. It is generally heavier and richer than sponge cake as it contains butter as well as flour, sugar and eggs. That is why it is preferable to fill tarts with fruit rather than confectioner's custard or butter cream.
It is best to make the Genoese sponge the night before, as then it is easier to cut and spread.
It is important for the appearance of the cake that the surface is even. If, while cooking, small bumps appear, they can be smoothed out when the cake is taken out of the oven using a very sharp knife. Another solution is simply to turn the sponge upside down so that the smoother side is uppermost.

There are two ways of cutting

Genoese sponges into layers: you can either use a very long-bladed knife, or you can run round the sides of the cake with a pointed knife, before cutting through the centre with a thread slipped into where the cut made by the knife (photographs opposite).

It is best to place the layers of sponge on stiff paper, such as greaseproof paper, when moving the layers of sponge.

The filling
Genoese sponges can be filled with whipped cream, butter cream, confectioner's custard or jam. When the cream has been prepared, it is spread over each layer using a spatula or broad-bladed knife, before being covered with the next layer. The top and sides of the cake can be decorated traditionally or you can use your own original ideas. Sachertorte is always coated in

chocolate. Malakoff has a white coating of cream decorated with glacé cherries and more cream. Other cakes can be covered with butter cream and then sprinkled with nibbed toasted almonds or walnuts.

For icing and decorating cakes, you do need some equipment, such as a spatula, an icing syringe or bag with

a variety of nozzles, not to mention a brush for coating with jam or icing, and a palette knife or other broad-bladed knife for smoothing out the filling and the icing.

The icing

Instead of filling a cake, it can be enough just to ice it. There are numerous sugar icings which can be flavoured as you like, usually with lemon or orange juice, rum, maraschino, kirsch or brandy. Nearly all fruit flavourings can be used to add taste or colour to icings.

The most popular icing is usually chocolate. You can make this yourself by melting grated chocolate, icing sugar and a little milk and butter in a bowl over a pan of hot water before spreading it over the cake. Other chocolate icings are available ready-made from the shops.

The chocolate must have a high cocoa content (more than 50%). For this reason, superfine cooking chocolate is best for icings. It must be melted in a bowl over a pan of hot water over a very low heat so that it does not lose its glossiness. Cool the coating slightly, then pour on to the middle of the warm cake and spread

over the top and sides using a broad-bladed knife.

American frosting uses egg whites whisked into stiff peaks. The frosting is put into an icing bag and then piped on to the cake.

Other icings

Confectioner's custard and butter cream are used both to fill and to decorate cakes.

When using an icing bag, the nozzle must be held absolutely upright. Squeeze the bag with one hand and guide the nozzle with the other.

It is important to work quickly so that the icing does not become warm and soft.

Stencils can also be used to decorate cakes. Simply cut out the stencils, position them on the cake and dredge with sifted cocoa powder or icing sugar.

Biscuits

Biscuits are very popular, whether they are made from sweet pastry or macaroon mixtures. They are just the right thing to have with a cup of tea or coffee and there is no end of variety: gingerbreadmen, coconut biscuits, macaroons, cinnamon stars and Viennese whirls.

Spiced cakes and biscuits

Spiced cakes and biscuits are often made using honey. It is essential that the honey is runny when it comes to be used. For real continental spiced biscuits to be eaten at Christmas, the mixture is made as early as September of October.

In that case, the only raising agent which can be used is bicarbonate of soda. If baking powder is used, the mixture must be baked immediately.

In England, such spice mixtures are used for gingerbread and gingerbread men. In France, pain d'épice is usually in the form of a cake, while the Germans make it into round sponge biscuits called Lebkuchen. Dijon is the French capital of spiced cakes, while Nuremberg is the German capital, but they are also a speciality of Basel (Switzerland), Deventer (The Netherlands), Metz (France) and Gdansk (Poland).

Macaroons

It must not be thought that macaroons have any connection with 'macaroni'. Originally, macaroons were almond biscuits, but over time the ingredients have changed and nowadays hazelnuts are used, as are walnuts or even desiccated coconut or almond paste. Macaroon mixture uses egg whites which must be of a suitable consistency for piping. It is best to bake them on greaseproof paper. They can also be piped on to a sweet pastry base. Macaroons are baked only for a short time. They must be taken out of the oven while still soft to the touch, as they continue to dry out as they cool. If they are baked for too long, they will be hard and dry.

If you like them moist and succulent, they are best eaten soon, although they will keep very well in a tin. Placing a slice of bread in the tin keeps them fresh for even longer.

Sweet pastry biscuits

The greatest variety of biscuits can be made using sweet pastry. All sorts of ingredients can be added, such as walnuts, almonds, chocolate or almond paste, and the pastry then used as you wish.

It can be rolled out, then cut into all sorts of shapes, such as hearts, stars, animals or half-moons, using a pastry cutter, or just into circles using different-sized cups.

Alternatively, instead of rolling out the dough, it can be shaped into balls, pretzels, plaits, fish-shapes or rings. Some biscuits can be piped using an icing bag or syringe, in which case it is important to chill the mixture before using. When cooked, biscuits made using sweet pastry must be removed from the baking sheet immediately and left to cool on a wire rack. They can then be stored in an air-tight tin.

Sweetmeats

If you are looking for that very special something to impress your guests or family, it is well worth taking the time to make your own sweetmeats. They are also a very original present, especially if wrapped up prettily.

It is best to put chocolate whirls in paper cases. They highlight the sweets, as well as separating them to prevent them from sticking together. When drying, chocolate sweetmeats do not respond well to sudden changes in temperature. They must therefore be left at room temperature and not in a refrigerator. This way, they will lose none of their gloss.

Biscuits stick to baking sheet

When cooked, it is important not only to take the biscuits out of the oven immediately, but also to take them off the baking sheet. If this is not done, they will stick and they will be hard to remove without spoiling them.

If you forget to take them off straight away, re-heat the oven to the correct temperature, return the baking sheet to the oven and let the biscuits warm

HOW TO AVOID PROBLEMS WHEN BAKING

Crumbly pastry

It just needs a little liquid. Make a well in the centre of the pastry and add a little milk.

Mix it in carefully, using a fork, then knead the pastry into a smooth ball.

Dough will not rise

Either your kitchen is too cold - it must be 22oC (72oF) - or you did not heat the milk before mixing it with the yeast. The yeast must be mixed with a liquid which is roughly at body temperature, i.e. 36° C (96.8° F).

through. You will then be able to remove them easily - but you must do so immediately!

Biscuits break when removed from the baking sheet
Bake them on greaseproof paper. Not only does this mean there is no need to grease the baking sheet, but it also avoids any problems when removing the biscuits from the baking sheet. A further advantage is that the baking sheet will not have to be washed. Greaseproof paper can be used several times.

Egg whites will not whisk into stiff peaks
A little egg yolk has probably got in with the whites. Remove it carefully using a piece of eggshell.

Lumpy gelatine
The mixture in which the gelatine is incorporated must not be too cold. It should be at room temperature. Gelatine does not dissolve at temperatures below 15oC (59oF).

Raisins sink to bottom while cooking
The mixture is too runny. If the mixture does not drop from a spoon, the raisins will stay where they are when you have transferred the mixture to the cake tin. The solution is to add a little mixture.
Macaroons stick to greaseproof paper when cooked
Remove the macaroons from the baking sheet with the greaseproof

paper. Place the paper on a damp tea towel. Leave for a short while, then the macaroons will come off easily.

Meringues sink when cooked
Take the meringues out of the oven as soon as they start to colour. Carefully remove them from the baking sheet with a knife and return them to the oven to finish baking.

Cake sinks while cooking
Perhaps you have used more liquid than the recipe stated. Alternatively, the mixture could have been beaten for too long with an electric mixer. In both cases, the mixture starts to rise, but sinks while cooking. It is therefore very important to stick to the quantities stated in the recipe and not to beat the mixture for too long with an electric mixer or spoon. In both cases, adding a little extra mixture will avoid disaster.

Oil and cream cheese pastry is too soft
This is often due to the cream or cottage cheese being too moist. It is therefore always advisable to drain the cheese carefully before use or to press it dry in a tea towel.

Baked cheesecake sinks
It is worth knowing that baked cheesecakes always shrink, particularly in the centre. For this reason, you should always put a little more mixture in the centre than at the sides. When the cooking time is over, the cheesecake must always be left in the oven with the door closed until the temperature has fallen.

Burnt cake
All you can do is scrape off the burnt crust with a very sharp knife or, if the damage is more serious, cut off the burnt layer. It is best to cover the cake with icing to disguise the damage.

Soggy fruit tart pastry
Many types of fruit make juice when cooking.
Sprinkling the pastry with bread-crumbs before adding the fruit will prevent it from becoming soggy.

Problems cutting cream-filled cakes
Dividing the top layer of the cake into the required number of portions before placing it on the layer of cream filling will stop the cake from being ruined.

Air bubbles in fluted ring cakes
You have beaten the mixture too vigorously when incorporating the flour. It is best to add 2-3 table-spoons flour at a time, giving each addition a short stir immediately.

Crumbly cake hard to cut
When cutting a cake, the knife must not be pressed down to the bottom, but moved across the cake in a sawing motion. It is best to use a serrated knife.

Glaze is no longer clear
The glaze must not be beaten too vigorously, otherwise small air bubbles are formed which make the mixture cloudy. It must be beaten with a spoon and not with a whisk.

Caramel sets too quickly
It will stay runny and smooth if you add a dash of hot lemon juice when cooked.

Discoloured baking powder
Baking powder should not be kept near to some spices. It often turns pink when stored next to cinnamon or vanilla sugar. It is best to store it

separately in an air-tight container. Any such discoloration does not affect its efficacy.

Curdled custard
Transfer the curdled custard to a bottle, 3 tablespoons at a time. Cool it down by placing the bottle in cold water. When cold, shake the bottle vigorously and the custard will stabilize.

Oil froths up when frying doughnuts
The oil has not yet reached the correct temperature. This can ruin delicate mixtures. To prevent this happening, check the temperature by dipping in the handle of a wooden spoon: the oil will be at the correct temperature when small bubbles form around the handle.

Handy hints
• Sprinkle hot cream with icing sugar to prevent a skin forming.

• To make tart pastry softer and lighter, mix 1 teaspoon bicarbonate of soda with 3 tablespoons water or milk and add to 250 g (8 oz) plain flour.
When it gets hot, it will release tiny bubbles of carbon dioxide, which makes the pastry lighter and easier to digest. It must be thoroughly incorporated if the pastry is to rise evenly.

• There is a choice of pastry, depending on whether you wish to make a fresh fruit or cooked fruit tart. Sweet pastry is good for fresh fruit.

Its sugar content goes well with soft fruits and slightly acid cream fillings.

Unsweetened shortcrust pastry is the most practical for cooked fruit, as sweet and puff pastry, which are more delicate, would have to be baked blind before adding the fruit, or an ingredient, such as breadcrumbs, would have to be placed between the pastry and the fruit to absorb the juices produced by the fruit while cooking.

SHORTCRUST PASTRY

Serves 4-6

250 g (8 oz) plain flour	125 g (4 oz) butter
1 teaspoon salt	

Put the flour and salt in a bowl and quickly rub in the butter with the fingertips until the mixture resembles breadcrumbs. Gradually add 150 ml (¼ pint) water. Quickly bind the mixture into a dough which is easy to roll out.
Wrap in a tea towel and leave to rest for at least 2 hours.

SWEET PASTRY

Serves 4-6

250 g (8 oz) plain flour	caster sugar 125 g (4 oz)
A pinch of salt	butter
125 g (4 oz)	2 egg yolks

Put the flour, salt, sugar and softened, but not melted, butter in a mixing bowl. Quickly bind together. Add the egg yolks one at a time. You should end up with a soft dough with a granular, sand-like texture. Make into a ball, wrap in a tea towel and leave to rest in a refrigerator for at least 2 hours. Before using, roll it out on a floured board. It must not be baked for more than 20 minutes in a preheated oven at 200° C (400° F, Gas Mark 6).

Tip: this pastry is delicate and difficult to roll out as it breaks easily. It can also puff up while cooking, so take care to prick the base with a fork before placing in the oven. When ready to use, roll it out on a floured board.

PANCAKE BATTER

Serves 4-6

250 g (8 oz) plain flour	A pinch of salt
3 eggs	3 tablespoons oil
200 ml (7 fl oz) milk	200 ml (7 fl oz) milk
100 ml (3½ fl oz) beer	200 ml (7 fl oz) milk

Put the flour in a mixing bowl. Make a well in the centre and add the eggs. Beat with a wooden spoon, adding the milk and beer gradually to avoid getting any lumps. When smooth, add the salt and oil.

CHOUX PASTRY

Serves 4-6

1 tablespoon caster sugar	butter
A pinch of salt	125 g (4 oz) plain flour
30 g (1¼ oz)	3 eggs

Put the sugar, salt and butter in a pan containing 250 ml (8 fl oz) water. Bring to the boil. Quickly add all the flour, remove from the heat and stir quickly to prevent lumps.
Continue stirring over a very low heat until a smooth dough is formed. Leave to cool. Add the eggs one at a time, beating the mixture constantly. Use the choux pastry when absolutely cold.

CREME AU BEURRE
(Extra-rich butter cream)

Serves 6-8

200 g (7 oz) granulated sugar	separated 225 g (7½ oz) butter
8 eggs,	

Put the sugar in a pan. Dissolve in 150 ml (¼ pint) hot water. Boil for 10 minutes. Beat the egg yolks in a bowl using an electric mixer. Incorporate the sugar syrup, beating constantly with the mixer. Do not pour the sugar syrup on to the sides of the bowl, as it will set immediately. Gradually add the butter cut into pieces, beating constantly for 5 minutes until the mixture has cooled. This rich butter cream is very useful for filling cakes. It can be flavoured with coffee, chocolate or vanilla, for example, and can easily be stored in an air-tight container in a refrigerator for five or six days.

GLOSSARY

Baking blind: pastry flan and tart bases which have a fruit filling or a topping which is then going to be baked should be 'baked blind' first. The empty flan or pastry case is filled with rice or dried peas while baking. When the pastry is sufficiently cooked, usually half-way through the total cooking time, these are removed and replaced by the filling or topping. This prevents the pastry base from becoming soggy.

Baking powder: only small quantities of this raising agent need be used. The heat and humidity produced during baking quickly cause it to release carbon dioxide, which makes the mixture rise.

Cornflour: many continental recipes replace part of the ordinary flour with cornflour, giving the cakes a particularly fine and delicate texture.

Praline: to make praline, slowly heat granulated sugar until golden brown. Add chopped almonds or other nuts and spread the mixture over a greased baking sheet. When cool, crush with a rolling pin. It adds texture and flavour to butter cream and cream cake fillings and can also be used to decorate cakes.

Spelt: a variety of wheat with small black grains that adhere strongly to the chaff. It is now rare, but was widely grown until the beginning of the twentieth century, especially in the upland regions of Germany, Switzerland and France, as it tolerates poor soils. Its nutritious value is comparable with soft wheat. A famous German bread is made with spelt and rye. After threshing, spelt is cooked like rice; it is still used in Switzerland and the Massif Central, as well as in certain country soups, especially in Provence.

Springform cake tin: the sides of a springform cake tin are joined with a buckle and can therefore be easily undone and removed, leaving the cake on the tin base. If you do not have one, a sliding-based cake tin can be used instead.

Sugar: there are two main types of sugar: cane or beet. Light or dark brown sugar is perfect for pancakes, waffles, apple puddings and gingerbread. There is a hint of rum in the flavour of demerara sugar. It is often used in cakes and pastries in the north of France.

Vanilla sugar: if you cannot find sachets of vanilla sugar, you can easily make your own. Simply split 1-2 vanilla pods and put in an air-tight jar containing 500 g (1 lb) caster sugar. Leave until the sugar is fragrant, then use instead of the caster sugar and sachet(s) of vanilla sugar specified in the recipes.

Wire rack: it is important to cool most cakes on a wire rack. As the cake is surrounded by air, it cools evenly and no condensation is formed. Leaving pastry or cakes to cool on a baking sheet or in the cake tin means they will stay slightly damp. This is desirable for cakes which are intended to be moist.

Yeast: there are three types of yeast.
Fresh yeast is a living organism and must be used while fresh. It can be kept in a refrigerator for 8 days, but must be discarded when it begins to look brown, as it will no longer work.
Dried yeast needs to be reconstituted with warm water and sugar, producing froth when active. As with fresh yeast, it is important that it does not become stale. If no froth is produced, the dried yeast is stale and the dough will not rise.
Powdered easy-blend yeast is perhaps the easiest option - simply combine it with the flour, then add the liquid. Once again, it is important that the powdered easy-blend yeast is not stale.
With all these types of yeast, the dough must be left to rise at a constant temperature of 35-37° C (95-98.6° F).

INDEX